CIMA Official *Learning System*

CIMA
PUBLISHING

Relevant for Computer-Based Assessment

C1 –
of M
Acc

CIMA C
Busines

Janet V

ELSEVIER

AMSTERDAM   BOSTON   HEIDELBERG   LONDON   NEW YORK   OXFORD
PARIS   SAN DIEGO   SAN FRANCISCO   SINGAPORE   SYDNEY   TOKYO

CIMA Publishing is an imprint of Elsevier
Linacre House, Jordan Hill, Oxford OX2 8DP, UK
30 Corporate Drive, Suite 400, Burlington, MA 01803, USA

First edition 2008

British Library Cataloguing in Publication Data
A catalogue record for this book is available from the British Library

Library of Congress Cataloguing in Publication Data
A catalogue record for this book is available from the Library of Congress

978-1-85617-792-4

For information on all CIMA publications visit
our website at www.elsevierdirect.com

Typeset by Macmillan Publishing Solutions.
www.macmillansolutions.com

Printed and bound in Italy

09 10 11   11 10 9 8 7 6 5 4 3 2 1

Contents

The CIMA
Learning System

How to use your CIMA *Learning System*

This *Fundamentals of Management Accounting Learning System* has been devised as a resource for students attempting to pass their CIMA computer-based assessments, and provides:

- a detailed explanation of all syllabus areas;
- extensive 'practical' materials;
- generous question practice, together with full solutions;
- a computer-based assessments preparation section, complete with computer-based assessment standard questions and solutions.

This Learning System has been designed with the needs of home-study and distance-learning students in mind. Such students require very full coverage of the syllabus topics, and also the facility to undertake extensive question practice. However, the Learning System is also ideal for fully taught courses.

The main body of the text is divided into a number of chapters, each of which is organised on the following pattern:

- *Detailed learning outcomes.* expected after your studies of the chapter are complete. You should assimilate these before beginning detailed work on the chapter, so that you can appreciate where your studies are leading.
- *Step-by-step topic coverage.* This is the heart of each chapter, containing detailed explanatory text supported where appropriate by worked examples and exercises. You should work carefully through this section, ensuring that you understand the material being explained and can tackle the examples and exercises successfully. Remember that in many cases knowledge is cumulative: if you fail to digest earlier material thoroughly, you may struggle to understand later chapters.
- *Question practice.* The test of how well you have learned the material is your ability to tackle assessment-standard questions. Make a serious attempt at producing your own answers, but at this stage do not be too concerned about attempting the questions in computer-based assessment conditions. In particular, it is more important to absorb the material thoroughly than to observe the time limits that would apply in the actual computer-based assessment.
- *Solutions.* Avoid the temptation merely to 'audit' the solutions provided. It is an illusion to think that this provides the same benefits as you would gain from a serious attempt

THE CIMA LEARNING SYSTEM

of your own. However, if you are struggling to get started on a question you should read the introductory guidance at the beginning of the solution, where provided, and then make your own attempt before referring back to the full solution.

Having worked through the chapters you are ready to begin your final preparations for the computer-based assessments. The final section of this CIMA Learning System provides you with the guidance you need. It includes the following features:

- A brief guide to revision technique.
- A note on the format of the computer-based assessment. You should know what to expect when you tackle the real computer-based assessment, and in particular the number of questions that you will be required to attempt.
- Guidance on how to tackle the computer-based assessment itself.
- A table mapping revision questions to the syllabus learning outcomes allowing you to quickly identify questions by subject area.
- Revision questions. These are of computer-based assessment standard and should be tackled in computer-based assessment conditions, especially as regards the time allocation.
- Solutions to the revision questions.

Two mock computer-based assessments. You should plan to attempt these just before the date of the real computer-based assessment. By this stage your revision should be complete and you should be able to attempt the mock computer-based assessments within the time constraints of the real computer-based assessment.

If you work conscientiously through this CIMA Learning System according to the guidelines above you will be giving yourself an excellent chance of success in your computer-based assessment. Good luck with your studies!

Guide to the Icons used within this text

Key term or definition

Assessment tip

Exercise

Question

Solution

Comment or Note

Formula to learn

Study technique

Passing exams is partly a matter of intellectual ability, but however accomplished you are in that respect you can improve your chances significantly by the use of appropriate study and revision techniques. In this section we briefly outline some tips for effective study during the earlier stages of your approach to the computer-based assessment. Later in the text we mention some techniques that you will find useful at the revision stage.

Planning

To begin with, formal planning is essential to get the best return from the time you spend studying. Estimate how much time in total you are going to need for each paper you are studying for the Certificate in Business Accounting. Remember that you need to allow time for revision as well as for initial study of the material. The amount of notional study time for any paper is the minimum estimated time that students will need to achieve the specified learning outcomes in the syllabus. This time includes all appropriate learning activities, for example, face-to-face tuition, private study, directed home study, learning in the workplace, revision time, etc. You may find it helpful to read Better Exam Results: a Guide for Business and Accounting Students by Sam Malone, Elsevier, ISBN: 9780750663571. This book will help you develop proven study and examination techniques. Chapter by chapter it covers the building blocks of successful learning and examination techniques.

The notional study time for the Certificate in Business Accounting Paper *Fundamentals of Management Accounting* is 130 hours. Note that the standard amount of notional learning hours attributed to one full-time academic year of approximately 30 weeks is 1,200 hours.

By way of example, the notional study time might be made up as follows:

	Hours
Face-to-face study: up to	40
Personal study: up to	65
'Other' study – e.g. learning in the workplace, revision, etc.: up to	25
	130

Note that all study and learning-time recommendations should be used only as a guideline and are intended as minimum amounts. The amount of time recommended for face-to-face tuition, personal study and/or additional learning will vary according to the type of course undertaken, prior learning of the student, and the pace at which different students learn.

Now split your total time requirement over the weeks between now and the assessment. This will give you an idea of how much time you need to devote to study each week. Remember to allow for holidays or other periods during which you will not be able to study (e.g. because of seasonal workloads).

With your study material before you, decide which chapters you are going to study in each week, and which weeks you will devote to revision and final question practice.

Prepare a written schedule summarising the above – and stick to it!

It is essential to know your syllabus. As your course progresses you will become more familiar with how long it takes to cover topics in sufficient depth. Your timetable may need to be adapted to allocate enough time for the whole syllabus.

Tips for effective studying

1. Aim to find a quiet and undisturbed location for your study, and plan as far as possible to use the same period of time each day. Getting into a routine helps to avoid wasting time. Make sure that you have all the materials you need before you begin so as to minimise interruptions.

2. Store all your materials in one place, so that you do not waste time searching for items every time you want to begin studying. If you have to pack everything away after each study period, keep your study materials in a box, or even a suitcase, which will not be disturbed until the next time.

3. Limit distractions. To make the most effective use of your study periods you should be able to apply total concentration, so turn off all entertainment equipment, set your phones to message mode, and put up your 'do not disturb' sign.

4. Your timetable will tell you which topic to study. However, before diving in and becoming engrossed in the finer points, make sure you have an overall picture of all the areas that need to be covered by the end of that session. After an hour, allow yourself a short break and move away from your Learning System. With experience, you will learn to assess the pace you need to work at.

5. Work carefully through a chapter, making notes as you go. When you have covered a suitable amount of material, vary the pattern by attempting a practice question. When you have finished your attempt, make notes of any mistakes you made.

6. Make notes as you study, and discover the techniques that work best for you. Your notes may be in the form of lists, bullet points, diagrams, summaries, 'mind maps', or the written word, but remember that you will need to refer back to them at a later date, so they must be intelligible. If you are on a taught course, make sure you highlight any issues you would like to follow up with your lecturer.

7. Organise your paperwork. Make sure that all your notes, calculations etc. can be effectively filed and easily retrieved later.

Computer-Based Assessment

CIMA uses computer-based assessment (CBAs) for all subjects for the Certificate in Business Accounting.

Objective test questions are used. The most common type is 'multiple choice', where you have to choose the correct answer from a list of possible answers, but there are a variety of other objective question types that can be used within the system. These include true/false questions, matching pairs of text and graphic, sequencing and ranking, labelling diagrams and single and multiple numeric entry.

Candidates answer the questions by either pointing and clicking the mouse, moving objects around the screen, typing numbers, or a combination of these responses. Try the online demo at www.cimaglobal.com/cba to see how the technology works.

In every chapter of this Learning System we have introduced these types of questions but obviously we have to label answers A, B, C etc. rather than using click boxes. For convenience we have retained quite a lot of questions where an initial scenario leads to a number of sub-questions. There will be questions of this type in the CBA but they will rarely have more than three sub-questions. In all such cases examiners will ensure that the answer to one part does not hinge upon a prior answer.

For further CBA practice, CIMA eSuccess CD's are available from www. cimapublishing.com.

Fundamentals of Management Accounting and Computer-Based Assessment

The assessment for Fundamentals of Management Accounting is a two-hour computer based assessment comprising 50 compulsory questions, each with one or more parts. Single part questions are generally worth 1–2 marks each, but two and three part questions may be worth 4 or 6 marks. There will be no choice and all questions should be attempted if time permits. CIMA are continuously developing the question styles within the CBA system and you are advised to try the on-line website demo at www.cimaglobal.com, to both gain familiarity with assessment software and examine the latest style of questions being used.

Syllabus (2006) – Paper C01 Fundamentals of Management Accounting

Syllabus Outline

The syllabus comprises:

Topic and Study Weighting

A	Cost Determination	25%
B	Cost Behaviour and Break-even Analysis	10%
C	Standard Costing	15%
D	Cost and Accounting Systems	30%
E	Financial Planning and Control	20%

The percentage study weightings are a guide to the amount of time you should spend studying each topic.

You must study all topics in the syllabus. All questions in the assessment are compulsory and the study weighting does not specify the number of marks that the topic will be given in the assessment.

Learning Aims

This syllabus aims to test student's ability to:

- explain and use concepts and processes to determine product and service costs;
- explain direct, marginal and absorption costs and their use in pricing;
- apply cost-volume-profit (CVP) analysis and interpret the results;
- apply a range of costing and accounting systems;
- explain the role of budgets and standard costing within organisations;
- prepare and interpret budgets, standard costs and variance statements.

Learning Outcomes and Indicative Syllabus Content

A Cost Determination – 25%

Learning Outcomes

On completion of their studies students should be able to:

(i) explain why organisations need to know how much products, processes and services cost and why they need costing systems;

(ii) explain the idea of a 'cost object';

(iii) explain the concept of a direct cost and an indirect cost;

(iv) explain why the concept of 'cost' needs to be qualified as direct, full, marginal etc. in order to be meaningful;

(v) distinguish between the historical cost of an asset and the economic value of an asset to an organisation;

(vi) apply first-in-first-out (FIFO), last-in-first-out (LIFO) and average cost (AVCO) methods of accounting for stock, calculating stock values and related gross profit;

(vii) explain why FIFO is essentially a historical cost method, while LIFO approximates economic cost;

(viii) prepare cost statements for allocation and apportionment of overheads, including between reciprocal service departments;

(ix) calculate direct, variable and full costs of products, services and activities using overhead absorption rates to trace indirect costs to cost units;

(x) explain the use of cost information in pricing decisions, including marginal cost pricing and the calculation of 'full cost' based prices to generate a specified return on sales or investment.

Indicative Syllabus Content:

- Classification of costs and the treatment of direct costs (specifically attributable to a cost object) and indirect costs (not specifically attributable) in ascertaining the cost of a 'cost object' (e.g. a product, service, activity, customer).
- Cost measurement: historical versus economic costs.
- Accounting for the value of materials on FIFO, LIFO and AVCO bases.
- Overhead costs: allocation, apportionment, re-apportionment and absorption of overhead costs. Note: The repeated distribution method only will be used for reciprocal service department costs.
- Marginal cost pricing and full-cost pricing to achieve specified return on sales or return on investment.

Note: students are not expected to have a detailed knowledge of activity based costing (ABC).

B Cost Behaviour and Break-even Analysis – 10%

Learning Outcomes

On completion of their studies students should be able to:

(i) explain how costs behave as product, service or activity levels increase or decrease;

(ii) distinguish between fixed, variable and semi-variable costs;

   (iii) explain step costs and the importance of time-scales in their treatment as either variable or fixed;

   (iv) compute the fixed and variable elements of a semi-variable cost using the high-low method and 'line of best fit' method;

   (v) explain the concept of contribution and its use in cost-volume-profit (CVP) analysis;

   (vi) calculate and interpret the break-even point, profit target, margin of safety and profit/volume ratio for a single product or service;

  (vii) prepare break-even charts and profit/volume graphs for a single product or service;

 (viii) calculate the profit maximising sales mix for a multi-product company that has limited demand for each product and one other constraint or limiting factor.

Indicative Syllabus Content:

- Fixed, variable and semi-variable costs.
- Step costs and the importance of time-scale in analysing cost behaviour.
- High-low and graphical methods to establish fixed and variable elements of a semi-variable cost. Note: regression analysis is not required.
- Contribution concept and CVP analysis.
- Break-even charts, profit volume graphs, break-even point, profit target, margin of safety, contribution/sales ratio.
- Limiting factor analysis.

C Standard Costing – 15%

Learning Outcomes

On completion of their studies students should be able to:

   (i) explain the difference between ascertaining costs after the event and planning by establishing standard costs in advance;

   (ii) explain why planned standard costs, prices and volumes are useful in setting a benchmark for comparison and so allowing managers' attention to be directed to areas of the business that are performing below or above expectation;

  (iii) calculate standard costs for the material, labour and variable overhead elements of cost of a product or service;

  (iv) calculate variances for materials, labour, variable overhead, sales prices and sales volumes;

  (v) prepare a statement that reconciles budgeted contribution with actual contribution;

  (vi) interpret statements of variances for variable costs, sales prices and sales volumes including possible inter-relations between cost variances, sales price and volume variances, and cost and sales variances;

  (vii) discuss the possible use of standard labour costs in designing incentive schemes for factory and office workers.

Indicative Syllabus Content:

- Principles of standard costing.
- Preparation of standards for the variable elements of cost: material, labour, variable overhead.
- Variances: materials – total, price and usage; labour – total, rate and efficiency; variable overhead – total, expenditure and efficiency; sales – sales price and sales volume contribution. Note: students will be expected to calculate the sales volume contribution variance.

- Reconciliation of budget and actual contribution.
- Piecework and the principles of incentive schemes based on standard hours versus actual hours taken. Note: the details of a specific incentive scheme will be provided in the examination.

D Costing and Accounting Systems – 30%

Learning Outcomes

On completion of their studies students should be able to:

(i) explain the principles of manufacturing accounts and the integration of the cost accounts with the financial accounting system;

(ii) prepare a set of integrated accounts, given opening balances and appropriate transactional information, and show standard cost variances;

(iii) compare and contrast job, batch, contract and process costing;

(iv) prepare ledger accounts for job, batch and process costing systems;

(v) prepare ledger accounts for contract costs;

(vi) explain the difference between subjective and objective classifications of expenditure and the importance of tracing costs both to products/services and to responsibility centres;

(vii) construct coding systems that facilitate both subjective and objective classification of costs;

(viii) prepare financial statements that inform management;

(ix) explain why gross revenue, value-added, contribution, gross margin, marketing expense, general and administration expense, etc. might be highlighted in management reporting;

(x) compare and contrast management reports in a range of organisations including commercial enterprises, charities and public sector undertakings.

Indicative Syllabus Content:

- Manufacturing accounts including raw material, work in progress, finished goods and manufacturing overhead control accounts.
- Integrated ledgers including accounting for over and under absorption of production overhead.
- The treatment of variances as period entries in integrated ledger systems.
- Job, batch, process and contract costing. Note: Only the average cost method will be examined for process costing but students must be able to deal with differing degrees of completion of opening and closing stocks, normal losses and abnormal gains and losses, and the treatment of scrap value.
- Subjective, objective and responsibility classifications of expenditure and the design of coding systems to facilitate these analyses.
- Cost accounting statements for management information in production and service companies and not-for-profit organisations.

E Financial Planning and Control – 20%

Learning Outcomes

On completion of their studies students should be able to:

(i) explain why organisations set out financial plans in the form of budgets, typically for a financial year;

(ii) prepare functional budgets for material usage and purchase, labour and overheads, including budgets for capital expenditure and depreciation;

(iii) prepare a master budget: income statement, balance sheet and cash flow statement, based on the functional budgets;

(iv) interpret budget statements and advise managers on financing projected cash shortfalls and/or investing projected cash surpluses;

(v) prepare a flexed budget based on the actual levels of sales and production and calculate appropriate variances;

(vi) compare and contrast fixed and flexed budgets;

(vii) explain the use of budgets in designing reward strategies for managers.

Indicative Syllabus Content:

- Budgeting for planning and control.
- Budget preparation, interpretation and use of the master budget.
- Reporting of actual against budget.
- Fixed and flexible budgeting.
- Budget variances.
- Interpretation and use of budget statements and budget variances.

Basic Aspects of
Cost Accounting

Basic Aspects of
Cost Accounting

1

LEARNING OUTCOMES

After completing this chapter, you should be able to:

▸ explain why organisations need to know how much products, processes and services cost and why they need costing systems;

▸ explain the idea of a 'cost object';

▸ explain the concept of a direct cost and an indirect cost;

▸ explain why the concept of cost needs to be qualified as direct, full, marginal, etc. in order to be meaningful;

▸ explain how costs behave as product, service or activity levels increase or decrease;

▸ distinguish between fixed, variable and semi-variable costs;

▸ explain step costs and the importance of time-scales in their treatment as either variable or fixed;

▸ compute the fixed and variable elements of a semi-variable cost using the high–low method and 'line of best fit' method.

1.1 Introduction

In this chapter, we will look at some of the fundamental concepts of the framework of cost accounting. You will learn some basic principles which underpin all of the material in your *Fundamentals of Management Accounting* syllabus.

1.2 Why organisations need costing systems

An organisation's costing system is the foundation of the internal financial information system for managers. It provides the information that management needs to plan and control the organisation's activities and to make decisions about the future. Examples of the type of information provided by a costing system and the uses to which it might be put include the following.

- Actual unit costs for the latest period; could be used for cost control by comparing with a predetermined unit standard cost, which would also be provided by the costing system. Could also be used as the basis for planning future unit costs and for decisions about pricing and production levels. For example, a manager cannot make a decision about the price to be charged to a customer without information which tells the manager how much it costs to produce and distribute the product to the customer.
- Actual costs of operating a department for the latest period; could be used for cost control by comparing with a predetermined budget for the department. Could also be used as the basis for planning future budgeted costs and for decisions such as outsourcing. For example, a manager might be considering the closure of the packing department and instead outsourcing the packing operations to another organisation. In order to make this decision the manager needs to know, among other things, the actual cost of operating the packing department.
- The forecast costs to be incurred at different levels of activity. Could be used for planning, for decision making and as a part of cost control by comparing the actual costs with the forecasts. For example, a manager cannot make a well-informed decision about the appropriate production level for the forthcoming period unless information is available about the costs that will be incurred at various possible output levels.

This is by no means an exhaustive list of the information that is provided by a costing system. However, it should serve to demonstrate that organisations need costing systems that will provide the basic information that management requires for planning, control and decision-making.

1.3 What is meant by 'cost'?

The word 'cost' can be used in two contexts. It can be used as a noun, for example, when we are referring to the cost of an item. Alternatively, it can be used as a verb, for example, we can say that we are attempting to cost an activity, when we are undertaking the tasks necessary to determine the costs of carrying out the activity.

The word 'cost' can rarely stand alone and should always be qualified as to its nature and limitations. You will be seeing throughout this text that there are many different types of cost and that each has its usefulness and limitations in different circumstances.

1.4 Cost units

 The CIMA *Terminology* defines a cost unit as 'a unit of product or service in relation to which costs are ascertained'.

This means that a cost unit can be anything for which it is possible to ascertain the cost. The cost unit selected in each situation will depend on a number of factors, including the purpose of the cost ascertainment exercise and the amount of information available.

Cost units can be developed for all kinds of organisations, whether manufacturing, commercial or public-service based. Some examples from the CIMA *Terminology* are as follows:

Industry sector	*Cost unit*
Brick-making	1,000 bricks
Electricity	Kilowatt-hour (KwH)
Professional services	Chargeable hour
Education	Enrolled student

Activity	*Cost unit*
Credit control	Account maintained
Selling	Customer call

 ## Exercise 1.1

Can you think of at least one other cost unit which could be used for each of these industries and activities? For example, in controlling the costs of the selling activity we might monitor the cost per order taken.

The above list is not exhaustive. A cost unit can be anything which is measurable and useful for cost control purposes. For example, with brick-making, 1,000 bricks is suggested as a cost unit. It would be possible to determine the cost per brick but perhaps in this case a larger measure is considered more suitable and useful for control purposes.

Notice that this list of cost units contains both tangible and intangible items. Tangible items are those which can be seen and touched, for example the 1,000 bricks. Intangible items cannot be seen and touched and do not have physical substance but they can be measured, for example a chargeable hour of accounting service.

1.4.1 Composite cost units

The cost units for services are usually intangible and they are often composite cost units, that is, they are often made up of two parts. For example, if we were attempting to monitor and control the costs of a delivery service we might measure the cost per tonne delivered. However, 'tonne delivered' would not be a particularly useful cost unit because it would not be valid to compare the cost per tonne delivered from London to Edinburgh with the cost per tonne delivered from London to Brighton. The former journey is much longer and it will almost certainly cost more to deliver a tonne over the longer distance.

Composite cost units assist in overcoming this problem. We could perhaps use a 'tonne-mile' instead. This means that we would record and monitor the cost of carrying one tonne for one mile. The cost per tonne-mile would be a comparable measure whatever the length of journey and this is therefore a valid and useful cost unit for control purposes.

Other examples of composite cost units might be as follows:

Business	*Cost unit*
Hotel	Bed night
Bus company	Passenger mile
Hospital	In-patient day

Exercise 1.2

Can you think of some other examples of composite cost units that could be used in these organisations and in other types of organisation?

1.5 Cost centres

A cost centre is a production or service location, a function, an activity or an item of equipment for which costs are accumulated.

A cost centre is used as a 'collecting place' for costs. The cost of operating the cost centre is determined for the period, and then this total cost is related to the cost units which have passed through the cost centre.

For instance, an example of a production cost centre could be the machine shop in a factory. The production overhead cost for the machine shop might be £100,000 for the period. If 1,000 cost units have passed through this cost centre we might say that the production overhead cost relating to the machine shop was £100 for each unit.

A cost centre could also be a service location, a function, an activity or an item of equipment. Examples of these might be as follows but you should try to think of some others:

Type of cost centre	*Examples*
Service location	Stores, canteen
Function	Sales representative
Activity	Quality control
Item of equipment	Packing machine

If you are finding it difficult to see how a sales representative could be used as a cost centre, then work carefully through the following points.

1. What are the costs which might be incurred in 'operating' a sales representative for one period?

   Examples might be the representative's salary cost, the cost of running a company car, the cost of any samples given away by the representative and so on. Say these amount to £40,000.

2. Once we have determined this cost, the next thing we need to know is the number of cost units that can be related to the sales representative.

   The cost unit selected might be £100 of sales achieved. If the representative has achieved £400,000 of sales, then we could say that the representative's costs amounted to £10 per £100 of sales. The representative has thus been used as a cost centre or collecting place for the costs, which have then been related to the cost units.

1.6 Cost objects

A cost object is anything for which costs can be ascertained. The CIMA *Terminology* contains the following description: 'For example a product, service, centre, activity, customer or distribution channel in relation to which costs are ascertained'.

All of the cost units and cost centres we have described earlier in this chapter are therefore types of cost object. We have seen the quality control activity being treated as a cost centre, and thus as a cost object.

 ## Exercise 1.3

Notice that CIMA's examples of cost objects include a customer. Can you think of costs that might be attributed to a supermarket which is a customer and is treated as a cost object by a supplier of processed foods?

 ## Solution

Costs that you might have thought of include the following:

- the cost of the food products supplied to the customer,
- the cost of delivering the food products to the customer,
- the cost of funding the credit taken by the customer,
- the cost of holding any inventories for the supermarket,
- the salary cost of the account manager responsible for the supermarket's account,
- the cost of dealing with the customer's queries.

1.7   Classification of costs

Costs can be classified in many different ways. It is necessary to be able to classify all costs, that is, to be able to arrange them into logical groups, in order to devise an efficient system to collect and analyse the costs. The classifications selected and the level of detail used in the classification groupings will depend on the purpose of the classification exercise.

 The CIMA *Terminology* defines classification as the 'arrangement of items in logical groups by nature, purpose or responsibility'.

1.7.1   Classification of costs according to their nature

This means grouping costs according to whether they are materials, labour or expense cost.

Material costs include the cost of obtaining the materials and receiving them within the organisation. The cost of having the materials brought to the organisation is known as *carriage inwards*.

Labour costs are those costs incurred in the form of wages and salaries, together with related employment costs. In the United Kingdom, there is an additional cost borne by the employer in respect of employees which is paid to the government: this is called National Insurance. These costs are documented internally, the amount of the wages and salary costs being determined by reference to agreed rates of pay and attendance time and output measures, depending on the method of remuneration being used.

Expense costs are external costs such as rent, business rates, electricity, gas, postages, telephones and similar items which will be documented by invoices from suppliers.

Within each of these classifications there is a number of subdivisions; for example, within the materials classification the subdivisions might include the following:

(a) Raw materials, that is, the basic raw material used in manufacture.
(b) Components, that is, complete parts that are used in the manufacturing process.
(c) Consumables, that is, cleaning materials, etc.
(d) Maintenance materials, that is, spare parts for machines, lubricating oils, etc.

This list of subdivisions is not exhaustive, and there may even be further subdivisions of each of these groups. For example, the raw materials may be further divided according to the type of raw material, for example, steel, plastic, glass, etc.

Exercise 1.4

Can you think of some possible subdivisions for the costs that are classified as labour costs and as expense costs?

1.7.2 Classification of costs according to their purpose: direct costs and indirect costs

When costs are classified having regard to their purpose, they are grouped according to the reason for which they have been incurred. The broadest classification of this type is to divide costs into *direct* costs and *indirect* costs.

A direct cost is one that can be clearly identified with the cost object we are trying to cost. For example, suppose that a furniture maker is determining the cost of a wooden table. The manufacture of the table has involved the use of timber, screws and metal drawer handles. These items are classified as *direct materials*. The wages paid to the machine operator, assembler and finisher in actually making the table would be classified as *direct labour costs*. The designer of the table may be entitled to a royalty payment for each table made, and this would be classified as a *direct expense*.

Other costs incurred would be classified as *indirect costs*. They cannot be directly attributed to a particular cost unit, although it is clear that they have been incurred in the production of the table. Examples of indirect production costs are as follows:

Cost incurred	Cost classification
Lubricating oils and cleaning materials	Indirect material
Salaries of supervisory labour	Indirect labour
Factory rent and power	Indirect expense

It is important for you to realise that a particular cost may sometimes be a direct cost and sometimes an indirect cost. It depends on the cost object we are trying to cost.

For example, the salary of the machining department supervisor is a direct cost of that department because it can be specifically identified with the department. However, it is an indirect cost of each of the cost units processed in the machining department because it cannot be specifically identified with any particular cost unit.

Exercise 1.5

State whether each of the following costs would be a direct cost or an indirect cost of the quality control activity which is undertaken in a company's factory.

- The salary of the quality control supervisor.
- The rent of the factory.
- The depreciation of the quality testing machine.
- The cost of the samples destroyed during testing.
- The insurance of the factory.

 ## Solution

- The salary of the quality control supervisor is a direct cost of the quality control activity because it can be specifically attributed to this cost object.
- The rent of the factory is an indirect cost of the quality control activity because it cannot be specifically attributed to this cost object but must also be attributed to other activities undertaken in the factory.
- The depreciation of the quality testing machine is a direct cost of the quality control activity because it can be specifically attributed to this cost object.
- The cost of the samples destroyed during testing is a direct cost of the quality control activity because it can be specifically attributed to this cost object.
- The insurance of the factory is an indirect cost of the quality control activity because it cannot be specifically attributed to this cost object but must also be attributed to other activities undertaken in the factory.

> In a later chapter we will return to consider the classification of costs by responsibility.

 ## 1.8 Elements of cost

The elements of cost are the constituent parts of cost which make up the total cost of a cost object.

In Figure 1.1, the outline cost statement for a single cost unit shows you how the total or full cost for a unit might be built up. Notice in particular that a number of subtotals can be highlighted before the total cost figure is determined.

The usefulness of each of these subtotals depends on the management action that is to be taken based on each of the totals.

Suppose that the cost analysis in Figure 1.1 has been provided by the management accountant to help us to decide on the selling price to be charged for a luxury wall-mounted hairdryer: the type that is fixed to the wall for customers' use in hotel bedrooms.

You have been negotiating with the procurement manager of a chain of hotels in an attempt to secure a contract to supply a batch of hairdryers. It is very important that you should win this contract because it is likely that, once this first order has been fulfilled successfully, the hotel chain will place future orders for hairdryers and for your company's other products, when refurbishing its other hotels. Furthermore, other hotel chains may become interested in your company's products once they discover that this major chain is one of your customers.

BASIC ASPECTS OF COST ACCOUNTING

	£	£
Direct material		15
Direct labour		5
Direct expenses		2
Prime cost or total direct cost		22
Production overhead:		
indirect material	4	
indirect labour	6	
indirect expenses	6	
		16
Total production/factory cost		38
Selling, distribution and administration overhead		2
Total (full) cost		40
Profit		10
Selling price		50

Figure 1.1 The build-up of cost

Unfortunately, the hotel's procurement manager is working within the constraints of a very strict budget and has made it clear that the highest price that the hotel is prepared to pay is £25 per hairdryer. The analysis in Figure 1.1 shows that your company's normal selling price is considerably higher than this.

The company cannot afford to sell its hairdryers for £25 each if they cost £40 to produce and sell. Or can it?

Let us look at the sort of costs that might be incurred in manufacturing and selling a hairdryer, and how each cost would be classified in terms of the above analysis of the elements of cost.

- *Direct materials*. This is the material that actually becomes part of the finished hairdryer. It would include the plastic for the case and the packaging materials. If we make another batch of hairdryers then we will need to purchase another batch of these and other direct materials.
- *Direct labour*. This is the labour cost incurred directly as a result of making one hairdryer. If we make another batch of hairdryers then we will need to pay more direct labour cost.
- *Direct expenses*. These are expenses caused directly as a result of making one more batch of hairdryers. For example, the company might be required to pay the designer of the hairdryer a royalty of £2 for each hairdryer produced.

The three direct costs are summed to derive the prime cost or total direct cost of a hairdryer. This is one measure of cost but there are still other costs to be added: production overheads and other overheads.

Production overheads are basically the same three costs as for direct cost, but they are identified as *indirect* costs because they cannot be specifically identified with any particular hairdryer or batch of hairdryers. Indirect costs must be shared out over all the cost objects using a fair and equitable basis.

 In a later chapter you will see how indirect costs can be shared over all the production for the period.

Indirect materials are those production materials that do not actually become part of the finished product. This might include the cleaning materials and lubricating oils for the machinery. The machines must be clean and lubricated in order to carry out production, but it will probably not be necessary to spend more on these materials in order to manufacture a further batch. This cost is therefore only indirectly related to the production of this batch.

Indirect labour is the production labour cost which cannot be directly associated with the production of any particular batch. It would include the salaries of supervisors who are overseeing the production of hairdryers as well as all the other products manufactured in the factory.

Indirect expenses are all the other production overheads associated with running the factory, including factory rent and rates, heating and lighting, etc. These indirect costs must be shared out over all of the batches produced in a period.

The share of indirect production costs is added to the prime cost to derive the total production cost of a hairdryer. This is another measure of cost but there are still more costs to be added: a share of the other overheads.

Selling and distribution overhead includes the sales force salaries and commission, the cost of operating delivery vehicles and renting a storage warehouse, etc. These are indirect costs which are not specifically attributable to a particular cost unit.

Administration overhead includes the rent on the administrative office building, the depreciation of office equipment, postage and stationery costs, etc. These are also indirect costs which are not specifically attributable to a particular cost unit.

Now that you understand the nature of each of the cost elements which make up the full cost we can think a bit more about the price to be charged to the hotel chain.

 ## Exercise 1.6

Which of the above costs would be incurred as a result of making another hairdryer?

 ## Solution

The direct cost of £22 would definitely be incurred if another hairdryer was produced. This is the extra material that would have to be bought, the extra labour costs that would have to be paid and the extra expenses for royalties that would be incurred.

The £16 production overhead cost would not be incurred additionally if another hairdryer was produced. This is the share of costs that would be incurred anyway, such as the cleaning materials, the factory rent and the supervisors' salaries.

The £2 share of selling, distribution and administration overhead would probably not be incurred if another hairdryer was produced. This includes the office costs, the depreciation on the delivery vehicles and the rent of warehousing facilities. This sort of cost would not increase as a result of producing another hairdryer or batch of hairdryers. However, there may be some incremental or extra selling and distribution costs, for example we would probably be entitled to a sales commission for all our hard work in winning the sale, and there would be some costs involved in delivering the goods to the hotel chain. For the sake of our analysis let us suppose that this incremental cost amounts to £1 per hairdryer, rather than the full amount of £2 shown in the cost analysis.

You can see from the discussion in this exercise that in fact the only extra or incremental cost to be incurred in producing another hairdryer is £23 (£22 direct cost plus assumed £1 incremental selling and distribution costs).

Therefore it may be possible to sell to the hotel chain for £25 per hairdryer, and still be better off than if the sale was not made at all! At least the extra £2 per hairdryer (£25 – £23 extra cost) would contribute towards the costs which are being incurred anyway – the production overheads, administration overheads, etc.

This discussion has illustrated that the concept of cost needs to be qualified if it is to be meaningful. We need to know to which cost we are referring when we state something like, 'The cost is £40'.

The £40 cost quoted is the full cost, which includes a fair share of all costs incurred on behalf of the cost object. In our discussion we derived the *marginal* or *incremental* cost of £23 which would be incurred as a direct result of making and selling another hairdryer.

Therefore, we have seen that different costs are useful in different circumstances and we must always qualify what we mean by 'cost'. Do we mean the direct cost, the marginal cost, the full cost or some other measure of cost?

When we consider the full cost in this example there is a profit of £10 on this particular cost unit if it is sold for £50. This is referred to as a profit *margin* on sales of 20 per cent (10/50) and a profit *mark-up* on full cost of 25 per cent (10/40). These are the 'strictly correct' definitions of margin and mark-up. However, in practice, the two terms tend to be used interchangeably.

> The important thing in an assessment question is that you should establish whether profit is to be calculated as a percentage of cost, or as a percentage of selling price.

1.9 Cost behaviour

Many factors affect the level of costs incurred; for instance inflation will cause costs to increase over a period of time. In management accounting, when we talk about cost behaviour we are referring to the way in which costs are affected by fluctuations in the level of activity.

The level of activity can be measured in many different ways. For example, we can record the number of units produced, miles travelled, hours worked, meals served, percentage of capacity utilised and so on.

An understanding of cost behaviour patterns is essential for many management tasks, particularly in the areas of planning, decision-making and control. It would be impossible for managers to forecast and control costs without at least a basic knowledge of the way in which costs behave in relation to the level of activity.

In this section we will look at the most common cost behaviour patterns and we will consider some examples of each.

1.9.1 Fixed cost

> The CIMA *Terminology* defines a fixed cost as a 'cost incurred for an accounting period, that, within certain output or turnover limits, tends to be unaffected by fluctuations in the levels of activity (output or turnover)'.

Another term that can be used to refer to a fixed cost is a period cost. This highlights the fact that a fixed cost is incurred according to the time elapsed, rather than according to the level of activity.

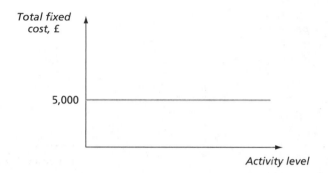

Figure 1.2 Fixed cost

A fixed cost can be depicted graphically as shown in Figure 1.2.

Examples of fixed costs are rent, rates, insurance and executive salaries.

The graph shows that the cost is constant (in this case at £5,000) for all levels of activity. However, it is important to note that this is only true for the relevant range of activity. Consider, for example, the behaviour of the rent cost. Within the relevant range it is possible to expand activity without needing extra premises and therefore the rent cost remains constant. However, if activity is expanded to the critical point where further premises are needed, then the rent cost will increase to a new, higher level.

This cost behaviour pattern can be described as a stepped fixed cost or step cost (Figure 1.3).

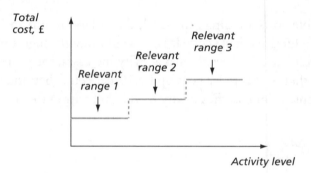

Figure 1.3 Stepped fixed cost

The cost is constant within the relevant range for each activity level but when a critical level of activity is reached, the total cost incurred increases to the next step.

The possibility of changes occurring in cost behaviour patterns means that it is unreliable to predict costs for activity levels which are outside the relevant range. For example our records might show the cost incurred at various activity levels between 100 units and 5,000 units. We should therefore try to avoid using this information as the basis for forecasting the level of cost which would be incurred at an activity of, say, 6,000 units, which is outside the relevant range.

> **!** This warning does not only apply to fixed costs: it is never wise to attempt to predict costs for activity levels outside the range for which cost behaviour patterns have been established.

When you are drawing or interpreting graphs of cost behaviour patterns, it is important that you pay great attention to the label on the vertical axis. In Figures. 1.2 and 1.3 the graphs depicted the total cost incurred. If the vertical axis had been used to represent the fixed cost per unit, then it would look as shown in Figure 1.4.

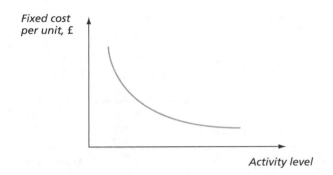

Figure 1.4 Fixed cost per unit

The fixed cost per unit reduces as the activity level is increased. This is because the same amount of fixed cost is being spread over an increasing number of units.

1.9.2 Variable cost

 The CIMA *Terminology* defines a variable cost as a 'cost that varies with a measure of activity'.

Examples of variable costs are direct material, direct labour and variable overheads.

Figure 1.5 depicts a linear variable cost. It is a straight line through the origin, which means that the cost is nil at zero activity level. When activity increases, the total variable cost increases in direct proportion, that is, if activity goes up by 10 per cent, then the total variable cost also increases by 10 per cent, as long as the activity level is still within the relevant range.

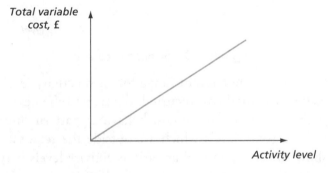

Figure 1.5 Linear variable cost

The gradient of the line will depend on the amount of variable cost per unit.

Exercise 1.7

Figure 1.5 depicts the total variable cost at each activity level. Can you draw a sketch graph of the variable cost per unit?

Your graph of variable cost per unit should look like Figure 1.6. The straight line parallel to the horizontal axis depicts a constant variable cost per unit, within the relevant range.

In most assessment situations, and very often in practice, variable costs are assumed to be linear. Although many variable costs do approximate to a linear function, this assumption

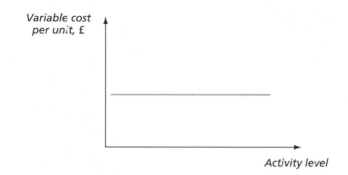

Figure 1.6 Variable cost per unit

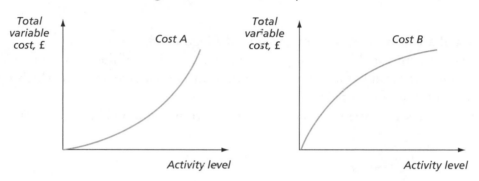

Figure 1.7 Non-linear variable costs

may not always be realistic. A variable cost may be non-linear as depicted in either of the diagrams in Figure 1.7.

These costs are sometimes called curvilinear variable costs.

The graph of cost A becomes steeper as the activity level increases. This indicates that each successive unit of activity is adding more to the total variable cost than the previous unit. An example of a variable cost which follows this pattern could be the cost of direct labour where employees are paid an accelerating bonus for achieving higher levels of output. The graph of cost B becomes less steep as the activity level increases. Each successive unit of activity adds less to total variable cost than the previous unit. An example of a variable cost which follows this pattern could be the cost of direct material where quantity discounts are available.

Exercise 1.8

Can you think of other variable costs which might follow the behaviour patterns depicted in Figure 1.7?

The important point is that managers should be aware of any assumptions that have been made in estimating cost behaviour patterns. They can then use the information which is based on these assumptions with a full awareness of its possible limitations.

1.9.3 Semi-variable cost

> A semi-variable cost is also referred to as a semi-fixed or mixed cost. The CIMA *Terminology* defines it as a 'cost containing both fixed and variable components and thus partly affected by a change in the level of activity'.

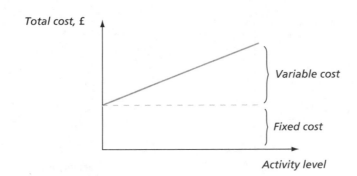

Figure 1.8 Semi-variable cost

A graph of a semi-variable cost might look like Figure 1.8.

Examples of semi-variable costs are gas and electricity. Both of these expenditures consist of a fixed amount payable for the period, with a further variable amount which is related to the consumption of gas or electricity.

Alternatively a semi-variable cost behaviour pattern might look like Figure 1.9.

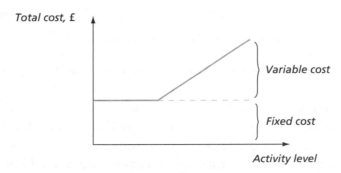

Figure 1.9 Semi-variable cost

This cost remains constant up to a certain level of activity and then increases as the variable cost element is incurred. An example of such a cost might be the rental cost of a photocopier where a fixed rental is paid and no extra charge is made for copies up to a certain number. Once this number of copies is exceeded, a constant charge is levied for each copy taken.

Exercise 1.9

Can you think of other examples of semi-variable costs with behaviour patterns like those indicated in Figures. 1.8 and 1.9?

1.9.4 Analysing semi-variable costs

The semi-variable cost behaviour pattern depicted in Figure 1.8 is most common in practice and in assessment situations.

When managers have identified a semi-variable cost they will need to know how much of it is fixed and how much is variable. Only when they have determined this will they be able to estimate the cost to be incurred at relevant activity levels. Past records of costs and their associated activity levels are usually used to carry out the analysis. Your *Fundamentals of Management Accounting* syllabus requires you to know how to use two common methods of separating the fixed and variable elements:

(1) The high–low method.
(2) The 'line of best fit' method.

The high–low method

This method picks out the highest and lowest activity levels from the available data and investigates the change in cost which has occurred between them. The highest and lowest points are selected to try to use the greatest possible range of data. This improves the accuracy of the result.

Example: The high–low method

A company has recorded the following data for a semi-variable cost:

Month	Activity level (units)	Cost incurred (£)
January	1,800	36,600
February	2,450	41,150
March	2,100	38,700
April	2,000	38,000
May	1,750	36,250
June	1,950	37,650

The highest activity level occurred in February and the lowest in May. Since the amount of fixed cost incurred in each month is constant, the extra cost resulting from the activity increase must be the variable cost.

	Activity level (units)	£
February	2,450	41,150
May	1,750	36,250
Increase	700	4,900

The extra variable cost for 700 units is £4,900. We can now calculate the variable cost per unit:

$$\text{Variable cost} = \frac{£4,900}{700} = £7 \text{ per unit}$$

Substituting back in the data for February, we can determine the amount of fixed cost:

February	£
Total cost	41,150
Variable cost (2,450 units × £7	17,150
Therefore, fixed cost per month	24,000

Now that the fixed and variable cost elements have been identified, it is possible to estimate the total cost for any activity level within the range 1,750 units to 2,450 units.

The scattergraph method

This method takes account of all available historical data and it is simple to use. However, it is very prone to inaccuracies that arise due to subjectivity and the likelihood of human error.

1. First a scattergraph is drawn which plots all available pairs of data on a graph.
2. Then a line of best fit is drawn by eye. This is the line which, in the judgement of the user, appears to be the best representation of the gradient of the sets of points on the graph. This is demonstrated in Figure 1.10.

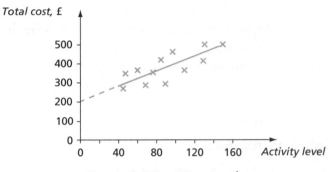

Figure 1.10 Scattergraph

> ❗ The inaccuracies involved in drawing the line of best fit should be obvious to you. If you had been presented with this set of data, your own line of best fit might have been slightly different from ours.

3. The point where the extrapolation of this line cuts the vertical axis (the intercept) is then read off as the total fixed cost element. The variable cost per unit is given by the gradient of the line.

   From Figure 1.10, the fixed cost contained within this set of data is adjudged to be £200. The variable cost is calculated as follows:

   Cost for zero units = £200
   Cost for 150 units = £500

   $$\text{Gradient (i.e. variable cost)} = \frac{500 - 200}{150 - 0} = £2 \text{ per unit}$$

1.9.5 Using historical data

The main problem which arises in the determination of cost behaviour is that the estimates are usually based on data collected in the past. Events in the past may not be representative of the future and managers should be aware of this if they are using the information for planning and decision-making purposes.

1.9.6 The importance of time scale in analysing cost behaviour

It is important to think about the time period under consideration when we are analysing cost behaviour patterns. For example, over a long period of time all costs might be considered to be variable.

Over a number of years, if activity reduces an organisation can move to smaller premises to reduce rent costs and they can reduce the number of supervisors to reduce supervisor salary cost. Thus costs which we might normally classify as fixed costs are, in the longer term, becoming more variable in relation to the level of activity.

However in the shorter term costs such as rent and supervisors' salaries are fixed. If demand for a product reduces, the expenditure on rent and on supervisors' salaries cannot be reduced immediately in response to the reduction in output. Such decisions require planning and consideration of factors such as whether the reduction in output is temporary or actions that might be taken to increase output again.

Similarly, over a number of years if activity increases then rent costs and supervisor salary costs will increase in response to the change in activity, again demonstrating more variable behaviour patterns in the longer term.

However the rent and salary cost is not likely to increase in the longer term in a linear fashion in the way that we have depicted linear variable costs earlier in this chapter. In fact the behaviour of such costs over a longer period of time is likely to follow the pattern of the stepped fixed cost depicted in Figure 1.3.

Think also about a cost that we would normally classify as variable, such as direct labour cost. In the very short term, for example one day, this cost could be regarded as a fixed cost. If for some reason, perhaps a machine breakdown, we do not produce any output on a particular day it is unlikely that at short notice we can send home all the work force and not pay them. Thus the direct labour cost is a fixed cost in the very short term.

> In an assessment you should assume that the time period under consideration is neither very long nor very short, unless you are given clear instructions to the contrary.

1.10 Summary

Having read this chapter the main points that you should understand are as follows.

1. Organisations need costing systems that will provide the basic information that management requires for planning, control and decision-making.
2. A cost unit is the basic unit of measurement selected for cost control purposes.
3. A cost centre is used as a 'collecting place' for costs, which may then be further analysed and related to individual cost units.
4. A cost object is anything for which costs can be ascertained. Examples are a product, a service, a centre, an activity, a customer and a distribution channel.
5. Costs may be classified in a number of different ways depending on the reason for the classification exercise. The main classifications are according to their nature (material, labour, expenses), according to their purpose (direct or indirect) or according to responsibility.
6. The concept of cost needs to be qualified as direct, full, marginal, etc. in order to be meaningful.
7. Costs which are not affected by changes in the level of activity are fixed costs or period costs.

8. A stepped fixed cost is constant within the relevant range for each activity level.
9. A variable cost increases or decreases in line with changes in the level of activity.
10. A cost which is partly fixed and partly variable is a semi-variable, semi-fixed or mixed cost.
11. Observed cost behaviour patterns apply only over the relevant range of activity levels.
12. The fixed and variable elements of a semi-variable cost can be determined using the high–low method or a scattergraph.
13. It is important to consider the time scale when analysing cost behaviour. In the longer term, fixed costs tend to become step fixed costs and in the very short term all costs are fixed.

Revision Questions

1

? Question 1 Multiple choice

In the multiple choice questions in the actual assessment each option would usually have an empty box or circle beside it. You would be required to simply place the cursor on the relevant box and click the mouse to select the correct answer. In this Learning System we have labelled the four options as A, B, C and D. These letters are for reference purposes only and to assist us in our discussion of the solutions.

You are advised to try the online demo of cba questions on CIMA's website at www.cimaglobal.com/cba so that you will be aware of the way in which the questions will be presented.

1.1 Cost centres are:

    (A) units of output or service for which costs are ascertained.
    (B) functions or locations for which costs are ascertained.
    (C) a segment of the organisation for which budgets are prepared.
    (D) amounts of expenditure attributable to various activities.

1.2 Prime cost is:

    (A) all costs incurred in manufacturing a product.
    (B) the total of direct costs.
    (C) the material cost of a product.
    (D) the cost of operating a department.

1.3 Fixed costs are conventionally deemed to be:

    (A) constant per unit of output.
    (B) constant in total when production volume changes.
    (C) outside the control of management.
    (D) those unaffected by inflation.

1.4 The following data relate to two activity levels of an out-patient department in a hospital:

Number of consultations by patients	4,500	5,750
Overheads	£269,750	£289,125

Fixed overheads are not affected by the number of consultations per period. The variable cost per consultation:

    (A) is approximately £15.50
    (B) is approximately £44.44
    (C) is approximately £59.94
    (D) cannot be calculated without more information.

1.5 P Ltd is preparing the production budget for the next period. Based on previous experience, it has found that there is a linear relationship between production volume and production costs. The following cost information has been collected in connection with production:

Volume (units)	Cost (£)
1,600	23,200
2,500	25,000

What would be the production cost for a production volume of 2,700 units?

(A) £5,400
(B) £25,400
(C) £27,000
(D) £39,150

1.6 The following is a graph of cost against volume of output:

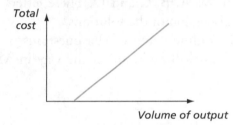

To which of the following costs does the graph correspond?

(A) Electricity bills made up of a standing charge and a variable charge.
(B) Bonus payments to employees when production reaches a certain level.
(C) Sales commission payable per unit up to a maximum amount of commission.
(D) Bulk discounts on purchases, the discount being given on all units purchased.

The following information relates to questions 1.7–1.11

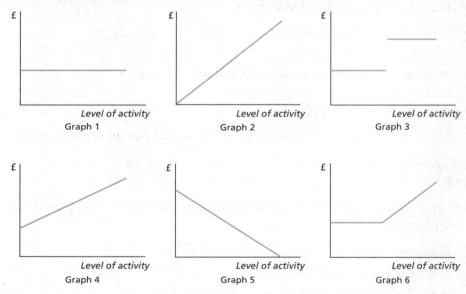

Which one of the above graphs illustrates the costs described in questions 1.7–1.11?

1.7   A linear variable cost – when the vertical axis represents cost incurred.

   (A) Graph 1
   (B) Graph 2
   (C) Graph 4
   (D) Graph 5

1.8   A fixed cost – when the vertical axis represents cost incurred.

   (A) Graph 1
   (B) Graph 2
   (C) Graph 3
   (D) Graph 6

1.9   A linear variable cost – when the vertical axis represents cost per unit.

   (A) Graph 1
   (B) Graph 2
   (C) Graph 3
   (D) Graph 6

1.10   A semi-variable cost – when the vertical axis represents cost incurred.

   (A) Graph 1
   (B) Graph 2
   (C) Graph 4
   (D) Graph 5

1.11   A step fixed cost – when the vertical axis represents cost incurred.

   (A) Graph 3
   (B) Graph 4
   (C) Graph 5
   (D) Graph 6

1.12   Over long-time periods of several years, factory rent costs will tend to behave as:

   (A) linear variable costs
   (B) fixed costs
   (C) step fixed costs
   (D) curvilinear variable costs

❓ **Question 2** Short objective-test questions

2.1   Which of the following are stepped fixed costs?

   ☐   Machine rental costs
   ☐   Direct material costs
   ☐   Royalties payable on units produced
   ☐   Depreciation on delivery vehicles

2.2 A company increases its activity within the relevant range. Tick the correct boxes below to indicate the effect on costs.

Total variable costs will:	increase	☐
	decrease	☐
	remain the same	☐
Total fixed cost will:	increase	☐
	decrease	☐
	remain the same	☐
The variable cost per unit will:	increase	☐
	decrease	☐
	remain the same	☐
The fixed cost per unit will:	increase	☐
	decrease	☐
	remain the same	☐

2.3 The variable production cost per unit of product B is £2 and the fixed production overhead for a period is £4,000. The total production cost of producing 3,000 units of B in a period is £⬚.

2.4 In a hotel, which of the following would be suitable cost units and cost centres?

	Suitable as cost centre	*Suitable as cost unit*
Restaurant	☐	☐
Guest night	☐	☐
Meal served	☐	☐
Fitness suite	☐	☐
Bar	☐	☐

2.5

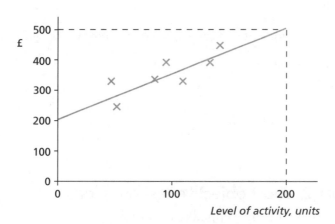

Based on the above scattergraph:

- the period fixed cost is £⬚.
- the variable cost per unit is £⬚.

2.6 The following data relates to the overhead costs of a commercial laundry for the latest two periods.

Overhead costs £	Number of items laundered
5,140	2,950
5,034	2,420

A formula that could be used to estimate the overhead costs for a forthcoming period is:

Overhead cost = £⬚ + (£⬚ × number of items laundered)

2.7 Spotless Limited is an office cleaning business which employs a team of part-time cleaners who are paid an hourly wage. The business provides cleaning services for a number of clients, ranging from small offices attached to high-street shops to large open-plan offices in high-rise buildings.

In determining the cost of providing a cleaning service to a particular client, which of the following costs would be a direct cost of cleaning that client's office and which would be an indirect cost?

	Direct cost	Indirect cost
(a) The wages paid to the cleaner who is sent to the client's premises	☐	☐
(b) The cost of carpet shampoo used by the cleaner	☐	☐
(c) The salaries of Spotless Ltd's accounts clerks	☐	☐
(d) Rent of the premises where Spotless Ltd stores its cleaning materials and equipment	☐	☐
(e) Travelling expenses paid to the cleaner to reach the client's premises	☐	☐
(f) Advertising expenses incurred in attracting more clients to Spotless Ltd's business	☐	☐

BASIC ASPECTS OF COST ACCOUNTING

 Question 3 Cost classification

A company manufactures and retails clothing.

When determining the cost of units produced, *you are required* to write the correct classification for each of the costs below into the box provided, using the following classifications (each cost is intended to belong to only one classification):

   (i) direct materials
  (ii) direct labour
 (iii) direct expenses
  (iv) indirect production overhead
   (v) research and development costs
  (vi) selling and distribution costs
 (vii) administration costs
(viii) finance costs

1. lubricant for sewing machines
2. floppy disks for general office computer
3. maintenance contract for general office photocopying machine
4. telephone rental plus metered calls
5. interest on bank overdraft
6. Performing Rights Society charge for music broadcast throughout the factory
7. market research undertaken prior to a new product launch
8. wages of security guards for factory
9. cost of denim fabric purchased
10. royalty payable on number of units of product XY produced
11. road fund licences for delivery vehicles
12. postage cost of parcels sent to customers
13. cost of advertising products on television
14. audit fees
15. chief accountant's salary
16. wages of operatives in the cutting department
17. cost of painting advertising slogans on delivery vans
18. wages of storekeepers in materials store
19. wages of fork lift truck drivers who handle raw materials
20. cost of developing a new product in the laboratory

Solutions to Revision Questions

✓ Solution 1

- The best way to approach multiple-choice questions is to work out your own answer first, before you look at the options. If your answer is not included in the options then you may be forced to guess. Improve your chances by eliminating the unlikely answers, or those that you know to be incorrect. Then take a guess from the remaining choices.
- Make sure that you answer every question. You will not be penalised for an incorrect answer – and you might guess correctly!

1.1 Answer: (B)

Cost centres act as 'collecting places' for costs before they are analysed further.

1.2 Answer: (B)

Answer (A) describes total production cost. Answer (C) is only a part of prime cost. Answer (D) is an overhead cost.

1.3 Answer: (B)

The total amount of fixed costs remains unchanged when production volume changes, therefore the unit rate fluctuates.

1.4 Answer: (A)

With the same amount of fixed overheads at both activity levels, the change in overheads must be due to extra variable cost.

	Overheads £	Consultations
High	289,125	5,750
Low	269,750	4,500
Change	19,375	1,250

$$\text{Variable overhead cost per consultation} = \frac{£19,375}{1,250} = £15.50$$

1.5   Answer: (B)

Units	£
2,500	25,000
1,600	23,200
900	1,800

$$\text{Variable cost per unit} = \frac{£1,800}{900} = £2$$

Substitute in high activity:

	£
Total cost	25,000
Variable cost = 2,500 units × £2	5,000
Therefore fixed cost	20,000

Forecast for 2,700 units:

	£
Fixed cost	20,000
Variable cost 2,700 × £2	5,400
Total cost	25,400

1.6   Answer: (B)

The graph shows a variable cost which starts to be incurred only beyond a certain volume of output. Only B fits this description of cost behaviour.

1.7   Answer: (B)

Graph 2 depicts a cost which increases in total by equal amounts for each increment in the level of activity.

1.8   Answer: (A)

Graph 1 depicts a cost which remains the same regardless of the level of activity.

1.9   Answer: (A)

The variable cost per unit remains constant regardless of the level of activity.

1.10   Answer: (C)

Graph 4 depicts a cost which contains a fixed element which is incurred even at zero activity. Thereafter the cost increases in total by equal amounts for each increment in the level of activity: this is the extra variable cost incurred.

1.11   Answer: (A)

Graph 3 depicts a cost which remains constant up to a critical level of activity. At that point the total cost increases by a step to a new, higher level.

1.12 Answer: (C)

As activity increases or decreases over a period of several years the rent cost will remain constant for a range of activity but will then increase or decrease in steps as critical activity levels are reached when larger or smaller premises are needed.

 Solution 2

- Always read the question carefully. For example, question 2.1 does *not* state 'which *one* of the following are stepped fixed costs?'. In fact, there is more than one correct answer.

2.1 Machine rental cost is a stepped fixed cost. For one machine the total rental cost stays constant until the machine is working at full capacity. Then two machines will be needed and the rental cost goes up a step to a new, higher level. When the two machines are at full capacity there will be a need to rent three machines and so on.

Depreciation on delivery vehicles is a stepped fixed cost. Depreciation is calculated on an annual basis and is unlikely to be affected by the level of activity in the short term. For one vehicle the annual depreciation is a constant amount. If two vehicles are required the depreciation cost goes up a step and so on.

Royalty costs and direct material costs are variable costs.

2.2 As activity increases within the relevant range, the total variable costs will *increase* and the total fixed cost will *remain the same*. The variable cost per unit will *remain the same* and the fixed cost per unit will *decrease*.

2.3 Total production cost = (3,000 × £2) + £4,000 = £10,000.

2.4

	Suitable as cost centre	*Suitable as cost unit*
Restaurant	✓	
Guest night		✓
Meal served		✓
Fitness suite	✓	
Bar	✓	

2.5 The period fixed cost is £200. The variable cost per unit is:

$$\frac{£500 - £200}{200 \text{ units}} = £1.50 \text{ per unit}$$

2.6

Overhead costs £	*Number of items laundered*
5,140	2,950
5,034	2,420
106	530

Variable cost per item laundered £106/530 = £0.20
Substitute in high activity:

	£
Total cost	5,140
Variable cost = 2,950 items × £0.20	590
Therefore fixed cost	4,550

A formula that could be used to estimate the overhead costs for a forthcoming period is:

Overhead cost = £4,550 + (£0.20 × number of items laundered)

2.7

		Direct cost	Indirect cost
(a)	The wages paid to the cleaner who is sent to the client's premises	✓	
(b)	The cost of carpet shampoo used by the cleaner	✓	
(c)	The salaries of Spotless Ltd's accounts clerks		✓
(d)	Rent of the premises where Spotless Ltd stores its cleaning materials and equipment		✓
(e)	Travelling expenses paid to the cleaner to reach the client's premises	✓	
(f)	Advertising expenses incurred in attracting more clients to Spotless Ltd's business		✓

The direct costs are (a), (b) and (e) because they can be directly identified with the cost object under consideration (this particular client). The other costs are indirect because they would have to be shared among all of the clients serviced by Spotless Limited.

 ## Solution 3

- When you are trying to determine whether a cost is direct or indirect in relation to a cost object, think about whether the cost would need to be shared over several cost objects or whether it can be attributed directly to a particular cost object. A cost that needs to be shared must be an indirect cost.

Item	Classification	Item	Classification
1	(iv)	11	(vi)
2	(vii)	12	(vi)
3	(vii)	13	(vi)
4	(vii)	14	(vii)
5	(viii)	15	(vii)
6	(iv)	16	(ii)
7	(vi)	17	(vi)
8	(iv)	18	(iv)
9	(i)	19	(iv)
10	(iii)	20	(v)

Accounting for the
Value of Inventories

Accounting for the Value of Inventories

2

LEARNING OUTCOMES

After completing this chapter, you should be able to:

▶ distinguish between the historical cost of an asset and the economic value of an asset to an organisation;

▶ apply first-in-first-out (FIFO), last-in-first-out (LIFO) and average cost (AVCO) methods of accounting for stock, calculating stock values and related gross profit;

▶ explain why first-in-first-out (FIFO) is essentially a historical cost method, while last-in-first-out (LIFO) approximates economic cost.

2.1 Introduction

In this chapter, you will learn about the different methods that can be used to value inventory and the impact of each of these on the profit reported for the period.

The valuation of inventory, although a cost accounting function, is also required for financial accounting and you should be aware that the regulations concerning the valuation of inventory which apply to financial accounting may be a significant influence in determining the valuation method used.

All of the inventory valuation methods described in this chapter can be applied to finished goods items ready for sale as well as to raw materials held in stores for use in production.

2.2 Valuing inventory at cost

The general principle is that inventory should be valued at cost. However, it can sometimes be difficult to determine which cost should be used. Have a look at the following example.

Example: Which cost should be used?

The following example illustrates the problem of determining the cost of the inventory held at a particular time. During September the following items were purchased and issued from stores.

September 1		Opening balance		Nil
	Bought	100 units		@ £5.00 each
2	Issued	50 units		
10	Bought	50 units		@ £5.50 each
20	Issued	60 units		
27	Bought	100 units		@ £5.60 each

It is easy to calculate the quantity of items remaining in the stores on 27 September by comparing the total quantity purchased (250) with the total number issued from stores (110). The closing inventory quantity is therefore 140 units (250 – 110). However what is the cost of the items in inventory?

Unless each item is individually marked with the price at which it was bought and the balance is identified by individual items at individual prices, it is difficult to know what value should be placed on the inventory items.

This method of individual pricing does exist (it is known as the *specific price* method), but because of the cost of operating such a system it is unsuitable for all but very expensive items where the inventory quantities and rates of usage are low. Alternative methods are used instead, each of which will now be explained using the data from the above example.

2.3 First in, first out (FIFO)

This method assumes for valuation purposes that the items received earliest are those which are issued first. This does not necessarily mean that these are the items which have physically been issued first.

A stores ledger record is maintained for each inventory item. This record shows the volume and value of the receipts and issues made during the period, and the remaining balance in stores after each receipt or issue.

The stores ledger record of the transactions using this method would appear as follows:

Stores ledger record

Date	Qty	Receipts Price	£	Qty	Issues Price	£	Qty	Balance Price	£
September									
1							Nil		Nil
1	100	5.00	500				100	5.00	500
2				50	5.00	250	50	5.00	250
10	50	5.50	275				50	5.00	250
							50	5.50	275
							100		525
20				50	5.00	250			
				10	5.50	55			
				60		305	40	5.50	220
27	100	5.60	560				40	5.50	220
							100	5.60	560
							140		780

Note that the issue made on 20 September is valued as 50 units at £5 each plus 10 units at £5.50 each. This is because the earliest price paid for any of the remaining inventory held at the time of issue was £5.

You should note the clarity of the entries, particularly those relating to the closing balances at the end of each day which are stated in chronological order.

> You must practice producing neat workings for your stores ledger record. Speed and accuracy are essential in the assessment and although you will not be awarded marks for your workings they will help to ensure that you arrive at the correct answer.

2.4 Last in, first out (LIFO)

This method assumes for valuation purposes that the latest price paid for items received is the one to be used to price issues. Using this method the stores ledger record of the same transactions would appear as follows:

Stores ledger record

Date	Qty	Receipts Price	£	Qty	Issues Price	£	Qty	Balance Price	£
September									
1							Nil		Nil
1	100	5.00	500				100	5.00	500
2				50	5 00	250	50	5.00	250
10	50	5.50	275				50	5.00	250
							50	5.50	275
							100		525
20				50	5.50	275			
				10	5.00	50			
				60		325	40	5.00	200
27	100	5.60	560				40	5.00	200
							100	5.60	560
							140		760

Using this valuation method, the first 50 items issued on 20 September are valued at £5.50 per unit. This is because the latest price paid at that date was the price paid for the delivery received on 10 September, which was £5.50 per unit. The remaining 10 units are valued at the price of £5 paid for the delivery received on 1 September.

2.5 Cumulative weighted average (AVCO)

This method calculates a weighted average price each time there is a receipt, using the formula:

$$\text{Weighted average price} = \frac{(\text{Value of inventory b/f} + \text{value of purchases})}{(\text{Quantity of inventory b/f} + \text{quantity purchased})}$$

This average value per unit is then used for all issues until another delivery is received, when the average is recalculated. The stores ledger record of the same transactions using this method is as follows:

Stores ledger record

Date	Qty	Receipts Price	£	Qty	Issues Price	£	Qty	Balance Price	£
September									
1							Nil		Nil
1	100	5.00	500				100	5.00	500
2				50	5.00	250	50	5.00	250
10	50	5.50	275				100	5.25	525
20				60	5.25	315	40	5.25	210
27	100	5.60	560				140	5.50	770

Note that the price per unit on 10 September is calculated by the formula shown above:

$$\frac{£(250 + 275)}{50 + 50} = £5.25 \text{ per unit}$$

The average value per unit of £5.50 calculated on 27 September (£770/140) would be used to value all issues after this date until another receipt occurs when the average would be recalculated.

2.6   Comparison of FIFO, LIFO and AVCO

The following table shows the closing inventory valuations and values of issues using each of the three methods. In each case the value of the issues is obtained by totalling the individual issue valuations.

	Closing inventory valuation £	Value of issues £
FIFO	780	555
LIFO	760	575
AVCO	770	565

Points to note about the different inventory valuation methods include the following:

- The values for AVCO in the table lie between those for LIFO and FIFO. This should always occur because AVCO is an averaging method.
- Both LIFO and FIFO require records to be kept of each batch of purchases so that the appropriate price may be attached to each issue.
- Price fluctuations are smoothed out with the AVCO method which makes the data easier to use for decision-making, although the rounding of the unit value might cause some difficulties.
- Many management accountants would argue that LIFO provides more relevant information for decision-making because it uses the most up-to-date price.
- However LIFO may sometimes confuse managers, since the pricing method represents the opposite to what is happening in reality, that is, the items in store will probably be physically issued on a FIFO basis.

The overriding consideration for the internal cost accounting system is that the information should be useful for management purposes.

Let us look in more detail at the assertion that LIFO provides more relevant information for decision-making. If we assume that the items in the above example are items for resale, then using the FIFO method the cost of the items issued on 20 September was £305. If a customer offered you £315 for them you might well accept the offer on the basis that you had made £10 profit. If the LIFO method is used the offer would be rejected because the cost of the issue is stated to be £325 and thus to accept the customer's offer would be to make a loss. Which is correct?

It is reasonable to believe that in order to make a profit you should be able to replace the items that you have sold and still have some of the sale proceeds left over. In this example, the latest price paid on 10 September was £5.50 per unit and with the benefit of hindsight we know that the price on 27 September is £5.60 per unit. It is reasonable therefore to expect that the cost of replacing the items sold will be at least £5.50 per unit, which totals £330.

Thus, it can be seen that the use of the FIFO method would lead you to a decision which would cause you to be unable to replace the items sold with the sale proceeds received. The use of the LIFO method is thus argued to be better for decision-making.

2.6.1 Historical cost compared with economic cost and economic value

Although we have seen that the LIFO method results in issues from stores being valued at the most recent prices paid, the costs used are still historical costs. By their nature, historical costs are out of date and might not reflect the current value of an item.

The economic value of an asset depends on current circumstances and we have just seen that it can even be misleading to rely on LIFO historical costs when assessing the worth of an item issued from stores. The issue cost was out of date and the company might have had difficulty replacing the item if did not make a sufficiently high charge against profit for the cost of replacement.

If the inflation rate is very high or if purchases of inventory are made only infrequently then even the charges to cost of sales resulting from the LIFO method do not provide a good approximation of economic cost.

However in many circumstances the LIFO method will use up-to-date values, whereas the FIFO method is essentially an historical cost method.

The economic cost of an asset such as an item of material might be measured in terms of the benefit forgone by not using the asset in the 'next best' way; this is its opportunity cost.

For example, an item of material might be obsolete. The 'next best' alternative for this item would be to sell it and the value of this option is its net realisable value. The application of this concept can be seen in the financial accounting rule that inventory items should be valued at the lower of cost and net realisable value.

Thus an asset's economic cost or economic value might be higher or lower than its historical cost, depending on current circumstances.

2.7 Inventory valuation and the effect on gross profit

An important point to realise is that since each of the inventory valuation methods produces a different valuation, the profit reported under each of the methods will be different. An example will help you to see the difference.

Example

Continuing with the example in Section 2.2, suppose that the units issued from inventory are sold direct to the customer for £8 per unit. The gross profit recorded under each of the inventory valuation methods would be as follows:

	FIFO £	LIFO £	AVCO £
Sales revenue: 110 × £8	880	880	880
Purchases	1,335	1,335	1,335
Less closing inventory	780	760	770
Cost of goods sold	555	575	565
Gross profit	325	305	315

The prices of receipts are rising during the month. Therefore the FIFO method, which prices issues at the older, lower prices, results in the highest value of closing inventory and the highest profit figure. The AVCO method produces results that lie between those for FIFO and LIFO.

2.8 Periodic weighted average

This method is similar to the cumulative weighted average method described earlier, except that instead of calculating a new average price every time a receipt occurs an average is calculated based on the total purchases for the period. This average is then applied to all issues in the period.

$$\text{Periodic weighted average price} = \frac{\text{cost of opening inventory} + \text{total cost of receipts in period}}{\text{units in opening inventory} + \text{total units received in period}}$$

Using the same data, the periodic weighted average cost per unit is:

$$\frac{(\pounds 500 + \pounds 275 + \pounds 560)}{(100 + 50 + 100)} = \frac{\pounds 1,335}{250} = \pounds 5.34 \text{ per unit}$$

Every issue is priced at £5.34 per unit. The total value of all issues would be 110 units @ £5.34 = £587.40, leaving a closing inventory of 140 units valued at £747.60.

> In an assessment you must always use the *cumulative* weighted average pricing method unless you are specifically instructed to use the periodic weighted average method.

2.9 Materials documentation

2.9.1 Perpetual inventory system

We have seen how a stores ledger record for a particular inventory item shows each receipt and issue from stores as it occurs. This provides a continuous record of the balance of each inventory item and is known as a *perpetual inventory system*.

In practice there are likely to be discrepancies between the actual physical balance in stores and the balance shown on the stores ledger record. For this reason the inventory in stores should be counted on a regular basis and checked against the total shown on the stores ledger record. This ensures that minor discrepancies are corrected as soon as possible and that the stores ledger record provides a reasonably accurate record of available inventory.

2.9.2 Recording the receipt of goods

When goods are delivered by a supplier they will normally be accompanied by a delivery note. It is common for all orders to be delivered to stores (unless there is good reason to have them delivered elsewhere) and for the storekeeper to be responsible for checking the delivery and acknowledging its receipt by signing the supplier's delivery note.

The storekeeper will then raise a *goods received note (GRN)*. This is the document which is used to record the receipt of goods for the purpose of updating the stores ledger record. The information recorded on the GRN will include the quantity, code number and description of the material received, as well as the date of the delivery and the supplier's details.

A copy of the *GRN* will be sent to the purchasing department (so that they know that the goods ordered have actually been delivered) and to the accounts department (so that when the time comes to pay the supplier's invoice the accounts department knows that the goods have been received).

2.9.3 Recording the movement of inventory items

Whether material is issued to production or issued for indirect purposes, it may only be issued from stores against a properly authorised *material requisition*. This document is used to record the issue of material on the stores ledger record.

The information shown on the material requisition will include the quantity, code number and description of the items issued, as well as the date of the issue, the cost of the items issued (based on whatever inventory valuation method is in use: FIFO, LIFO, etc.) and the cost centre or the job number to be charged with the cost of the items issued.

Sometimes, materials may be issued and subsequently found to be surplus to requirements. These will be returned to the stores and this movement of materials must be recorded on a *material returned note*. This ensures that the recorded inventory quantity is increased to its correct level and that the recorded cost value of the materials issued to production is reduced.

This transaction can be thought of as the opposite of an issue to production and the information contained on a material returned note is similar to that on a material requisition note. The returned note will indicate which cost centre or job is to be credited with the cost of the materials returned to stores.

Occasionally, a cost centre might transfer material to another cost centre, without the material first being sent back to the stores. To ensure that the correct cost centre or job is charged with the cost of the materials a *material transfer note* is raised. This note details the material being transferred, giving the same information as a material requisition/material returned note, that is description, quantity, cost and so on. The transfer note also shows which cost centre or job is to be credited with the cost of the material and which is to be debited. The stores ledger record is not altered because the items transferred do not physically return to the stores.

2.10 Summary

Having read this chapter the main points that you should understand are as follows:

1. The stores ledger record for each inventory item shows the quantity, cost and total value of each issue and receipt and of the balance in stores after each movement of inventory.
2. The pricing of issues from inventory has a direct effect on cost of sales, inventory valuations and reported profits.
3. The FIFO method prices issues at the price of the oldest items remaining in stores. The LIFO method prices issues at the price of the items in stores that were received most recently.
4. The weighted average method uses an average price that can be calculated using two different bases: the cumulative weighted average and the periodic weighted average. The cumulative weighted average calculates a new average price every time a new batch is received into stores. The periodic weighted average calculates an average price at the end of each period. Unless you receive instructions to the contrary you should use the cumulative weighted average method in an assessment.
5. The inventory valuation methods can be applied to finished goods for sale as well as to raw materials held in stores for use in production.
6. A number of documents are used to record the receipt and movement of inventory items. These include a goods received note, material requisition, material returned note and a material transfer note.

Revision Questions

Question 1 Multiple choice
Data for questions 1.1 and 1.2

P Ltd had an opening inventory value of £2,640 (300 units valued at £8.80 each) on 1 April. The following receipts and issues were recorded during April:

10 April	Receipt	1,000 units	£8.60 per unit
23 April	Receipt	600 units	£9.00 per unit
29 April	Issues	1,700 units	

1.1 Using the LIFO method, what was the total value of the issues on 29 April?

(A) £14,840
(B) £14,880
(C) £14,888
(D) £15,300

1.2 Using the FIFO method, the value of the closing inventory was:

(A) £1,680
(B) £1,760
(C) £1,800
(D) £14,840

1.3 A firm has a high level of inventory turnover and uses the FIFO issue pricing system. In a period of rising purchase prices, the closing inventory valuation is:

(A) close to current purchase prices.
(B) based on the prices of the first items received.
(C) much lower than current purchase prices.
(D) the average of all goods purchased in the period.

1.4 Using the FIFO system for pricing issues from stores means that when prices are rising:

(A) product costs are overstated and profits understated.
(B) product costs are kept in line with price changes.
(C) product costs are understated and profits understated.
(D) product costs are understated and profits overstated.

1.5 During a period of rising prices, which *one* of the following statements is correct?

(A) The LIFO method will produce lower profits than the FIFO method, and lower closing inventory values.

(B) The LIFO method will produce lower profits than the FIFO method, and higher closing inventory values.

(C) The FIFO method will produce lower profits than the LIFO method, and lower closing inventory values.

(D) The FIFO method will produce lower profits than the LIFO method, and higher closing inventory values.

? **Question 2** Short objective-test questions

2.1 Opening inventory for a particular component at the beginning of April was zero. The following receipts and issues were recorded during April.

April 1	Received 100 components at a price of £6.00 each
April 2	Issued 30 components
April 8	Received 30 components at a price of £6.50 each
April 10	Issued 60 components
April 15	Received 100 components at a price of £6.50 each
April 16	Issued 40 components

The weighted average pricing method is used.
Complete the following boxes.
The total value of the components issued on April 10 was £ ⬚.
The cost per component issued on April 16 was £ ⬚.

2.2 In a period of rising prices, which of the following statements are *true*? Tick the box for any statement that is true.

☐ (a) Reported profits will be higher with FIFO than with LIFO.

☐ (b) The value of closing inventory will be higher with FIFO than with LIFO.

☐ (c) LIFO would be the preferable method for financial accounting purposes because it uses the oldest price.

2.3 BB imports product U and sells the product to retail customers at a price of £14 per case. BB had no inventory at the beginning of February and during February the following receipts and sales were recorded.

6 February	Received	1,400 cases @ £8.20 per case
15 February	Received	900 cases @ £9.10 per case
20 February	Sold	780 cases
22 February	Received	330 cases @ £9.90 per case
28 February	Sold	860 cases

(a) Using the FIFO method of inventory valuation, the gross profit reported for February would be £ ⬚.

(b) Using the LIFO method of inventory valuation, the gross profit reported for February would be £ ⬚.

2.4 Which of the following documents will be used to record the receipt of materials from stores by a production cost centre, ready for use in production?

☐ Goods received note
☐ Material requisition

2.5 Tick the correct box below to indicate whether the following statement is true or false. Economic cost is always higher than historical cost.

☐ True
☐ False

2.6 A retailer currently uses the weighted average pricing method to value his inventory. In a period of rising prices, the retailer decides instead to use the FIFO method. Tick the correct box to complete the statement below.

The gross profit for the period will be:

☐ higher
☐ lower

Question 3 Longer revision question: inventory valuation

Three students, K, L and M, are equal partners in a joint venture which involves them, on a part-time basis, in buying and selling sacks of product F. The transactions for the 3 months ended on 30 June were as stated below. You are to assume that purchases at unit costs given were made at the beginning of each month and that the sales were made at the end of each month at the fixed price of £1.50 per sack.

Month	Purchases Sacks	Unit cost £	Sales Sacks
April	1,000	1.00	500
May	500	1.20	750
June	1,000	1.00	200

In July, the student partners held a meeting to review their financial position and share out the profits but there was disagreement because each partner had priced the issues on a different basis. K had used FIFO, L had used LIFO and M had used a weighted average, basing his weighted average on the whole of the 3 months' purchases.

Shown below is an extract from K and L's stores ledger records.

Month	Receipts Qty	Price	£	Sales Qty	Price	£	Balance Qty	Price	£
April	1,000	1.00	1,000	500			500		
May	500	1.20	600	750		A	250		B
June	1,000	1.00	1,000	200		C	1,050		D

Requirements

(a) The values shown as A, B, C and D in K's records, using a FIFO system, would be:

A: £ [   ]
B: £ [   ]
C: £ [   ]
D: £ [   ]

(b) The values shown as A, B, C and D in L's records, using a LIFO system, would be:

A: £ [   ]
B: £ [   ]
C: £ [   ]
D: £ [   ]

(c) The value of the closing inventory in M's records, using a weighted average based on the whole of the 3 months' purchases, would be £ [   ].

(d) The profit reported by each of the students for the 3-month period would be:

K (FIFO):   £ [   ]
L (LIFO):   £ [   ]
M (wt. ave.): £ [   ]

(e) The pricing method being used by student M is known as a: (*tick the correct box*)

☐ periodic weighted average method
☐ cumulative weighted average method.

(f) Show how the stores ledger record of student M would appear if he recalculated a revised weighted average price every time sacks are received into stores.

Solutions to Revision Questions

2

✓ Solution 1

- You will need to think carefully when you are selecting the answer for the narrative multiple-choice questions. Read each option slowly and ensure that all aspects of the description are correct before you make your final selection.

1.1 Answer: (B)

With the LIFO method the latest prices are used first to price issues:

	£
600 units from 23 April × £9.00 per unit	5,400
1,000 units from 10 April × £8.60 per unit	8,600
100 units from opening inventory × £8.80 per unit	880
Total	14,880

1.2 Answer: (C)

With the FIFO method the earliest prices are used first to price issues. Therefore, the remaining inventory is valued at the latest prices.

Closing inventory = 200 units × £9 = £1,800

1.3 Answer: (A)

Using FIFO, the inventory will be valued at the latest prices paid for the items. If inventory turnover is high, then the items in stores will have been purchased fairly recently. Therefore, they will be valued at prices which are close to current purchase prices.

1.4 Answer: (D)

FIFO charges cost of production with the price of the oldest items in stores. When prices are rising, the charges made to product costs lag behind current prices. Product costs and charges to cost of sales are therefore understated and profits are overstated.

1.5 Answer: (A)

LIFO charges the latest prices to cost of sales. Therefore, during a period of rising prices the LIFO method will produce a higher cost of sales and a lower profit. Since inventory is valued using the older prices, the LIFO closing inventory values will be lower.

Solution 2

2.1 The total value of the components issued on April 10 was £369.00
The cost per component issued on April 16 was £6.40

Workings:

		Receipts			Issues			Balance	
Date	Qty	Price	£	Qty	Price	£	Qty	Price	£
1							Nil		Nil
1	100	6.00	600.00				100	6.00	600.00
2				30	6.00	180.00	70	6.00	420.00
8	30	6.50	195.00				100	6.15[1]	615.00
10				60	6.15	369.00	40	6.15	246.00
15	100	6.50	650.00				140	6.40[2]	896.00

Notes

1. $\dfrac{£420 + £195}{100} = £6.15$

2. $\dfrac{£246 + £650}{140} = £6.40$

2.2 (a) *True*. The FIFO issues from inventory, to be charged as a part of cost of sales, will be made at the older, lower prices.
   (b) *True*. The FIFO closing inventory will be valued at the most recent prices.
   (c) *False*. The LIFO valuation method is not acceptable under the accounting standard which regulates the valuation of inventory for financial accounting purposes.

2.3 (a) Using the FIFO method of inventory valuation, the gross profit reported for February would be £9,296.
   (b) Using the LIFO method of inventory valuation, the gross profit reported for February would be £8,141.

Workings:
(a) FIFO

		Receipts			Sales			Balance	
Date	Qty	Price	£	Qty	Price	£	Qty	Price	£
6	1,400	8.20	11,480				1,400	8.20	11,480
15	900	9.10	8,190				1,400	8.20	11,480
							900	9.10	8,190
							2,300		19,670
20				780	8.20	6,396	620	8.20	5,084
							900	9.10	8,190
							1,520		13,274
22	330	9.90	3,267				620	8.20	5,084
							900	9.10	8,190
							330	9.90	3,267
							1,850		16,541
28				620	8.20	5,084	660	9.10	6,006
				240	9.10	2,184	330	9.90	3,267
				860		7,268	990		9,273

Gross profit $= (£14 \times (780 + 860)) - £(6,396 + 7,268) = £9,296$

(b) LIFO

| | | Receipts | | | Sales | | | Balance | |
Date	Qty	Price	£	Qty	Price	£	Qty	Price	£
6	1,400	8.20	11,480				1,400	8.20	11,480
15	900	9.10	8,190				1,400	8.20	11,480
							900	9.10	8,190
							2,300		19,670
20				780	9.10	7,098	1,400	8.20	11,480
							120	9.10	1,092
							1,520		12,572
22	330	9.90	3,267				1,400	8.20	11,480
							120	9.10	1,092
							330	9.90	3,267
							1,850		15,839
28				330	9.90	3,267			
				120	9.10	1,092			
				410	8.20	3,362			
				860		7,721	990	8.20	8,118

Gross profit = (£14 × (780 + 860)) − £(7,098 + 7,721) = £8,141

2.4 The issue of material from stores to a production cost centre will be recorded on a material requisition. A goods received note is used to record the original receipt into stores of goods from the supplier.

2.5 False.

Economic cost can be lower than historical cost. For example a manufacturer might have purchased a certain item of raw material for £20. This is its historical cost. If the material has now become obsolete and can be sold for only £12 this is its economic cost, which is lower than the historical cost.

2.6 If the retailer uses FIFO instead of the weighted average pricing method in a period of rising prices, the gross profit for the period will be higher.

The FIFO method charges to cost of sales the price of the oldest, lower priced goods. The weighted average price charged to cost of sales will be higher because of the effect on the average of the higher prices of items received into inventory most recently. Thus the gross profit will be higher with FIFO than with the weighted average pricing method.

✓ Solution 3

- Probably the best approach is to draft your own rough stores records as workings.
- Remember the need for accuracy; it is your final answer that counts. You will not receive marks for your workings.

(a) A £800
B £300
C £240
D £1,060

Workings: K's records using FIFO

Month	Receipts Qty	Price	£	Sales Qty	Price	£	Balance Qty	Price	£
April	1,000	1.00	1,000	500	1.00	500	500	1.00	500
May	500	1.20	600	500	1.00	500			
				250	1.20	300			
				750		800	250	1.20	300
June	1,000	1.00	1,000	200	1.20	240	50	1.20	60
							1,000	1.00	1,000
							1,050		1,060

(b) A £850

B £250

C £200

D £1,050

Workings: L's records using LIFO

Month	Receipts Qty	Price	£	Sales Qty	Price	£	Balance Qty	Price	£
April	1,000	1.00	1,000	500	1.00	500	500	1.00	500
May	500	1.20	600	500	1.20	600			
				250	1.00	250			
				750		850	250	1.00	250
June	1,000	1.00	1,000	200	1.00	200	1,050	1.00	1,050

(c) £1,092

Workings:

$$\text{Weighted average price for 3 months} = \frac{£(1,000 + 600 + 1,000)}{1,000 + 500 + 1,000} = £1.04 \text{ per unit}$$

Value of closing inventory = 1,050 units × £1.04 = £1,092

(d) K (FIFO)   £635

L (LIFO)   £625

M (wt. ave.)   £667

Workings:

	K £	L £	M £
Sales (1,450 @ £1.50)	2,175	2,175	2,175
Cost of sales:			
Purchases	2,600	2,600	2,600
Less closing inventory	1,060	1,050	1,092
	1,540	1,550	1,508
Profit	635	625	667

(e) The pricing method being used by student M is known as a *periodic weighted average method.*

M's weighted average is based on the whole of the 3 month's purchases, so this is a periodic average. The method that recalculates the weighted average price every time a receipt occurs is called the cumulative or perpetual weighted average method.

(f) This is the perpetual weighted average method.

 Remember that you should use the perpetual weighted average in the assessment unless you are specifically told otherwise.

Month	Receipts Qty	Receipts Price	Receipts £	Sales Qty	Sales Price	Sales £	Balance Qty	Balance Price	Balance £
April	1,000	1.00	1,000				1,000	1.00	1,000
April				500	1.00	500	500	1.00	500
May	500	1.20	600				1,000	1.10[1]	1,100
May				750	1.10	825	250	1.10	275
June	1,000	1.00	1,000				1,250	1.02[2]	1,275
June				200	1.02	204	1,050	1.02	1,071

1. £1,100/1,000 units = £1.10 weighted average price
2. £1,275/1,250 units = £1.02 weighted average price

3

The Analysis of Overhead

The Analysis of Overhead

3

LEARNING OUTCOMES

After completing this chapter, you should be able to:

▶ prepare cost statements for allocation and apportionment of overheads, including between reciprocal service departments:

▶ calculate direct, variable and full costs of products, services and activities using overhead absorption rates to trace indirect costs to cost units;

▶ explain the use of cost information in pricing decisions, including marginal cost pricing and the calculation of 'full cost'-based prices to generate a specified return on sales or investment.

3.1 Introduction

In this chapter you will learn about the analysis of indirect costs or overheads. We will be looking at the three-stage process of attributing overheads to individual cost units: allocation, apportionment and absorption.

You will need a thorough understanding of the contents of this chapter for your studies of the *Fundamentals of Management Accounting* syllabus and for many of the syllabuses at later stages in the CIMA examinations.

3.2 What is an overhead cost?

3.2.1 Definition

An overhead cost is defined in the CIMA *Terminology* as 'expenditure on labour, materials or services that cannot be economically identified with a specific saleable cost unit'.

Overhead costs are also referred to as *indirect costs* which we discussed in Chapter 1. Therefore, overhead cost comprises indirect material, indirect labour and indirect expenses. The indirect nature of overheads means that they need to be 'shared out' among the cost units as fairly and as accurately as possible.

In this chapter, you will be learning how this 'sharing out', or *attribution*, is accomplished for production overheads, using a costing method known as *absorption costing*.

One of the main reasons for absorbing overheads into the cost of units is for inventory valuation purposes. Accounting standards recommend that inventory valuations should include an element of fixed production overheads incurred in the normal course of business. We therefore have to find a fair way of sharing out the fixed production overhead costs among the units produced.

3.2.2 Functional analysis of overhead costs

Overhead costs may be classified according to the function of the organisation responsible for incurring the cost. Examples of overhead cost classifications include production overhead, selling and distribution overhead, and administration overhead. It is usually possible to classify the majority of overhead cost in this way, but some overhead costs relate to the organisation generally and may be referred to as general overhead.

In this chapter we shall focus mainly on production overhead. Production is that function of the business which converts raw materials into the organisation's finished product. The production department is usually divided into a number of departments or cost centres. Some of these cost centres are directly involved with the production process. These are called *production cost centres* and might include, for example, the cutting department and the finishing department.

Other cost centres in the production department are not directly involved with the production process but provide support services for the production cost centres. These are called *service cost centres*, and examples include the maintenance department and the stores.

3.3 Overhead allocation and apportionment

The first stage in the analysis of production overheads is the selection of appropriate cost centres. The selection will depend on a number of factors, including the level of control required and the availability of information.

Having selected suitable cost centres, the next stage in the analysis is to determine the overhead cost for each cost centre. This is achieved through the process of allocation and apportionment.

Cost allocation is possible when we can identify a cost as specifically attributable to a particular cost centre. For example, the salary of the manager of the packing department can be allocated to the packing department cost centre. It is not necessary to share the salary cost over several different cost centres.

Cost apportionment is necessary when it is not possible to allocate a cost to a specific cost centre. In this case, the cost is shared out over two or more cost centres according to the estimated benefit received by each cost centre. As far as possible the basis of apportionment is selected to reflect this benefit received. For example, the cost of rent and rates might be apportioned according to the floor space occupied by each cost centre.

The following example illustrates the allocation and apportionment of production overhead costs.

Example

The information given below relates to a four-week accounting period of WHW Ltd.

	Machining	Assembly	Finishing	Stores
Area occupied (square metres)	24,000	36,000	16,000	4,000
Plant and equipment at cost (£000)	1,400	200	60	10
Number of employees	400	800	200	20
Direct labour hours	16,000	32,000	4,000	
Direct wages (£)	32,600	67,200	7,200	
Machine hours	32,000	4,000	200	
Number of requisitions on stores	310	1,112	100	
Allocated costs	£	£	£	£
Indirect wages	9,000	15,000	4,000	6,000
Indirect materials	394	1,400	600	
Maintenance	1,400	600	100	
Power	1,600	400	200	

Other costs (in total)	
Rent	2,000
Business rates	600
Insurance on building	200
Lighting and heating	400
Depreciation on plant and equipment	16,700
Wage-related costs	28,200
Factory administration and personnel	7,100
Insurance on plant and equipment	1,670
Cleaning of factory premises	800
	57,670

The data above distinguishes between those costs which can and those which cannot be allocated to a cost centre. The first step is to construct an overhead analysis sheet having separate columns for each cost centre, together with a column for the total costs, a description of the cost item and the basis upon which the cost has been apportioned between the cost centres if applicable.

An explanation of the apportionment method is given beneath the analysis.

Item	Basis of apportionment	Machining £	Assembly £	Finishing £	Stores £	Total £
Indirect wages	Allocation	9,000	15,000	4,000	6,000	34,000
Indirect materials	Allocation	394	1,400	600	–	2,394
Maintenance	Allocation	1,400	600	100	–	2,100
Power	Allocation	1,600	400	200	–	2,200
Rent	Area occupied	600	900	400	100	2,000
Business rates	Area occupied	180	270	120	30	600
Building insurance	Area occupied	60	90	40	10	200
Lighting/heating	Area occupied	120	180	80	20	400
Depreciation on plant/equipment	Plant/equipment at cost	14,000	2,000	600	100	16,700
Wage-related costs	Total wages	8,320	16,440	2,240	1,200	28,200
Factory administration and personnel	No. of employees	2,000	4,000	1,000	100	7,100
Insurance on plant/equipment	Plant/equipment at cost	1,400	200	60	10	1,670
Factory cleaning	Area occupied	240	360	160	40	800
		39,314	41,840	9,600	7,610	98,364

You should note that the direct wages costs are not included in the analysis because they are not overhead costs. Also notice that the apportionment of wage-related costs is based on total wages – that is, the sum of the direct and indirect wages for each cost centre.

The apportioned costs are all calculated using the general formula:

$$\frac{\text{Total overhead cost}}{\text{Total value of apportionment base}} \times \text{Value of apportionment base of the cost centre being calculated}$$

For example, in the case of depreciation apportioned to the machining cost centre:

$$\frac{£16,700}{£1,670,000} = £1,400,000 = £14,000$$

The result of the initial allocation and apportionment is that the organisation's production overhead costs have been identified with cost centres associated with production. However, the service cost centre (stores) is not directly involved in the manufacture of the saleable cost unit. Nevertheless, it is part of the production function and the total cost of operating the stores should be attributed to the saleable cost units. The total cost of the stores must be shared or apportioned between those production cost centres which derive benefit from the stores service.

If we now return to our example, the next step is to apportion the cost of the stores department to the production cost centres.

Item	Basis of apportionment	M/c £	Ass'y £	Finish £	Stores £	Total £
B/fwd		39,314	41,840	9,600	7,610	98,364
Stores costs	No. of requisitions on stores	1,550	5,560	500	(7,610)	–
		40,864	47,400	10,100	–	98,364

We have now achieved the objective of allocating and apportioning all of the production overhead costs to the departments directly involved in the manufacture of the saleable cost unit.

3.4 Absorption of overheads into saleable cost units

3.4.1 General principles

The last stage in the analysis of overheads is their absorption into the cost units produced in the production cost centres. This is sometimes referred to as *overhead recovery*.

To begin with, we need to measure the level of production achieved. There are many measures which may be used, but the most common are:

- physical units produced;
- labour hours worked;
- machine hours operated.

It is quite likely that different production departments will measure their production in different ways. The objective is to use a measure which reflects the nature of the work involved. The physical unit measure is in theory the simplest but it is only valid if all of the items produced require the same amount of resources.

The overhead costs of each production cost centre are then divided by the quantity of production achieved to calculate the amount of overhead cost to be attributed to each unit.

This is the technique of overhead absorption and we shall illustrate it by extending our example on allocation and apportionment.

The output of the machining department is to be measured using the number of machine hours produced, while the output of the assembly and finishing departments is to be measured using the number of direct labour hours produced. The reasons for this can be seen from the number of machine and direct labour hours for each department shown in the original data for the example. The machining department is clearly machine-intensive, whereas the other departments are labour-intensive.

The absorption rates are calculated by dividing the costs attributed to the department by its appropriate measure of output.

	Machining	Assembly	Finishing
Production overhead costs obtained by allocation and apportionment	£40,864	£47,400	£10,100
Number of:			
machine hours	32,000		
direct labour hours		32,000	4,000
Absorption rates:			
per machine hour	£1.277		
per direct labour hour		£1.48125	£2.525

3.4.2 Applying the overhead absorption rate

When using an absorption method based either on direct labour hours or on machine hours the cost attributed to each unit is obtained by multiplying the time taken per unit by the absorption rate per hour.

For example, if a particular cost unit took three machine hours in the machining department, and five direct labour hours in each of the assembly and finishing departments, the overhead cost absorbed by the cost unit would be as follows:

	£
Machining: 3 hours × £1.277	3.83
Assembly: 5 hours × £1.48125	7.41
Finishing: 5 hours × £2.525	12.63
Overhead absorbed by cost unit	23.87

3.4.3 Other absorption bases

In addition to the three bases of absorption mentioned above, a percentage rate based on any of the following may be used:

- direct material cost;
- direct labour cost;
- prime cost.

For example, if a direct labour cost percentage is used the absorption rates would be as follows:

	Machining £	Assembly £	Finishing £
Production overhead costs	40,864	47,400	10,100
Direct wages cost	32,600	67,200	7,200
Direct labour cost percentage	125%	71%	140%

If our cost unit had a labour cost of £12 in the machining department, and £20 in each of the assembly and finishing departments, the overhead cost absorbed by the cost unit using this method would be as follows:

	£
Machining: 125% × £12=	15.00
Assembly: 71% × £20=	14.20
Finishing: 140% × £20=	28.00
Overhead absorbed by cost unit	57.20

The direct material cost and the prime cost methods work in a similar way.

3.4.4 Selecting the most appropriate absorption rate

The data in the last example demonstrate how the calculated total production cost of a particular cost unit can be dramatically different, depending on the overhead absorption method selected. It is important that the selected method results in the most realistic charge for overhead, reflecting the incidence of overheads in the cost centre as closely as possible within the limits of available data.

You must not make the common mistake of thinking that the best absorption method in this example would be the one which results in the lowest overhead charge to our cost unit. Remember that the same total cost centre overhead is being shared out over the cost units produced, whichever absorption method is selected. If this unit is given a lower charge for overhead, then other cost units will be charged with a higher amount so that the total overhead is absorbed overall.

A major factor in selecting the absorption rate to be used is a consideration of the practical applicability of the rate. This will depend on the ease of collecting the data required to use the selected rate.

It is generally accepted that a time-based method should be used wherever possible, that is, the machine hour rate or the labour hour rate. This is because many overhead costs increase with time, for example indirect wages, rent and rates. Therefore, it makes sense to attempt to absorb overheads according to how long a cost unit takes to produce. The longer it takes, the more overhead will have been incurred in the cost centre during that time.

In addition to these general considerations, each absorption method has its own advantages and disadvantages:

(a) *Rate per unit*. This is the easiest method to apply but it is only suitable when all cost units produced in the period are identical. Since this does not often happen in practice this method is rarely used.

(b) *Direct labour hour rate*. This is a favoured method because it is time-based. It is most appropriate in labour-intensive cost centres, which are becoming rarer nowadays and so the method is less widely used than it has been in the past.

(c) *Machine hour rate*. This is also a favoured method because it is time-based. It is most appropriate in cost centres where machine activity predominates and is therefore more widely used than the direct labour hour rate. As well as absorbing the time-based over-heads mentioned earlier, it is more appropriate for absorbing the overheads related to machine activity, such as power, maintenance, repairs and depreciation.

(d) *Direct wages cost percentage*. This method may be acceptable because it is to some extent time-based. A higher direct wages cost may indicate a longer time taken and therefore a greater incidence of overheads during this time. However, the method will not produce equitable overhead charges if different wage rates are paid to individual employees in the cost centre. If this is the case, then there may not be a direct relation-ship between the wages paid and the time taken to complete a cost unit.

(e) *Direct materials cost percentage*. This is not a very logical method because there is no reason why a higher material cost should lead to a cost unit apparently incurring more production overhead cost. The method can be used if it would be too costly and inconvenient to use a more suitable method.

(f) *Prime cost percentage*. This method is not recommended because it combines methods (d) and (e) and therefore suffers from the combined disadvantages of both.

3.5 Predetermined overhead absorption rates

Overhead absorption rates are usually predetermined, that is, they are calculated in advance of the period over which they will be used.

The main reason for this is that overhead costs are not incurred evenly throughout the period. In some months the actual expenditure may be very high and in others it may be relatively low. The actual overhead rate per hour or per unit will therefore be subject to wide fluctuations. If the actual rate was used in product costing, then product costs would also fluctuate wildly. Such product costs would be very difficult to use for planning and control purposes.

Fluctuations in the actual level of production would also cause the same problem of fluctuating product costs.

To overcome this problem the absorption rate is determined in advance of the period, using estimated or budget figures for overhead and for the number of units of the absorp-tion base (labour hours or machine hours, etc.).

A further advantage of using predetermined rates is that managers have an overhead rate permanently available which they can use in product costing, price quotations and so on. The actual overhead costs and activity levels are not known until the end of the period. It would not be desirable for managers to have to wait until after the end of the period before they had a rate of overhead that they could use on a day-to-day basis.

3.5.1 Under- or over-absorption of overheads

The problem with using predetermined overhead absorption rates is that the actual figures for overhead and for the absorption base are likely to be different from the estimates used in calculating the absorption rate. It is this difference which causes an under-/over-absorption of production overhead. We will now return to our example in Section 3.4 to see how this is calculated, assuming that machine/labour hour rates have been used to absorb the overheads.

We will assume that all of the values used in the calculations in our example are estimates based on WHW Limited's budgets.

The *actual* costs for the same four-week period have now been allocated and apportioned using the same techniques and bases as shown in our earlier example, with the following total actual costs being attributed to each cost centre:

	Machining £	Assembly £	Finishing £
Actual costs	43,528	49,575	9,240

Actual labour and machine hours recorded against each cost centre were:

	Machining	Assembly	Finishing
Number of:			
machine hours	32,650		
labour hours		31,040	3,925

The amount of overhead cost absorbed into each department's total number of saleable cost units will be calculated by multiplying the absorption rate calculated in Section 3.4 (using the budget data) by the actual number of hours. The amounts absorbed are thus:

	Machining £	Assembly £	Finishing £
Amount absorbed:			
32,650 hours × £1.277	41,694		
31,040 hours × £1.48125		45,978	
3,925 hours × £2.525			9,911

This is compared with the actual cost incurred and the difference is the under-/over-absorption of production overhead:

	Machining £	Assembly £	Finishing £
Amount absorbed	41,694	45,978	9,911
Actual cost incurred	43,528	49,575	9,240
Over-absorption			671
Under-absorption	1,834	3,597	

If the amount absorbed exceeds the amount incurred, then an over-absorption arises; the opposite is referred to as an under-absorption. The terms *under-recovery* and *over-recovery* are sometimes used.

3.5.2 The reasons for under- or over-absorption

The under- or over-absorption has arisen because the actual overhead incurred per hour was different from the predetermined rate per hour. There are two possible causes of this:

1) The actual number of hours (machine or direct labour) was different from the number contained in the budget data. If this happens, then we would expect the variable element of the overhead to vary in direct proportion to the change in hours, so this part of the absorption rate would still be accurate. However, the fixed overhead would not alter with the hours worked and this means that the actual overhead cost per hour would be different from the predetermined rate.

2) The actual production overhead incurred may be different from the estimate contained in the predetermined rate. Apart from the expected change in variable overhead referred to in (1), this would also cause an under- or over-absorption of overhead.

 We will return in a later chapter to learn how any under- or over-absorption is accounted for in the bookkeeping records.

3.5.3 The problems caused by under- or over-absorption of overheads

If overheads are under-absorbed then managers have been working with unit rates for overheads which are too low. Prices may have been set too low and other similar decisions may have been taken based on inaccurate information. If the amount of under-absorption is significant, then this can have a dramatic effect on reported profit.

Do not make the common mistake of thinking that over-absorption is not such a bad thing because it leads to a boost in profits at the period end. If overhead rates have been unnecessarily high, then managers may have set selling prices unnecessarily high, leading to lost sales. Other decisions would also have been based on inaccurate information.

Although it is almost impossible to avoid under- and over-absorption altogether, it is possible to minimise the amount of adjustment necessary at the year end. This is achieved by conducting regular reviews of the actual expenditure and activity levels which are arising. The overhead absorption rate can thus be reviewed to check that it is still appropriate to absorb the overheads sufficiently accurately by the year end. If necessary the overhead absorption rate can be adjusted to reflect more recent estimates of activity and expenditure levels.

3.6 Illustrative example

You can use the following short example to practise the techniques which we have covered so far in this chapter.

The information given below relates to the forthcoming period for a manufacturer's operation. There are four cost centres of which two are involved in production and two are service cost centres.

	Total £	Production depts A £	B £	Service depts Canteen £	Stores £
Allocated costs	70,022	21,328	29,928	8,437	10,329
Other costs:					
Rent and rates	4,641				
Buildings insurance	3,713				
Electricity and gas	6,800				
Plant depreciation	28,390				
Plant insurance	8,517				
	122,083				
Area occupied (square metres)		7,735	6,188	1,547	3,094
Plant at cost (£000)		1,845	852	–	142
Number of employees		600	300	30	70
Machine hours		27,200	800	–	–
Direct labour hours		6,800	18,000	–	–
Number of stores requisitions		27,400	3,400	–	–

Use this information to calculate a production overhead absorption rate for departments A and B.

3.6.1 Solution

The first step is to prepare an overhead analysis sheet which shows the apportionment of the overheads, using the most appropriate basis for each.

Overhead item	Basis of apportionment	Total £	Dept A £	Dept B £	Canteen £	Stores £
Allocated costs	–	70,022	21,328	29,928	8,437	10,329
Rent and rates[1]	Area	4,641	1,934	1,547	387	773
Buildings insurance	Area	3,713	1,547	1,238	309	619
Electricity and gas	Area	6,800	2,833	2,267	567	1,133
Depreciation	Plant cost	28,390	18,450	8,520	–	1,420
Insurance	Plant cost	8,517	5,535	2,556	–	426
		122,083	51,627	46,056	9,700	14,700
Canteen[2]	Employees	–	6,000	3,000	(9,700)	700
Stores[3]	Requisitions	–	13,700	1,700	–	(15,400)
		122,083	71,327	50,756	–	–

Notes

1. The rent and rates cost is apportioned as follows. Total area occupied is 18,564 square metres. Therefore, rent and rates cost £4,641/18,564 = £0.25 per square metre.

   All of the other apportionments are calculated in the same way.

2. Since the canteen serves all other departments, its costs must be apportioned first, over the 970 employees in the other departments.

3. Once the stores have received a charge from the canteen, the total stores costs can be apportioned to the production departments.

Looking at the data for machine hours and direct labour hours in each of the departments, it appears that the most appropriate absorption base for department A is machine hours and for department B is direct labour hours. The absorption rates can now be calculated.

Production department A = £71,327/27,200 = £2.62 per machine hour

Production department B = £50,756/18,000 = £2.82 per direct labour hour

We can now extend the example a little further to practise using the calculated absorption rates. What is the total production cost of the following job?

	Job 847
Direct material cost	£487
Direct labour cost	£317
Machine hours in department A	195
Direct labour hours in department B	102

The overhead absorption rates can be applied as follows:

	Job 847
	£
Direct material cost*	487.00
Direct labour cost*	317.00
Prime cost	804.00
Production overhead:	
Department A 195 hours × £2.62	510.90
Department B 102 hours × £2.82	287.64
Total production cost	1602.54

*Remember that direct costs are not affected by the overhead absorption rate selected.

See if you can calculate the under- or over-absorbed overhead in each of the departments using the following data. The actual overhead incurred would have been determined by the allocation and apportionment of the actual overhead costs.

	Department A	Department B
Actual results		
Overhead incurred	£70,483	£52,874
Direct labour hours	6,740	18,300
Machine hours	27,900	850

The first step is to calculate how much overhead would have been absorbed, based on the actual hours and the predetermined overhead absorption rate for each department. This total can then be compared with the actual overhead incurred.

	Department A £	Department B £
Overhead absorbed		
27,900 × £2.62	73,098	
18,300 × £2.82		51,606
Overhead incurred	70,483	52,874
(Under-)/over-absorption	2,615	(1,268)

3.7 Reciprocal servicing

3.7.1 Taking account of reciprocal servicing

In the previous example there were two service cost centres: the canteen and the stores. The stores personnel made use of the canteen and it was therefore equitable to charge some of the canteen costs to the stores cost centre. It was not necessary to charge any of the stores costs to the canteen because there was no indication that the canteen made use of the stores facilities.

If the canteen had used the stores facilities, then we would say that reciprocal servicing was taking place, that is, that the service cost centres each used the other's facilities.

This can lead to a complicated situation because we do not know the total of the stores costs until a proportion of the canteen costs has been charged to it. Similarly, we do not know the total of the canteen costs until the total of the stores costs has been apportioned.

There are two methods which can be used to solve this problem. Your *Fundamentals of Management Accounting* syllabus requires you to be able to use only the repeated distribution method. We will use the following example to illustrate this. The other method, using algebra, is outside the scope of your syllabus.

Example

A company reapportions the costs incurred by two service cost centres – materials handling and inspection – to three production cost centres – machining, finishing and assembly.

The following are the overhead costs which have been allocated and apportioned to the five cost centres:

	£000
Machining	400
Finishing	200
Assembly	100
Materials handling	100
Inspection	50

Estimates of the benefits received by each cost centre are as follows:

	Machining %	Finishing %	Assembly %	Materials handling %	Inspection %
Materials handling	30	25	35	–	10
Inspection	20	30	45	5	–

These percentages indicate the use which each of the cost centres makes of the materials handling and inspection facilities. Calculate the charge for overhead to each of the three production cost centres, including the amounts reapportioned from the two service centres.

Solution: repeated distribution method

The task of allocating and apportioning the overheads to all cost centres has already been done (the primary apportionment). The problem now is to reapportion the costs of the service centres (the secondary apportionment).

Using the repeated distribution method the service cost centre costs are apportioned backwards and forwards between the cost centres until the figures become very small. At this stage it might be necessary to round the last apportionments.

In the workings that follow we have chosen to begin the secondary apportionment by apportioning the inspection costs first. The £50,000 inspection cost is reapportioned according to the percentages provided, then the total of the materials handling department is reapportioned and so on. The final result would have been the same if we had chosen instead to begin by apportioning the materials handling costs first.

	Machining £	Finishing £	Assembly £	Materials handling £	Inspection £
Initial allocation	400,000	200,000	100,000	100,000	50,000
Apportion inspection	10,000	15,000	22,500	2,500	(50,000)
Apportion materials handling	30,750	25,625	35,875	(102,500)	10,250
Apportion inspection	2,050	3,075	4,612	513	(10,250)
Apportion materials handling	154	128	180	(513)	51
Apportion inspection*	11	16	24	–	(51)
Total charge for overhead	442,965	243,844	63,191	0	0

* When the service department cost reduces to a small amount the final apportionment is adjusted for roundings.

The objective has been achieved and all of the overheads have been apportioned to the production cost centres, using the percentages given. A spreadsheet or similar software package would obviously be helpful here!

3.7.2 The usefulness of reapportioned service centre costs

The task of accounting for reciprocal servicing can be fairly laborious, particularly if it must be performed manually. Managers must therefore ensure that the effort is worthwhile.

Generally, if the service centre costs are significant and they make considerable use of each other's services, then accounting for reciprocal servicing is probably worthwhile. In other cases the reciprocal servicing could be ignored, or alternatively the service centre which does the most work for the other service centres could be apportioned first. The other service centres could then be apportioned direct to the production cost centres.

The overriding consideration must be the usefulness to managers of the resulting information. If the improved accuracy of the overhead absorption rates is deemed to be worthwhile, then reciprocal servicing should be taken into account in service cost reapportionment.

 In the assessment, you must never ignore the existence of reciprocal servicing unless you are specifically instructed to do so.

THE ANALYSIS OF OVERHEAD

3.8 Activity-based costing (ABC)

Activity-based costing (ABC) is a more recent development in cost analysis. It is based on the idea that to use a single absorption base of either labour or machine hours does not accurately reflect the cause of the overhead costs being incurred.

Supporters of ABC argue that overhead costs are only loosely related to time and are not often related to the volume of production. They argue that overheads in a modern manufacturing environment are related to the complexity of production. The more complex the production process for a product, the higher are the overheads incurred on its behalf. For example, a product might require a number of complicated machine set-ups, or quality control activity might be more intense for some products than for others. An ABC approach attempts to ensure that overheads are traced to products in a way which more adequately reflects the overhead cost which has been incurred on their behalf.

Using an ABC approach, overhead costs are accumulated initially in activity *cost pools*. These might include, for example, order placing or material handling. Costs would then be collected and analysed for each activity cost pool and a *cost driver* would be identified for each activity. Cost drivers are the factors which cause the cost of an activity to increase.

Using estimates of the costs attributed to each activity cost pool and the number of cost drivers associated with it, a cost driver rate is calculated. This is similar in principle to the calculation of absorption rates. For example, if the total cost of the activity of setting up a machine is £5,000 for a period and the number of machine set-ups for the period is 250, the cost per set-up is £20 (£5,000/250). Each product that requires the use of this machine is regarded as having incurred £20 of overhead cost each time the machine is set up for the product.

This analysis of overhead costs into activities, and their absorption using a variety of cost drivers, is believed to produce more accurate product costs. The ABC technique can also be applied to non-production costs as well as to the determination of the costs of services provided.

3.9 The use of cost information in pricing decisions

3.9.1 Marginal cost pricing

In Chapter 1, we saw how knowledge of the extra or *marginal* cost of making and selling a hairdryer provided a manager with important information when deciding what selling price should be charged for a special order.

If the price charged is higher than the marginal or incremental cost of making and selling a cost unit then some contribution is earned towards the costs which are being incurred anyway. These include costs such as certain production and administration overheads.

The problem with marginal cost pricing is that it is difficult to decide on the mark-up that must be added to the marginal cost in order to ensure that the other costs such as administration overheads are covered and that the organisation makes a profit.

Marginal cost pricing is useful in a one-off special price decision such as that discussed concerning the hairdryer in Chapter 1, but it does not help us to decide on the price to be charged in routine product pricing decisions, in order to cover all costs and earn a profit.

3.9.2 Full cost-plus pricing

We have seen how the overhead absorption rate can be used to trace indirect costs to cost units in order to obtain the unit's full cost.

Full cost-plus pricing involves adding a mark-up to the total cost of a cost unit in order to arrive at the selling price. Your syllabus requires you to know how to calculate full cost-based prices to generate a specified return on sales or on investment.

3.9.3 Example: full-cost pricing to achieve a specified return on sales

This pricing method involves determining the full cost of a cost unit and then adding a mark-up that represents a specified percentage of the final selling price. The following example will demonstrate how the method works.

WP Limited manufactures product A.

Data for product A are as follows:

Direct material cost per unit	£7
Direct labour cost per unit	£18
Direct labour hours per unit	2 hours
Production overhead absorption rate	£6 per direct labour hour
Mark-up for non-production overhead costs	5% of total production cost

WP Limited requires a 15 per cent return on sales revenue from all products.
Calculate the selling price for product A, to the nearest penny.

Solution

	£ per unit
Direct material cost	7.00
Direct labour cost	18.00
Total direct cost	25.00
Production overhead absorbed = 2 hours × £6	12.00
Total production cost	37.00
Mark-up for non-production costs = 5% × £37.00	1.85
Full cost	38.85
Profit mark-up = 15/85* × £38.85	6.86
Selling price	45.71

*Always read the question data carefully. The 15 per cent required return is expressed as a percentage of the sales revenue, not as a percentage of the cost.

3.9.4 Example: full-cost pricing to achieve a specified return on investment

This method involves determining the amount of capital invested to support a product. For example, some fixed or non-current assets and certain elements of working capital such as inventory and trade receivables can be attributed to individual products.

The selling price is then set to achieve a specified return on the capital invested on behalf of the product. The following example will demonstrate how the method works.

LG Limited manufactures product B.

Data for product B are as follows:

Direct material cost per unit	£62
Direct labour cost per unit	£14
Direct labour hours per unit	4 hours
Production overhead absorption rate	£16 per direct machine hour
Mark-up for non-production overhead costs	8% of total production cost

LG Limited sells 1,000 units of product B each year. Product B requires an investment of £400,000 and the target rate of return on investment is 12% per annum.

Calculate the selling price for one unit of product B, to the nearest penny.

Solution

	£ per unit
Direct material cost	62.00
Direct labour cost	14.00
Total direct cost	76.00
Production overhead absorbed = 4 hours × £16	64.00
Total production cost	140.00
Mark-up for non-production costs = 8% × £140.00	11.20
Full cost	151.20
Profit mark-up (see working)	48.00
Selling price	199.20

Working

Target return on investment in product B = £400,000 × 12% = £48,000
Target return per unit of product B = £48,000/1,000 units = £48

3.9.5 Second example: full-cost pricing to achieve a specified return on investment

This example demonstrates how the profit mark-up can be determined as a percentage of the total budgeted cost for a period.

The following data relate to a company which produces a range of products.

Capital invested in company	£800,000
Required return on investment each period	15%
Budgeted total cost for next period	£1,500,000

One of the company's products, R, incurs a total cost of £35 per unit.
Calculate the cost-plus selling price of one unit of product R.

Solution

Required profit in period = £800,000 × 15% = £120,000

Profit as a percentage of budgeted total cost = (£120,000/£1,500,000) × 100%

= 8%

This percentage is applied to calculate the mark up for all products produced.

Profit mark-up for one unit of product R = £35 × 8% = £2.80
Selling price for one unit of product R = £35 + £2.80 = £37.80

3.10 Summary

Having read this chapter the main points you should understand are as follows:

1. The three stages in attributing overheads to cost units are allocation, apportionment and absorption. Allocation involves allotting whole items of cost to a single cost centre. Apportionment is necessary when it is not possible to allot the whole cost to a single cost centre. The cost must then be apportioned between cost centres using a suitable basis.
2. The primary apportionment of production overheads involves apportioning the overhead costs to all cost centres. The secondary apportionment is then necessary to reapportion the service cost centre costs to the production cost centres.
3. The final totals of the production cost centre overheads are absorbed into product costs using a predetermined production overhead absorption rate. The absorption basis should reflect the type of activity undertaken within each production cost centre.
4. The production overhead absorption rate is calculated by dividing the budgeted cost centre overheads by the budgeted number of units of the absorption base (machine hours, direct labour hours, etc.).
5. Under- or over-absorption arises at the end of a period when the amount of production overhead absorbed into cost units is lower than or higher than the actual production overhead incurred during the period.
6. Reciprocal servicing occurs where service cost centres each do work for the other. In this situation the service cost centre overheads are reapportioned using the repeated distribution method.
7. Activity-based costing uses a variety of cost drivers to trace overhead costs to products and services.
8. The full cost of a cost unit can be used as a basis for determining its selling price. The required return from each cost unit can be calculated to achieve a specified return on sales or return on investment.

Revision Questions

? Question 1 Multiple choice

1.1 A method of dealing with overheads involves spreading common costs over cost centres on the basis of benefit received. This is known as:

(A) overhead absorption.
(B) overhead apportionment.
(C) overhead allocation.
(D) overhead analysis.

1.2 An overhead absorption rate is used to:

(A) share out common costs over benefiting cost centres.
(B) find the total overheads for a cost centre.
(C) charge overheads to products.
(D) control overheads.

1.3 Over-absorbed overheads occur when:

(A) absorbed overheads exceed actual overheads.
(B) absorbed overheads exceed budgeted overheads.
(C) actual overheads exceed budgeted overheads.
(D) budgeted overheads exceed absorbed overheads.

Data for questions 1.4 and 1.5

Budgeted labour hours   8,500
Budgeted overheads   £148,750
Actual labour hours   7,928
Actual overheads   £146,200

1.4 Based on the data given above, what is the labour hour overhead absorption rate?

(A) £17.50 per hour.
(B) £17.20 per hour.
(C) £18.44 per hour.
(D) £18.76 per hour.

1.5 Based on the data given above, what is the amount of overhead under-/over-absorbed?

(A) £2,550 under-absorbed.
(B) £2,529 over-absorbed.
(C) £2,550 over-absorbed.
(D) £7,460 under-absorbed.

1.6 A management consultancy recovers overheads on chargeable consulting hours. Budgeted overheads were £615,000 and actual consulting hours were 32,150. Overheads were under-recovered by £35,000.

   If actual overheads were £694,075, what was the budgeted overhead absorption rate per hour?

   (A) £19.13
   (B) £20.50
   (C) £21.59
   (D) £22.68

1.7 P Ltd absorbs overheads on the basis of direct labour hours. The overhead absorption rate for the period has been based on budgeted overheads of £150,000 and 50,000 direct labour hours.

   During the period, overheads of £180,000 were incurred and 60,000 direct labour hours were used.

   Which of the following statements is correct?

   (A) Overhead was £30,000 over-absorbed.
   (B) Overhead was £30,000 under-absorbed.
   (C) No under- or over-absorption occurred.
   (D) None of the above.

❓ **Question 2** Short objective-test questions

2.1 Match the overhead costs to the most appropriate basis of cost apportionment. Write the correct letter in the box provided beside each apportionment basis. An apportionment basis may be selected more than once.

Overhead cost
(a) Canteen costs
(b) Cleaning of factory premises
(c) Power
(d) Rent
(e) Insurance of plant and machinery

Apportionment bases
☐ Floor area
☐ Plant and equipment at cost
☐ Number of employees
☐ Machine running hours
☐ Direct labour hours

2.2 Maintenance costs are to be apportioned to production cost centres on the basis of the following number of maintenance hours worked in each cost centre.

	Machining	*Assembly*	*Finishing*
Maintenance hours worked	1,000	700	300

Complete the following extract from the overhead analysis sheet:

Overhead cost item	Total £	Machining £	Assembly £	Finishing £
Maintenance cost	38,000			

2.3 After the initial overhead allocation and apportionment has been completed, the overhead analysis sheet for a car repair workshop is as follows:

Total overhead cost £	Vehicle servicing £	Crash repairs £	Tyre fitting £	Canteen and vending £
233,000	82,000	74,000	61,000	16,000

The costs of the canteen and vending activity are to be reapportioned to the other activities on the basis of the number of personnel employed on each activity.

	Vehicle servicing	Crash repairs	Tyre fitting	Canteen and vending
Number of personnel	20	15	5	2

The canteen and vending cost to be apportioned to the crash repair activity is £ ☐

2.4 The budgeted fixed overhead absorption rate for last period was £5 per direct labour hour. Other data for the period are as follows:

Actual fixed overhead expenditure	£234,500
Actual direct labour hours	51,300
Budgeted fixed overhead expenditure	£212,900

The number of direct labour hours budgeted to be worked last period was ☐

2.5 *Tick the correct box.*

Activity in the packing department of a company manufacturing fine china involves operatives bubble-wrapping finished items and placing them in boxes which are then sealed and labelled. Most of the boxes are sealed and labelled by specialised machines, but about a quarter of them have to be sealed and labelled by hand. Budgeted activity levels for next period are 3,800 machine hours and 3,600 direct labour hours. The most appropriate production overhead absorption rate for the packing department would be a:

Machine hour rate ☐
Direct labour hour rate ☐

2.6 Data for the machining cost centre are as follows:

Budgeted cost centre overhead	£210,000
Actual cost centre overhead	£230,000
Budgeted machine hours	42,000
Actual machine hours	43,000

Complete the following calculation.

	£
Overhead absorbed	[ ]
Actual overhead incurred	[ ]
Overhead under-/over-absorbed	[ ]

Tick correct box:

under-absorbed ☐

over-absorbed ☐

2.7 The number of machine and labour hours budgeted for three production cost centres for the forthcoming period is as follows:

	Machining	*Assembly*	*Finishing*
Machine hours	50,000	4,000	5,000
Labour hours	10,000	30,000	20,000

The most appropriate production overhead absorption basis for each cost centre would be (tick the correct box):

	Machining	*Assembly*	*Finishing*
Rate per machine hour	☐	☐	☐
Rate per labour hour	☐	☐	☐

2.8 Production overhead in department A is absorbed using a predetermined rate per machine hour. Last period, the production overhead in department A was under-absorbed. Which of the following situations could have contributed to the under absorption? (tick all that apply)

☐ the actual production overhead incurred was lower than budgeted.
☐ the actual production overhead incurred was higher than budgeted.
☐ the actual machine hours were lower than budgeted.
☐ the actual machine hours were higher than budgeted.

2.9 The Crayfield Hotel has completed its initial allocation and apportionment of overhead costs and has established that the total budgeted annual overhead cost of its linen services activity is £836,000.

The cost unit used to plan and control costs in the hotel is an occupied room night. The hotel expects the occupancy rate of its 400 rooms, which are available for 365 nights each year, to be 85 per cent for the forthcoming year.

To the nearest penny, the overhead absorption rate for the linen services activity is £[   ] per occupied room night.

2.10 GY Limited budgets to produce and sell 3,800 units of product R in the forthcoming year. The amount of capital investment attributable to product R will be £600,000 and GY Limited requires a rate of return of 15 per cent on all capital invested.

Further details concerning product R are as follows:

Direct material cost per unit	£14
Direct labour cost per unit	£19
Variable overhead cost per unit	£3
Machine hours per unit	8

Fixed overhead is absorbed at a rate of £11 per machine hour.

Calculate all answers to the nearest penny.

(a) The variable cost of product R is £ ☐ per unit.

(b) The total(full) cost of product R is £ ☐ per unit.

(c) The selling price of product R which will achieve the specified return on investment is £ ☐ per unit.

2.11 A company manufactures a range of products one of which, product Y, incurs a total cost of £20 per unit. The company incurs a total cost of £600,000 each period and the directors wish to achieve a return of 18% on the total capital of £800,000 invested in the company.

Based on this information the cost-plus selling price of one unit of product Y should be £ ☐

Question 3 Overhead analysis and absorption

The Utopian Hotel is developing a cost accounting system. Initially it has been decided to create four cost centres: Residential and Catering deal directly with customers, while Housekeeping and Maintenance are internal service cost centres.

The management accountant is in the process of calculating overhead absorption rates for the next period. An extract from the overhead analysis sheet is as follows:

	Basis of apportionment £	Residential £	Catering £	Housekeeping £	Maintenance £	Total £
Consumables	Allocated	14,000	23,000	27,000	9,000	73,000
Staff costs	Allocated	16,500	13,000	11,500	5,500	46,500
Rent and rates				A		37,500
Contents ins.	Value of equip.		B			14,000
Heat and light		C				18,500

Other information

The following information is also available:

	Residential	Catering	Housekeeping	Maintenance	Total
Floor area (sq. metres)	2,750	1,350	600	300	5,000
Value of equipment, etc.	£350,000	£250,000	£75,000	£75,000	£750,000

Requirements

(a) The entries on the overhead analysis sheet shown as A to C are:

A £ ☐ (to the nearest £)

B £ ☐ (to the nearest £)

C £ ☐ (to the nearest £)

(b) The initial overhead allocation and apportionment has now been completed. The cost centre overhead totals are as follows:

	Residential £	Catering £	Housekeeping £	Maintenance £	Total £
Initial allocation and apportionment	85,333	68,287	50,370	23,010	227,000

Housekeeping works 70 per cent for Residential and 30 per cent for Catering, and Maintenance works 20 per cent for Housekeeping, 30 per cent for Catering and 50 per cent for Residential.

After the reapportionment of the Housekeeping and Maintenance cost centres, the total cost centre overheads for Residential and Catering will be, to the nearest £:

Residential £ _____
Catering £ _____

Question 4 Overhead absorption rates

QRS Ltd has three main departments – Casting, Dressing and Assembly – and has prepared the following production overhead budgets for period 3.

Department	Casting	Dressing	Assembly
Production overheads	£225,000	£175,000	£93,000
Expected production hours	7,500	7,000	6,200

During period 3, actual results were as follows:

Department	Casting	Dressing	Assembly
Production overheads	£229,317	£182,875	£92,500
Production hours	7,950	7,280	6,696

Requirements

(a) The departmental overhead absorption rates per production hour for period 3 are:

Casting £ _____
Dressing £ _____
Assembly £ _____

(b) (i) The overheads in the Casting department were (tick the correct box and insert the value of the over-/under-absorption):

under-absorbed ☐   over-absorbed ☐
by £ _____

(ii) The overheads in the Dressing department were (tick the correct box and insert the value of the over-/under-absorption):

under-absorbed ☐   over-absorbed ☐
by £ _____

(c) The overheads in the Assembly department were over-absorbed. Which of the following factors contributed to the over absorption?

☐ the actual overheads incurred were lower than budgeted.
☐ the actual production hours were higher than budgeted.

Question 5 Overhead analysis

DC Ltd is an engineering company which uses job costing to attribute costs to individual products and services provided to its customers. It has commenced the preparation of its fixed production overhead cost budget for year 2 and has identified the following costs:

	£000
Machining	600
Assembly	250
Finishing	150
Stores	100
Maintenance	80
	1,180

The stores and maintenance departments are production service departments. An analysis of the services they provide indicates that their costs should be apportioned as follows:

	Machining	Assembly	Finishing	Stores	Maintenance
Stores	40%	30%	20%	–	10%
Maintenance	55%	20%	20%	5%	–

Requirements

(a) After the apportionment of the service department costs, the total overheads of the production departments will be (*to the nearest £500*):

Machining £ _____
Assembly £ _____
Finishing £ _____

(b) DC Ltd's overhead absorption rates for year 1 are as follows:

Machining   £13.83 per machine hour
Assembly   £9.98 per labour hour
Finishing   £9.45 per labour hour

Job no. XX34 is to be started and completed in year 1. Data for the job is as follows:

Direct materials cost £2,400
Direct labour cost £1,500

Machine hours and labour hours required for the job are:

	Machine hours	Labour hours
Machining department	45	10
Assembly department	5	15
Finishing department	4	12

DC Ltd adds 10 per cent to total production cost in order to absorb non-production overhead costs, and profit is calculated as 20 per cent of selling price.

Requirement

Complete the following statements (to the nearest penny):

(i) The total production overhead cost of job no. XX34 is £ ☐

(ii) The total production cost of job no. XX34 is £ ☐

(iii) The selling price of job no. XX34 is £ ☐

Solutions to Revision Questions

☑ Solution 1

- Always remember that production overhead absorption rates are predetermined, that is, they are based on budgeted production overhead and budgeted activity levels.
- Over- or under-absorbed overhead = overhead absorbed − actual overhead incurred. If actual overhead exceeds the amount absorbed, then there is an under-absorption. If actual overhead is less than the amount absorbed, there is an over-absorption.

1.1 Answer: (B)

Answer (A) describes the final stage of charging overheads to cost units. (C) describes the allotment of whole items of cost to a single cost unit or cost centre. (D) describes the whole process of overhead allocation, apportionment and absorption.

1.2 Answer: (C)

An overhead absorption rate is a means of attributing overhead to a product or service-based, for example, on direct labour hours.

1.3 Answer: (A)

Over- or under-absorption of overhead is the difference between absorbed overheads and actual overheads. Under-absorption occurs when actual overheads exceed absorbed overheads.

1.4 Answer: (A)

Labour hour overhead absorption rate = £148,750/£8,500 = £17.50 per hour.

1.5 Answer: (D)

	£
Overhead incurred	146,200
Overhead absorbed = £17.50 × 7,928 hours	138,740
Under-absorption	7,460

THE ANALYSIS OF OVERHEAD

1.6 Answer: (B)

Let $£x$ = budgeted overhead absorption rate per hour:

	£
Actual overheads	694,075
Less: absorbed overheads	32,150x
Difference = under-absorption	35,000

$$\therefore x = \frac{694,075 - 35,000}{32,150} = 20.5$$

1.7 Answer: (C)

	£
Absorbed: (£150,000/50,000) = £3/hour × 60,000	180,000
Actual incurred	180,000
Under-/over-absorption	–

 Solution 2

2.1 (a) Number of employees
  (b) Floor area
  (c) Machine running hours
  (d) Floor area
  (e) Plant and equipment at cost

2.2 Overhead cost per maintenance hour $= \dfrac{£38,000}{1,000 + 700 + 300} = £19$

Overhead cost item	Total	Machining	Assembly	Finishing
	£	£	£	£
Maintenance cost	38,000	19,000	13,300	5,700

2.3 Canteen and vending cost per
personal member in production activities* $= \dfrac{£16,000}{20 + 15 + 5} = £400$

*The canteen and vending personnel are not included because the canteen cannot give a charge to itself.

   The canteen and vending cost apportioned to the crash repair activity is £400 × 15 = £6,000.

2.4 Direct labour hours budgeted to be worked last period = 42,580.

$$\text{Budgeted overhead absorption rate} = \frac{\text{budgeted fixed overhead expenditure}}{\text{budgeted direct labour hours}}$$

$$£5 = \frac{£212,900}{\text{budgeted direct labour hours}}$$

Budgeted direct labour hours = £212,900/£5 = 42,580.

2.5 The most appropriate production overhead absorption rate for the packing department would be a *direct labour hour rate*.

Although the number of machine hours in the cost centre is significant, we are told that a quarter of the output is not placed on the machines. No machine hours would be recorded for this output and the use of a machine hour rate would mean that this part of the output received no charge for the overheads of the packing cost centre.

2.6 Overhead absorption rate $= \dfrac{£210,000}{42,000} = £5$ per machine hour

	£
Overhead absorbed (£5 × 43,000)	215,000
Actual overhead incurred	230,000
Overhead under-absorbed	15,000

2.7 Looking at the number of machine and labour hours budgeted for each cost centre it is clear that the machining department is machine intensive. Therefore, a *rate per machine hour* would be most appropriate for this cost centre.

The assembly and finishing departments are labour intensive. Therefore, a *rate per labour hour* would be most appropriate for each of these cost centres.

2.8 Two of the stated factors could have contributed to the under absorption:

- *the actual production overhead incurred was higher than budgeted*; if this did happen then the predetermined absorption rate would be too low and there would be a potential under absorption;
- *the actual machine hours were lower than budgeted*; if this occurred then there would be fewer than expected hours to absorb the production overhead, potentially leading to under absorption.

2.9 Budgeted number of occupied room nights = 400 rooms × 365 nights × 85% = 124,100 occupied room nights.

Overhead absorption rate for linen services activity = £836,000/124,100 = £6.74 per occupied room night.

2.10 (a) The variable cost per unit of product R is £36.00 per unit.

Direct material £14 + direct labour £19 + variable overhead £3 = £36

(b) The total (full) cost of product R is £124.00 per unit.

Variable cost £36 + fixed overhead (8 hours × £11) = £124

(c) The selling price of product R which will achieve the specified return on investment is £147.68 per unit.

Required return from investment in product R = £600,000 × 15% = £90,000

Required return per unit sold = £90,000/3,800 units = £23.68

Required selling price = £124.00 full cost + £23.68 = £147.68

2.11 The cost-plus selling price of one unit of product Y should be £24.80.

Required annual return = £800,000 × 18% = £144,000

Return as a percentage of total cost = £144,000/£600,000 = 24%

Required cost-plus selling price = £20 + (24% × £20) = £24.80

THE ANALYSIS OF OVERHEAD

 Solution 3

- This is an example of an application of absorption costing in a non-manufacturing situation. Do not be put off by this. In an assessment you must be prepared to deal with all sorts of unfamiliar situations. The principles of overhead analysis that you have learned in this chapter can be applied in the same way in this non-manufacturing environment. Residential and Catering are the equivalent of the production cost centres that you have learned about, whereas Housekeeping and Maintenance are internal service departments whose costs will need to be reapportioned.
- Maintenance does work for Housekeeping, but notice that Housekeeping does not provide any service to Maintenance. Therefore, in part (b), if you apportion the total of Maintenance first, including the appropriate charge to Housekeeping, you can then apportion the new total for Housekeeping straight to the departments which deal directly with customers, that is, Residential and Catering.

(a) A £4,500
     B £4,667
     C £10,175

Workings:

A: Using floor area as the apportionment basis, the rent and rates cost apportioned to Housekeeping = (600/5,000) × £37,500 = £4,500.
B: (250,000/750,000) × £14,000 = £4,667.
C: Using floor area as the apportionment basis, the heat and light cost apportioned to Residential = (2,750/5,000) × £18,500 = £10,175.

(b) Residential   £135,318
     Catering   £91,682

Workings:

	Residential £	Catering £	Housekeeping £	Maintenance £	Total £
Initial allocation and appt.	85,333	68,287	50,370	23,010	227,000
Maintenance reapportioned					
50% to Residential	11,505				
30% to Catering		6,903			
20% to Housekeeping			4,602	(23,010)	
	96,838	75,190	54,972	–	
Housekeeping reapportioned					
70% to Residential	38,480				
30% to Catering		16,492	(54,972)		
	135,318	91,682	–		

 Solution 4

- A common mistake in part (b) would be to compare the actual overheads with the budgeted overheads instead of with the absorbed overheads when calculating the under- or over-absorption.

(a) Predetermined departmental overhead absorption rates for period 3 (per production hour).

$$\underset{\text{Casting}}{\frac{£225,000}{7,500} = £30} \qquad \underset{\text{Dressing}}{\frac{£175,000}{7,000} = £25} \qquad \underset{\text{Assembly}}{\frac{£93,000}{6,200} = £15}$$

(b) (i) The overheads in the Casting department were over-absorbed by £9,183
    (ii) The overheads in the Dressing department were under-absorbed by £875.

Workings:

	Casting £	Dressing £
Overheads absorbed:		
£30/hour × 7,950	238,500	
£25/hour × 7,280		182,000
Actual overheads	(229,317)	(182,875)
Over/(under) absorption	9,183	(875)

(c) Both factors would have contributed to the over-absorption. The amount of overhead absorbed increased in line with the production hours, which would have led to over absorption even if the overhead expenditure had remained constant. The fact that the overhead expenditure was below budget would have increased the amount of over-absorption.

 ## Solution 5

- You will need to use the repeated distribution method to deal with the reciprocal servicing in part (a).
- The question mentions job costing, which is the subject of Chapter 8. For now, all you need to know is that an individual job – in this case job XX34 – is simply treated as a cost unit for the purposes of overhead absorption.

(a) Machining: £691,500
    Assembly: £299,500
    Finishing: £189,000
    Workings:

	Machining £000	Assembly £000	Finishing £000	Stores £000	Maintenance £000
Allocated costs	600.00	250.00	150.00	100.00	80.00
Stores apportionment	40.00	30.00	20.00	(100.00)	10.00
Maintenance apportionment	49.50	18.00	18.00	4.50	(90.00)
Stores apportionment	2.00	1.50	1.00	(4.50)	–
Total	691.50	299.50	189.00	–	–

THE ANALYSIS OF OVERHEAD

(b) (i) £885.45
   (ii) £4,785.45
  (iii) £6,580.00

Workings:

	£	£
Direct material		2,400.00
Direct labour		1,500.00
Prime cost		3,900.00
Overhead cost:		
Machining (45 × £13.83)	622.35	
Assembly (15 × £9.98)	149.70	
Finishing (12 × £9.45)	113.40	
		885.45
Total production cost		4,785.45
Non-production overhead (10%)		478.55
Total cost		5,264.00
Profit mark-up (25%)*		1,316.00
Price for Job XX34		6,580.00

*A profit margin of 20 per cent of selling price is the same as a mark-up of 25 per cent of cost. Check for yourself that the calculated profit margin is in fact 20 per cent of the selling price.

4

Cost–Volume–Profit Analysis

Cost–Volume–Profit Analysis

4

LEARNING OUTCOMES

After completing this chapter, you should be able to:

► explain the concept of contribution and its use in cost–volume–profit (CVP) analysis;

► calculate and interpret the breakeven point, profit target, margin of safety and profit/volume ratio for a single product or service;

► prepare breakeven charts and profit/volume graphs for a single product or service;

► calculate the profit maximising sales mix for a multi-product company that has limited demand for each product and one other constraint or limiting factor.

4.1 Introduction

In this chapter, you will see how an understanding of cost behaviour patterns and a focus on identifying the costs that will alter as the result of a course of action are important in providing effective information as the basis for management decision-making.

4.2 Breakeven or cost–volume–profit analysis

> *Cost–volume–profit (CVP) analysis* is defined in CIMA's *Terminology* as the 'study of the effects on future profit of changes in fixed cost, variable cost, sales price, quantity and mix'.

A common term used for this type of analysis is *breakeven analysis*. However, this is somewhat misleading, since it implies that the focus of the analysis is the *breakeven point* – that is, the level of activity which produces neither profit nor loss. You will see in this chapter that the scope of CVP analysis is much wider than this, as indicated in the definition. However, you should be aware that the terms 'breakeven analysis' and 'CVP analysis' tend to be used interchangeably.

4.2.1 The concept of contribution

In chapter 1 you learned that variable costs are those that vary with the level of activity. If we can identify the variable costs associated with producing and selling a product or service we can highlight a very important measure: *contribution.*

Contribution = sales value − variable costs

 Variable costs are sometimes referred to as marginal costs and the two terms are often used interchangeably.

Contribution is so called because it literally does contribute towards fixed costs and profit. Once the contribution from a product or service has been calculated, the fixed costs associated with the product or service can be deducted to determine the profit for the period.

4.2.2 Calculating the breakeven point

As sales revenues grow from zero, the contribution also grows until it just covers the fixed costs. This is the breakeven point where neither profits nor losses are made.

It follows that to break even the amount of contribution must exactly match the amount of fixed costs. If we know how much contribution is earned from each unit sold, then we can calculate the number of units required to break even as follows:

$$\text{Breakeven point in units} = \frac{\text{Fixed costs}}{\text{Contribution per unit}}$$

For example, suppose that an organisation manufactures a single product, incurring variable costs of £30 per unit and fixed costs of £20,000 per month. If the product sells for £50 per unit, then the breakeven point can be calculated as follows:

$$\text{Breakeven point in units} = \frac{£20,000}{£50 − £30} = 1,000 \text{ units per month}$$

4.3 The margin of safety

 The margin of safety is the difference between the expected level of sales and the breakeven point. The larger the margin of safety, the more likely it is that a profit will be made, that is, if sales start to fall there is more leeway before the organization begins to incur losses. (Obviously, this statement is made on the assumption that projected sales volumes are above the breakeven point.)

In the above example, if forecast sales are 1,700 units per month, the margin of safety can be easily calculated.

$$
\begin{aligned}
\text{Margin of safety} &= \text{projected sales} − \text{breakeven point} \\
&= 1,700 \text{ units} − 1,000 \text{ units} \\
&= 700 \text{ units per month, or } 41\% \text{ of sales } (700\,/\,1,700 \times 100\%)
\end{aligned}
$$

The margin of safety should be expressed as a percentage of projected sales to put it in perspective. To quote a margin of safety of 700 units without relating it to the projected sales figure is not giving the full picture.

The margin of safety can also be used as one route to a profit calculation. We have seen that the contribution goes towards fixed costs and profit. Once breakeven point is reached the fixed costs have been covered. After the breakeven point there are no more fixed costs to be covered and all of the contribution goes towards making profits grow.

In our example, the monthly profit from sales of 1,700 units would be £14,000.

$$\text{Margin of safety} = 700 \text{ units per month}$$
$$\text{Monthly profit} = 700 \times \text{contribution per unit}$$
$$= 700 \times £20$$
$$= £14,000.$$

4.4 · The contribution to sales (C/S) ratio

The contribution to sales ratio is usually expressed as a percentage. It can be calculated for the product in our example as follows.

$$\text{Contribution to sales ratio (C/S ratio)} = £20 / £50 \times 100\%$$
$$= 40\%$$

A higher contribution to sales ratio means that contribution grows more quickly as sales levels increase. Once the breakeven point has been passed, profits will accumulate more quickly than for a product with a lower contribution to sales ratio.

You might sometimes see this ratio referred to as the profit−volume (P/V) ratio.

If we can assume that a unit's variable cost and selling price remain constant then the C/S ratio will also remain constant. It can be used to calculate the breakeven point as follows (using the data from the earlier example):

π $\quad$ $$\text{Breakeven point in sales value} = \frac{\text{Fixed costs}}{\text{C/S ratio}} = \frac{£20,000}{0.40} = £50,000$$

This can be converted to 1,000 units as before by dividing by the selling price of £50 per unit.

Exercise 4.1

A company manufactures and sells a single product which has the following cost and selling price structure:

	£/unit	£/unit
Selling price		120
Direct material	22	
Direct labour	36	
Variable overhead	14	
Fixed overhead	12	
		84
Profit per unit		36

The fixed overhead absorption rate is based on the normal capacity of 2,000 units per month. Assume that the same amount is spent each month on fixed overheads.

Budgeted sales for next month are 2,200 units.

You are required to calculate:

(i) the breakeven point, in sales units per month;
(ii) the margin of safety for next month;
(iii) the budgeted profit for next month;
(iv) the sales required to achieve a profit of £96,000 in a month.

☑ Solution

(i) The key to calculating the breakeven point is to determine the contribution per unit.

$$\text{Contribution per unit} = £120 - (£22 + £36 + £14) = £48$$

$$\text{Breakeven point} = \frac{\text{Fixed overhead}}{\text{Contribution per unit}}$$

$$= \frac{£12 \times 2,000}{£48} = 500 \text{ units}$$

(ii) Margin of safety = budgeted sales − breakeven point
= 2,200 − 500
= 1,700 units (or 1,700 / 2,2000 × 100% = 77% of budgeted sales)

(iii) Once breakeven point has been reached, all of the contribution goes towards profits because all of the fixed costs have been covered.

$$\text{Budgeted profit} = 1,700 \text{ units margin of safety} \times £48 \text{ Contribution per unit}$$
$$= £81,600$$

(iv) To achieve the desired level of profit, sufficient units must be sold to earn a contribution which covers the fixed costs and leaves the desired profit for the month.

$$\text{Number of sales units required} = \frac{\text{Fixed overhead} + \text{desired profit}}{\text{Contribution per unit}}$$

$$= \frac{(£12 \times 2,000) + £96,000}{£48} = 2,500 \text{ units.}$$

4.5 Drawing a basic breakeven chart

A basic breakeven chart records costs and revenues on the vertical axis and the level of activity on the horizontal axis. Lines are drawn on the chart to represent costs and sales revenue. The breakeven point can be read off where the sales revenue line cuts the total cost line.

We will use our basic example to demonstrate how to draw a breakeven chart. The data is:

Selling price	£50 per unit
Variable cost	£30 per unit
Fixed costs	£20,000 per month
Forecast sales	1,700 units per month

> ! While you will not be required to draw a graph to scale in the assessment, you may need to do so in your working life or in future examinations for other subjects. Learning to draw a chart to scale will provide a firm foundation for your understanding of breakeven charts. To give yourself some practice, it would be a good idea to follow the step-by-step guide which follows to produce your own chart on a piece of graph paper.

- *Step 1. Select appropriate scales for the axes and draw and label them.* Your graph should fill as much of the page as possible. This will make it clearer and easier to read. You can make sure that you do this by putting the extremes of the axes right at the end of the available space.

  The furthest point on the vertical axis will be the monthly sales revenue, that is,

  1,700 units × £50 = £85,000

  The furthest point on the horizontal axis will be monthly sales volume of 1,700 units. Make sure that you do not need to read data for volumes higher than 1,700 units before you set these extremes for your scales.

- *Step 2. Draw the fixed cost line and label it.* This will be a straight line parallel to the horizontal axis at the £20,000 level.

  The £20,000 fixed costs are incurred in the short term even with zero activity.

- *Step 3. Draw the total cost line and label it.* The best way to do this is to calculate the total costs for the maximum sales level, which is 1,700 units in our example. Mark this point on the graph and join it to the cost incurred at zero activity, that is, £20,000.

	£
Variable costs for 1,700 units (1,700 × £30)	51,000
Fixed costs	20,000
Total cost for 1,700 units	71,000

- *Step 4. Draw the revenue line and label it.* Once again, the best way is to plot the extreme points. The revenue at maximum activity in our example is 1,700 × £50 = £85,000. This point can be joined to the origin, since at zero activity there will be no sales revenue.

- *Step 5. Mark any required information on the chart and read off solutions as required.* Check that your chart is accurate by reading off the measures that we have already calculated in this chapter: the breakeven point, the margin of safety, the profit for sales of 1,700 units.

The completed graph is shown in Figure 4.1.

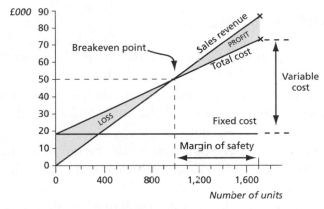

Figure 4.1   Basic breakeven chart

> ❗ Your own graph should be considerably larger than this: a full A4 graph-ruled sheet is recommended to facilitate ease of interpretation.

4.6 The contribution breakeven chart

One of the problems with the conventional or basic breakeven chart is that it is not possible to read contribution directly from the chart. A contribution breakeven chart is based on the same principles but it shows the variable cost line instead of the fixed cost line (Figure 4.2). The same lines for total cost and sales revenue are shown so the breakeven point and profit can be read off in the same way as with a conventional chart. However, it is possible also to read the contribution for any level of activity.

Using the same basic example as for the conventional chart, the total variable cost for an output of 1,700 units is 1,700 × £30 = £51,000. This point can be joined to the origin since the variable cost is nil at zero activity.

The contribution can be read as the difference between the sales revenue line and the variable cost line.

This form of presentation might be used when it is desirable to highlight the importance of contribution and to focus attention on the variable costs.

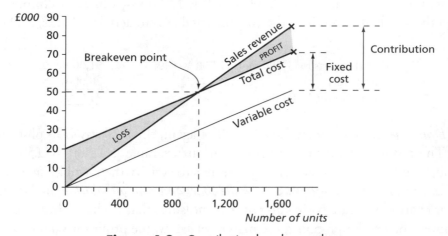

Figure 4.2 Contribution breakeven chart

4.7 The profit–volume chart

Another form of breakeven chart is the profit–volume chart. This chart plots a single line depicting the profit or loss at each level of activity. The breakeven point is where this line cuts the horizontal axis. A profit–volume graph for our example will look like Figure 4.3.

The vertical axis shows profits and losses and the horizontal axis is drawn at zero profit or loss.

At zero activity the loss is equal to £20,000, that is, the amount of fixed costs. The second point used to draw the line could be the calculated breakeven point or the calculated profit for sales of 1,700 units.

The profit–volume graph is also called a profit graph or a contribution–volume graph.

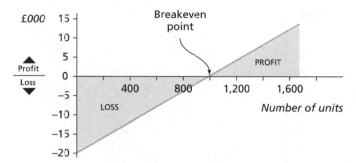

Figure 4.3   Profit–volume chart

 ## Exercise 4.2

Make sure that you are clear about the extremes of the profit–volume chart axes. Practise drawing the chart to scale on a piece of graph paper.

4.7.1   The advantage of the profit–volume chart

The main advantage of the profit–volume chart is that it is capable of depicting clearly the effect on profit and breakeven point of any changes in the variables. An example will show how this can be done.

Example

A company manufactures a single product which incurs fixed costs of £30,000 per annum. Annual sales are budgeted to be 70,000 units at a sales price of £30 per unit. Variable costs are £28.50 per unit.

(a) Draw a profit–volume graph, and use it to determine the breakeven point.

The company is now considering improving the quality of the product and increasing the selling price to £35 per unit. Sales volume will be unaffected, but fixed costs will increase to £45,000 per annum and variable costs to £33 per unit.

(b) Draw, on the same graph as for part (a), a second profit–volume graph and comment on the results.

Solution

The profit–volume chart is shown in Figure 4.4.
The two lines have been drawn as follows:

- *Situation (a).* The profit for sales of 70,000 units is £75,000.

	£000
Contribution 70,000 × £(30 − 28.50)	105
Fixed costs	30
Profit	75

This point is joined to the loss at zero activity, £30,000, that is, the fixed costs.
- *Situation (b).* The profit for sales of 70,000 units is £95,000.

	£000
Contribution 70,000 × £(35 − 33)	140
Fixed costs	45
Profit	95

This point is joined to the loss at zero activity, £45,000, that is, the fixed costs.

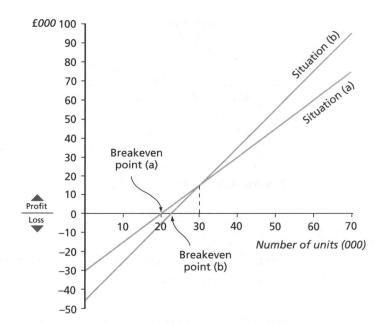

Figure 4.4   Showing changes with a profit–volume chart

Comment on *the results*. The graph depicts clearly the larger profits available from option (b). It also shows that the breakeven point increases from 20,000 units to 22,500 units but that this is not a large increase when viewed in the context of the projected sales volume. It is also possible to see that for sales volumes above 30,000 units the profit achieved will be higher with option (b). For sales volumes below 30,000 units option (a) will yield higher profits (or lower losses).

The profit–volume graph is the clearest way of presenting information like this. If we attempted to draw two conventional breakeven charts on one set of axes the result would be a jumble, which is very difficult to interpret.

4.8   The limitations of breakeven (or CVP) analysis

The limitations of the practical applicability of breakeven analysis and breakeven charts stem mostly from the assumptions which underlie the analysis:

(a) Costs are assumed to behave in a linear fashion. Unit variable costs are assumed to remain constant and fixed costs are assumed to be unaffected by changes in activity levels. The charts can in fact be adjusted to cope with non-linear variable costs or steps in fixed costs but too many changes in behaviour patterns can make the charts very cluttered and difficult to use.

(b) Sales revenues are assumed to be constant for each unit sold. This may be unrealistic because of the necessity to reduce the selling price to achieve higher sales volumes. Once again the analysis can be adapted for some changes in selling price but too many changes can make the charts unwieldy.

(c) It is assumed that activity is the only factor affecting costs, and factors such as inflation are ignored. This is one of the reasons why the analysis is limited to being essentially a short-term decision aid.

(d) Apart from the unrealistic situation of a constant product mix, the charts can only be applied to a single product or service. Not many organisations have a single product or service and if there is more than one, then the apportionment of fixed costs between them becomes arbitrary.

(e) The analysis seems to suggest that as long as the activity level is above the breakeven point, then a profit will be achieved. In reality certain changes in the cost and revenue patterns may result in a second breakeven point after which losses are made. This situation will be depicted in the next section of this chapter.

4.9 The economist's breakeven chart

An economist would probably depict a breakeven chart as shown in Figure 4.5.

The total cost line is not a straight line which climbs steadily as in the accountant's chart. Instead it begins to reduce initially as output increases because of the effect of economies of scale. Later it begins to climb upwards according to the law of diminishing returns.

The revenue line is not a straight line as in the accountant's chart. The line becomes less steep to depict the need to give discounts to achieve higher sales volumes.

However, you will see that within the middle range the economist's chart does look very similar to the accountant's breakeven chart. This area is marked as the relevant range in Figure 4.5.

For this reason, it is unreliable to assume that the cost–volume–profit relationships depicted in breakeven analysis are relevant across a wide range of activity. In particular, Figure 4.5 shows that the constant cost and price assumptions are likely to be unreliable at very high or very low levels of activity. Managers should therefore ensure that they work within the relevant range, that is, within the range over which the depicted cost and revenue relationships are more reliable.

> ❗ You may recall that we discussed the relevant range in the context of cost behaviour patterns in Chapter 1.

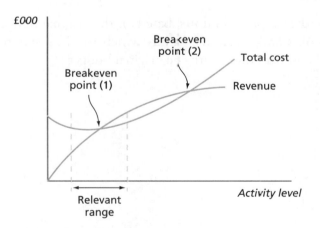

Figure 4.5 The economist's breakeven chart

COST-VOLUME-PROFIT ANALYSIS

4.10   Using CVP analysis to evaluate proposals

Use your understanding of breakeven analysis and cost behaviour patterns to evaluate the proposals in the following exercise.

Exercise 4.3

A summary of a manufacturing company's budgeted profit statement for its next financial year, when it expects to be operating at 75 per cent of capacity, is given below.

	£	£
Sales 9,000 units at £32		288,000
Less:		
direct materials	54,000	
direct wages	72,000	
production overhead – fixed	42,000	
– variable	18,000	
		186,000
Gross profit		102,000
Less: admin., selling and dist'n costs:		
– fixed	36,000	
– varying with sales volume	27,000	
		63,000
Net profit		39,000

It has been estimated that:

(i) if the selling price per unit were reduced to £28, the increased demand would utilise 90 per cent of the company's capacity without any additional advertising expenditure;

(ii) to attract sufficient demand to utilise full capacity would require a 15 per cent reduction in the current selling price and a £5,000 special advertising campaign.

You are required to:

(a) calculate the breakeven point in units, based on the original budget;

(b) calculate the profits and breakeven points which would result from each of the two alternatives and compare them with the original budget.

Solution

(a) First calculate the current contribution per unit.

	£000	£000
Sales revenue		288
Direct materials	54	
Direct wages	72	
Variable production overhead	18	
Variable administration etc.	27	
		171
Contribution		117
Contribution per unit ($\div$9,000 units)		£13

Now you can use the formula to calculate the breakeven point.

$$\text{Breakeven point} = \frac{\text{Fixed costs}}{\text{Contribution per unit}} = \frac{£42,000 + £36,000}{£13} = 6,000 \text{ units}$$

(b) *Alternative (i)*

Budgeted contribution per unit	£13
Reduction in selling price (£32 − £28)	£4
Revised contribution per unit	£9
Revised breakeven point = £78,000/£9	8,667 units
Revised sales volume = 9,000 × (90/75)	10,800 units
Revised contribution = 10,800 × £9	£97,200
Less fixed costs	£78,000
Revised profit	£19,200

Alternative (ii)

Budgeted contribution per unit	£13.00
Reduction in selling price (15% × £32)	£4.80
Revised contribution per unit	£8.20
Revised breakeven point $= \dfrac{£78,000 + £5,000}{£8.20}$	10,122 units
Revised sales volume = 9,000 units × (100/75)	12,000 units
Revised contribution = 12,000 × £8.20	£98,400
Less fixed costs	£83,000
Revised profit	£15,400

Neither of the two alternative proposals is worthwhile. They both result in lower forecast profits. In addition, they will both increase the breakeven point and will therefore increase the risk associated with the company's operations.

This exercise has shown you how an understanding of cost behaviour patterns and the manipulation of contribution can enable the rapid evaluation of the financial effects of a

COST–VOLUME–PROFIT ANALYSIS

proposal. We can now expand it to demonstrate another aspect of the application of CVP analysis to short-term decision-making.

 Exercise 4.4

The manufacturing company decided to proceed with the original budget and has asked you to determine how many units must be sold to achieve a profit of £45,500.

 Solution

Once again, the key is the required contribution. This time the contribution must be sufficient to cover both the fixed costs and the required profit. If we then divide this amount by the contribution earned from each unit, we can determine the required sales volume.

$$\text{Required sales} = \frac{\text{Fixed costs} + \text{required profit}}{\text{Contribution per unit}}$$

$$= \frac{(£42{,}000 + £36{,}000 + £45{,}500)}{£13} = 9{,}500 \text{ units}$$

4.11 Limiting factor analysis

> 🔑 A limiting factor is any factor which is in scarce supply and which stops the organisation from expanding its activities further, that is, it limits the organisation's activities.

The limiting factor for many trading organisations is sales volume because they cannot sell as much as they would like. However, other factors may also be limited, especially in the short term. For example, machine capacity or the supply of skilled labour may be limited for one or two periods until some action can be taken to alleviate the shortage.

The concept of contribution can be used to make decisions about the best use of a limited resource.

4.11.1 Decisions involving a single limiting factor

If an organisation is faced with a single limiting factor, for example machine capacity, then it must ensure that a production plan is established which maximises the profit from the use of the available capacity. Assuming that fixed costs remain constant, this is the same as saying that the contribution must be maximised from the use of the available capacity. The machine capacity must be allocated to those products which earn the most contribution per machine hour.

This decision rule can be stated as 'maximising the contribution per unit of limiting factor'.

Example

LMN Ltd manufactures three products L, M and N. The company which supplies the two raw materials which are used in all three products has informed LMN that their employees are refusing to work overtime. This means that supply of the materials is limited to the following quantities for the next period:

Material A	1,030 kg
Material B	1,220 kg

No other source of supply can be found for the next period.

Information relating to the three products manufactured by LMN Ltd is as follows:

	L	M	N
Quantity of material used per unit manufactured:			
Material A (kg)	2	1	4
Material B (kg)	5	3	7
Maximum sales demand (units)	120	160	110
Contribution per unit sold	£15	£12	£17.50

Owing to the perishable nature of the products, no finished goods are held.

Requirements

(a) Recommend a production mix which will maximise the profits of LMN Ltd for the forthcoming period.

(b) LMN Ltd has a valued customer to whom they wish to guarantee the supply of 50 units of each product next period. Would this alter your recommended production plan?

Solution

(a) The first step is to check whether the supply of each material is adequate or whether either or both of them represent a limiting factor.

	L	M	N	Total
Maximum sales demand (units)	120	160	110	
Material A required per unit (kg)	2	1	4	
Total material A required (kg)	240	160	440	840
Material B required per unit (kg)	5	3	7	
Total material B required (kg)	600	480	770	1,850

There will be sufficient material A to satisfy the maximum demand for the products but material B will be a limiting factor.

The next step is to rank the products in order of their contribution per unit of limiting factor. The available material B can then be allocated according to this ranking.

	L	M	N
Contribution per unit sold	£15	£12	£17.50
Material B consumed (kg)	5	3	7
Contribution per kg of material B	£3	£4	£2.50
Ranking	2	1	3

The available material B will be allocated to the products according to this ranking, to give the optimum production plan for the next period.

Product	Recommended production (units)	Material B utilised (kg)
M	160 (maximum)	480
L	120 (maximum)	600
N	20	140 (balance)
		1,220

The available material B is allocated to satisfy the maximum market demand for products M and L. The balance of available material is allocated to the last product in the ranking, product N.

(b) The recommended production plan in part (a) does not include sufficient product N to satisfy the requirement of 50 units for the valued customer. Some of the material allocated to product L (second in the ranking) must be allocated to product N. The recommended production plan will now be as follows:

Product	Recommended production (units)	Material B utilised (kg)
N	50	350
M	160	480
L	78	390 (balance)
		1,220

This recommendation makes the best use of the available material B within the restriction of the market requirements for each product.

> The identification of a limiting factor and the ranking of products to maximise contribution has been a favourite topic in the multiple-choice questions on past papers. Make sure that you are well prepared in case this topic comes up in your assessment.

Exercise 4.5

Gill Ltd manufactures three products E, F and G. The products are all finished on the same machine. This is the only mechanised part of the process. During the next period the production manager is planning an essential major maintenance overhaul of the machine. This will restrict the available machine hours to 1,400 hours for the next period. Data for the three products are:

	Product E £ per unit	Product F £ per unit	Product G £ per unit
Selling price	30	17	21.00
Variable cost	13	6	9.00
Fixed production cost	10	8	6.00
Other fixed cost	2	1	3.50
Profit	5	2	2.50
Maximum demand (units/period)	250	140	130

No inventories are held.

Fixed production costs are absorbed using a machine hour rate of £2 per machine hour.

You are required to determine the production plan that will maximise profit for the forthcoming period.

 ### Solution

The first step is to calculate how many machine hours are required for each product. We can then determine whether machine hours are really a limiting factor.

	Product E	Product F	Product G	Total
Fixed production cost per unit	£10	£8	£6	
@ £2 per hour				
Machine hours per unit	5	4	3	
Maximum demand (units)	250	140	130	
Maximum hours required	1,250	560	390	2,200

Since 2,200 machine hours are required and only 1,400 hours are available, machine hours are a limiting factor.

The optimum production plan is the plan which maximises the *contribution* from the *limiting factor*.

Do not make the common mistake of allocating the available hours according to the profit per unit of product or according to the profit per hour.

The next step is to calculate the contribution per hour from each of the products.

	Product E	Product F	Product G
	£	£	£
Selling price per unit	30	17	21
Variable cost per unit	13	6	9
Contribution per unit	17	11	12
Machine hours per unit	5	4	3
Contribution per hour	£3.40	£2.75	£4.00
Ranking	2	3	1

The available hours can be allocated according to this ranking.

	Units to be produced	Machine hours required
Product G (maximum demand)	130	390
Product E (balance of hours)	202	1,010
		1,400

COST–VOLUME–PROFIT ANALYSIS

4.12 Summary

Having read this chapter the main points that you should understand are as follows.

1. Cost–volume–profit (CVP) analysis is the study of the effect on profit of changes in costs and sales price, quantity and mix. Another common term used in this context is 'breakeven analysis'.
2. Contribution is calculated as sales value minus variable cost.
3. The ratio of a cost unit's contribution to its selling price is usually assumed to be constant. This ratio may be referred to as the contribution to sales (C/S) ratio or the profit–volume (P/V) ratio, both of which are usually expressed as a percentage.
4. The breakeven point can be calculated as (fixed costs/contribution per unit) or (fixed costs/PV ratio).
5. The margin of safety is the difference between the expected level of sales and the breakeven point. It may be expressed as a percentage of the expected sales.
6. Contribution required to achieve a target profit = fixed costs + target profit.
7. A breakeven chart is a pictorial representation of costs and revenues depicting the profit or loss for the relevant range of activity.
8. A contribution breakeven chart shows the variable cost line instead of the fixed cost line, so that contribution can be read directly from the chart.
9. A profit–volume (PV) chart depicts a single line indicating the profit or loss for the relevant range of activity. It is particularly useful for demonstrating the effect on profit of changes in costs or revenues.
10. Breakeven or CVP analysis has a number of limitations and managers should be aware of these if they are to apply the technique effectively.
11. A limiting factor is any factor which is in scarce supply and stops the organisation from expanding its activities further. The decision rule in this situation is to maximise the contribution per unit of limiting factor.

Revision Questions

Question 1 Multiple choice

1.1 A Ltd has fixed costs of £60,000 per annum. It manufactures a single product which it sells for £20 per unit. Its contribution to sales ratio is 40 per cent.

A Ltd's breakeven point in units is:

- (A) 1,200
- (B) 3,000
- (C) 5,000
- (D) 7,500.

1.2 B Ltd manufactures a single product which it sells for £9 per unit. Fixed costs are £54,000 per month and the product has a variable cost of £6 per unit.

In a period when actual sales were £180,000, B Ltd's margin of safety, in units, was:

- (A) 2,000
- (B) 14,000
- (C) 18,000
- (D) 20,000.

1.3 For the forthcoming year, E plc's variable costs are budgeted to be 60 per cent of sales value and fixed costs are budgeted to be 10 per cent of sales value.

If E plc increases its selling prices by 10 per cent, but if fixed costs, variable costs per unit and sales volume remain unchanged, the effect on E plc's contribution would be:

- (A) a decrease of 2 per cent.
- (B) an increase of 5 per cent.
- (C) an increase of 10 per cent.
- (D) an increase of 25 per cent.

1.4 An organisation currently provides a single service. The cost per unit of that service is as follows:

	£
Selling price	130
Direct materials	22
Direct labour	15
Direct expenses	3
Variable overheads	10
Total variable cost	50

Total fixed costs for the period amount to £1,600,000. How many units of service (to the nearest whole unit) will the organisation need to provide to customers to generate a profit of £250,000?

(A) 20,000
(B) 20,555
(C) 23,125
(D) 26,428.

1.5 P Ltd provides plumbing services. Due to a shortage of skilled labour next period the company is unable to commence all the plumbing jobs for which customers have accepted estimates.

When deciding which plumbing jobs should be commenced, the jobs should be ranked according to the:

(A) Contribution to be earned from each job.
(B) Profit to be earned from each job.
(C) Contribution to be earned per hour of skilled labour on each job.
(D) Profit to be earned per hour of skilled labour on each job.

1.6 Z Ltd manufactures three products, the selling price and cost details of which are given below:

	Product X £	Product Y £	Product Z £
Selling price per unit	75	95	95
Costs per unit:			
Direct materials (£5/kg)	10	5	15
Direct labour (£8/hour)	16	24	20
Variable overhead	8	12	10
Fixed overhead	24	36	30

In a period when direct materials are restricted in supply, the most and the least profitable uses of direct materials are:

	Most profitable	Least profitable
(A)	X	Z
(B)	Y	Z
(C)	Z	Y
(D)	Y	X

? **Question 2** Short objective-test questions

2.1 OT Ltd plans to produce and sell 4,000 units of product C each month, at a selling price of £18 per unit. The unit cost of product C is as follows:

	£ per unit
Variable cost	8
Fixed cost	4
	12

To the nearest whole number, the monthly margin of safety, as a percentage of planned sales is ☐_____☐%.

2.2 The P/V ratio is the ratio of profit generated to the volume of sales.

True ☐
False ☐

2.3 Product J generates a contribution to sales ratio of 30 per cent. Fixed costs directly attributable to product J amount to £75,000 per month. The sales revenue required to achieve a monthly profit of £15,000 is £ ☐_____☐.

2.4 Match the following terms with the labels **a** to **d** on the graph. Write a, b, c or d in the relevant boxes.

☐ Margin of safety
☐ Fixed cost
☐ Contribution
☐ Profit

2.5 Select *true* or *false* for each of the following statements about a profit–volume chart.

(a) The profit line passes through the origin.

True ☐
False ☐

(b) Other things being equal, the angle of the profit line becomes steeper when the selling price increases.

True ☐
False ☐

(c) Contribution cannot be read directly from the chart.

True ☐
False ☐

(d) The point where the profit line crosses the vertical axis is the breakeven point.

True ☐
False ☐

(e) Fixed costs are shown as a line parallel to the horizontal axis.

True ☐
False ☐

(f) The angle of the profit line is directly affected by the P/V ratio.

True ☐
False ☐

2.6 PH Ltd has spare capacity in its factory. A supermarket chain has offered to buy a number of units of product XZ each month, and this would utilise the spare capacity. The supermarket is offering a price of £8 per unit and the cost structure of XZ is as follows:

	£ per unit
Direct material	3
Direct labour	2
Variable overhead	1
Fixed overhead	3
	9

Fixed costs would not be affected.
On a purely financial basis, should the supermarket's offer be accepted or rejected?

Accept the offer ☐
Reject the offer ☐

2.7 The following tasks are undertaken when deciding on the optimum production plan when a limiting factor exists. Write 1, 2, 3 or 4 in the boxes to indicate the correct sequence of tasks.

☐ Rank the products according to the contribution per unit of limiting factor used.
☐ Calculate each product's contribution per unit of limiting factor used.
☐ Identify the limiting factor.
☐ Allocate the limited resource according to the ranking.

2.8 A manufacturer of cell phones is considering the following actions. Which of these is likely to increase the manufacturer's C/S (contribution/sales) ratio (tick all that apply)?

(i) ☐ taking advantage of quantity discounts for bulk purchases of material;
(ii) ☐ introducing training programmes designed to improve labour efficiency;
(iii) ☐ following the actions of a competitor who has cut prices substantially;
(iv) ☐ reducing exports to countries where there is intense price competition;
(v) ☐ offering retailers a lower price if they display the product more prominently.

? **Question 3** Profit statements and breakeven analysis

BSE Veterinary Services is a specialist laboratory carrying out tests on cattle to ascertain whether the cattle have any infection. At present, the laboratory carries out 12,000 tests each period but, because of current difficulties with the beef herd, demand is expected to increase to 18,000 tests a period, which would require an additional shift to be worked.

The current cost of carrying out a full test is:

	£ per test
Materials	115
Technicians' wages	30
Variable overhead	12
Fixed overhead	50

Working the additional shift would:

(i) require a shift premium of 50 per cent to be paid to the technicians on the additional shift;

(ii) enable a quantity discount of 20 per cent to be obtained for all materials if an order was placed to cover 18,000 tests;

(iii) increase fixed costs by £700,000 per period.

The current fee per test is £300.

Requirements

(a) The profit for the period at the current capacity of 12,000 tests is £ _____ .

(b) A framework for a profit statement if the additional shift was worked and 18,000 tests were carried out is as follows (complete the boxes to derive the period profit):

		£000
(i)	Sales	_____
(ii)	Direct materials	_____
(iii)	Direct labour	_____
(iv)	Variable overhead	_____
(v)	Fixed costs	_____
(vi)	Profit	_____

(c) It has been determined that for a capacity of 15,000 tests per period, the test fee would be £300. Variable costs per test would amount to £140, and period fixed costs would be £1,200,000. The breakeven number of tests at this capacity level is _____ tests.

Question 4 Profit–volume graphs

MC Limited manufactures one product only, and for the last accounting period has produced the simplified income statement below:

	£	£
Sales		300,000
Costs:		
Direct materials	60,000	
Direct wages	40,000	
Prime cost	100,000	
Variable production overhead	10,000	
Fixed production overhead	40,000	
Fixed administration overhead	60,000	
Variable selling overhead	40,000	
Fixed selling overhead	20,000	
		270,000
Net profit		30,000

Requirements

(a) A profit–volume graph is to be drawn for MC Ltd's product.

   (i) The profit line drawn on the graph would cut the vertical axis (y-axis) at the point where y is equal to £ ⬚.

   (ii) The profit line drawn on the graph would cut the horizontal axis (x-axis) at the point where x is equal to £ ⬚.

   (iii) The margin of safety indicated by the graph would be £ ⬚.

(b) The effect of various changes in variables is to be indicated separately on the profit–volume graph. For each change, indicate whether the angle of the profit line and the breakeven point will increase, decrease or remain unchanged.

	The angle of the profit line will:		
Variable changed	*Increase*	*Decrease*	*Remain unchanged*
(i) Increase in selling price	☐	☐	☐
(ii) Increase in fixed cost	☐	☐	☐
(iii) Decrease in variable cost per unit	☐	☐	☐

	The breakeven point will:		
	Increase	*Decrease*	*Remain unchanged*
(i) Increase in selling price	☐	☐	☐
(ii) Increase in fixed cost	☐	☐	☐
(iii) Decrease in variable cost per unit	☐	☐	☐

? Question 5 Breakeven charts

The following data is available concerning HF Ltd's single service Q.

	£ per hour of service	*£ per hour of service*
Selling price		50
Variable cost		
Direct material	7	
Direct labour	8	
Variable overhead	5	
		20
Contribution		30
Fixed overhead		15
Profit		15

1,000 hours of service Q are provided to customers each month.

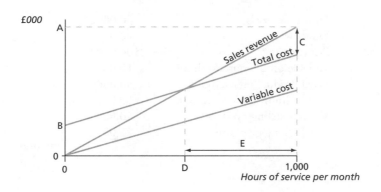

Requirements

The management accountant of HF Ltd has prepared the above contribution breakeven chart for service Q:

The values or quantities indicated by A to E on the chart are:

A £ ☐

B £ ☐

C £ ☐

D ☐ hours

E ☐ hours

Question 6 Decision-making, limiting factor

ABC Ltd makes three products, all of which use the same machine, which is available for 50,000 hours per period.

The standard costs of the product, per unit, are:

	Product A £	Product B £	Product C £
Direct materials	70	40	80
Direct labour:			
Machinists (£8/hour)	48	32	56
Assemblers (£6/hour)	36	40	42
Total variable cost	154	112	178
Selling price per unit	200	158	224
Maximum demand (units)	3,000	2,500	5,000

Fixed costs are £300,000 per period.

Requirements

(a) The deficiency in machine hours for the next period is ☐ hours.

(b) The optimum production plan that will maximise ABC Ltd's profit for the next period is:

Product A ☐ units

Product B ☐ units

Product C ☐ units.

Solutions to Revision Questions

4

 Solution 1

- Question 1.3 is quite tricky. Try setting up a table of the selling price, variable cost and contribution before and after the change, perhaps using a selling price of £100. Remember that fixed costs are not relevant because they do not affect contribution.

1.1   Answer: (D)

Contribution per unit = 40% of selling price = £8

$$\text{Breakeven point} = \frac{£60,000}{£8} = 7,500 \text{ units}$$

1.2   Answer: (A)

Contribution per unit = £9 − £6 = £3

$$\text{Breakeven point} = \frac{\text{Fixed costs}}{\text{Contribution per unit}} = \frac{£54,000}{£3} = 18,000 \text{ units}$$

$$\text{Margin of safety} = \text{Actual sales} - \text{breakeven sales} = \frac{£180,000}{£9} - 18,000$$
$$= 2,000 \text{ units}$$

1.3   Answer: (D)

Fixed costs are not relevant because they do not affect contribution. Taking a selling price of, say, £100 per unit, the cost structures will look like this:

	Before change £ per unit		After change £ per unit
Sales price	100	+10%	110
Variable cost	60		60
Contribution	40		50

Contribution per unit increases by 25 per cent. If sales volume remains unchanged then total contribution will also increase by 25 per cent.

1.4 Answer: (C)

$$\frac{£1,600,000 + £250,000}{£80} = 23,125 \text{ units}$$

Working:	
Contribution per unit	£
Selling price	130
Variable cost	(50)
Contribution/unit	80

1.5 Answer: (C)

The decision rule in a limiting factor situation is to maximise the contribution per unit of limiting factor.

1.6 Answer: (B)

Product	*X*	*Y*	*Z*
Contribution/unit	£41	£54	£50
Materials (kg/unit)	2	1	3
Contribution/kg	£20.50	£54	£16.66
Ranking	2	1	3

☑ Solution 2

2.1 Monthly fixed costs = 4,000 units × £4 = £16,000.

$$\text{Breakeven point} = \frac{\text{Fixed costs}}{\text{Contribution per unit}} = \frac{£16,000}{£18 - £8} = 1,600 \text{ units}$$

$$\text{Margin of safety \%} = \frac{\text{Planned sales} - \text{breakeven sales}}{\text{Planned sales}} \times 100\%$$
$$= \frac{4,000 - 1,600}{4,000} \times 100\% = 60\%.$$

2.2 *False*. The P/V ratio is another term for the C/S ratio. It measures the ratio of the contribution to sales.

2.3 $$\text{Required sales revenue} = \frac{\text{Required contribution}}{\text{C/S ratio}} = \frac{£75,000 + £15,000}{0.30}$$
$$= £300,000.$$

2.4 **c** Margin of safety
 a Fixed cost
 b Contribution
 d Profit.

2.5 (a) *False.* The profit line passes through the breakeven point on the horizontal axis, and cuts the vertical axis at the point where the loss is equal to the fixed costs.

(b) *True.* Profits increase at a faster rate if the selling price is higher.

(c) *True.* A contribution breakeven chart is needed for this.

(d) *False.* The breakeven point is where the profit line cuts the horizontal axis.

(e) *False.* No fixed cost line is shown on a profit–volume chart.

(f) *True.* The higher the P/V ratio or contribution to sales ratio, the higher will be the contribution earned per £ of sale and the steeper will be the angle of the profit line.

2.6 *Accept the offer.* On a purely financial basis, the price of £8 per unit exceeds the variable cost of £6 per unit. Since the fixed cost would not be affected, the units sold to the supermarket will each earn a contribution of £2.

2.7 1. Identify the limiting factor.
2. Calculate each product's contribution per unit of limiting factor used.
3. Rank the products according to the contribution per unit of limiting factor used.
4. Allocate the limited resource according to the ranking.

2.8 (i), (ii) and (iv) will increase the contribution/sales ratio.

(i) Lower variable costs per unit, higher contribution per unit = higher C/S ratio
(ii) Lower variable costs per unit, higher contribution per unit = higher C/S ratio
(iii) Lower selling price per unit, lower contribution per unit = lower C/S ratio
(iv) Higher average contribution per unit = higher C/S ratio
(v) Lower selling price per unit, lower contribution per unit = lower C/S ratio

✅ Solution 3

- In part (b) do not be tempted to use unit rates to calculate the new level of fixed costs. The current level of fixed costs is £600,000 *per period*. This will increase by £700,000.
- Also in part (b), notice that the shift premium applies only to the technicians working on the additional shift. It does not apply to all technicians' wages.

(a) £1,116,000
Workings: profit statement for current 12,000 capacity

		£000
Sales	12,000 tests @ £300/test	3,600
Direct materials	12,000 tests @ £115/test	(1,380)
Direct labour	12,000 tests @ £30/test	(360)
Variable overhead	12,000 tests @ £12/test	(144)
Contribution		1,716
Fixed costs	12,000 tests @ £50/test	(600)
Profit		1,116

(b) *Profit statement for 18,000 capacity, with additional shift*

			£000	£000	
Sales	18,000 tests @ £300/test			5,400	**(i)**
Direct materials	18,000 tests @ £92/test			(1,656)	**(ii)**
Direct labour	12,000 tests @ £30/test	(360)			
	6,000 tests @ £45/test	(270)			
				(630)	**(iii)**
Variable overhead	18,000 tests @ £12/test			(216)	**(iv)**
Contribution				2,898	
Fixed costs				(1,300)	**(v)**
Profit				1,598	**(vi)**

(c) Breakeven volume $= \dfrac{£1,200,000}{(£300 - £140)} = 7,500$ tests.

✅ Solution 4

- The profit line cuts the vertical axis at the point equal to the fixed costs, that is, the loss when no sale is made.
- The profit line cuts the horizontal axis at the breakeven point. Therefore, for (a)(ii) you will need to calculate the breakeven point. For (a)(iii), the margin of safety is the difference between £300,000 sales and the breakeven point.

(a) (i) $-£120,000$
   (ii) £240,000
   (iii) £60,000.

Workings:

$$\text{Contribution-to-sales ratio} = \frac{£(300,000 - 100,000 - 10,000 - 40,000)}{£300,000} \times 100 = 50\%$$

$$\text{Breakeven point} = \frac{\text{Fixed costs}}{\text{C/S ratio}} = \frac{£(40,000 + 60,000 + 20,000)}{0.5} = £240,000$$

$$\text{Margin of safety} = £(300,000 - 240,000) = £60,000$$

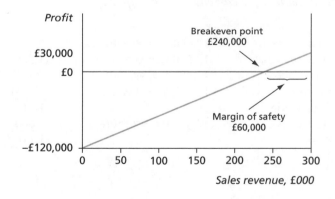

(b)

	The angle of the profit line will:	The breakeven point will:
(i) Increase in selling price	Increase	Decrease
(ii) Increase in fixed cost	Remain unchanged	Increase
(iii) Decrease in variable cost per unit	Increase	Decrease

 ## Solution 5

- Remember that a contribution breakeven chart shows the variable cost line instead of the fixed cost line.
- This means that contribution can be read directly from the chart, as the difference between the sales value and the variable cost. This is the main advantage of the contribution breakeven chart.

A   £50,000 (1,000 hours × £50 selling price)
B   £15,000 (fixed cost at zero activity)
C   £15,000 (profit for 1,000 hours – see below)
D   500 hours (breakeven point – see below)
E   500 hours (margin of safety (1,000 hours − 500 hours breakeven))

Workings:

	£	£
Sales value for 1,000 hours = 1,000 × £50		50,000
Total cost for 1,000 hours:		
variable cost 1,000 × £20	20,000	
fixed cost 1,000 × £15	15,000	
		35,000
Profit for 1,000 hours		15,000

$$\text{Breakeven point} = \frac{\text{Fixed costs}}{\text{Contribution per hour}} = \frac{£15,000}{£30} = 500 \text{ hours}$$

 ## Solution 6

- In part (b) remember to rank the products according to their contribution per machine hour. Then allocate the available machine hours according to this ranking.

(a) The deficiency in machine hours for the next period is 13,000 hours.
(b) Product A 3,000 units
   Product B 2,500 units
   Product C 3,142 units

Workings:

(a) Deficiency in machine hours for next period

	Product A	Product B	Product C	Total
Machine hours required per unit	48/8 = 6	32/8 = 4	56/8 = 7	
Maximum demand (units)	3,000	2,500	5,000	
Total machine hours to meet maximum demand	18,000	10,000	35,000	63,000
Machine hours available				50,000
Deficiency of machine hours				13,000

(b)

	Product A £	Product B £	Product C £
Selling price per unit	200	158	224
Variable cost per unit	(154)	(112)	(178)
Contribution per unit	46	46	46
Machine hours required per unit	6	4	7
Contribution per machine hour	£7.67	£11.50	£6.57
Order of production	2	1	3

Therefore, make:

	Machine hours
2,500 units of product B, using machine hours of (4 × 2,500)	10,000
3,000 units of product A, using machine hours of (6 × 3,000)	18,000
	28,000
Machine hours left to make product C	22,000
	50,000

Therefore, the company should make 3,142, that is, (22,000/7) units of product C.

5

Standard Costing and
Variance Analysis

Standard Costing and Variance Analysis

5

LEARNING OUTCOMES

After completing this chapter, you should be able to:

▶ explain the difference between ascertaining costs after the event and planning by establishing standard costs in advance;

▶ explain why planned standard costs, prices and volumes are useful in setting a benchmark for comparison and so allowing managers' attention to be directed to areas of the business that are performing below or above expectation;

▶ calculate standard costs for the material, labour and variable overhead elements of cost of a product or service;

▶ calculate variances for materials, labour, variable overhead, sales prices and sales volumes.

5.1 Introduction

In this chapter, we will be looking at standard costs: how they are set and how they are used as the basis of variance analysis to monitor and control an organisation's performance.

> The CIMA *Terminology* defines standard costing as a 'control technique that reports variances by comparing actual costs to pre-set standards facilitating action through management by exception'.

The pre-set standards require managers to plan in advance the amount and price of each resource that will be used in providing a service or manufacturing a product. These pre-set standards, for selling prices and sales volumes as well as for costs, provide a basis for planning, a target for achievement and a benchmark against which the actual costs and revenues can be compared.

The actual costs and revenues recorded after the event are then compared with the pre-set standards and the differences are recorded as variances. If resource price or usage is above standard, or if sales volume or selling price is below standard, an adverse variance will result. If resource price or usage is below standard, or if sales volume or selling price is above standard, a favourable variance will result.

Careful analysis of the variances and their presentation to management can help to direct managers' attention to areas of the business that are performing below or above expectation.

If certain variances are large or significant then managers can concentrate their attention on these activities where any corrective action is likely to be most worthwhile. If other variances are small or not significant then managers can ignore these activities, knowing that they appear to be conforming to expectations. This is the principle of management by exception that is mentioned in CIMA's definition of standard costing.

5.2 What is a standard cost?

A standard cost is a carefully predetermined unit cost which is prepared for each cost unit. It contains details of the standard amount and price of each resource that will be utilised in providing the service or manufacturing the product.

In order to be able to apply standard costing it must be possible to identify a measurable cost unit. This can be a unit of product or service but it must be capable of standardising, for example, standardised tasks must be involved in its creation. The cost units themselves do not necessarily have to be identical. For example, standard costing can be applied in situations such as costing plumbing jobs for customers where every cost unit is unique. However, the plumbing jobs must include standardised tasks for which a standard time and cost can be determined for monitoring purposes.

 It can be difficult to apply standard costing in some types of service organisation, where cost units may not be standardised and they are more difficult to measure.

The standard cost may be stored on a standard cost card like the one shown below but nowadays it is more likely to be stored on a computer, perhaps in a database. Alternatively it may be stored as part of a spreadsheet so that it can be used in the calculation of variances.

A standard cost card showing the variable elements of production cost might look like this.

Standard cost card: product 176

	£ per unit
Direct materials: 30 kg @ £4.30	129.00
Direct wages: 12 hours @ £11.80	141.60
Prime cost	270.60
Variable production overhead:	
12 hours @ £0.75	9.00
Variable production cost	279.60

For every variable cost the standard amount of resource to be used is stated, as well as the standard price of the resource. This standard data provides the information for a detailed variance analysis, as long as the actual data is collected in the same level of detail.

Standard costs and standard prices provide the basic unit information which is needed for valuing budgets and for determining total expenditures and revenues.

Exercise 5.1

From the information given below, prepare a standard cost card extract for one unit and enter on the standard cost card the costs to show subtotals for:

(a) prime cost;
(b) variable production cost.

The following data is given for the standard details for one unit:

Direct materials: 40 square metres @ £6.48/sq m

Direct wages:

Bonding department–48 hours @ £12.50/hour

Finishing department–30 hours @ £11.90/hour

Budgeted costs and labour hours per annum:	*£*	*hours*
Variable production overhead:		
Bonding department	375,000	500,000
Finishing department	150,000	300,000

 Solution

Standard cost card extract

	£ per unit
Direct materials: 40 sq m @ £6.48	259.20
Direct wages:	
Bonding – 48 hours @ £12.50	600.00
Finishing – 30 hours @ £11.90	357.00
Prime cost	1,216.20
Variable production overhead:	
Bonding – 48 hours @ £0.75	36.00
Finishing – 30 hours @ £0.50	15.00
Variable production cost	1,267.20

5.3 Performance levels

5.3.1 A standard

 CIMA's *Terminology* defines a standard as a 'benchmark measurement of resource usage or revenue or profit generation, set in defined conditions'.

The definition goes on to describe a number of bases which can be used to set the standard. These bases include:

- a prior period level of performance by the same organisation;
- the level of performance achieved by comparable organisations;
- the level of performance required to meet organisational objectives.

Use of the first basis indicates that management feels that performance levels in a prior period have been acceptable. They will then use this performance level as a target and control level for the forthcoming period.

When using the second basis management is being more outward looking, perhaps attempting to monitor their organisation's performance against 'the best of the rest'.

The third basis sets a performance level which will be sufficient to achieve the objectives which the organisation has set for itself.

5.3.2 Ideal standard

Standards may be set at ideal levels, which make no allowance for inefficiencies such as losses, waste and machine downtime. This type of ideal standard is achievable only under the most favourable conditions and can be used if managers wish to highlight and monitor the full cost of factors such as waste, etc. However, this type of standard will almost always result in adverse variances since a certain amount of waste, etc., is usually unavoidable. This can be very demotivating for individuals who feel that an adverse variance suggests that they have performed badly.

5.3.3 Attainable standard

Standards may also be set at attainable levels which assume efficient levels of operation, but which include allowances for factors such as losses, waste and machine downtime. This type of standard does not have the negative motivational impact that can arise with an ideal standard because it makes some allowance for unavoidable inefficiencies. Adverse variances will reveal whether inefficiencies have exceeded this unavoidable amount.

5.3.4 Current standard

Standards based on current performance levels (current wastage, current inefficiencies) are known as current standards. Their disadvantage is that they do not encourage any attempt to improve on current levels of efficiency.

5.4 Setting standard costs

You have already seen that each element of a unit's standard cost has details of the price and quantity of the resources to be used. In this section of the chapter, we will list some of the sources of information which may be used in setting the standard costs.

5.4.1 Standard material price

Sources of information include:

(a) quotations and estimates received from potential suppliers;
(b) trend information obtained from past data on material prices;
(c) details of any bulk discounts which may be available;
(d) information on any charges which will be made for packaging and carriage inwards;
(e) the quality of material to be used: this may affect the price to be paid;
(f) for internally manufactured components, the predetermined standard cost for the component will be used as the standard price.

5.4.2 Standard material usage

Sources of information include:

(a) the basis to be used for the level of performance (see Section 5.3);
(b) if an attainable standard is to be used, the allowance to be made for losses, wastage, etc. (work study techniques may be used to determine this);
(c) technical specifications of the material to be used.

5.4.3 Standard labour rate

Sources of information include:

(a) the personnel department, for the wage rates for employees of the required grades with the required skills;
(b) forecasts of the likely outcome of any trades union negotiations currently in progress;
(c) details of any bonus schemes in operation. For example, employees may be paid a bonus if higher levels of output are achieved.

5.4.4 Standard labour times

Sources of information include:

(a) the basis to be used for the level of performance (see Section 5.3);
(b) if an attainable standard is to be used, the allowance to be made for downtime, etc.;
(c) technical specifications of the tasks required to manufacture the product or provide the service;
(d) the results of work study exercises which are set up to determine the standard time to perform the required tasks and the grades of labour to be employed.

5.4.5 Variable production overhead costs

In Chapter 3, you learned how predetermined hourly rates were derived for production overhead. These overhead absorption rates represent the standard hourly rates for overhead in each cost centre. They can be applied to the standard labour hours or machine hours for each cost unit.

The overheads will be analysed into their fixed and variable components so that a separate rate is available for fixed production overhead and for variable production overhead. This is necessary to achieve adequate control over the variable and fixed elements. Your *Fundamentals of Management Accounting* syllabus requires you to deal only with standard variable overhead costs.

5.5 Updating standards

The main purpose of standard costs is to provide a yardstick or benchmark against which actual performance can be monitored. If the comparison between actual and standard cost is to be meaningful, then the standard must be valid and relevant.

It follows that the standard cost should be kept as up to date as possible. This may necessitate frequent updating of standards to ensure that they fairly represent the latest methods and operations, and the latest prices which must be paid for the resources being used.

The standards may not be updated for *every* small change: however, any significant changes should be adjusted as soon as possible.

5.6 Standard costing in the modern business environment

There has recently been some criticism of the appropriateness of standard costing in the modern business environment. The main criticisms include the following:

(a) Standard costing was developed when the business environment was more stable and operating conditions were less prone to change. In the present dynamic environment, such stable conditions cannot be assumed.

If conditions are not stable, then it is difficult to set a standard cost which can be used to control costs over a period of time.

(b) Performance to standard used to be judged as satisfactory, but in today's climate constant improvement must be aimed for in order to remain competitive.

(c) The emphasis on labour variances is no longer appropriate with the increasing use of automated production methods.

An organisation's decision to use standard costing depends on its effectiveness in helping managers to make the correct decisions. It can be used in areas of most organisations, whether they are involved with manufacturing, or with services such as hospitals or insurance. For example, a predetermined standard could be set for the labour time to process an insurance claim. This would help in planning and controlling the cost of processing insurance claims.

Standard costing may still be useful even where the final product or service is not standardised. It may be possible to identify a number of standard components and activities for which standards may be set and used effectively for planning and control purposes. In addition, the use of demanding performance levels in standard costs may help to encourage continuous improvement.

5.7 What is variance analysis?

You already know that a variance is the difference between the expected standard cost and the actual cost incurred. You also know that a unit standard cost contains detail concerning both the usage of resources and the price to be paid for the resources.

Variance analysis involves breaking down the total variance to explain how much of it is caused by the usage of resources being different from the standard, and how much of it is caused by the price of resources being different from the standard. These variances can be combined to reconcile the total cost difference revealed by the comparison of the actual and standard cost.

5.8 Variable cost variances

We will use a simple example to demonstrate how the variances are calculated for direct material, direct labour and variable overhead.

Example

A company manufactures a single product for which the standard variable cost is:

	£ per unit
Direct material: 81 kg × £7 per kg	567
Direct labour: 97 hours × £8 per hour	776
Variable overhead: 97 hours × £3 per hour	291
	1,634

During January, 530 units were produced and the costs incurred were as follows:

Direct material:	42,845 kg purchased and used; cost £308,484
Direct labour:	51,380 hours worked; cost £400,764
Variable overhead:	cost £156,709

You are *required* to calculate the variable cost variances for January.

5.8.1 Direct material cost variances

(a) Direct material total variance

	£
530 units should cost (×£567)	300,510
But did cost	308,484
Total direct material cost variance	7,974 adverse

 You should always remember to indicate whether a variance is adverse or favourable.

This direct material total variance can now be analysed into its 'price' and 'quantity' elements.

(b) Direct material price variance

The direct material price variance reveals how much of the direct material total variance was caused by paying a different price for the materials used.

	£
42,845 kg purchased should have cost (×£7)	299,915
But did cost	308,484
Direct material price variance	8,569 adverse

The adverse price variance indicates that expenditure was £8,569 more than standard because a higher than standard price was paid for each kilogram of material.

(c) Direct material usage variance

The direct material usage variance reveals how much of the direct material total variance was caused by using a different quantity of material, compared with the standard allowance for the production achieved.

	kg	
530 units produced should have used (×81 kg)	42,930	
But did use	42,845	
Variance in kg	85	favourable
× standard price per kg (£7):		
Direct material usage variance	£595	favourable

The favourable usage variance of £595 is the saving in material cost (at standard prices) resulting from using a lower amount of material than the standard expected for this level of output.

Check: £8,569 adverse + £595 favourable = £7,974 adverse (the correct total variance).

> **!** All of the 'quantity' variances are always valued at the standard price. Later in this example you will see that the 'quantity' variances for labour and for variable overhead – the efficiency variances – are valued at the standard rate per hour.

5.8.2 The direct material price variance and inventory valuation

One slight complication sometimes arises with the calculation of the direct material price variance. In this example, the problem did not arise because the amount of material purchased was equal to the amount used.

However, when the two amounts are not equal then the direct material price variance could be based either on the material purchased or on the material used. In the example we used the following method – we will call it method A:

Method A Direct material price variance

	£
Material purchased should have cost	X
But did cost	X
Direct material price variance	X

Alternatively, we could have calculated the variance as follows – we will call it method B.

Method B Direct material price variance

	£
Material used should have cost	X
But did cost	X
Direct material price variance	X

Obviously, if the purchase quantity is different from the usage quantity, then the two methods will give different results.

So how do you know which method to use? The answer lies in the inventory valuation method.

If inventory is valued at standard cost, then method A is used. This will ensure that all of the variance is eliminated as soon as purchases are made and the inventory will be held at standard cost.

If inventory is valued at actual cost, then method B is used. This means that the variance is calculated and eliminated on each bit of inventory as it is used up. The remainder of the inventory will then be held at actual price, with its price variance still 'attached', until it is used and the price variance is calculated.

If this seems confusing you might find it easier to return and consider the reasoning after you have studied standard cost bookkeeping in chapter 7, when you will learn which method is generally preferred.

5.8.3   Direct labour cost variances

(a)   Direct labour total variance

	£	
530 units should cost (×£776)	411,280	
But did cost	400,764	
Total direct labour cost variance	10,516	favourable

This variance can now be analysed into its 'price' and 'quantity' elements. The 'price' part is called the labour rate variance and the 'quantity' part is called the labour efficiency variance.

(b)   Direct labour rate variance

The direct labour rate variance reveals how much of the direct labour total variance was caused by paying a different rate per hour for the labour hours worked.

	£	
51,380 hours should have cost (×£8)	411,040	
But did cost	400,764	
Direct labour rate variance	10,276	favourable

The favourable rate variance indicates that expenditure was £10,276 less than standard because a lower than standard rate was paid for each hour of labour.

 Notice the similarity between the method used to calculate the labour rate variance and the method used to calculate the material price variance.

(c) Direct labour efficiency variance

The direct labour efficiency variance reveals how much of the direct labour total variance was caused by using a different number of hours of labour, compared with the standard allowance for the production achieved.

	Hours	
530 units produced should take (×97 hours)	51,410	
But did take	51,380	
Variance in hours	30	favourable
× standard labour rate per hour (£8)		
Direct labour efficiency variance	£240	favourable

The favourable efficiency variance of £240 is the saving in labour cost (at standard rates) resulting from using fewer labour hours than the standard expected for this level of output.

   Check: £10,276 favourable + £240 favourable = £10,516 favourable (the correct total variance).

 In the next chapter you will see that a further analysis of the efficiency variance can be carried out when idle time occurs.

5.8.4 Variable overhead cost variances

(a) Variable overhead total variance

	£	
530 units should cost (×£291)	154,230	
But did cost	156,709	
Total variable overhead cost variance	2,479	adverse

This variance can now be analysed into its 'price' and 'quantity' elements. The 'price' part is called the variable overhead expenditure variance and the 'quantity' part is called the variable overhead efficiency variance.

(b) Variable overhead expenditure variance

The variable overhead expenditure variance reveals how much of the variable overhead total variance was caused by paying a different hourly rate of overhead for the hours worked.

	£	
51,380 hours of variable overhead should cost (×£3)	154,140	
But did cost	156,709	
Variable overhead expenditure variance	2,569	adverse

The adverse expenditure variance indicates that expenditure was £2,569 more than standard because a higher than standard hourly rate was paid for variable overhead.

(c) Variable overhead efficiency variance

The variable overhead efficiency variance reveals how much of the variable overhead total variance was caused by using a different number of hours of labour, compared with the standard allowance for the production achieved. Its calculation is very similar to the calculation of the labour efficiency variance.

Variance in hours (from labour efficiency variance)	<u>30 hours</u>	favourable
× standard variable overhead rate per hour (£3)		
Variable overhead efficiency variance	<u>£90</u>	favourable

The favourable efficiency variance of £90 is the saving in variable overhead cost (at standard rates) resulting from using fewer labour hours than the standard expected for this level of output.

Check: £2,569 adverse + £90 favourable = £2,479 adverse (the correct total variance)

> **!** Notice that the method used to calculate the variable overhead variances is identical to the method used to calculate the direct labour variances. In the next chapter you will see that the calculation of the variable overhead efficiency variance may be affected by idle time.

5.9   Sales variances

Now that we have seen how to analyse the variable cost variances we will turn our attention to sales variances. Your syllabus requires you to be able to calculate two variances for sales: the sales price variance and the sales volume contribution variance. We will demonstrate the calculation of these variances using the following data.

Budget	Sales and production volume	81,600 units
	Standard selling price	£59 per unit
	Standard variable cost	£24 per unit
Actual results	Sales and production volume	82,400 units
	Actual selling price	£57 per unit
	Actual variable cost	£23 per unit

5.9.1   Sales price variance

The sales price variance reveals the difference in total revenue caused by charging a different selling price from standard.

	£	
82,400 units should sell for (×£59)	4,861,600	
But did sell for (82,400 units ×£57)	4,696,800	
Sales price variance	<u>164,800</u>	adverse

The adverse sales price variance indicates that the 82,400 units were sold for a lower price than standard, which we can see from the basic data.

5.9.2 Sales volume contribution variance

The sales volume contribution variance reveals the contribution difference which is caused by selling a different quantity from that budgeted.

> **!** Since the analysis of variable cost variances explains all of the variations caused by differences between actual costs and standard costs, the calculation of the sales volume variance is based on the standard contribution not on the actual contribution.

Actual sales volume	32,400	units
Budget sales volume	81,600	units
Sales volume variance in units	800	favourable
× standard contribution per unit £(59 − 24)	×£35	
Sales volume contribution variance	£28,000	favourable

5.10 Summary

Having read this chapter the main points that you should understand are as follows:

1. A standard cost is a carefully predetermined unit cost. It is established in advance to provide a basis for planning, a target for achievement and a benchmark against which the actual costs and revenues can be compared.
2. The difference between the standard cost and the actual result is called a variance.
3. The analysis of variances facilitates action through management by exception, whereby managers concentrate on those areas of the business that are performing below or above expectations and ignore those that appear to be conforming to expectations.
4. A number of different performance levels can be used in setting standards. The most common are ideal, attainable and current.
5. The direct material total variance can be analysed between the direct material price variance and the direct material usage variance.
6. If inventories are valued at standard cost then the material price variance should be based on the quantity purchased. If inventories are valued at actual cost the material price variance should be based on the quantity used during the period.
7. The direct labour total variance can be analysed between the direct labour rate variance and the direct labour efficiency variance.
8. The variable overhead total variance can be analysed between the variable overhead expenditure variance and the variable overhead efficiency variance.
9. The sales price variance reveals the difference in total revenue caused by charging a different selling price from standard.
10. The sales volume contribution variance reveals the contribution difference which is caused by selling a different quantity from that budgeted. The calculation of the variance is based on the standard contribution not on the actual contribution.

Revision Questions

 **Question 1** Multiple choice

1.1 A standard cost is:

(A) the planned unit cost of a product, component or service in a period.
(B) the budgeted cost ascribed to the level of activity achieved in a budget centre in a control period.
(C) the budgeted production cost ascribed to the level of activity in a budget period.
(D) the budgeted non-production cost for a product, component or service in a period.

Data for questions 1.2–1.7

Budgeted production of product V is 650 units each period. The standard cost card for product V contains the following information.

		£ per unit
Ingredients	12 litres @ £4 per litre	48
Direct labour	3 hours @ £9 per hour	27
Variable production overhead	3 hours @ £2 per hour	6

During the latest period 670 units of product V were produced. The actual results recorded were as follows:

Ingredients purchased and used	8,015 litres	£33,663
Direct labour	2,090 hours	£17,765
Variable production overhead		£5,434

1.2 The ingredients price variance is:

(A) £1,503 favourable
(B) £1,503 adverse
(C) £1,603 favourable
(D) £1,603 adverse

1.3 The ingredients usage variance is:

(A) £100 favourable
(B) £100 adverse
(C) £105 favourable
(D) £860 adverse

1.4 The labour rate variance is

(A) £325 favourable
(B) £325 adverse
(C) £1,045 favourable
(D) £1,045 adverse

1.5 The labour efficiency variance is

(A) £680 adverse
(B) £720 adverse
(C) £720 favourable
(D) £1,260 adverse

1.6 The variable overhead expenditure variance is:

(A) £1,254 favourable
(B) £1,254 adverse
(C) £1,534 favourable
(D) £1,534 adverse

1.7 The variable overhead efficiency variance is:

(A) £151 adverse
(B) £160 adverse
(C) £160 favourable
(D) £280 adverse

1.8 ABC Ltd uses standard costing. It purchases a small component for which the following data are available:

Actual purchase quantity	6,800 units
Standard allowance for actual production	5,440 units
Standard price	85p per unit
Purchase price variance (adverse)	(£544)

What was the actual purchase price per unit?

(A) 75p
(B) 77p
(C) 93p
(D) 95p.

1.9 During a period 17,500 labour hours were worked at a standard cost of £6.50 per hour. The labour efficiency variance was £7,800 favourable. The number of standard labour hours expected for the output achieved was:

(A) 1,200
(B) 16,300
(C) 17,500
(D) 18,700.

1.10 XYZ Ltd uses standard costing. It makes an assembly for which the following standard data are available:

Standard labour hours per assembly	24
Standard labour cost per hour	£8

During a period 850 assemblies were made, there was a nil rate variance and an adverse efficiency variance of £4,400.

How many actual labour hours were worked?

(A) 19,850
(B) 20,400
(C) 20,950
(D) 35,200.

Data for questions 1.11 and 1.12

The standard cost of providing a meal in a fast food restaurant is as follows.

	£
Ingredient cost	1.80
Direct labour cost	0.30
Variable overhead cost	0.20

The standard price of the meal is £4.50 and the budgeted sales volume is 4,650 meals each period.

During period 9 a total of 4,720 meals were sold for £20,768. The actual total variable cost per meal was £2.30.

1.11 The sales price variance for period 9 was:

(A) £465 favourable
(B) £465 adverse
(C) £472 favourable
(D) £472 adverse

1.12 The sales volume contribution variance for period 9 was:

(A) £147 favourable
(B) £147 adverse
(C) £154 favourable
(D) £154 adverse

Question 2 Short objective-test questions

2.1 *Tick the correct box.*

A standard which assumes efficient levels of operation, but which includes allowances for factors such as waste and machine downtime, is known as an:

attainable standard ☐
ideal standard ☐

2.2 The standard cost card for product F shows that each unit requires 3 kg of material at a standard price of £9 per kilogram. Last period, 200 units of F were produced and £5,518 was paid for 620 kg of material that was bought and used. Calculate the following variances and tick the correct box to indicate whether each variance is adverse or favourable.

	Adverse	Favourable
(a) the direct material price variance is £ [　　　　　]	☐	☐
(b) the direct material usage variance is £ [　　　　]	☐	☐

2.3 The standard cost card for product K shows that each unit requires four hours of direct labour at a standard rate of £8 per hour. Last period, 420 units were produced and the direct labour cost amounted to £15,300. The direct labour efficiency variance was £160 adverse.

The actual rate paid per direct labour hour is £ [　　　　　].

2.4 Is the following statement *true* or *false*?

Standard costing cannot be applied in an organisation that manufactures specialist furniture to customers' specifications because every cost unit is unique.

True ☐

False ☐

2.5 The following extract is taken from the standard cost card of product H.

		£ per unit
Direct labour	4 hours @ £12 per hour	48
Variable production overhead		8

During the latest period the number of direct labour hours worked to produce 490 units of product H was 1,930. The variable production overhead cost incurred was £3,281.

The variable production overhead variances for the period are:

	Adverse	Favourable
(a) Variable production overhead expenditure variance £ [　　　　]	☐	☐
(b) Variable production overhead efficiency variance £ [　　　]	☐	☐

2.6 The following data relate to product R for the latest period.

Budgeted sales revenue	£250,000
Standard selling price per unit	£12.50
Standard contribution per unit	£5.00
Actual sales volume (units)	19,500
Actual sales revenue	£257,400

The sales variances for the period are:

	Adverse	Favourable
(a) Sales price variance £ [　　　　]	☐	☐
(b) Sales volume contribution variance £ [　　　]	☐	☐

2.7 The budgeted sales of product Y are 230 units per period at a standard sales price of £43 per unit. Last period the sales volume contribution variance was £1,100 favourable and all units were actually sold for £46 per unit. The sales price variance was £840 favourable.

The standard variable cost per unit of product Y is £ [　　　　].

? **Question 3** Direct cost variances

XYZ Ltd is planning to make 120,000 units per period of a new product. The following standards have been set:

	Per unit
Direct material A	1.2 kg at £11 per kg
Direct material B	4.7 kg at £6 per kg
Direct labour:	
Operation 1	42 minutes
Operation 2	37 minutes
Operation 3	11 minutes

All direct operatives are paid at the rate of £8 per hour. Attainable work hours are less than clock hours, so the 500 direct operatives have been budgeted for 400 hours each in the period.

Actual results for the period were:

Production	126,000 units
Direct labour	cost £1.7 m for 215,000 clock hours
Material A	cost £1.65 m for 150,000 kg
Material B	cost £3.5 m for 590,000 kg

Requirements

(a) (i) A realistic labour efficiency variance for the period is £ [   ]

adverse ☐
favourable ☐

(ii) The labour rate variance for the period is £ [   ]

adverse ☐
favourable ☐

(b) (i) The material price variances for the period are

Material A £ [   ]   Material B £ [   ]
adverse ☐   adverse ☐
favourable ☐   favourable ☐

(ii) The material usage variances for the period are:

Material A £ [   ]   Material B £ [   ]
adverse ☐   adverse ☐
favourable ☐   favourable ☐

Solutions to Revision Questions

5

✓ Solution 1

- Select your answer carefully from the available options. You may in haste select an option that has the correct absolute value for the variance but is adverse when you should have selected favourable, or vice versa.
- In some of the questions you will need to 'work backwards' from variance information to determine the actual results. This will enable you to test yourself to see if you really understand how the variances are calculated!
- The second question asks for an ingredients price variance. This is calculated in exactly the same way as a direct material price variance.

1.1 Answer: (A)

A standard cost is a carefully predetermined unit cost which is prepared for each cost unit.

1.2 Answer: (D)

	£	
8,015 litres should cost (×£4)	32,060	
But did cost	33,663	
Ingredients price variance	1,603	adverse

1.3 Answer: (A)

	Litres	
670 units produced should use (×12)	8,040	
But did use	8,015	
Variance in litres	25	favourable
× standard price per litre (£4)		
Ingredients usage variance	£100	favourable

1.4 Answer: (C)

	£	
2,090 hours should cost (×£9)	18,810	
But did cost	17,765	
Labour rate variance	1,045	favourable

137

1.5   Answer: (B)

	Hours	
670 units produced should take (×3)	2,010	
But did take	2,090	
Variance in hours	80	adverse
× standard labour rate per hour (£9)		
Labour efficiency variance	£720	adverse

1.6   Answer: (B)

	£	
2,090 hours should cost (×£2)	4,180	
But did cost	5,434	
Variable overhead expenditure variance	1,254	adverse

1.7   Answer: (B)

Variance in hours (from labour efficiency variance)	80 hours	adverse
× standard variable overhead rate per hour (£2)		
Variable overhead efficiency variance	£160	adverse

1.8   Answer: (C)

Purchase price variance per unit purchased = £544/6,800 = 8p adverse per unit.
Actual purchase price = 85p standard + 8p = 93p per unit.

1.9   Answer: (D)

Number of hours saved compared with standard = £7,800/£6.50 = 1,200.
Number of standard labour hours expected = 17,500 + 1,200 = 18,700.

1.10   Answer: (C)

Standard labour cost = 24 hours × 850 × £8 = £163,200
Actual cost = £163,200 + £4,400 = £167,600
@£8/hour = 20,950 hours

1.11   Answer: (D)

	£	
4,720 meals should sell for(×£4.50)	21,240	
But did sell for	20,768	
Sales price variance	472	adverse

1.12   Answer: (C)

Actual sales volume	4,720	meals
Budget sales volume	4,650	meals
Sales volume variance in meals	70	favourable
× standard contribution per meal	×£2.20	
£(4.50 − 1.80 − 0.30 − 0.20)		
Sales volume contribution variance	£154	favourable

 # Solution 2

2.1   A standard which assumes efficient levels of operation, but which includes allowances for factors such as waste and machine downtime is known as an *attainable* standard.

2.2

	£	
620 kg should have cost (×£9)	5,580	
But did cost	5,518	
Direct material price variance	62	favourable

	Kg	
200 units produced should have used (×3 kg)	600	
But did use	620	
Variance in kg	(20)	adverse
× standard price per kg (£9)		
Direct material usage variance	(£180)	adverse

2.3   Efficiency variance in hours = £160/£8 = 20 hours adverse
Actual hours worked = 20 + 1,680 standard hours (420 × 4) = 1,700
Actual rate paid per hour = £15,300/1,700 = £9 per hour

2.4   *False.* Even though each cost unit is unique, each could involve standardised tasks for which a standard time and/or cost can be determined for control purposes.

2.5

	£	
1,930 hours should cost (×£8/4)	3,860	
But did cost	3,281	
Variable production overhead expenditure variance	579	favourable

	Hours	
490 units should take (×4)	1,960	
But did take	1,930	
Efficiency variance in hours	30	favourable
× standard variable overhead rate per hour (×£8/4)		
Variable production overhead efficiency variance	£60	favourable

STANDARD COSTING AND VARIANCE ANALYSIS

2.6

	£	
19,500 units should sell for (£12.50)	243,750	
But did sell for	257,400	
Sales price variance	13,650	favourable
Actual sales volume	19,500	
Budget sales volume (£250,000/£12.50)	20,000	
Sales volume variance in units	500	adverse
× standard contribution per unit	×£5	
Sales volume contribution variance	£2,500	adverse

2.7 The standard variable cost per unit of product Y is £21.

Sales price variance per unit sold = £46 actual price − £43 std. price = £3 favourable
Number of units sold = £840 sales price variance/£3 = 280 units

Sales volume variance in units = 280 actual sales − 230 budget sales
$$= 50 \text{ units favourable}$$

Standard contribution per unit = £1,100 volume variance/50 = £22
Standard variable cost per unit = £43 standard price − £22 standard contribution = £21

 ## Solution 3

- There is an unusual request in part (a): for a *realistic* labour efficiency variance. This means that you need to take account of the difference between attainable work hours and actual clock hours. A realistic efficiency variance should be based on attainable hours rather than on clock hours.
- The question gives you a hint about the difference between attainable hours and clock hours: the clock hours budgeted for 120,000 units are more than the standard time allowance of 1.5 hours per unit. The difference is the lost time or idle time, for which an allowance should be made when the efficiency variance is calculated.
- Do not forget to indicate whether your calculated variances are adverse or favourable.

(a) (i) £36,000 adverse

(ii) £20,000 favourable

Workings:
Standard labour hours per unit = (42 + 37 + 11)/60 = 1.5 hours
Budgeted attainable work hours for the period = 120,000 units × 1.5 hours
= 180,000 hours
Budgeted clock hours for the period = 500 operatives × 400 hours = 200,000 hours
Attainable hours = 90 per cent of clock hours

Labour efficiency variance

	Hours	
126,000 units should have taken (×1.5 hours)	189,000	
But did take (215,000 × 90%)	193,500	
Variance in hours	4,500	adverse
× standard labour rate per hour (£8)		
Labour efficiency variance	£36,000	adverse

Labour rate variance

	£	
215,000 hours paid for should have cost (×£8)	1,720,000	
But did cost	1,700,000	
Labour rate variance	20,000	favourable

	Material A		*Material B*	
(b) (i)	£0		£60,000	adverse
(ii)	£13,200	favourable	£13,200	favourable

Workings:
Direct material price variance

Material A	£	
150,000 kg should have cost (×£11)	1,650,000	
And did cost	1,650,000	
Direct material price variance	—	

Material B	£	
590,000 kg should have cost (×£6)	3,540,000	
But did cost	3,600,000	
Direct material price variance	60,000	adverse

Direct material usage variance

Material A	Kg	
126,000 units produced should have used (×1.2 kg)	151,200	
But did use	150,000	
Variance in kg	1,200	favourable
× standard price per kg (£11)		
Direct material usage variance	£13,200	favourable

Material B	Kg	
126,000 units produced should have used (×4.7 kg)	592,200	
But did use	590,000	
Variance in kg	2,200	favourable
× standard price per kg (£6)		
Direct material usage variance	£13,200	favourable

6

Further Standard Costing

Further Standard Costing

6

6.1 Introduction

In this chapter you will be continuing your studies of standard costing and variance analysis. You will learn how to put all the variances together in a statement which reconciles the budgeted contribution for a period with the actual contribution achieved.

You will also be learning how to interpret variances and how standard labour costs can be used in designing incentive schemes.

6.2 Reconciling actual contribution with budgeted contribution

Now that you have seen how to calculate all the main variable cost and sales variances, you should be in a position to produce a statement which reconciles the actual and budget contribution for the period.

First, to get some important practice, you should calculate all of the variances using the data given in the following example. Then you can learn to put all the variances together in a reconciliation statement like the one shown at the end of the solution.

Example

A company produces and sells one product only, the standard variable cost for which is:

	£ per unit
Direct material 11 litres at £2	22
Direct labour 5 hours at £6	30
Variable production overhead	10
Total standard variable cost	62
Standard contribution	58
Standard selling price	120

The variable production overhead is incurred in direct proportion to the direct labour hours worked. The budgeted sales volume for May was 2,000 units.

The following were the actual results recorded during May:

Number of units produced and sold: 1,750

	£	£
Sales revenue		218,750
Direct materials: 19,540 litres purchased and used	41,034	
Direct labour: 8,722 hours	47,971	
Variable production overhead	26,166	
		115,171
Contribution		103,579

You are required to calculate the operating variances and present them in a statement which reconciles the budget and actual contribution for May.

Solution

Direct material price variance

	£	
19,540 litres purchased should have cost (×£2)	39,080	
But did cost	41,034	
Direct material price variance	1,954	adverse

Direct material usage variance

	Litres	
1,750 units produced should have used (×11 litres)	19,250	
But did use	19,540	
Variance in litres	290	adverse
× standard price per litre (£2)		
Direct material usage variance	£580	adverse

Direct labour rate variance

	£	
8,722 hours should have cost (×£6)	52,332	
But did cost	47,971	
Direct labour rate variance	4,361	favourable

Direct labour efficiency variance

	Hours	
1,750 units produced should take (×5 hours)	8,750	
But did take	8,722	
Variance in hours	28	favourable
× standard labour rate per hour (£6)		
Direct labour efficiency variance	£168	favourable

Variable production overhead expenditure variance

	£	
8,722 hours of variable production overhead should cost (×£2)	17,444	
But did cost	26,166	
Variable production overhead expenditure variance	8,722	adverse

Variable production overhead efficiency variance

Variance in hours (from labour efficiency variance)	28	favourable
× standard variable overhead rate per hour (£2)		
Variable production overhead efficiency variance	£56	favourable

Sales price variance

	£	
1,750 units should sell for (×£120)	210,000	
But did sell for	218,750	
Sales price variance	8,750	favourable

Sales volume contribution variance

Actual sales volume	1,750	units
Budget sales volume	2,000	units
Sales volume variance in units	250	adverse
× standard contribution per unit	×£58	
Sales volume contribution variance	£14,500	adverse

A reconciliation statement, known as an *operating statement*, begins with the original budgeted contribution. It then adds or subtracts the variances (depending on whether they are favourable or adverse) to arrive at the actual contribution for the month.

Contribution reconciliation statement for May

		£	£
Original budgeted contribution: 2,000 units × £58			116,000
Sales volume contribution variance			(14,500)
Standard contribution from actual sales volume			101,500
Sales price variance			8,750
Cost variances			110,250
Direct material:	price	(1,954)	
	usage	(580)	
			(2,534)
Direct labour:	rate	4,361	
	efficiency	168	
			4,529
Variable production overhead:	expenditure	(8,722)	
	efficiency	56	
			(8,666)
Actual contribution			103,579

Note: Variances in brackets are adverse.

6.3 Idle time variances

You may come across a situation which involves idle time. Idle time occurs when labour is available for production but is not engaged in active production due to, for example, shortage of work or material.

During idle time, direct labour wages are being paid but no output is being produced. The cost of this can be highlighted separately in an idle time variance, so that it is not 'hidden' in an adverse labour efficiency variance. In this way, management attention can be directed towards the cost of idle time.

Variable production overhead variances can also be affected by idle time. It is usually assumed that variable production overhead expenditure is incurred in active hours only – for example, only when the machines are actually running, incurring power costs, etc. – therefore variable production overhead expenditure is not being incurred during idle hours. The variable production overhead efficiency variance is affected in the same way as the labour efficiency variance.

Example

To demonstrate this, suppose that in the last example you were given the following additional information about the actual results recorded during May.

Of the 8,722 hours of direct labour paid for, 500 hours were idle because of a shortage of material supplies. An idle time variance could be calculated as follows:

Idle time variance

Idle hours × standard labour rate per hour

= 500 × £6
= £3,000 adverse

This is the standard cost of wages incurred during the idle time.

These idle hours must be eliminated from the calculation of the labour efficiency variance, so that the efficiency of labour is being measured only during the hours when they were actually working. This gives a much more meaningful measure of labour efficiency.

Direct labour efficiency variance

	Hours	
1,750 units produced should have taken (×5 hours)	8,750	
But did take (active hours)	8,222	
Variance in hours	528	favourable
× standard labour rate per hour (£6)		
Direct labour efficiency variance	£3,168	favourable

The total of these two variances is the same as the original labour efficiency variance (£168 favourable). The effect on the variable production overhead variances would be as follows:

Variable production overhead expenditure variance

	£	
8,222 active hours of variable production overhead should cost (×£2)	16,444	
But did cost	26,166	
Variable production overhead expenditure variance	9,722	adverse

Variable production overhead efficiency variance

	Hours	
1,750 units produced should have taken (×5 hours)	8,750	
But did take (active hours)	8,222	
Variance in hours	528	favourable
× standard variable overhead rate per hour (£2)		
Variable production overhead efficiency variance	£1,056	favourable

The total of £8,666 adverse for the two variable production overhead variances is not affected by the idle time (you should check this for yourself). However, we have now measured efficiency during active hours only, and we have allowed variable production overhead expenditure only for active hours.

6.4 Interpreting variances

6.4.1 The reasons for variances

There are many possible causes of variances, ranging from errors in setting the standard cost to efficiencies and inefficiencies of operations. Table 6.1 shows the possible causes of variances. This table is not exhaustive, but it will give you an idea of the range of possible causes.

> In an assessment question, you should review the information given and select any feasible cause that is consistent with the variance in question: that is, if the variance is favourable you must select a cause that would result in a favourable variance.

Table 6.1 Causes of variances

Variance	Favourable	Adverse
Material price	Standard price set too high	Standard price set too low
	Unexpected discounts available	Unexpected general price increase
	Lower-quality material used	Higher-quality material used
	Careful purchasing	Careless purchasing
	Gaining bulk discounts by buying larger quantities	Losing bulk discounts by buying smaller quantities
Material usage	Standard usage set too high	Standard usage set too low
	Higher-quality material used	Lower-quality material used
	A higher grade of worker used the material more efficiently	A lower grade of worker used the material less efficiently
	Stricter quality control	Theft
Labour rate	Standard rate set too high	Standard rate set too low
	Lower grade of worker used	Higher grade of worker used
		Higher rate due to wage award
Labour efficiency	Standard hours set too high	Standard hours set too low
	Higher grade of worker	Lower grade of worker
	Higher grade of material was quicker to process	Lower grade of material was slower to process
	More efficient working through improved motivation	Less efficient working due to poor motivation
Idle time		Shortage of work
		Machine breakdown
		Shortage of material
Variable overhead expenditure	Standard hourly rate set too high	Standard hourly rate set too low
	Overheads consist of a number of items: indirect materials, indirect labour, maintenance costs, power, etc., which may change because of rate changes or variations in consumption. Consequently, any meaningful interpretation of the expenditure variance must focus on individual cost items.	
Variable overhead efficiency	See labour efficiency variance	
Sales price	Higher quality product commanded higher selling price than standard	Increased competition forced a reduction in selling price below standard
Sales volume contribution	Increased marketing activity led to higher than budgeted sales volume	Quality control problems resulted in lower than budgeted sales volumes

6.4.2 The significance of variances

Once the variances have been calculated, management has the task of deciding which variances should be investigated. It would probably not be worthwhile or cost effective to investigate every single variance. Some criteria must be established to guide the decision as to whether or not to investigate a particular variance.

Factors which may be taken into account include the following:

(a) *The size of the variance*. Costs tend to fluctuate around a norm and therefore 'normal' variances may be expected on most costs. The problem is to decide how large a variance must be before it is considered 'abnormal' and worthy of investigation.

A rule of thumb may be established that any variance which exceeds, say, five per cent of its standard cost may be worthy of investigation. Alternatively, control limits may be set statistically and if a cost fluctuates outside these limits it should be investigated.

(b) *The likelihood of the variance being controllable.* Managers may know from experience that certain variances may not be controllable even if a lengthy investigation is undertaken to determine their causes. For example, it might be argued that a material price variance is less easily controlled than a material usage variance because it is heavily influenced by external factors.

(c) *The likely cost of an investigation.* This cost would have to be weighed against the cost which would be incurred if the variance was allowed to continue in future periods.

(d) *The interrelationship of variances.* Adverse variances in one area of the organisation may be interrelated with favourable variances elsewhere. For example, if cheaper material is purchased this may produce a favourable material price variance. However, if the cheaper material is of lower quality and difficult to process, this could result in adverse variances for material usage and labour efficiency.

(e) *The type of standard that was set.* You have already seen that an ideal standard will almost always result in some adverse variances, because of unavoidable waste, etc. Managers must decide on the 'normal' level of adverse variance which they would expect to see.

Another example is where a standard price is set at an average rate for the year. Assuming that inflation exists, favourable price variances might be expected at the beginning of the year, to be offset by adverse price variances towards the end of the year as actual prices begin to rise.

A detailed knowledge of the significance of variances is outside the scope of your *Fundamentals of Management Accounting* syllabus. However, you should now be aware that the use of standard costing systems for control purposes does not end with the calculation of the variances.

 ## Exercise

In (d) above we mention one possible interrelationship that might exist between cost variances. Following this example, can you think of a possible interrelationship that might exist:

 (i) between other cost variances;
 (ii) between the sales price and sales volume contribution variance;
(iii) between cost and sales variances.

 ## Solution

You might have thought of other, equally valid suggestions in addition to those below.

 (i) *Possible interrelationship between cost variances*
   Employing a higher grade of labour than standard might produce an adverse labour rate variance. However, if these employees are more skilled than standard they may work more quickly and efficiently, resulting in a favourable labour efficiency variance and a favourable variable overhead efficiency variance.

(ii) *Possible interrelationship between the sales price and sales volume contribution variance*

Charging a higher selling price than standard will produce a favourable sales price variance. However, the higher price might deter customers and thus sales volumes might fall below budget, resulting in an adverse sales volume contribution variance.

(iii) *Possible interrelationship between cost and sales variances*

Purchasing a higher quality material than standard might produce an adverse material price variance. However, the quality of the finished product might be higher than standard and it might be possible to command higher selling prices, thus producing a favourable sales price variance. Furthermore, the higher quality product might attract more customers to buy which could result in a favourable sales volume contribution variance.

6.5 Standard hour

Sometimes it can be difficult to measure the output of an organisation which manufactures a variety of dissimilar items. For example, if a company manufactures metal saucepans, utensils and candlesticks, it would not be meaningful to add together these dissimilar items to determine the total number of units produced. It is likely that each of the items takes a different amount of time to produce and utilises a different amount of resource.

A standard hour is a useful way of measuring output when a number of dissimilar items are manufactured. A standard hour or minute is the amount of work achievable, at standard efficiency levels, in an hour or minute.

The best way to see how this works is to look at an example.

Example

A company manufactures tables, chairs and shelf units. The standard labour times allowed to manufacture one unit of each of these are as follows:

	Standard labour hours per unit
Table	3 hours
Chair	1 hour
Shelf unit	5 hours

Production output during the first two periods of this year was as follows:

	Units produced	
	Period 1	Period 2
Table	7	4
Chair	5	2
Shelf unit	3	5

It would be difficult to monitor the trend in total production output based on the number of units produced. We can see that 15 units were produced in total in period 1 and 11 units in period 2. However, it is not particularly meaningful to add together tables, chairs and shelf units because they are such dissimilar items. You can see that the mix of the three products changed over the two periods and the effect of this is not revealed by simply monitoring the total number of units produced.

Standard hours present a useful output measure which is not affected by the mix of products. The standard hours of output for the two periods can be calculated as follows:

		Period 1		Period 2	
	Standard hours per unit	Units produced	Standard hours	Units produced	Standard hours
Table	3	7	21	4	12
Chair	1	5	5	2	2
Shelf unit	5	3	15	5	25
Total standard labour hours produced			41		39

Expressing the output in terms of standard labour hours shows that in fact the output level for period 2 was very similar to that for period 1.

It is important for you to realise that the actual labour hours worked during each of these periods was probably different from the standard labour hours produced. The standard hours figure is simply an expression of how long the output should have taken to produce, to provide a common basis for measuring output.

> The difference between the actual labour hours worked and the standard labour hours produced will be evaluated as the labour efficiency variance.

6.6 Labour incentive schemes

Standard labour times can be useful in designing incentive schemes for factory and office workers. For example, if a standard time has been established for a particular task an employee might be paid a bonus if the task is completed in less than the standard time.

Knowledge of the standard labour costs can assist managers in devising a labour incentive scheme that provides an incentive for the employee while at the same time being cost-effective for the organisation.

6.6.1 Bonus schemes

A variety of bonus and incentive schemes exist in practice. They are all similar and are designed to increase productivity.

The schemes rely on the setting of a standard time to achieve a task and the comparison of the actual time taken with the standard time. The savings which result from the employee's greater efficiency are usually shared between the employee and the employer on a proportionate basis. Usually the employee receives between 30 and 60 per cent of the time saved as a bonus number of hours paid at the normal hourly rate.

Example

John is a skilled engineer, paid £15 per hour. Each job he does has a standard time allowance and he is paid 50 per cent of any time he saves each week as a bonus paid at his hourly rate.

During week 11 John worked for 40 hours and completed jobs having a total standard time allowed of 47 hours.

John's earnings were:

	£
40 hours × £15	600.00
Bonus 3.5 hours* × £15	52.50
Total earnings	652.50

* Seven hours were saved against the total standard hours allowed, so 3.5 bonus hours are paid.

> ✏️ A wide variety of incentive and bonus schemes exist. In the assessment you must read the description of the scheme carefully before you apply it to the data supplied.

Note that incentive schemes based on a standard time allowance can be applied to office workers as well as to factory workers. For example, a standard time might be set for processing an invoice. At the end of a period the number of standard hours of work represented by the number of invoices processed by a particular employee can be measured. If the employee has saved time against this standard allowance then a bonus can be paid to the employee as a reward for performance above standard.

6.6.2 Piecework systems

If remuneration is based on piecework an employee is paid according to the output achieved, regardless of the time taken.

A payment rate per unit produced is agreed in advance. Knowledge of standard labour times will help managers to decide on the amount that will be paid for each unit produced.

A variation of the basic piecework principle is for the organisation to set a daily target level of activity, based on the standard labour time per unit. The employee is then paid a higher rate per unit for those completed in excess of the target.

Example

Dave is employed on a part-time basis by K Limited. He is paid £0.40 for each unit he produces up to 100 units per shift. Any units produced above this target are paid at £0.50 per unit. Last shift he produced 108 units. His earnings that shift were:

	£
100 @ £0.40	40
8 @ £0.50	4
	44

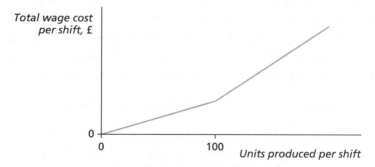

A sketch graph of this piecework system would look like this (not to scale):
The gradient of the graph becomes steeper when output exceeds 100 units per shift.

6.6.3 Guaranteed minimum wage

A guaranteed minimum wage may be included within a piecework system. It protects employees by guaranteeing them a minimum weekly wage based on an hourly rate multiplied by the employee's number of attendance hours. Note that this is only applied if the level of piecework earnings is below this guaranteed minimum level.

Example

If Dave (see Section 6.6.2) had only produced 50 units but was entitled to a guaranteed minimum wage of £30 per shift, he would receive £30 even though his piecework earnings were only 50 × £0.40 = £20.

A sketch graph of this piecework system would look like this (not to scale):

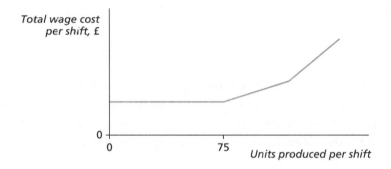

The wages cost remains constant at £30 per shift, until output reaches 75 units (75 × £0.40 = £30). After this point the wages cost increases according to the rate per unit, as before

---

6.6.4 Differential piece rate

Using this system a target number of units is set and different rates per unit are paid depending upon the total number of units achieved. Usually a daily target is used. For example:

Units produced in a day	£
1–100 units	0.40 each
101–129 units	0.42 each
130 units and above	0.44 each

You should note that it is usual for the higher rates to apply only to the additional units, not to all of the units achieved.

A sketch graph of a differential piece-rate system would look like this (not to scale):

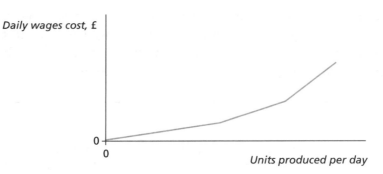

The gradient of the graph becomes progressively steeper with each successive increase in the rate paid per unit.

6.6.5 Piecework hours

A piecework hour is the same in principle as the standard hour that you learned about earlier in this chapter. Piecework hours are used to measure the output when employees are paid according to a piecework scheme and dissimilar items are produced. A standard piecework time allowance is determined for each unit produced.

Example

Employee number 297 is paid a guaranteed wage of £170 per week plus £3 per piecework hour produced. Last week the employee produced the following output.

Product	Number of units produced	Standard piecework hours per unit
R	40	0.7
T	30	0.3

The number of standard piecework hours produced is $(40 \times 0.7) + (30 \times 0.3) = 37$

Wages for last week = £170 + (37 piecework hours × £3) = £281

6.6.6 Group incentive schemes

Bonus or incentive schemes based on standard time allowances can be applied to groups as well as to individuals. Group incentive schemes might be appropriate in circumstances such as:

- when it is not possible to set a standard for and to measure individual performance – for example, in an office;
- when operations are performed by a group or team and not by individuals working alone – for example, road repairs or refuse collections;
- where production is integrated and increased output depends on a number of people all making extra effort – for example, in production line manufacture such as that in the automobile industry.

Example

A team of three clerks produces a detailed credit control report for a company's monthly management meeting. The standard time allowed for production of the report is 18 labour hours. A bonus of £9 per hour saved against this time allowance is paid to the team, divided equally between the three clerks. The time taken to produce the report last month was as follows:

Clerk no.	Time taken (hours)
1	2
2	3
3	5

$$\text{Time saved against standard allowance} = 18 \text{ hours allowance} - 10 \text{ hours taken}$$
$$= 8 \text{ hours}$$
$$\text{Bonus payable per clerk} = (8 \times £9)/3 = £24$$

6.7 Summary

Having read this chapter the main points that you should understand are as follows:

1. Sales and variable cost variances can be combined in a statement that reconciles the budgeted contribution with the actual contribution achieved during a period. Favourable variances are added to the budgeted contribution and adverse variances are deducted to arrive at the actual contribution.
2. The idle time variance is always adverse. It is calculated as the number of hours idle multiplied by the standard labour rate per hour. If there is idle time then the variances for labour efficiency, variable production overhead efficiency and variable production overhead expenditure should be based on active hours only.
3. It is not always worth investigating every variance. Some criteria must be established to guide the decision as to whether or not to investigate a particular variance.
4. Variances might be interrelated so that one variance might be a direct result of another variance. It is important to consider possible interrelationships between variances before embarking on detailed investigations as to their cause.
5. Knowledge of the standard labour cost can provide the basis for designing incentive schemes based on standard time allowances or on piecework.
6. A differential piece rate system pays different rates per unit depending on the output achieved.

Revision Questions

❓ Question 1 Multiple choice

1.1 The following data relates to an employee in production department A:

Normal working day	7 hours
Hourly rate of pay	£8
Standard time allowed to produce one unit	6 minutes
Bonus payable at basic hourly rate	50% of time saved

What would be the gross wages payable in a day when the employee produces 82 units?

(A) £33.60
(B) £60.80
(C) £65.60
(D) £84.00

1.2

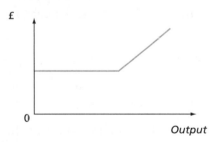

The labour cost graph above depicts:

(A) a piece-rate scheme with a minimum guaranteed wage.
(B) a straight piece-rate scheme.
(C) a time-rate scheme, where the employee is paid for each hour of attendance.
(D) a differential piece-rate scheme.

Data for questions 1.3–1.5

The standard direct labour cost of one unit of product Q is £3.00 (0.25 hours × £12.00).

The eight employees who make product Q work a 7-hour day. In a recent 3-day period, results were as follows:

Actual units produced	650 units
Actual labour cost	£2,275

During this period, there was a power failure. This meant that all work had to stop for 2 hours.

1.3 If the company reports idle time separately, the labour efficiency variance for the period is:

(A) £126 favourable
(B) £142 favourable
(C) £66 adverse
(D) £126 adverse

1.4 The labour rate variance for the period is:

(A) £259 favourable
(B) £259 adverse
(C) £325 favourable
(D) £325 adverse

1.5 The idle time variance for the period is:

(A) £24 adverse
(B) £24 favourable
(C) £192 adverse
(D) £192 favourable

Question 2 Short objective-test questions

2.1 The direct material usage variance for last period was £3,400 adverse. Which of the following reasons could have contributed to this variance? (Tick all that apply.)

(a) Output was higher than budgeted. ☐
(b) The purchasing department bought poor quality material. ☐
(c) The original standard usage was set too high. ☐
(d) Market prices for the material were higher than expected. ☐
(e) An old, inefficient machine was causing excess wastage. ☐

2.2 If employees are more skilled than had been allowed for in the original standard cost, which *four* of the following variances are most likely to result?

(a) favourable material usage; ☐
(b) adverse material usage; ☐
(c) favourable labour efficiency; ☐
(d) adverse labour efficiency; ☐
(e) favourable labour rate; ☐
(f) adverse labour rate; ☐
(g) favourable variable overhead efficiency; ☐
(h) adverse variable overhead efficiency; ☐

2.3   The budgeted contribution for last month was £43,900 but the following variances arose:

	£	
Sales price variance	3,100	adverse
Sales volume contribution variance	1,100	adverse
Direct material price variance	1,986	favourable
Direct material usage variance	2,200	adverse
Direct labour rate variance	1,090	adverse
Direct labour efficiency variance	512	adverse
Variable overhead expenditure variance	1,216	favourable
Variable overhead efficiency variance	465	adverse

The actual contribution for last month was £ ☐

2.4   Extracts from the standard cost card for product N are as follows:

	£
Direct labour: 14 hours @ £11 per hour	154
Variable production overhead: 14 hours @ £3 per hour	42

During the latest period, 390 units of product N were produced. Details concerning direct labour and variable production overhead are as follows:

Direct labour: amount paid for 5,720 hours = £68,640
Variable production overhead cost incurred = £16,280

Of the 5,720 labour hours paid for, 170 hours were recorded as idle time due to a machine breakdown.

Calculate the following variances and tick the correct box to indicate whether each variance is adverse or favourable:

	Adverse	Favourable
(a) the direct labour rate variance is £ ☐	☐	☐
(b) the direct labour efficiency variance is £ ☐	☐	☐
(c) the idle time variance is £ ☐	☐	☐
(d) the variable production overhead expenditure variance is £ ☐	☐	☐
(e) the variable production overhead efficiency variance is £ ☐	☐	☐

2.5   An office worker who processes insurance claims is paid an hourly wage of £9 per hour plus a bonus based on the time saved to process claims compared with a standard time allowance. The bonus paid is 40 per cent of the time saved, at the basic hourly rate.

Last week the employee worked 30 hours and processed the following claims.

	Number of claims processed	Standard hours allowed per claim
Motor insurance	11	2
Household contents	15	1
Travel insurance	4	0.5

(a) The number of standard hours of work produced last week was ☐ .

(b) The total wage payable to the employee for the week is (to the nearest penny) £ ☐ .

? **Question 3** Standard costing in a service organisation

Carshine Services employs a number of people providing a car cleaning and valeting service which operates in the car parks of local supermarkets and railway stations. In an attempt to control costs and revenues the company has established the following standard cost and fee per car cleaned and valeted:

	£ per car
Materials: shampoo/polish: 0.5 litres @ £2.00 per litre	1.00
Labour: 0.75 hour @ £6 per hour	4.50
Total variable cost	5.50
Standard contribution	4.50
Standard fee per car	10.00

Carshine services expects to clean and valet 3,000 cars each month. In March, a total of 2,800 cars were cleaned and the following costs and revenues were recorded:

	£	£
Sales revenue		28,050
Shampoo/polish: 1,460 litres	2,800	
Labour: 2,020 hours	12,726	
		15,526
Contribution		12,524

Requirements

The following cost and sales variances will be recorded for March. Tick the box to indicate whether each variance is adverse or favourable

		Adverse	Favourable
(a) material price:	£ ☐	☐	☐
(b) material usage:	£ ☐	☐	☐
(c) labour rate:	£ ☐	☐	☐
(d) labour efficiency:	£ ☐	☐	☐
(e) sales price:	£ ☐	☐	☐
(f) sales volume contribution:	£ ☐	☐	☐

Solutions to Revision Questions

 Solution 1

- Every bonus scheme is different. In question 1.1 you will need to read the information carefully to ensure that you understand the principles, then follow these principles to calculate the correct bonus – and do not forget to add the basic pay to the bonus to arrive at the total amount payable!

1.1 Answer: (B)

	Minutes
Time allowed: 82 units × 6 min	492
Time taken: 7 hours	420
Time saved	72

	£
Bonus payable:	
50% × 72 min × £8 per hour	4.80
Basic wage: 7 hours × £8	56.00
Gross wages payable	60.80

1.2 Answer: (A)

The minimum guaranteed wage is shown as a fixed cost up to a certain output. Thereafter, the total cost increases at a steady rate, as piecework rates are paid for increased output.

1.3 Answer: (A)

650 units should take (×0.25)	162.5 active hours
But did take (7 hours × 3 days × 8 employees) − (8 × 2 hours)	152.0 active hours
	10.5 (F) h × £12.00
Labour efficiency variance	£126 (F)

1.4 Answer: (B)

	£
168 hours should cost (×£12.00)	2,016
But did cost	2,275
Labour rate variance	259 adverse

1.5 Answer: (C)

Idle time variance = 2 hours × 8 employees = 16 hours idle × £12 per hour = £192 adverse.

 Solution 2

2.1 (b) Poor quality material could have led to higher wastage.

(e) Excess wastage causes an adverse material usage variance.

A higher output (a) would not in itself cause an adverse usage variance, because the expected usage of material would be flexed according to the actual output achieved.

Setting the original standard usage too high (c) is likely to lead to favourable usage variances.

Higher market prices (d) would cause adverse material price variances.

2.2 (a) Highly skilled employees may use material more efficiently.

(c) Highly skilled employees may work more quickly.

(f) Highly skilled employees are likely to be paid a higher hourly rate.

(g) Highly skilled employees may work more quickly.

2.3 The actual contribution for last month was £38,635.

Workings:

When working from the budgeted contribution to the actual contribution, adverse variances are deducted from the budgeted contribution; favourable variances are added to the budgeted contribution.

£(43,900 − 3,100 − 1,100 + 1,986 − 2,200 − 1,090 − 512 + 1,216 − 465) = £38,635.

2.4 (a) Direct labour rate variance = £5,720 adverse

(b) Direct labour efficiency variance = £990 adverse

(c) Idle time variance = £1,870 adverse

(d) Variable production overhead expenditure variance = £370 favourable

(e) Variable production overhead efficiency variance = £270 adverse

Workings

(a)

	£	
5,720 hours paid for should cost (×£11)	62,920	
But did cost	68,640	
Direct labour rate variance	5,720	adverse

(b)

	Hours	
390 units should take (×14)	5,460	
But did take (active hours = 5,720 − 170)	5,550	
Variance in hours	90	adverse
× standard labour rate per hour (£11)		
Direct labour efficiency variance	£990	adverse

(c)   Idle time variance = 170 hours × £11 standard rate = £1,870   adverse

(d)

	£	
Variable overhead cost of 5,550 active hours should be (×£3)	16,650	
Actual variable overhead cost	16,280	
Variable production overhead expenditure variance	370	favourable

(e)

Efficiency variance in hours (from labour efficiency variance)	90	adverse
× standard variable production overhead rate per hour	£3	
Variable production overhead efficiency variance	£270	adverse

2.5   (a) The number of standard hours of work produced last week was 39.

(b) The total wage payable to the employee for the week is £302.40.

	Number of claims processed	*Standard hours allowed per claim*	*Standard hours produced*
Motor insurance	11	2	22
Household contents	15	1	15
Travel insurance	4	0.5	2
Total standard hours produced			39
Time taken			30
Time saved (hours)			9

Basic wage payable = 30 hours × £9 = £270
Bonus = 40% × 9 hours saved × £9 = £32.40
Total wage payable = £270 + £32.40 = £302.40

Solution 3

- Do not be put off by the fact that this is a service organisation. An important point to learn from this question is that the variance calculations in a service organisation are no different from those in a manufacturing organisation.
- Remember to indicate whether your calculated variances are adverse or favourable.
- As an additional exercise, have a go at putting together all your calculated variances into a statement which reconciles the budgeted contribution with the actual contribution for the month.

(a) £120 favourable
(b) £120 adverse
(c) £606 adverse
(d) £480 favourable
(e) £50 favourable
(f) £900 adverse

Workings:
Material price variance

	£	
1,460 litres should have cost (×£2)	2,920	
But did cost	2,800	
Material price variance	120	favourable

Material usage variance

	Litres	
2,800 cars should have used (×0.5 litres)	1,400	
But did use	1,460	
Variance in litres	60	adverse
× standard price per litre (£2)		
Material usage variance	£120	adverse

Labour rate variance

	£	
2,020 hours should have cost (×£6)	12,120	
But did cost	12,726	
Labour rate variance	606	adverse

Labour efficiency variance

	Hours	
2,800 cars should have taken (×0.75 hour)	2,100	
But did take	2,020	
Variance in hours	80	favourable
× standard rate per hour (£6)		
Labour efficiency variance	£480	favourable

Sales price variance

	£	
Revenue for 2,800 cars should be (×£10)	28,000	
But actual revenue was	28,050	
Sales price variance	50	favourable

Sales volume contribution variance

Actual cars cleaned	2,800	cars
Budgeted cars cleaned	3,000	cars
Sales volume variance in cars	200	adverse
× standard contribution per car	×£4.50	
Sales volume contribution variance	£900	adverse

Solution to additional exercise

Statement reconciling the budgeted contribution for March with the actual contribution achieved

		£
Budgeted contribution (3,000 cars × £4.50)		13,500
Sales volume contribution variance		(900)
Standard contribution from actual		
volume achieved		12,600
Sales price variance		50
		12,650
Cost variances		
Material price	120	
Material usage	(120)	
		–
Labour rate	(606)	
Labour efficiency	480	
		(126)
Actual contribution		12,524

Note: variances in brackets are adverse

Integrated Accounting
Systems

Integrated Accounting Systems

LEARNING OUTCOMES

After completing this chapter, you should be able to:

▶ explain the principles of manufacturing accounts and the integration of the cost accounts with the financial accounting system;

▶ prepare a set of integrated accounts, given opening balances and appropriate transactional information, and show standard cost variances.

7.1 Introduction

The systems that are used to account for costs will vary between organisations. Each organisation will design its system to suit its own needs, taking into account factors such as statutory accounting requirements and management information needs. The accounting systems that are in use range from very simple manual systems to sophisticated computerised systems capable of producing detailed reports on a regular or an *ad hoc* basis.

In this chapter, you will learn about the principal accounting entries within integrated accounting systems. You will also be applying your knowledge of standard cost variances when you learn how to record variances in an integrated accounting system.

7.2 An integrated accounting system

> The CIMA *Terminology* defines integrated accounts as a 'set of accounting records that integrates both financial and cost accounts using a common input of data for all accounting purposes'.

Therefore, in an integrated system the cost accounting function and the financial accounting function are combined in one system, rather than separating the two sets of accounts in two separate ledgers.

be identified with any particular cost unit and will be shared out over all units, using the methods described in Chapter 3.

7.4 Integrated accounts in operation

The following example will demonstrate the double-entry principles involved in an integrated system. Make sure that you understand which accounts are used to record each type of transaction, before you move on to the next example, which contains figures.

7.4.1 Example: the main accounting entries in an integrated system

Figure 7.1 shows the flow of accounting entries within an integrated system for the following transactions:

(i) The purchase of raw materials on credit terms.

    Debit   Raw materials control
    Credit   Payables control

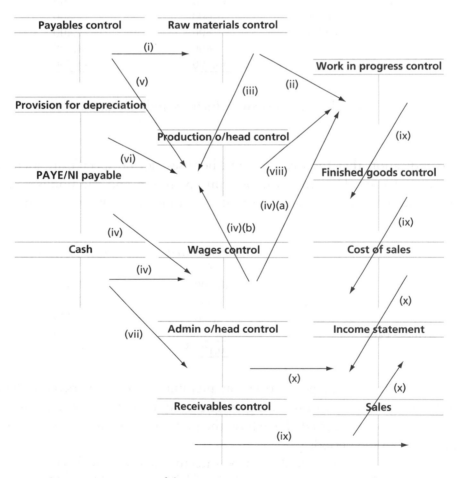

Figure 7.1 Some of the accounting entries in an integrated system

(ii) The issue to production of part of the consignment received in (i) above.

Debit   Work in progress control
Credit   Raw materials control

Direct materials costs are charged to the work in progress account.

(iii) The issue, as indirect materials, of part of the consignment received in (i) above.

Debit   Production overhead control
Credit   Raw materials control

Indirect production costs (in this case indirect materials costs) are collected in the production overhead control account for later absorption into production costs.

(iv) A cash payment of wages, after deduction of PAYE and National Insurance (a) to direct workers; and (b) to indirect workers associated with production.

Debit   Wages control
Credit   Cash/Bank

with the net amount of wages actually paid, after deductions.

Debit   Wages control
Credit   PAYE/NI payable

with the deductions for PAYE and National Insurance.

The wages control account has now been debited with the gross amount of total wages. This gross amount must then be charged out according to whether it is direct or indirect wages. The direct wages are charged to work in progress (a). The indirect wages are collected with other indirect costs in the production overhead control account (b) for later absorption into production costs.

Later in the period when the payment is made of the amount owing for PAYE/NI, the relevant entries will be:

Debit   PAYE/NI payable
Credit   Cash/Bank

(v) Electricity for production purposes, obtained on credit.

Debit   Production overhead control
Credit   Payables control

(vi) Depreciation of machinery used for production.

Debit   Production overhead control
Credit   Provision for depreciation

These last two items are both production overhead costs which are being accumulated for later absorption into production costs.

(vii) Cash paid for office expenses.

Debit   Administration overhead control
Credit   Cash account

(viii) Absorption of production overhead, using a predetermined rate.

Debit   Work in progress control
Credit   Production overhead control

Once all of the production overhead has been accumulated in the overhead control account, a predetermined rate is used to absorb it into the cost of work in progress. The work in progress account now contains charges for direct costs and for absorbed production overheads.

(ix) The sale, on credit, of all goods produced in the month.

Debit   Receivables control
Credit   Sales account

with the sales value achieved.

Debit   Finished goods control
Credit   Work in progress control

This transfers the cost of the completed goods to the finished goods inventory account. This is usually done in stages as production is completed during the month. For demonstration purposes this has been simplified to show one transfer at the end of the month.

Debit   Cost of sales account
Credit   Finished goods control

This transfers the cost of the goods sold from the inventory account. This is also usually done in stages as inventory is sold during the month.

(x) The summary income statement is prepared for the month.

Debit   Income statement
Credit   Cost of sales account

Debit   Income statement
Credit   Administration overhead control

(Alternatively, the administration overhead control account balance may first be transferred to the cost of sales account and from there to the income statement.)

This transfers the costs for the month to the income statement, to be offset against the sales revenue which is transferred from the sales account:

Debit   Sales account
Credit   Income statement

This illustration has been simplified to demonstrate the main accounting flows. For example, in practice there would be more items of production overhead and administration overhead. There would also be expenditure on other types of overhead such as selling and distribution costs. Control accounts would be opened for these costs and they would be dealt with in the same way as the administration overhead in this example.

7.4.2 Accounting for under- or over-absorbed overheads

Take a moment to look back at the production overhead control account in the example you have just studied.

You will see that the production overhead control account has acted as a collecting place for the production overheads incurred during the period. In this simplified example the account has been debited with the following overhead costs:

- indirect materials issued from stores
- the wages cost of indirect workers associated with production
- the cost of electricity for production purposes
- the depreciation of machinery used for production.

At the end of the period the production overhead cost is absorbed into work in progress costs using the predetermined overhead absorption rate. The amount absorbed is credited in the production overhead control account and debited in the work in progress account.

The remaining balance on the production overhead control account represents the amount of production overhead which is under-absorbed (debit balance) or over-absorbed (credit balance).

If overheads are under-absorbed it effectively means that product costs have been understated. It is not usually considered necessary to adjust individual unit costs and therefore inventory values are not altered. However, the cost of units sold will have been understated and therefore the under-absorption is charged to the income statement for the period.

The reverse is true for any over absorption, which is credited in the income statement for the period.

Some organisations do not charge or credit the under or over absorption to the income statement every period. Instead, the balance is carried forward in the control account and at the end of the year the net balance is transferred to the income statement. This procedure is particularly appropriate when activity fluctuations cause under and over absorptions which tend to cancel each other out over the course of the year.

> **!** Note that under-absorbed or over-absorbed overhead is sometimes referred to as under-recovered or over-recovered overhead.

7.4.3 Example: integrated accounts

You should now be in a position to tackle a fully worked example on integrated accounts.

Although you would not be required to prepare a full set of ledger accounts in your assessment, it is still important for you to work carefully through the example. This will ensure that you have a sound knowledge of how to account for all of the main transactions in an integrated accounting system.

Exercise 7.1

See if you can complete the relevant ledger accounts yourself before looking at the solution.

IA Ltd produces a product in two processes. Output from process 1 is transferred to process 2 and from there to finished goods stores.

IA Ltd operates an integrated accounting system and, based on the data given below, you are required to prepare the relevant ledger accounts for the month ended 31 October, year 2, close the accounts at the end of the month and draw up the income statement for the period and the balance sheet as at 31 October year 2.

Account balances at 1 October, year 2

	£
Receivables	60,000
Payables	75,000
Provision for depreciation, plant and machinery	60,000
Inventories:	
Raw materials	350,000
Work in process 1	120,000
Work in process 2	150,000
Finished goods	30,000
Bank	31,000
Sales	500,000
Cost of sales	370,000
Administration overhead	60,000
Selling and distribution overhead	40,000
Production overhead, over-/ under-absorbed (credit balance brought forward)	10,500
Share capital and reserves	735,500
Plant and machinery at cost	170,000

Transactions for the month ended 31 October, year 2 included:

	£
Direct wages incurred:	
Process 1	42,400
Process 2	64,600
Direct wages paid	100,000
Production salaries paid	85,000
Production expenses paid	125,000
Paid to suppliers	165,000
Received from credit customers	570,000
Administration overhead paid	54,000
Selling and distribution overhead paid	42,000
Materials purchased on credit	105,000
Materials returned to suppliers	5,000
Materials issued to:	
Process 1	68,000
Process 2	22,000
Goods sold on credit:	
At sales prices	550,000
At cost	422,400
Transfer from process 1 to process 2	242,200
Transfer from process 2	448,400

Provision for depreciation of plant and machinery is £4,000 for the month.
The predetermined overhead absorption rates are:

Process 1 – 250% of direct wages cost
Process 2 – 150% of direct wages cost

 Solution

The first step is to open a ledger account for each balance listed. Enter the opening balances, which are all labelled as item 1 in the solution which follows. All of the other transaction numbers relate to the explanatory notes which you will find at the end of the ledger accounts.

Receivables

	£		£
1 Balance b/f	60,000	Bank	570,000
7 Sales	550,000	13 Balance c/f	40,000
	610,000		610,000

Payables

	£		£
Bank	165,000	1 Balance b/f	75,000
Raw materials	5,000	Raw materials	105,000
13 Balance c/f	10,000		
	180,000		180,000

Provision for depreciation

	£		£
13 Balance c/f	64,000	1 Balance b/f	60,000
		10 Production o/h control	4,000
	64,000		64,000

Raw materials inventory

	£		£
1 Balance b/f	350,000	Payables	5,000
Payables	105,000	6 Process 1	68,000
		6 Process 2	22,000
		13 Balance c/f	360,000
	455,000		455,000

Finished goods inventory

	£		£
1 Balance b/f	30,000	8 Cost of sales	422,400
9 Process 2	448,400	13 Balance c/f	56,000
	478,400		478,400

Work in process 1

	£		£
1 Balance b/f	120,000	Process 2	242,200
2 Wages control	42,400	13 Balance c/f	94,200
6 Raw materials	68,000		
11 Overhead control	106,000		
	336,400		336,400

Work in process 2

	£		£
1 Balance b/f	150,000	9 Finished goods	448,400
2 Wages control	64,600	13 Balance c/f	127,300
6 Raw materials	22,000		
Process 1	242,200		
11 Overhead control	96,900		
	575,700		575,700

Bank

	£		£
1 Balance b/f	31,000	3 Wages control	100,000
Receivables	570,000	4 Production overhead control	85,000
		5 Production overhead control	125,000
		Payables	165,000
		Admin. Overhead	54,000
		Selling overhead	42,000
		13 Balance c/f	30,000
	601,000		601,000

Sales

	£		£
13 Income statement	1,050,000	1 Balance b/f	500,000
	550,000	7 Receivables	550,000
	1,050,000		1,050,000

Cost of sales

	£		£
1 Balance b/f	370,000	13 Income statement	792,400
8 Finished goods	422,400		
	792,400		792,400

Administration overhead

	£		£
1 Balance b/f	60,000	13 Income statement	114,000
Bank	54,000		
	114,000		114,000

Selling and distribution overhead

	£		£
1 Balance b/f	40,000	13 Income statement	82,000
Bank	42,000		
	82,000		82,000

Production overhead over-/under-absorbed

	£		£
12 Overhead control	11,100	1 Balance b/f	10,500
		13 Income statement	600
	11,100		11,100

Share capital and reserves

	£		£
Balance c/f	796,500	1 Balance b/f	735,500
		Profit for the period	61,000
	796,500		796,500

Plant and machinery at cost

	£		£
1 Balance b/f	170,000	13 Balance c/f	170,000

Wages control

	£		£
3 Bank	100,000	2 Process 1	42,400
Balance c/f	7,000	2 Process 2	64,600
	107,000		107,000

The control accounts for wages and for production overheads are opened as 'collecting places' for these costs. The wages can then be analysed and charged out as appropriate. The production overhead can be absorbed into the work in progress accounts.

	Production overhead control		
	£		£
4 Bank	85,000	11 Process 1	106,000
5 Bank	125,000	11 Process 2	96,900
10 Depreciation	4,000	12 Under-absorbed	11,100
	214,000		214,000

Explanatory notes

1. These are the opening balances as given in the trial balance.
2. Direct wages incurred are credited to the wages control account and debited to the relevant work in process account. This looks strange at first because there is not yet any debit entry in the wages control account.
3. Now that the direct wages actually paid have been debited to the control account, you can see that there is a difference of £7,000 between the wages paid and wages incurred. This represents a £7,000 accrual for direct wages owing, which is carried down as a credit balance.
4. Production salaries are charged to the production overhead control account for later absorption into work in process costs.

     The production salaries could alternatively have been charged first to the wages control account. They would then be transferred from there to the production overhead account, so the net effect is the same.
5. Production expenses are also collected in the production overhead control account for later absorption into work in process costs.
6. Direct materials issued from inventory are charged to the relevant work in process account.

     Materials used for indirect production purposes (there are none in this example) would be debited to the production overhead control account.
7. The sales value of goods sold is credited to the sales account and debited to receivables.
8. The cost of the goods sold is transferred from finished goods inventory to the cost of sales account.
9. The output from process 2 is transferred to the finished goods inventory account.
10. The depreciation provision for plant and machinery is a production overhead cost. It must therefore be collected in the production overhead control account for later absorption into work in process costs.
11. Once all of the transactions from the question data have been entered, the next step is to absorb the production overhead into the two work in process accounts. Use the predetermined overhead absorption rates that you are given.

     Process 1: Wages £42,400 × 250% = £106,000
     Process 2: Wages £64,600 × 150% = £96,900

12. The last control account to be dealt with is the one which you opened as a collecting place for production overhead costs. All of the production overhead costs incurred, including depreciation, have been debited to this account. The production overheads have been absorbed into the work in process accounts using the predetermined rates.

Therefore, the balance on this account represents the under- or over-absorbed production overhead for the period. In this example, it is transferred to a separate account and accumulated to be transferred to the income statement.

The debit balance on the production overhead control account means that the overhead was under-absorbed for this month.

13. Now that all the transactions have been recorded the relevant balances can be transferred to the income statement and balance sheet. Before you read on, try to complete the final income statement and balance sheet for yourself, using the ledger accounts we have produced.

Income statement for the period ended 31 October year 2

	£	£
Sales		1,050,000
Cost of sales	792,400	
Under absorbed production overhead	600	
		793,000
Gross profit		257,000
Administration overhead	114,000	
Selling and distribution overhead	82,000	
		196,000
Profit to reserves		61,000

Balance sheet as at 31 October year 2

	£	£	£
Plant and machinery at cost			170,000
Provision for depreciation			64,000
			106,000
Current assets			
Raw material inventory		360,000	
Work in process 1 inventory		94,200	
Work in process 2 inventory		127,300	
Finished goods inventory		56,000	
Receivables		40,000	
Bank		30,000	
		707,500	
Current liabilities			
Payables	10,000		
Accrued wages	7,000	17,000	
			690,500
			796,500
Share capital and reserves			796,500

 The layout of your balance sheet might be different from ours; but it should balance!

How did you get on?

If this is the first time that you have studied integrated accounts, it is important that you understand all of the entries in this example. Once you have checked each one carefully and understood it, put the example aside for a few days and then return to try it again without looking at the solution. You should be able to work all the way through without any errors (!)

7.5 Standard cost bookkeeping

In the remainder of this chapter you will learn how to record standard costs and variances in the ledger accounts. To be able to study this material effectively you must have a sound understanding of:

(a) the workings of an integrated accounting system;
(b) the calculation of cost variances in a standard costing system.

If you are not confident that you have a sound understanding of both of these subjects, then you should return and study them carefully before you begin on this section of the chapter.

7.6 Recording variances in the ledger accounts

A ledger account is usually kept for each cost variance. As a general rule, all variances are entered in the accounts at the point at which they arise. For example:

(a) labour rate variances arise when the wages are paid. Therefore, they are entered in the wages control account. An adverse variance is debited in the account for wage rate variance and credited in the wages control account. For a favourable variance the entries would be the opposite way round;
(b) labour efficiency variances arise as the employees are working. Therefore, the efficiency variance is entered in the work in progress account. An adverse variance is debited in the account for labour efficiency variance and credited in the work in progress account. For a favourable variance the entries would be the opposite way round.

7.6.1 General rules for recording variances

Although variations do exist, you will find the following general rules useful when you are recording variances in the ledger accounts:

(a) The materials price variance is recorded in the materials inventory account. This is the procedure if the materials inventory is held at standard cost. We will learn more about this later in the chapter.
(b) The labour rate variance is recorded in the wages control account.
(c) The 'quantity' variances, that is, material usage, labour efficiency and variable production overhead efficiency, are recorded in the work in progress account.
(d) The variance for variable production overhead expenditure is usually recorded in the production overhead control account.
(e) Sales values are usually recorded at actual amounts and the sales variances are not shown in the ledger accounts.

> | Remember that the amount of variance is recorded in the relevant variance account (a debit for an adverse variance and a credit for a favourable variance). The 'other side' of the entries are those detailed in this list.

7.6.2 The income statement

You will see from this list that all of the variances are eliminated before any entries are made in the finished goods inventory account. The finished goods inventory is therefore held at standard cost and the transfer to the cost of sales account and to the income statement will be made at standard cost.

At the end of the period the variance accounts are totalled and transferred to the income statement. Adverse variances are debited to the income statement and favourable variances are credited.

In this way the actual cost (standard cost, plus or minus the variances) is charged against the sales value in the income statement for the period.

7.7 Standard cost bookkeeping: an example

Work carefully through the following example of integrated standard cost bookkeeping. It will also give you some useful practice at calculating cost variances.

JC Ltd produces and sells one product only, product J, the standard variable cost of which is as follows for one unit:

	£
Direct material X: 10 kg at £20	200
Direct material Y: 5 litres at £6	30
Direct wages: 5 hours at £6	30
Variable production overhead	10
Total standard variable cost	270
Standard contribution	130
Standard selling price	400

During April, the first month of the financial year, the following were the actual results for production and sales of 800 units:

	£	£
Sales on credit: 800 units at £400		320,000
Direct materials:		
X 7,800 kg	159,900	
Y 4,300 litres	23,650	
Direct wages: 4,200 hours	24,150	
Variable production overhead	10,500	
		218,200
Contribution		101,800

The material price variance is extracted at the time of receipt and the raw materials stores control account is maintained at standard prices. The purchases, bought on credit, during the month of April were:

X 9,000 kg at £20.50 per kg from K Ltd
Y 5,000 litres at £5.50 per litre from C plc

Assume no opening inventories, and no opening bank balance.
All wages and production overhead costs were paid from the bank during April.

You are required to:

(a) Calculate the variable cost variances for the month of April.
(b) Show all the accounting entries in T-accounts for the month of April. The work in progress account should be maintained at standard variable cost and each balance on the separate variance accounts is to be transferred to an income statement which you are also required to show.
(c) Explain the reason for the difference between the actual contribution given in the question and the contribution shown in your income statement extract.

Exercise 7.2

See if you can calculate all the variances before you look at the solution. You might also like to try to complete the bookkeeping entries yourself, using the earlier list of general rules to guide you.

Solution

(a) *Direct material price variance*

Material X	£	
9,000 kg purchased should have cost (×£20)	180,000	
But did cost (9,000 × £20.50)	184,500	
Direct material price variance	4,500	adverse

Material Y	£	
5,000 litres purchased should have cost (×£6)	30,000	
But did cost (5,000 × £5.50)	27,500	
Direct material price variance	2,500	favourable

Direct material usage variance

Material X	kg	
800 units produced should have used (×10 kg)	8,000	
But did use	7,800	
Variance in kg	200	favourable
× standard price per kg (£20)		
Direct material usage variance	£4,000	favourable

Material Y	Litres	
800 units produced should have used (×5 litres)	4,000	
But did use	4,300	
Variance in litres	300	adverse
× standard price per litre (£6)		
Direct material usage variance	£1,800	adverse

Direct labour rate variance

	£	
4,200 hours should have cost (×£6)	25,200	
But did cost	24,150	
Direct labour rate variance	1,050	favourable

Direct labour efficiency variance

	Hours	
800 units produced should have taken (×5 hours)	4,000	
But did take	4,200	
Variance in hours	200	adverse
×standard labour rate per hour (£6)		
Direct labour efficiency variance	£1,200	adverse

Variable overhead expenditure variance

	£	
4,200 hours of variable overhead should cost (×£2)	8,400	
But did cost	10,500	
Variable overhead expenditure variance	2,100	adverse

Variable overhead efficiency variance

	£	
Variance in hours (from labour efficiency variance)	200	adverse
× standard variable overhead rate per hour	×£2	
Variable overhead efficiency variance	£400	adverse

(b) The easiest way to approach this question is probably to follow the production through: deal first with the purchase and then the issue of the material; then move on to deal with the information about the wages. Lastly, prepare the control account for overheads, before dealing with the transfer from the work in progress account.

Numbers in brackets refer to the notes following the accounts.

Raw materials stores control

	£		£
K Ltd: material X (1)	184,500	Direct material price variance:	
C plc: material Y (2)	27,500	material X (1)	4,500
Direct material price variance:		Work in progress (3)	
material Y (2)	2,500	material X (7,800 × £20)	156,000
		material Y (4,300 × £6)	25,800
		Closing inventory c/f	28,200
	214,500		214,500

K Ltd

	£		£
Balance c/f	184,500	Raw materials stores control (1)	184,500

C plc

	£		£
Balance c/f	27,500	Raw materials stores control (2)	27,500

Work in progress control

	£		£
Raw material stores: (3)		Direct material usage variance: (3)	
material X	156,000	material Y	1,800
material Y	25,800	Direct labour efficiency variance (6)	1,200
		Variable overhead efficiency variance (7)	400
Direct material usage variance: (3)		Finished goods: (8)	
material X	4,000	800 units × £270	216,000
Wages control (5)	25,200		
Production overhead control (7)	8,400		
	219,400		219,400

Wages control

	£		£
Bank (4)	24,150	Work in progress (4,200 × £6) (5)	25,200
Labour rate variance (5)	1,050		
	25,200		25,200

Bank

	£		£
		Wages control (4)	24,150
		Production overhead control (7)	10,500

Production overhead control

	£		£
Bank (7)	10,500	Work in progress (7) (4,200 × £2)	8,400
		Variable overhead expenditure variance (7)	2,100
	10,500		10,500

Finished goods control

	£		£
Work in progress (8)	216,000	Cost of sales (8)	216,000

Cost of sales

	£		£
Finished goods (8)	216,000	Income statement (8)	216,000

Sales

	£		£
Income statement	320,000	Receivables	320,000

Receivables

	£		£
Sales	320,000		

Direct material price variance

	£		£
Raw material stores control (1)	4,500	Raw material stores control (2)	2,500
		Income statement (9)	2,000
	4,500		4,500

Direct material usage variance

	£		£
Work in progress: material Y (3)	1,800	Work in progress: material X (3)	4,000
Income statement (9)	2,200		
	4,000		4,000

	Direct labour rate variance		
	£		£
Income statement (9)	1,050	Wages control (5)	1,050

	Direct labour efficiency variance		
	£		£
Work in progress control (6)	1,200	Income statement (9)	1,200

	Variable overhead expenditure variance		
	£		£
Production overhead control (7)	2,100	Income statement (9)	2,100

	Variable overhead efficiency variance		
	£		£
Production overhead control (7)	400	Income statement (9)	400

The income statement could also be shown as a T-account. However, a vertical presentation is probably preferable.

Income statement for April (extract)

	£	£	£
Sales			320,000
Cost of sales (8)			216,000
			104,000
Cost variances			
Direct material price	(2,000)		
Direct material usage	2,200		
		200	
Direct labour rate	1,050		
Direct labour efficiency	(1,200)		
		(150)	
Variable production overhead expenditure	(2,100)		
Variable production overhead efficiency	(400)		
		(2,500)	
			(2,450)
Contribution			101,550

Note: Variances in brackets are adverse.

Explanatory notes

1. The actual cost of material X purchases is debited to the raw materials stores control and credited to K Ltd. The adverse price variance is credited to the raw materials stores control and debited to the variance account. The net effect of these two entries is that the material is held in the stores account at standard cost.

2. The actual cost of material Y purchases is debited to the raw materials stores control and credited to C plc. To bring the inventory value of material Y up to standard cost, the favourable price variance is debited to the stores control account and credited to the variance account.

3. The standard cost of the actual material usage is transferred from the raw materials inventory to work in progress. The usage variances are transferred from work in progress to the material usage variance account. An adverse variance is debited to the variance account and credited to work in progress. A favourable variance is credited to the variance account and debited to work in progress.

   The net balance for materials cost in the work in progress account is now equal to the standard material cost for 800 units. Check this for yourself.

4. The wages paid are collected in the control account.

5. The standard wages cost of the hours worked is debited to work in progress. The favourable labour rate variance is credited to the variance account.

6. The adverse labour efficiency variance is transferred from work in progress to the relevant variance account.

   The net balance for wages cost in the work in progress account is now equal to the standard wages cost for 800 units. Check this for yourself.

7. The variable production overhead paid is collected in the production overhead control account. The standard variable overhead cost of the hours worked is then debited to work in progress. The adverse variable overhead expenditure variance is debited to the variance account.

   The adverse variable overhead efficiency variance is transferred from work in progress to the relevant variance account.

   Notice the similarity between the accounting entries for labour and for variable overhead.

8. The standard variable production cost of 800 units (800 × £270 = £216,000) is transferred from work in progress to finished goods. Since no finished goods inventories are held (production is equal to sales), this amount is transferred at the end of the month to cost of sales, and from there to the income statement.

9. At the end of April, the balances on the variance accounts are transferred to the income statement.

   (c) The difference between the actual contribution given in the question and the contribution shown in the income statement extract in the solution to part (b) is £250.

	£
Actual contribution given in question	101,800
Contribution shown in solution to part (b)	101,550
Difference	250

This difference is caused by the treatment of the direct material price variance.

In the actual results given in the question, the material price variance on only the material actually used has been charged against the sales value. In the bookkeeping entries in part (b), the material price variances on all of the purchases for the month have been recorded and transferred to the income statement.

The difference is therefore represented by the price variance on the materials in inventory at the end of April.

Direct material	Purchases	Usage	Inventory balance	Price variance per unit	Price variance in inventory
X	9,000 kg	7,800 kg	1,200 kg	£20 − £20.50 = (£0.50)	£ (600)
Y	5,000 litres	4,300 litres	700 litres	£6 − £5.50 = £0.50	£ 350
					£ (250)

Note: Variances in brackets are adverse.

7.8 Valuing material inventory at actual cost

In chapter 5 you saw that the material price variance is calculated using a different method if inventory is valued at actual cost. If material inventory had been valued at actual cost in the previous example the material price variance would have been calculated as:

Direct material price variance

Material X	£	
7,800 kg used should have cost (×£20)	156,000	
But did cost	159,900	
Direct material price variance	3,900	adverse

Material Y	£	
4,300 litres used should have cost (×£6)	25,800	
But did cost	23,650	
Direct material price variance	2,150	favourable

The raw materials stores control account would look like this:

Raw materials stores control

	£		£
K Ltd: material X		Work in progress:	
(9,000 × £20.50)	184,500	material X (7,800 × £20)	156,000
C plc: material Y		material Y (4,300 × £6)	25,800
(5,000 × £5.50)	27,500	Direct material price variance:	
Direct material price variance:		material X	3,900
material Y	2,150	Closing inventory c/f	28,450
	214,150		214,150

Notice that the transfer to the work in progress account is the same as before, therefore that account will not be altered by the raw material inventory valuation method.

Check that the raw material inventory balance carried forward into May is correctly valued at actual cost.

	£
Material X: 1,200 kg × £20.50	24,600
Material Y: 700 litres × £5.50	3,850
Actual cost of material inventory	28,450

7.8.1 Which inventory valuation method is generally preferred?

It is generally accepted that it is better to value the raw material inventory at standard cost, for the following reasons:

(a) The whole of the price variance is eliminated as soon as the raw materials are purchased. This means that inventories are valued at a uniform rate and that the price variances are highlighted earlier for management attention.

(b) Raw materials are often purchased in single batches, then broken into several smaller batches for issue to production. If raw materials inventories are valued at actual cost, then a separate variance calculation is required for each issue. With valuation at standard cost, one single calculation is required on purchase.

7.9 Summary

Having read this chapter the main points that you should understand are as follows:

1. An integrated accounting system contains both financial and cost accounts and uses the same data for all accounting purposes.

2. Overtime premium is the extra rate paid per hour for working above an agreed number of hours in a period. It is usually an indirect cost unless the overtime has been worked at the specific request of a customer.

3. The wages control account acts as a collecting place for wage costs. The direct wages are then transferred to work in progress and the indirect wages are transferred to the production overhead control account.

4. The production overhead control account act as a collecting place for production overheads. At the end of the period the production overhead is absorbed into work in progress using the predetermined overhead absorption rate. The balance on the production overhead control account represents the under or over absorbed overhead for the period.

5. As a general rule, in a standard cost bookkeeping system, variances are entered in the accounts at the point at which they arise. A favourable variance is credited in the relevant variance account. An adverse variance is debited in the relevant variance account.

Revision Questions

? Question 1 Multiple choice

1.1 A firm operates an integrated cost and financial accounting system. The accounting entries for an issue of direct materials to production would be:

	Debit	*Credit*
(A)	Work in progress control account	Stores control account
(B)	Finished goods account	Stores control account
(C)	Stores control account	Work in progress control account
(D)	Cost of sales account	Work in progress control account

1.2 During a period £35,750 was incurred for indirect labour. In a typical cost ledger, the double entry for this is:

	Debit	*Credit*
(A)	Wages control account	Overhead control account
(B)	WIP control account	Wages control account
(C)	Overhead control account	Wages control account
(D)	Wages control account	WIP control account

1.3 In an integrated cost and financial accounting system, the accounting entries for factory overhead absorbed would be:

	Debit	*Credit*
(A)	Work in progress control account	Overhead control account
(B)	Overhead control account	Work in progress control account
(C)	Overhead control account	Cost of sales account
(D)	Cost of sales account	Overhead control account

1.4 At the end of a period, in an integrated cost and financial accounting system the accounting entries for £18,000 overheads under-absorbed would be:

	Debit	*Credit*
(A)	Work in progress control account	Overhead control account
(B)	Income statement	Work in progress control account
(C)	Income statement	Overhead control account
(D)	Overhead control account	Income statement

1.5 In the cost ledger the factory cost of finished production for a period was £873,190. The double entry for this is

	Debit	*Credit*
(A)	Cost of sales account	Finished goods control account
(B)	Finished goods control account	Work in progress control account
(C)	Costing income statement	Finished goods control account
(D)	Work in progress control account	Finished goods control account

1.6 XYZ Ltd operates an integrated accounting system. The material control account at 31 March shows the following information:

Material control account

	£		£
Balance b/d	50,000	Production overhead control account	10,000
Payables	100,000	?	125,000
Bank	25,000	Balance c/d	40,000
	175,000		175,000

The £125,000 credit entry represents the value of the transfer to the

(A) cost of sales account.

(B) finished goods account.

(C) income statement.

(D) work in progress account.

1.7 In an integrated cost and financial accounting system the correct entries for the provision for depreciation of production machinery are:

	Debit	*Credit*
(A)	Provision for depreciation account	Work in progress account
(B)	Work in progress account	Provision for depreciation account
(C)	Overhead control account	Provision for depreciation account
(D)	Provision for depreciation account	Overhead control account.

1.8 Data for the finishing department for the last quarter are as follows:

Budgeted cost centre overhead	£320,000
Actual cost centre overhead	£311,250
Budgeted direct labour hours	40,000
Actual direct labour hours	41,500

The accounting entries to record the under- or over-absorbed overhead for the quarter would be:

	Debit		*Credit*	
(A)	Overhead control account	£20,750	Income statement	£20,750
(B)	Overhead control account	£8,750	Income statement	£8,750
(C)	Income statement	£20,750	Overhead control account	£20,750
(D)	Income statement	£8,750	Overhead control account	£8,750

1.9 Q Ltd uses an integrated standard costing system. In October, when 2,400 units of the finished product were made, the actual material cost details were:

Material purchased	5,000 units @ £4.50 each
Material used	4,350 units

The standard cost details are that two units of the material should be used for each unit of the completed product, and the standard price of each material unit is £4.70.

The entries made in the variance accounts would be:

	Material price *variance account*	*Material usage* *variance account*
(A)	Debit £970	Debit £225
(B)	Debit £1,000	Debit £225
(C)	Credit £970	Debit £235
(D)	Credit £1,000	Debit £235

1.10 The bookkeeping entries in a standard cost system when the actual price for raw materials is less than the standard price are:

	Debit	*Credit*
(A)	Raw materials control account	Raw materials price variance account
(B)	WIP control account	Raw materials control account
(C)	Raw materials price variance account	Raw materials control account
(D)	WIP control account	Raw materials price variance account

1.11 A firm uses standard costing and an integrated accounting system. The double entry for an adverse material usage variance is:

	Debit	*Credit*
(A)	Stores control account	Work in progress control account
(B)	Material usage variance account	Stores control account
(C)	Work in progress control account	Material usage variance account
(D)	Material usage variance account	Work in progress control account

1.12 In a standard cost bookkeeping system, when the actual hourly rate paid for labour is less than the standard hourly rate, the double entry to record this is:

(A) debit wages control account; credit labour rate variance account.
(B) debit work in progress control account; credit labour rate variance account.
(C) debit labour rate variance account; credit wages control account.
(D) debit labour rate variance account; credit work in progress control account.

1.13 Gross wages incurred in department 1 in June were £54,000. The wages analysis shows the following summary breakdown of the gross pay:

	Paid to direct labour £	Paid to indirect labour £
Ordinary time	25,185	11,900
Overtime		
basic pay	5,440	3,500
premium	1,360	875
Shift allowance	2,700	1,360
Sick pay	1,380	300
	36,065	17,935

What is the direct wages cost for department 1 in June?

(A) £25,185
(B) £30,625
(C) £34,685
(D) £36,065

1.14 A manufacturing firm is very busy and overtime is being worked.

The amount of overtime premium contained in direct wages would normally be classified as:

(A) part of prime cost.
(B) production overheads.
(C) direct labour costs.
(D) administrative overheads.

? Question 2 Short objective-test questions

2.1 A company purchased materials costing £30,000. Of these, materials worth £1,000 were issued to the maintenance department and materials worth £22,000 were issued to the production department. Which of the following accounting entries would arise as a result of these transactions? (Tick all that are correct.)

			£	
(a)	Debit	Raw materials control	29,000	☐
(b)	Debit	Raw materials control	30,000	☐
(c)	Debit	Work in progress control	22,000	☐
(d)	Debit	Work in progress control	23,000	☐
(e)	Debit	Work in progress control	30,000	☐
(f)	Debit	Production overhead control	1,000	☐
(g)	Credit	Raw materials control	23,000	☐
(h)	Credit	Raw materials control	30,000	☐

2.2 Look at the following account and then identify whether statements (a) to (c) are true or false.

Wages control account

	£		£
Bank	82,500	Work in progress control	52,500
PAYE/NI payable	9,500	Production overhead control	39,500
	92,000		92,000

	True	False
(a) Gross wages for the period amounted to £82,500.	☐	☐
(b) Indirect wages incurred amounted to £39,500.	☐	☐
(c) Direct wages incurred amounted to £92,000.	☐	☐

2.3 The production overhead absorption rate is £3 per direct labour hour. During the period 23,000 direct labour hours were worked.

Production overhead control account

	£		£
Wages control	44,000	Work in progress control	A
Bank	22,000		
Depreciation	8,000		
Raw materials control	2,000		
	76,000		

(a) In the production overhead control account for the period shown above, the value to be inserted at A is £ ☐

(b) Production overhead for the period was:

under-absorbed   ☐
over-absorbed   ☐

(c) The value of the under-/over-absorption was £ ☐

2.4 Details of the production wages for a company last period are as follows:

	Gross wages £000	PAYE/NI £000	£000
Direct wages paid	40	10	30
Indirect wages paid	20	6	14

Which of the following accounting entries would be used to record this data? (Tick all that are correct.)

		£000	
(a)	Debit Wages control	44	☐
(b)	Debit Work in progress	30	☐
(c)	Debit Work in progress	40	☐
(d)	Debit Production overhead control	14	☐
(e)	Debit Production overhead control	20	☐
(f)	Debit Wages control	16	☐
(g)	Debit Wages control	60	☐
(h)	Credit Bank	44	☐
(i)	Credit Wages control	60	☐
(j)	Credit PAYE/NI payable	16	☐
(k)	Credit Bank	60	☐

2.5 Is the following statement *true* or *false*?

If material inventory is valued at standard cost then the material price variance calculation should be based on the materials actually used during the period.

True ☐
False ☐

2.6 Inventories of material W are valued at their standard price of £7 per kilogram. Last period, 900 kg of W were purchased for £5,400, of which 800 kg were issued to production. Which of the following accounting entries would arise as a result of these transactions? (Tick all that apply.)

		£	
(a)	Raw material inventory	5,400 debit	☐
(b)	Raw material inventory	6,300 debit	☐
(c)	Work in progress	4,800 debit	☐
(d)	Work in progress	5,600 debit	☐
(e)	Material price variance	800 credit	☐
(f)	Material price variance	800 debit	☐
(g)	Material price variance	900 credit	☐
(h)	Material price variance	900 debit	☐

? **Question 3** Cost bookkeeping

D Ltd operates an integrated accounting system, preparing its annual accounts to 31 March each year. The following balances have been extracted from its trial balance at 31 October, year 3:

	£
Raw material control account	34,789 Dr
Wages control account	5,862 Cr
Production overhead control account	3,674 Cr
Work in progress control account	13,479 Dr

During the first week of November, year 3, the following transactions occurred:

	£
Purchased materials on credit	4,320
Incurred wages	6,450
Issued direct materials to production	2,890
Issued indirect materials to production	560
Incurred production overheads on credit	1,870
Absorbed production overhead cost	3,800
Cost of units completed	12,480
Paid wages	5,900

An analysis of the wages incurred shows that £5,200 is direct wages.

Requirements

(a) The balance shown on the production overhead control account means that the production overhead at 31 October was:

under-absorbed ☐

over-absorbed ☐

(b) The raw material control account has been prepared for the first week of November:

Raw material control account

	£		£
Balance b/d	34,789	Work in progress	B
Payables	A	Production overhead	C
		Balance c/d	35,659

The values that would be entered as A, B and C would be:

A £ [   ]

B £ [   ]

C £ [   ]

(c) The wages control account has been prepared for the first week of November:

Wages control account

	£		£
Bank	A	Balance b/d	5,862
		Work in progress	B
		Production overhead	C

The values that would be entered as A, B and C would be:

A £ [   ]

B £ [   ]

C £ [   ]

(d) At the end of the week, the balance brought down on the production overhead control account will be a:

debit balance ☐
credit balance ☐

The value of the balance will be £ ☐

(e) The work in progress control account has been prepared for the first week of November:

Work in progress control account			
	£		£
Balance b/d	13,479	Finished goods	D
Raw materials	A	Balance c/d	12,889
Wages	B		
Production overhead	C		

The values shown in the account as A, B, C and D are:

A £ ☐
B £ ☐
C £ ☐
D £ ☐

Solutions to Revision Questions

 Solution 1

- If you are having trouble identifying the correct entries for each type of transaction, look back to the flowchart of entries at the beginning of this chapter to refresh your memory.
- Take your time and think carefully before selecting the correct option. In many cases, one of the distractors states the correct accounts but the entries are the 'wrong way round'. It is easy to rush into selecting the wrong option.
- An adverse variance is always debited in the relevant variance account. A favourable variance is always credited in the variance account.

1.1 Answer: (A)

Direct costs of production are debited to the work in progress control account.

1.2 Answer: (C)

Indirect costs, including indirect labour, are collected in the debit side of the overhead control account pending their later absorption into work in progress.

1.3 Answer: (A)

The factory overhead is first collected in the overhead control account. It is then absorbed into production costs by debiting the work in progress account using the predetermined overhead absorption rate.

1.4 Answer: (C)

Under-absorbed overhead is transferred from the overhead control account as a debit to the income statement.

1.5 Answer: (B)

Answer (A) is the double entry for the production cost of goods sold. Answer (C) is also the entry for the production cost of goods sold, if a cost of sales account is not used. Answer (D) has entries in the correct accounts but they are reversed.

1.6 Answer: (D)

Materials are issued from stores as either direct materials (to work in progress) or indirect materials (charged to the production overhead control account). The entry for the issue of indirect materials is already shown (£10,000 to production overhead). Therefore, the £125,000 must be the value of the issue of direct materials to work in progress.

1.7 Answer: (C)

The provision for depreciation of production machinery is a production overhead cost. Therefore, it is debited to the production overhead control account to be accumulated with all other production overheads for the period. At the end of the period the production overhead will be absorbed into work in progress using the predetermined overhead absorption rate.

1.8 Answer: (A)

Overhead absorption rate = £320,000/40,000 = £8 per direct labour hour

	£
Overhead absorbed = £8 × 41,500	332,000
Overhead incurred	311,250
Over absorption	20,750

The over absorption is credited to the income statement and debited to the overhead control account.

1.9 Answer: (D)

Price variance:	£
5,000 units should cost each	4.70
But actually cost	4.50
Saving	0.20

5,000 × £0.20 = £1,000 (F) – credited to variance account

Usage variance	*Material units*
2,400 finished units should use	4,800
Actual material usage	4,850
Which is an extra	50 units

50 units @ £4.70 (standard price) = £235(A) − debited to variance account

1.10 Answer: (A)

If the actual price for raw materials is less than the standard price then the raw material price variance is favourable. The variance account would therefore be credited. The corresponding debit entry is made in the raw materials control account.

1.11 Answer: (D)

An adverse variance is debited to the relevant variance account. This leaves us with options (B) or (D). The usage variance is eliminated where it arises, that is, in the work in progress account. Therefore, (D) is the correct answer.

1.12 Answer: (A)

The actual hourly rate is less than standard. Therefore, the rate variance is favourable and is credited to the variance account.

1.13   Answer: (B)

£25,185 + £5,440 = £30,625. The only direct costs are the wages paid to direct workers for ordinary time, plus the basic pay for overtime. Overtime premium and shift allowances are usually treated as overheads. However, if and when the overtime and shiftwork are incurred specifically for a particular cost unit, they are classified as direct costs of that cost unit. Sick pay is treated as an overhead and is therefore classified as an indirect cost.

1.14   Answer: (B)

Overtime premium is usually treated as an overhead cost if the overtime cannot be specifically indentified with a particular cost unit.

 # Solution 2

2.1   The correct entries are:

(b) The purchased materials are debited in the raw materials control account.

(c) The direct materials are issued to the production department (work in progress).

(f) Materials issued to maintenance are indirect materials, debited to the production overhead control account.

(g) The total amount of materials issued is credited in the materials control account.

2.2   (a) *False*. Gross wages are £92,000.

(b) *True*. Indirect wages are transferred to the production overhead control account.

(c) *False*. Direct wages are £52,500: the amount transferred to work in progress.

2.3   (a) The value to be inserted at A is **£69,000** (£3 × 23,000 hours)

(b) Production overhead for the period was *under-absorbed* (see workings in (c)).

		£
(c)	Overhead incurred	76,000
	Overhead absorbed into production	69,000
	Overhead under-absorbed	7,000

2.4   Remember that the wages control account acts as a collecting place for the gross wages before they are transferred to work in progress or to production overhead control, according to whether they are direct wages or indirect wages. The gross wages are made up of two parts: the net wages that are paid from the bank, plus the PAYE/NI deductions. The correct entries are:

(a) and (h)   The net wages paid are 'collected' in the wages control account and credited to the bank.

(f) and (j)   The deductions are 'collected' in the wages control account and credited to the PAYE/NI payable.

The total gross wages have now been debited to the wages control account.

(c), (e) and (i)   The gross wages are transferred to work in progress or to production overhead control according to whether they are direct or indirect wages.

2.5   *False*. When material inventory is valued at standard cost, the material price variance is based on the materials purchased.

2.6 (b) Standard price of purchases is debited to the inventory account (900 × £7).

(d) Standard price of material issues is debited to work in progress (800 × £7).

(g) Favourable material price variance is credited to variance account:

	£	
900 kg purchased should cost (×£7)	6,300	
But did cost	5,400	
Material price variance	900	favourable

 Solution 3

● Use the flowchart of entries at the beginning of this chapter if you need help with remembering the correct double entry for each item.

(a) The credit balance shown on the production overhead control account means that there was *over-absorption* of production overhead at 31 October. A debit balance would have indicated an under-absorption of production overheads at that date.

(b) A £4,320

  B £2,890

  C £560

(c) A £5,900

  B £5,200

  C £1,250

Workings:

	£
Wages incurred	6,450
Direct wages to WIP	5,200
Indirect wages to production overhead	1,250

(d) At the end of the week, the balance on the production overhead control account will be a *credit* balance of £**3,794**.

Working:

Production overhead control account			
	£		£
Raw materials	560	Balance b/d	3,674
Wages	1,250	Work in progress*	3,800
Payables	1,870		
Balance c/d	3,794		
	7,474		7,474

*Production overhead absorbed is transferred to work in progress. The over-absorbed balance is now £3,794, which is carried down to the next week.

(e) A £2,890

  B £5,200

  C £3,800

  D £12,480.

Specific Order Costing

Specific Order Costing

8

LEARNING OUTCOMES

After completing this chapter, you should be able to:

▶ compare and contrast job, batch and contract costing;

▶ prepare ledger accounts for job and batch costing systems;

▶ prepare ledger accounts for contract costs.

8.1 Introduction

Every organisation will have its own costing system with characteristics which are unique to that particular system. However, although each system might be different, the basic costing method used by the organisation is likely to depend on the type of activity that the organisation is engaged in. The costing system would have the same basic characteristics as the systems of other organisations which are engaged in similar activities.

Specific order costing methods are appropriate for organisations which produce cost units which are separately identifiable from one another. Job costing, batch costing and contract costing are all types of specific order costing that you will learn about in this chapter. In organisations which use these costing methods, each cost unit is different from all others and each has its own unique characteristics.

8.2 Job costing

Job costing applies where work is undertaken according to specific orders from customers to meet their own special requirements. Each order is of relatively short duration. For example, a customer may request the manufacture of a single machine to the customer's own specification. Other examples, this time from service organisations, might be the repair of a vehicle or the preparation of a set of accounts for a client.

The job costing method can also be applied to monitor the costs of internal work done for the organisation's own benefit. For example, job cost sheets can be used to collect the costs of property repairs carried out by the organisation's own employees, or they may be used in the costing of internal capital expenditure jobs.

8.2.1 Job cost sheets and databases

The main feature of a job costing system is the use of a job cost sheet or job card which is a detailed record used to collect the costs of each job. In practice this would probably be a file in a computerised system but the essential feature is that each job would be given a specific job number which identifies it from all other jobs. Costs would be allocated to this number as they are incurred on behalf of the job. Since the sales value of each job can also be separately identified, it is then possible to determine the profit or loss on each job.

The job cost sheet would record details of the job as it proceeds. The items recorded would include:

- job number;
- description of the job; specifications, etc.;
- customer details;
- estimated cost, analysed by cost element;
- selling price, and hence estimated profit;
- delivery date promised;
- actual costs to date, analysed by cost element;
- actual delivery date, once the job is completed;
- sales details, for example, delivery note no., invoice no.

An example of a job cost sheet prepared for a plumbing job is shown in Figure 8.1. This job would have been carried out on the customer's own premises. The sheet has a separate section to record the details of each cost element. There is also a summary section where the actual costs incurred are compared with the original estimate. This helps managers to control costs and to refine their estimating process.

8.2.2 Collecting the direct costs of each job

(a) Direct labour

The correct analysis of labour costs and their attribution to specific jobs depends on the existence of an efficient time recording and analysis system. For example, daily or weekly timesheets may be used to record how each employee's time is spent, using job numbers where appropriate to indicate the time spent on each job. The wages cost can then be charged to specific job numbers (or to overhead costs, if the employee was engaged on indirect tasks). Figure 8.1 shows that a total of nine direct labour hours were worked by two different employees on job number 472. The remainder of the employees' time spent on direct tasks, as analysed on their individual timesheets for the period, will be shown on the job cost sheets for other jobs.

(b) Direct material

All documentation used to record movements of material within the organisation should indicate the job number to which it relates.

For example a material requisition note, which is a formal request for items to be issued from stores, should have a space to record the number of the job for which the material is being requisitioned. If any of this material is returned to stores, then the material returned note should indicate the original job number which is to be credited with the cost of the returned material. Figure 8.1 shows that two separate material requisitions were raised for material used on job number 472.

JOB COST SHEET

Job no.: 472

Estimate no.: 897

Job description: Instal shower
Model no. 5856

Details: Mrs. P. Johnson
01734 692174
30 Hillside, Whyteham
Price estimate: £330

Date started: 15 June 20×6

MATERIALS					LABOUR						PRODUCTION OVERHEAD		
Date	Req. no.	Qty	Price £	Value £	Date	Emp. no.	Cost ctr	Hrs	Rate	£	Hours	Overhead absorption rate	£
14/6	641	1	128.00	128.00	15/6	17	4	8	10	80.00	9	4.50	40.50
15/6	644	2	3.10	6.20	15/6	12	3	1	10	10.00			
			Total c/f	134.20				Total c/f		90.00		Total c/f	40.50

EXPENSES	
Description	Cost £
Total c/f	

Job card completed by: _(signature)_

JOB COST SUMMARY		
Cost element	Actual £	Estimate £
Direct materials b/f	134.20	150.00
Direct labour b/f	90.00	80.00
Direct expenses b/f	–	–
Total direct cost	224.20	230.00
Production o/h b/f	40.50	36.00
Total production cost	264.70	266.00
Admin. o/h (5%)	13.24	13.30
Total cost	277.94	279.30
Price estimate	330.00	330.00
Job profit/loss)	52.06	50.70

Figure 8.1 Job cost sheet

Sometimes items of material might be purchased specifically for an individual job, without the material first being delivered to general stores and then requisitioned from stores for the job. In this situation the job number must be recorded on the supplier's invoice or on the relevant cash records. This will ensure that the correct job is charged with the cost of the material purchased.

(c) Direct expenses

Although direct expenses are not as common as direct material and direct labour costs, it is still essential to analyse them and ensure that they are charged against the correct job number.

For example, if a machine is hired to complete a particular job, then this is a direct expense of the job. The supplier's invoice should be coded to ensure that the expense is charged to the job. Alternatively, if cash is paid, then the cash book analysis will show the job number which is to be charged with the cost. We can see from Figure 8.1 that no direct expenses were incurred on behalf of job number 472.

8.2.3 Attributing overhead costs to jobs

(a) Production overheads

The successful attribution of production overhead costs to cost units depends on the existence of well-defined cost centres and appropriate absorption bases for the overhead costs of each cost centre.

It must be possible to record accurately the units of the absorption base which are applicable to each job. For example if machine hours are to be used as the absorption base, then the number of machine hours spent on each job must be recorded on the job cost sheet. The relevant cost centre absorption rate can then be applied to produce a fair overhead charge for the job.

The production overhead section of the job cost sheet in Figure 8.1 shows that the absorption rate is £4.50 per labour hour. The labour analysis shows that 9 hours were worked on this job, therefore the amount of production overhead absorbed by the job is £40.50.

(b) Non-production overheads

The level of accuracy achieved in attributing costs such as selling, distribution and administration overheads to jobs will depend on the level of cost analysis which an organisation uses.

Many organisations simply use a predetermined percentage to absorb such costs, based on estimated levels of activity for the forthcoming period. The following example will demonstrate how this works.

Example

A company uses a predetermined percentage of production cost to absorb distribution costs into the total cost of its jobs. Based on historical records and an estimate of activity and expenditure levels in the forthcoming period, they have produced the following estimates:

Estimated distribution costs to be incurred	£13,300
Estimated production costs to be incurred on all jobs	£190,000
Therefore, predetermined overhead absorption rate for	
distribution costs = £13,300/£190,000 × 100% = 7% of production costs	

The plumbing company that has produced the job cost sheet in Figure 8.1 uses a predetermined percentage of five per cent of total production cost to absorb administration overhead into job costs. You can see the calculations in the job cost summary on the sheet.

The use of predetermined rates will lead to the problems of under- or over-absorbed overhead which we discussed in earlier chapters. The rates should therefore be carefully monitored throughout the period to check that they do not require adjusting to more accurately reflect recent trends in costs and activity.

8.2.4   A worked example

The following example will help you to practise presenting a cost analysis for a specific job.

Jobbing Limited manufactures precision tools to its customers' own specifications. The manufacturing operations are divided into three cost centres: A, B and C.

An extract from the company's budget for the forthcoming period shows the following data:

Cost centre	Budgeted production overhead	Basis of production overhead absorption
A	£38,500	22,000 machine hours
B	£75,038	19,760 machine hours
C	£40,954	41,800 labour hours

Job number 427 was manufactured during the period and its job cost sheet reveals the following information relating to the job:

Direct material requisitioned	£6,780.10
Direct material returned to stores	£39.60

Direct labour recorded against job number 427:

Cost centre A:	146 hours at £4.80 per hour
Cost centre B:	39 hours at £5.70 per hour
Cost centre C:	279 hours at £6.10 per hour

Special machine hired for this job: hire cost £59.00

Machine hours recorded against job number 427:

Cost centre A:	411 hours
Cost centre B:	657 hours
Price quoted and charged to customer, including delivery	£17,200

Jobbing Limited absorbs non-production overhead using the following predetermined overhead absorption rates:

Administration and general overhead	10% of production cost
Selling and distribution overhead	12% of selling price

You are required to present an analysis of the total cost and profit or loss attributable to job number 427.

Solution

First, we need to calculate the predetermined overhead absorption rates for each of the cost centres, using the basis indicated.

$$\text{Cost centre A} = \frac{£38,500}{22,000} = £1.75 \text{ per machine hour}$$

$$\text{Cost centre B} = \frac{£75,088}{19,760} = £3.80 \text{ per machine hour}$$

$$\text{Cost centre C} = \frac{£40,964}{41,800} = £0.98 \text{ per labour hour}$$

Now we can prepare the cost and profit analysis, presenting the data as clearly as possible.

Cost and profit analysis: job number 427	£	£
Direct material (note 1)		6,740.50
Direct labour:		
Cost centre A 146 hours × £4.80	700.80	
Cost centre B 39 hours × £5.70	222.30	
Cost centre C 279 hours × £6.10	1,701.90	
		2,625.00
Direct expenses: hire of machine		59.00
Prime cost		9,424.50
Production overhead absorbed:		
Cost centre A 411 hours × £1.75	719.25	
Cost centre B 657 hours × £3.80	2,496.60	
Cost centre C 279 hours × £0.98	273.42	
		3,489.27
Total production cost		12,913.77
Administration and general overhead		1,291.38
(10% × £12,913.77)		
Selling and distribution overhead		2,064.00
(12% × £17,200)		
Total cost		16,269.15
Profit		930.85
Selling price		17,200.00

Note 1

The figure for material requisitioned has been reduced by the amount of returns to give the correct value of the materials actually used for the job.

8.2.5 Preparing ledger accounts for job costing systems

In job costing systems a separate work in progress account is maintained for each job, as well as a summary work in progress control account for all jobs worked on in the period.

   The best way to see how this is done is to work carefully through the following exercise and ensure that you understand each entry that is made in every account. You will need to apply the principles of integrated accounts that you learned in the previous chapter.

Exercise 8.1

JC Limited operates a job costing system. All jobs are carried out on JC's own premises and then delivered to customers as soon as they are completed.

Direct employees are paid £10 per hour and production overhead is absorbed into job costs using a predetermined absorption rate of £24 per hour. General overhead is charged to the income statement on completed jobs using a rate of 12 per cent of total production cost.

Details of work done during the latest period are as follows:

Work in progress at beginning of period

Job number 308 was in progress at the beginning of the period.

Job number 308

Cost incurred up to beginning of period:

	£
Direct material	1,790
Direct labour	960
Production overhead absorbed	2,304
Production cost incurred up to beginning of period	5,054

Activity during the period

Job numbers 309 and 310 were commenced during the period.
The following details are available concerning all work done this period.

Job number:	**308**	**309**	**310**
Direct materials issued from stores	£169	£2,153	£452
Excess materials returned to stores	–	£23	–
Direct labour hours worked	82	53	28
Status of job at the end of the period	Completed	Completed	In progress
Invoice value	£9,900	£6,870	–

Cost of material transferred from job 309 to job 310	£43
Production overhead cost incurred on credit	£4,590
General overhead cost incurred on credit	£1,312

Requirements

(a) Prepare the ledger account for the period for each job, showing the production cost of sales transferred on completed jobs.

(b) Prepare the following accounts for the period:

- work in progress control
- production overhead control
- general overhead control
- overhead under- or over-absorbed control
- income statement

(c) Calculate the profit on each of the completed jobs.

Solution

(a) The figures in brackets refer to the explanatory notes below the accounts.

Job 308	£		£
Balance b/f (1)	5,054	Production cost of sales	8,011
Material stores	169		
Wages control (82 × £10)	820		
Production overhead (82 × £24)	1,968		
	8,011		8,011

Job 309	£		£
Material stores	2,153	Material stores (2)	23
Wages control (53 × £10)	530	Job 310 (3)	43
Production overhead (53 × £24)	1,272	Production cost of sales	3,889
	3,955		3,955

Job 310	£		£
Job 309 (3)	43	Balance c/f (4)	1,447
Material stores	452		
Wages control (28 × £10)	280		
Production overhead (28 × £24)	672		
	1,447		1,447

(b)

Work in progress control	£		£
Balance b/f (1)	5,054	Material stores control (2)	23
Material stores control (5)	2,774	Production cost of sales to income statement (6)	11,900
Wages control (163 hours × £10)	1,630		
Prod'n o'head control (163 × £24)	3,912	Balance c/f (7)	1,447
	13,370		13,370

Production overhead control	£		£
Payables control (8)	4,590	Work in progress control (9)	3,912
		Overhead under-/over-absorbed control (10)	678
	4,590		4,590

General overhead control

	£		£
Payables control (8)	1,312	General overhead cost to	1,428
Overhead under-/over-absorbed		income statement (11)	
control (10)	116		
	1,428		1,428

Overhead under-/over-absorbed control

	£		£
Production overhead control (10)	678	General overhead control (10)	116
		Income statement	562
	678		678

Income statement

	£		£
Production cost of sales (6)	11,900	Sales (9,900 + 6,870)	16,770
General overhead control (11)	1,428		
Under-absorbed overhead	562		
Profit for the period	2,880		
	16,770		16,770

Notes

1. The cost of the opening work in progress is shown as a brought forward balance in the individual job account and in the work in progress control account.
2. The cost of materials returned to stores is credited in the individual job account and in the work in progress control account.
3. The cost of materials transferred between jobs is credited to the job from which the material is transferred and debited to the job that actually uses the material.
4. Job 310 is incomplete. The production cost incurred this period is carried down as an opening work in progress balance for next period.
5. The total cost of all materials issued is debited to the work in progress control account.
6. The production cost of both completed jobs (£3,889 + £8,011) is transferred to the income statement.
7. The balance carried forward to next period is the cost of the work in progress represented by job 310.
8. The overhead cost incurred is debited in the control account.
9. The production overhead absorbed into work in progress is credited to the overhead control account.
10. Production overhead is under-absorbed and general overhead is over-absorbed this period.
11. The general overhead cost charged to the income statement on completed jobs = $12\% \times £(3,889 + 8,011) = £1,428$

(c)

	Job 308	Job 309
	£	£
Production cost	8,011.00	3,889.00
General overhead absorbed at 12%	961.32	466.68
	8,972.32	4,355.68
Invoice value	9,900.00	6,870.00
Profit	927.68	2,514.32

The total profit on the two jobs is £3,442. The difference of £562 between this total and the profit shown in the income statement is the result of the under-absorbed overhead of £562.

8.3 Batch costing

> The CIMA *Terminology* defines a batch as a 'group of similar units which maintains its identity throughout one or more stages of production and is treated as a cost unit'. Examples include a batch of manufactured shoes or a batch of programmes printed for a local fete.

You can probably see that a batch is very similar in nature to the jobs which we have been studying so far in this chapter. It is a separately identifiable cost unit for which it is possible to collect and monitor the costs.

The job costing method can therefore be applied in costing batches. The only difference is that a number of items are being costed together as a single unit, instead of a single item or service.

Once the cost of the batch has been determined, the cost per item within the batch can be calculated by dividing the total cost by the number of items produced.

Batch costing can be applied in many situations, including the manufacture of furniture, clothing and components. It can also be applied when manufacturing is carried out for the organisation's own internal purposes, for example, in the production of a batch of components to be used in production.

8.3.1 Example: batch costing

Needlecraft Limited makes hand embroidered sweat shirts to customer specifications.
The following detail is available from the company's budget.

Cost centre	Budgeted overheads	Budgeted activity
Cutting and sewing	£93,000	37,200 machine hours
Embroidering and packing	£64,000	16,000 direct labour hours

Administration, selling and distribution overhead is absorbed into batch costs at a rate of 8 per cent of total production cost. Selling prices are set to achieve a rate of return of 15 per cent of the selling price.

An order for 45 shirts, Batch No. 92, has been produced for Shaldene Community Choir. Details of activity on this batch are as follows:

Direct materials	£113.90
Direct labour	
Cutting and sewing 0.5 labour hours at £9 per hour	£4.50
Embroidering and packing 29 labour hours at £11 per hour	£319.00
Machine hours worked in cutting and sewing	2
Fee paid to designer of logo for sweat shirts	£140.00

Required

Calculate the selling price per shirt in Batch No. 92.

Solution

Batch No. 92

	£	£
Direct material		113.90
Direct labour:		
Cutting and sewing	4.50	
Embroidering and packing	319.00	
		323.50
Direct expense: design costs		140.00
Total direct cost		577.40
Production overhead absorbed:		
Cutting and sewing (W1) 2 machine hours × £2.50	5.00	
Embroidering and packing (W1) 29 labour hours × £4	116.00	
		121.00
Total production cost		698.40
Administration, etc. overhead £698.40 × 8%		55.87
Total cost		754.27
Profit margin 15/85 × £754.27		133.11
Total selling price of batch		887.38
Selling price per shirt £887.38/45		£19.72

Workings

Calculation of production overhead absorption rates:

Cutting and sewing = £93,000/37,200 = £2.50 per machine hour
Embroidering and packing = £64,000/16,000 = £4 per direct labour hour

8.4 Contract costing

Contract costing is another form of specific order costing. It is usually applied to construction contracts which are of relatively long duration in comparison with the jobs and batches which we have so far considered. The contracts are undertaken according to specific customer requirements and they are usually carried out on sites away from the organisation's own premises. Contract costing can be used in bridge-building, tunnel construction, motorway construction, shipbuilding and similar long-term works.

8.4.1 Architect's certificates and progress payments

Because of the long-term nature of building work, it is usual for the contract to provide for the customer to make payments as the contract proceeds. These interim payments are known as progress payments.

A surveyor or architect will visit the contract at various stages of its completion. Having inspected the progress of the work, the architect will issue a certificate which states the sales value of the work which has been completed to date. An appropriate invoice can then be sent to the customer, with a copy of the architect's certificate attached to verify the value of the work certified.

8.4.2 Retention money

The contract will usually provide for the customer to pay only a percentage of the value of the work certified. The balance which is not paid is called retention money. The retention percentage varies depending on the terms of the contract, but it is often about 10 per cent of the certified value. The customer retains this amount until an agreed time after the contract is completed, to guard against monetary loss due to unforeseen circumstances arising.

8.4.3 Contract accounts

The objective of contract costing is much the same as that of job costing. The costs of each contract must be systematically collected and monitored. For this purpose a separate account is maintained for each contract. All of the costs of the contract are collected in the account, which can then be used to assist in determining the contract profit.

The long-term nature of contracts means that they often span more than one accounting period. If a contract is still in progress at the end of the company's financial year, then it is necessary to value the contract work in progress for balance sheet purposes. In addition a calculation is performed to determine how much profit has been earned on the contract during the year and this amount is credited to the total company's income statement for the year. The profit on a contract is thus recognised in stages as the contract progresses, instead of waiting until the contract is completed to recognise any profit.

The reason for this is to attempt to present a true and fair view of the company's performance. It avoids the excessive fluctuations in reported profits which may arise if profits are recognised only when contracts are completed. For example, if several contracts were completed in one year, then the reported profits would be very high. In the next year there may be no contracts completed at all and excessive losses would be reported. Anybody who was trying to use the company's accounts to assess its performance would find it very difficult to make any judgements based on such wildly fluctuating reported profits. Reporting the profits as the contract progresses helps to smooth out these fluctuations.

8.4.4 Accounting for contract materials

Materials delivered to the contract site could come from the organisation's own stores or they could be delivered direct to the site by the supplier. In both cases, the movement of the materials must be carefully documented so that the correct contract is charged with the receipt of the materials. The contract account would be debited with the cost of the materials delivered. If any material is returned to stores or to the supplier, then the necessary documentation would be raised and the cost of these materials would be credited to the contract account.

At the end of the accounting period there will often be some material still on site which is to be used in the next period. The cost of this material will be credited to the contract account for the period and carried down as a debit balance at the start of the next period.

8.4.5 Accounting for plant used on the contract

Various types of heavy plant are used on building contracts, for example cranes, bulldozers and cement mixers. The plant is often transferred from one contract to another as it is needed. As with the movements of materials, it is important that plant movements are carefully documented and controlled. The objective is to ensure that the contract receives a fair charge for the depreciation of the plant while it has been used on the contract. There are two main ways in which this can be accomplished.

(1) Valuing the plant on transfer

With this method the plant is valued when it is transferred to the contract and this amount is debited to the contract account. The plant is then valued again when it is transferred from the contract and the value is credited to the contract account. The difference between these two amounts represents the depreciation which has been charged to the contract.

If the plant is still in use on the contract at the end of an accounting period, then the value of the plant remaining on site is credited to the account and carried forward as a debit balance into the next period. In this way, each accounting period will receive a fair charge for plant depreciation.

(2) Calculating the depreciation charge

With this method the contract is simply charged a proportion of the annual depreciation for the plant, depending on the length of time it was used on the contract. This method would be more appropriate for a plant which is moved frequently and which does not stay on any one contract for a long time.

8.4.6 Cost classification in contract costing

An important point to appreciate is that, because of the nature of the work undertaken when contract costing is applied, many costs that would in most circumstances be indirect costs are, in fact, direct costs of the contract.

Contract work is usually undertaken on a large scale at the customer's own premises – for example, when building a hospital or constructing a new road. Each contract will often be large enough to merit the employment of a full-time supervisor and perhaps the installation of its own telephone line and electricity services. This means that costs such as supervisors' salaries and telephone and electricity expenses would be a direct cost of the contract, because they can be specifically identified with it. Contrast this with the more common situation, with other costing methods, where these items are classified as indirect costs and it is necessary to attribute them as fairly as possible to several different cost centres or cost units.

8.4.7 Calculating contract profit and preparing balance sheet entries

When calculating the profit to be recognised on uncompleted contracts, it is essential that the requirements of the prudence concept are adhered to, that is, that profits are not overstated and a conservative view is taken. Indeed if a loss is foreseen on completion of the project, then the whole of the future loss should be taken into account as soon as possible.

The best way to see how contract costing works is to study it in the context of the following example.

8.4.8 Contract costing: a worked example

On 3 January, year 8, B Construction Ltd started work on the construction of an office block for a contracted price of £750,000 with completion promised by 31 March, year 9. The construction company's financial year end was 31 October, year 8, and on that date the accounts appropriate to the contract contained the following balances:

	£000
Materials issued to site	161
Materials returned from site	14
Wages paid	68
Own plant in use on site, at cost	96
Hire of plant and scaffolding	72
Supervisory staff:	
direct	10
indirect	12
Head office charges	63
Cash received related to work certified	330
Estimated cost to complete contract	240

Depreciation on own plant to be provided at the rate of 12.5 per cent per annum on cost. £2,000 is owing for wages.

Estimated value of materials on site is £24,000.

No difficulties are envisaged during the remaining time to complete the contract.

You are required to:

(a) prepare the contract account for the period ended 31 October, year 8, and show the amount to be included in the construction company's income statement for that period;

(b) show extracts from the construction company's balance sheet at 31 October, year 8, so far as the information provided will allow.

Solution

The first thing that we need to know is the total cost incurred on the contract in the period.

A contract account is used to collect the costs incurred. Work carefully through the entries in the account below.

The figures in brackets refer to the explanatory notes which follow the account.

Office block contract account to 31 October, year 8			
	£000		£000
Materials issued	161	Material returned (2)	14
Wages paid	68	Materials on site c/d (4)	24
Plant at cost (1)	96	Plant on site c/d (1)	86
Hire of plant and scaffolding	72	Cost to date c/d (5)	360
Supervisory staff:			
direct	10		
indirect	12		
Head office charges	63		
Wages accrued c/d (3)	2		
	484		484

Notice that the cash received from the customer is not entered in the contract account. This is not an item of cost information.

Office block contract account from 1 November, year 8			
	£000		£000
Material on site b/d (4)	24	Wages accrued b/d	2
Plant on site b/d (1)	86		
Cost to date (5)	360		

At the start of the next financial year the account contains all of the brought-forward balances from the previous year.

Explanatory notes

1. *Depreciation of plant.* As explained earlier in this chapter, the depreciation charge can be calculated and charged to the contract, or the remaining value of plant on site can be carried forward into the next period. The net effect is the same, but in this example it seems more logical to show the value of the plant carried forward, to reflect the continuing nature of the contract.

   Make sure that you do not make the common mistake of including the value of the plant *and* the depreciation charge. This would be double-counting.

	£000
Value of plant delivered to site	96
Depreciation while in use:	
10/12 × (£96,000 × 12.5%)	10
Value of plant carried down to next period	86

Did you notice that the plant was in use for only ten months of the year, *not* for the whole year?

The net effect of the debit of £96,000 and the credit of £86,000, in the contract account to 31 October, is to charge the correct amount of £10,000 for depreciation.

2. *Materials returned.* The materials returned from the site are credited to the contract and debited to the central stores account.

3. *Wages accrued.* This entry ensures that the correct amount is charged for wages in the period. The credit entry is carried down into the account for next period. Therefore when the wages are actually paid next period, the credit entry brought down will be netted against the payment and there will be no effect on next period's costs.

4. *Materials on site.* These materials have not yet been used and their cost is carried down into the next period. If this was not done, then the cost of the work for the period would be overstated.

5. *Cost to date.* Now that all of the adjustments have been made to carry forward the costs that do not relate to this period, the balance on the account must be the cost incurred to date.

Before any profit can be recognised on a contract, two questions must be asked:

1. *Are any losses evident on this contract?* If a loss is foreseen on completion of the contract, then all of the foreseen loss must be recognised now. The answer to this question is 'no', and we can proceed to the second question.

2. *Are any difficulties foreseen?* It may be possible to foresee difficulties arising during the remaining time to complete the contract. These difficulties may not actually result in losses, but any costs should be provided for in full as soon as they are foreseen. In this example there are no difficulties envisaged.

Since the answer to both these questions is 'no', it seems reasonable to proceed and calculate an amount of profit to be recognised in B Construction Ltd's accounts for the year ending 31 October, year 8. Later in this chapter you will see how to deal with the situations when the answers to these questions are 'yes'.

The amount of profit to be recognised on the contract will depend on its degree of completion. Two common formulae that might be used to calculate the profit to be recognised are based on the cost incurred to date or on the revenue earned to date as follows:

$$\text{Profit to be recognised} = \text{estimated final profit on contract} \times \frac{\text{cost incurred to date}}{\text{estimated final contract cost}}$$

or

$$\text{Profit to be recognised} = \text{estimated final profit on contract} \times \frac{\text{revenue earned to date}}{\text{estimated final contract revenue}}$$

> Many different methods could be used to determine the amount of profit to be recognised. The most important thing from the point of view of the assessment is to read the question carefully to check what information is available and follow any instructions given concerning the calculation of profit.

In this example we will determine the degree of completion by reference to the cost incurred to date as a proportion of the estimated final contract cost.

	£	£
Contracted price		750,000
Cost incurred to date	360,000	
Estimated cost to complete contract	240,000	
Estimated final contract cost		600,000
Estimated final profit on contract		150,000

Stage of completion = cost incurred to date/estimated final contract cost
= 360,000 / 600,000 = 60%

Profit to be recognised on contract = £150,000 × 60% = £90,000

This is an acceptable solution to the remainder of part (a) in our example: the amount to be included in the construction company's income statement for the period ended 31 October, year 8 is £90,000. This would affect the construction company's accounts as follows:

	£
Revenue to be credited to income statement (£750,000 × 60%)	450,000
Cost to be charged to income statement (£600,000 × 60%)	360,000
Profit recognised	90,000

Now you need to learn how to deal with part (b) of the question: showing the relevant extracts from the company's balance sheet.

There will be three items in the company's balance sheet in respect of this contract. (Figures in brackets refer to the explanatory notes which follow.)

(a) The receivable account for the contract

The receivable account for the contract will look like this:

Office block contract account receivable

	£000		£000
Sales (1)	450	Bank (2)	330
		Balance c/d	120
	450		450

Explanatory notes

1. The revenue of £450,000, as calculated above, will be credited to the sales account and debited to the receivable account.
2. The cash received related to the work certified, as specified in the question data, will be debited to the bank account and credited to the receivable account.

The balance of £120,000 on the receivable account will be shown within receivables on the company's balance sheet.

The other balance sheet extracts will relate to the remaining balances brought down on the contract account which you saw earlier, excluding the £360,000 cost which has been transferred to the income statement.

Office block contract account from 1 November, year 8			
	£000		*£000*
Material on site b/d	24	Wages accrued b/d	2
Plant on site b/d	86		

(b) The plant on site

The £86,000 book value of the plant on site will be shown under non-current assets on the balance sheet.

(c) The other contract balances

The remaining balances of material inventory £24,000 and wages accrued £2,000 will be shown on the company's balance sheet as an asset and a liability, respectively.

8.4.9 Accounting for a loss-making contract

If a loss is foreseen on the contract, then the whole of the loss should be recognised immediately, even if revenues received exceed the costs to date.

Suppose that because of problems envisaged before completion, the estimated costs to complete the office block contract are £410,000. A loss can be foreseen on the contract as follows:

	£	£
Contracted price		750,000
Cost incurred to date	360,000	
Estimated cost to complete contract	410,000	
Estimated final contract cost		770,000
Estimated final loss on contract		(20,000)

The whole of the loss would be recognised immediately and the effect on the income statement would be as follows. For demonstration purposes we will use the same degree of completion as before.

	£
Revenue to be credited to income statement (£750,000 × 60%)	450,000
Cost to be charged to income statement (£600,000 × 60%)	(360,000)
Provision for future losses (balancing figure)	(110,000)
Contract loss	(20,000)

The relevant ledger accounts would look like this:

Office block contract receivable			
	£000		*£000*
Sales	450	Bank	330
		Balance c/d	120
	450		450

Company cost of sales account (extract)		
	£000	*£000*
Office block contract:		
Cost of work completed	360	
Provision for losses	110	
	470	

Provision for contract losses		
	£000	*£000*
		Cost of sales	110

8.4.10 Contract costing: a second example

Work carefully through this next example, checking that you understand all the workings.

E Ltd, a construction company, has two sites on which it is building residential homes. Site A was started on 1 November year 4 and is expected to be completed by 30 June year 6. Site B was started on 1 October year 5 and is not due for completion until 30 April year 7.

The company's financial year ends on 31 December.

The following details relate to the contracts as at 31 December year 5.

	Site A	Site B
	£000	*£000*
Work in progress (1 January year 5)	51	
Materials sent to site	193	63
Materials returned from site	11	3
Plant sent to site	75	40
Material on site (31 December year 5)	6	25
Direct wages paid	142	48
Other site expenses paid	46	13
Cash received from clients	475	38

Notes:

1. The plant was sent to site at the commencement of the contract. For site A, the value shown is its net book value at 1 January year 5 and for site B, the value shown is that at the commencement of the contract. Depreciation is to be provided using the reducing balance method at an annual rate of 20 per cent.

2. At 31 December year 5 there were wages outstanding of £2,000 at site A and £1,000 at site B.

3. The cash received from clients represents the value of work certified and invoiced less an agreed retention of 5 per cent.

4. The total contract prices are £600,000 for site A and £400,000 for site B.

5. The estimated costs to complete the work at the sites is £110,000 at site A and £240,000 at site B.
6. No profit was recognised in respect of site A in the financial year ended 31 December year 4.

Solution

The first step is to prepare a contract account for each of the sites. For ease of presentation our solution shows the accounts side by side in a columnar format.

	Contract accounts to 31 December year 5				
	A	*B*		*A*	*B*
	£000	*£000*		*£000*	*£000*
Work in progress b/d	51		Materials returned from site	11	3
Materials sent to site	193	63	Material on site c/d	6	25
Plant sent to site	75	40	Plant on site c/d (see note)	60	38
Direct wages paid	142	48	Cost incurred to date	432	99
Other site expenses paid	46	13			
Wages accrued c/d	2	1			
	509	165		509	165

Note: Depreciation of plant

$$\text{Site A} = £75,000 \times 20\% = £15,000$$

Value of plant on site c/d = £75,000 − £15,000 = £60,000

$$\text{Site B} = £40,000 \times 20\% \times \frac{3}{12} = £2,000$$

Value of plant on site c/d = £40,000 − £2,000 = £38,000

Note that the plant is in use at site B for only 3 months.
The next step is to calculate the profit to be taken on each contract.
The degree of completion can be measured using either sales values or costs.

	Site A	Site B
Using sales values		
Value certified (note 1):		
$£475,000 \times \dfrac{100}{95}$	£500,000	
$£38,000 \times \dfrac{100}{95}$		£40,000
Contract price	£600,000	£400,000
Degree of completion:		
$\dfrac{500}{600}$	83.3%	
$\dfrac{40}{400}$		10.0%
Using cost values		
Cost incurred/estimated total cost (note 2):		
$\dfrac{£432,000}{£542,000}$	79.7%	
$\dfrac{£99,000}{£339,000}$		29.2%

Notes

1. The agreed retention is 5 per cent. Therefore, the cash received from clients is multiplied by $\frac{100}{95}$ to determine the value certified.

2.

	Site A £000	Site B £000
Estimated total costs:		
costs incurred to date	432	99
estimated costs to complete	110	240
	542	339

You can see that there is a difference in the estimated degree of completion calculated using each method. Whichever method is used it must be applied consistently.

You can also see that the degree of completion at site B is small. Therefore, it is not prudent to recognise any profit on this contract at this stage. As a general guide, no profit should be recognised until a contract is at least 30 per cent complete.

For contract A, the profit to be recognised is as follows:

	Site A £000
Contract price	600
Estimated total cost	542
Estimated final profit on contract	58
Degree of completion*: ×79.7%	
Profit to be recognised = £46,000	(to the nearest £000)

*The most prudent figure is taken for degree of completion (i.e. the lowest figure).

This would affect E Ltd's accounts as follows:

	Site A £000	Site B £000
Cost to be charged to income statement (542 × 79.7%)	432	44
Profit to be recognised	46	–
Revenue to be credited to income statement (600 × 79.7%)	478	44

Contract accounts receivable

	Site A £000	Site B £000		Site A £000	Site B £000
Sales	478	44	Bank	475	38
			Balance c/d	3	6
	478	44		478	44

Balance sheet extracts

	Site A	Site B	Total
	£000	£000	£000
Material on site	6	25	31
Receivables	3	6	9
Contract in progress (site B = 99 cost incurred less 44 transferred to income statement)		55	55
Plant on site	60	38	98

8.4.11 Contract costing: a final example

Try to produce your own answer to this example before you read the solution.

S Ltd is building an extension to a local factory. The agreed contract price is £300,000. The contract commenced on 1 March year 2 and is scheduled for completion on 30 June year 3.

S Ltd's financial year ends on 31 December.

The following details are available concerning the factory contract as at 31 December year 2.

	£000
Materials sent to site from central stores	15
Materials delivered to site direct from suppliers	70
Plant delivered to site (net book value)	40
Direct wages paid	85
Direct site expenses paid	38
Head office charges	12
Material returned from site to central stores	6
Net book value of plant on site, 31 December year 2	32
Materials on site, 31 December year 2	4
Direct wages owing at 31 December year 2	3
Cash received from customer	207
Estimated cost to complete the contract	119

You are required to prepare the contract account for the period ended 31 December year 2, and to show the amount to be included in S Ltd's income statement in respect of the contract for that period.

Solution

Factory extension contract account to 31 December, year 2			
	£000		*£000*
Materials from stores	15	Materials returned to stores	6
Materials from suppliers	70	Plant on site c/d	32
Plant delivered to site	40	Material on site c/d	4
Direct wages paid	85	Cost of work to date (balancing figure)	221
Direct site expenses paid	38		
Head office charges	12		
Wages accrued c/d	3		
	263		263
Plant on site b/d	32	Wages accrued b/d	3
Materials on site b/d	4		

In order to decide whether a profit should be recognised on the contract we will refer to the questions detailed in Section 8.4.8.

1. *Are any losses evident on the contract?* Yes, the following calculation shows that a loss is foreseen, therefore the whole of the future loss should be taken into account now.

	£000
Cost of work to date (from contract account)	221
Estimated cost to complete the contract	119
Total cost of contract	340
Agreed contract price	300
Expected loss on contract	(40)

The charge to cost of sales must allow for the full amount of the loss.

The degree of completion of the contract, based on the costs incurred to date as a percentage of the final contract cost, is 221/340 = 65%.

The sales revenue and cost of sales in the income statement are therefore as follows.

	£
Revenue to be credited to income statement (£300,000 × 65%)	195,000
Cost to be charged to income statement (£340,000 × 65%)	(221,000)
Provision for future losses (balancing figure)	(14,000)
Contract loss	(40,000)

8.5 Summary

Having read this chapter the main points that you should understand are as follows:

1. Specific order costing methods are appropriate for organisations that produce cost units which are separately identifiable from each other. Job costing, batch costing and contract costing are all specific order costing methods.

2. Job costing applies where work is undertaken according to individual customer requirements. Each job is of relatively short duration and may be undertaken on the customer's premises or on the contractor's premises.

3. Contract costing also applies where work is undertaken according to individual customer requirements, but each contract is usually of longer duration. Contracts frequently span more than one accounting period and are often constructional in nature.

4. Batch costing is a form of job costing where each batch of similar items is a separately identifiable cost unit.

5. In a job costing system, each job is given a unique number and the costs of each job are collected and analysed on a job cost sheet.

6. As a contract progresses the work completed is certified at various stages by an architect and the customer will make progress payments to the contractor. The customer might not pay the full amount of the value certified because retention monies are often held in case unforeseen circumstances arise.

7. In order to avoid wide fluctuations in reported profits an estimate may be made of the profit earned on an incomplete contract to date and this profit may be recognised in the contractor's income statement.

8. Profit may be recognised on an incomplete contract as long as its outcome can be reasonably foreseen and no adverse circumstances are expected. If a loss is expected on a contract then the whole of the loss must be provided for immediately.

Revision Questions

Question 1 Multiple choice

1.1 Which of the following are characteristics of job costing?

(i) Customer-driven production.
(ii) Complete production possible within a single accounting period.
(iii) Homogeneous products.

(A) (i) and (ii) only.
(B) (i) and (iii) only.
(C) (ii) and (iii) only.
(D) All of them.

1.2 Which of the following are characteristics of contract costing?

(i) Homogeneous products.
(ii) Customer-driven production.
(iii) Short timescale from commencement to completion of the cost unit.

(A) (i) and (ii) only.
(B) (ii) and (iii) only.
(C) (i) and (iii) only.
(D) (ii) only.

1.3 The following items may be used in costing jobs:

(i) Actual material cost.
(ii) Actual manufacturing overheads.
(iii) Absorbed manufacturing overheads.
(iv) Actual labour cost.

Which of the above are contained in a typical job cost?

(A) (i), (ii) and (iv) only.
(B) (i) and (iv) only.
(C) (i), (iii) and (iv) only.
(D) All four of them.

Data for questions 1.4 and 1.5

A firm uses job costing and recovers overheads on direct labour cost.
Three jobs were worked on during a period, the details of which were:

	Job 1	Job 2	Job 3
	£	£	£
Opening work-in-progress	8,500	0	46,000
Material in period	17,150	29,025	0
Labour for period	12,500	23,000	4,500

The overheads for the period were exactly as budgeted: £140,000.

1.4 Jobs 1 and 2 were the only incomplete jobs. What was the value of closing work in progress?

- (A) £81,900
- (B) £90,175
- (C) £140,675
- (D) £214,425

1.5 Job 3 was completed during the period and consisted of a batch of 2,400 identical circuit boards. The firm adds 50 per cent to total production costs to arrive at a selling price. What is the selling price of a circuit board?

- (A) It cannot be calculated without more information.
- (B) £31.56
- (C) £41.41
- (D) £58.33

1.6 BH Ltd is currently undertaking a contract to build an apartment block. The contract commenced on 1 January year 2 and is expected to take 13 months to complete. The contract value is £54 m. The contractor's financial year ends on 30 September.

The contract account for the building of the apartment block indicates the following situation at 30 September year 2:

Value of work certified	£30 m
Costs incurred to date	£20 m
Future costs to completion	£20 m

The amount of profits to be recognised is based on the cost incurred to date. It is company policy not to recognise profit on contracts unless the cost incurred is at least 30 per cent of the total contract cost.

The maximum amount of profit 5 loss for the contract that can be taken to the income statement for the year ended 30 September year 2 is:

- (A) Nil
- (B) £5 m
- (C) £7 m
- (D) £10 m.

? **Question 2** Short objective-test questions

2.1 Match the organisational activities below to the most appropriate costing method by writing (a), (b) or (c) in the box provided.

Costing methods

(a) Job costing
(b) Batch costing
(c) Contract costing

Organisational activities

- Accounting and taxation services ☐
- Shoe manufacturing ☐
- Plumbing and heating repairs ☐
- Road building ☐
- Building maintenance and repairs ☐

2.2 Calculate the selling price for each job (a) to (c) (to the nearest penny), and write the correct answer in the box provided.

(a) Total cost of job = £45. Profit mark-up = 25 per cent of cost. Job selling price = £ ☐ .

(b) Production cost of job = £38. Percentage to be added to production cost to absorb general overheads = 10 per cent. Profit mark-up = 20 per cent of total cost. Job selling price = £ ☐ .

(c) Total cost of job = £75. Profit margin = 15 per cent of selling price. Job selling price = £ ☐ .

2.3 Is the following sentence *true* or *false?* Tick the correct box.

Interim payments that are received from a customer as a contract progresses are known as retention monies.

True ☐
False ☐

2.4 A plant with a net book value of £40,000 is delivered to contract ZX on 31 March. The plant is still in use on the contract at the company's year end, 31 December. Company policy is to depreciate all contract plant on a reducing balance basis, at a rate of 25 per cent per annum.

Complete the box in the contract account to show how the plant would be accounted for.

Contract ZX [extract]				
		£		£
31 Mar.	Plant delivered to contract	40,000	31 Dec. Plant c/d	☐

2.5 The cost incurred on contract D372 to date is £465,000. The cost to be incurred to complete the contract is £116,250 and no problems are foreseen before its completion. The value of work certified is £545,000 and the cash received from the customer is £517,750. The final contract value is £640,000. The profit to be recognised on the contract is to be calculated as follows:

$$\text{Profit to be recognised} = \text{Final contract profit} \times \frac{\text{cost incurred to date}}{\text{final contract cost}}$$

The revenue to be credited to the company income statement in respect of contract D372 is £ [ ].

2.6 A company calculates the prices of jobs by adding overheads to the prime cost and adding 30 per cent to total costs as a profit margin. Complete the following job cost summary information:

Job Y256	£
Prime cost	[ ]
Overheads	694
Total cost	[ ]
Profit margin	[ ]
Selling price	1,690

2.7 A particular contract has earned a nominal profit to date but the contract overall is expected to incur a loss by the time it is completed. The loss should not be recognised in the accounts until the period when the loss actually occurs.

True ☐
False ☐

2.8 A commercial decorating organisation budgets for 4 per cent idle time on all its jobs.
The estimated number of active labour hours required to complete decorating job no. D47 is 120 hours. The hourly labour rate is £11.
The estimated labour cost of job no. D47 is (to the nearest £) £ [ ].

❓ **Question 3** Batch costing

Jetprint Ltd specialises in printing advertising leaflets and is in the process of preparing its price list. The most popular requirement is for a folded leaflet made from a single sheet of A4 paper. From past records and budgeted figures, the following data has been estimated for a typical batch of 10,000 leaflets.

Artwork	£65
Machine setting	4 hours at £22 per hour
Paper	£12.50 per 1,000 sheets
Ink and consumables	£40
Printers' wages	4 hours at £8 per hour (*Note*: Printers' wages vary with volume.)

General fixed overheads are £15,000 per period, during which a total of 600 labour hours are expected to be worked.
The firm wishes to achieve 30 per cent profit on sales.

Requirements

(a) The selling prices (*to the nearest pound*) per thousand leaflets for quantities of:

(i) 10,000 leaflets is £ [_____]

(ii) 20,000 leaflets is £ [_____]

(b) During the period, the firm printed and sold 64 batches of 10,000 leaflets and 36 batches of 20,000 leaflets. All costs were as expected.

(i) General fixed overhead for the period was (tick the correct box):

☐ under-absorbed
☐ over-absorbed

(ii) The value of the under-/over-absorption of general fixed overhead was £ [_____].

? Question 4 Contract costing

HR Construction plc makes up its accounts to 31 March each year. The following details have been extracted in relation to two of its contracts as at 31 March 20×5:

	Contract A	Contract B
Commencement date	1 April 20×4	1 December 20×4
Target completion date	31 May 20×5	30 June 20×5
	£000	£000
Contract price	2,000	550
Materials sent to site	700	150
Materials returned to stores	80	30
Plant sent to site	1,000	150
Materials transferred to contract B	40	–
Materials transferred from contract A	–	40
Materials on site 31 March 20×5	75	15
Cost incurred to date	1,200	406
Estimated additional cost to completion	400	174

Depreciation is charged on plant using the straight-line method at the rate of 12 per cent p.a.

Requirements

(a) The net book value of the plant on site at 31 March 20×5 is:

(i) Contract A: £ [_____]

(ii) Contract B: £ [_____]

(b) The total cost of materials for the contracts to 31 March 20×5 is:

(i) Contract A: £ [_____]

(ii) Contract B: £ [_____]

(c) HR's policy is to recognise profit on uncompleted contracts as:

$$\text{Estimated total contract profit} \times \frac{\text{Cost incurred}}{\text{Estimated total contract cost}}$$

(i) The profit to be recognised on contract A to date is £ ☐

(ii) The charge to the income statement as a provision for future losses in respect of contract B is £ ☐

Solutions to Revision Questions

8

✓ Solution 1

- If you are reduced to guessing the answer to a multiple-choice question, remember to eliminate first those answers that you know to be incorrect. Then, select an answer from the remaining options. This technique would be particularly useful for questions 1.1 and 1.2.
- In question 1.5 read the information you are given carefully to determine whether the profit percentage is calculated as a percentage of cost or as a percentage of selling price.

1.1 Answer: (A)

Job costing applies to situations where work is carried out to customer specifications, and each order is of relatively short duration. Each job is separately identifiable, therefore characteristic (iii) is incorrect.

1.2 Answer: (D)

Contract costing applies to situations where work is carried out to customer specifications, and typically each contract takes more than one year to complete. Thus, only (ii) is correct.

1.3 Answer: (C)

Overheads are absorbed into the cost of each job as the period progresses, using a predetermined overhead absorption rate. It is not usually possible to identify the actual overhead cost for each individual job – therefore option A is incorrect. Option (B) is incorrect because it does not include any overhead cost. Option (D) is incorrect because it includes a double charge for overhead.

1.4 Answer: (D)

$$\text{Overhead absorption rate} = \frac{£140,000}{£40,000} \times 100\% = 350\% \text{ of direct labour.}$$

239

Work in progress valuation	£	£
Costs given in question:		
Job 1	38,150	
Job 2	52,025	
		90,175
Overhead absorbed:		
Job 1 £12,500 × 350%	43,750	
Job 2 £23,000 × 350%	80,500	
		124,250
		214,425

1.5 Answer: (C)

	£
Costs given in question	50,500
Overhead absorbed: £4,500 × 350%	15,750
Total production cost	66,250
Mark up 50%	33,125
Sales value of batch	99,375

Selling price per circuit board $\left(\dfrac{99,375}{2,400}\right) = £41.41.$

1.6 Answer: (C)

The cost incurred is more than 30 per cent of the total contract cost therefore a profit can be recognised on this contract. The maximum amount of profit that might be recognised at 30 September is as follows:

	£m
Contract value	54
Less:	
Costs to date	(20)
Future costs	(20)
Expected profit	14

Profit to be recognised $= £14\,\mathrm{m} \times (£20\,\mathrm{m}/£40\,\mathrm{m}) = £7\,\mathrm{m}.$

 Solution 2

2.1
- Accounting and taxation services   (a)
- Shoe manufacturing   (b)
- Plumbing and heating repairs   (a)
- Road building   (c)
- Building maintenance and repairs   (a)   (the cost units are probably of relatively short duration)

2.2 (a) £45 + 25% = £56.25

(b) £38 + 10% = £41.80 total cost + 20% = £50.16

(c) Note that the margin is expressed as a percentage of selling price:

$$£75 \times \frac{100}{85} = £88.24$$

2.3 *False.* This is a description of progress payments.

2.4

CONTRACT ZX (extract)

	£			£
31 Mar. Plant delivered to contract	40,000	31 Dec.	Plant c/d*	32,500

*Depreciation for 9 months $= £40,000 \times 25\% \times \dfrac{9}{12} = £7,500$

∴ Net book value of plant at 31 December = £40,000 − £7,500 = £32,5000

2.5 The revenue to be credited to the company income statement in respect of contract D372 is £512,000. The contract is 80 per cent complete and no problems are foreseen, therefore it is acceptable to recognise a profit on the contract.

Stage of completion = cost incurred to date/estimated final contract cost
= 465,000/581,250 = 80%

Revenue to be credited to income statement = £640,000 × 80% = £512,000

2.6
• In this question the profit is calculated as a percentage of cost. Sometimes the profit is expressed as a percentage of selling price so be sure to read the question carefully.
• Calculate the total cost first, then the remaining answers can be slotted in as balancing figures.

Job Y256	£
Prime cost	606
Overheads	694
	1,300
Total cost $\left(1,690 \times \dfrac{100}{130}\right)$	
Profit margin	390
Selling price	1,690

2.7 *False.* A contract loss should be allowed for in the accounts as soon as it is foreseen.

2.8 The estimated labour cost of job no. D47 is £1,375.

Workings:
The idle time would be stated as a percentage of the *paid* labour hours.

	Hours
Active labour hours required	120
Idle time (×4/96)	5
Total paid hours required	125
Labour cost @ £11 per hour	£1,375

Solution 3

- You will need to recognise that some costs are fixed and others are variable – note that you cannot simply double the cost of 10,000 leaflets to obtain the cost for 20,000.
- In part (b), not all the capacity is utilised and consequently there is an under-absorption of fixed overheads.

(a) (i) £64
   (ii) £53

Workings:	*Cost of batch 10,000 leaflets*	*Cost of batch 20,000 leaflets*
	£	£
Artwork[1]	65.00	65.00
Machine setting[1]	88.00	88.00
Paper	125.00	250.00
Ink and consumables	40.00	80.00
Printers' wages	32.00	64.00
	350.00	547.00
General fixed overheads[2]	100.00	200.00
Total cost	450.00	747.00
Profit $\left(\dfrac{30}{70} \times \text{cost}\right)$	192.86	320.14
Sales revenue required	642.86	1,067.14
Selling price per 1,000	£64.00	£53.00

Notes:

1. Machine setting and artwork costs are not affected by the size of the batch.
2. General fixed overhead = £15,000/600 = £25 per hour.

(b) (i) General fixed overhead for the period was *under-absorbed*.
     Actual labour hours worked = (64 × 4 hours) + (36 × 8 hours) = 544 hours. This is less than the budgeted labour hours of 600 and all costs were as expected therefore the overhead would be under-absorbed.

   (ii) Overhead absorbed = 544 hours × £25 = £13,600
       Overhead incurred   £15,000
       Under-absorbed overhead   £1,400

 # Solution 4

- You will need to produce a lot of workings. These will be for your own benefit because workings do not earn marks in the assessment.
- Note that contract B has been in operation for only 4 months.

(a) (i) £880,000
   (ii) £144,000

Workings:

	Contract A £000	Contract B £000
Plant sent to site	1,000	150
Depreciation		
(12%)	120	
$\left(12\% \times \dfrac{4}{12}\right)$		6
Net book value	880	144

(b) (i) £505,000

(ii) £145,000

Workings:

	Contract A £000	Contract B £000
Materials sent to site	700	150
Materials returned to stores	(80)	(30)
Materials transferred	(40)	40
Materials on site at 31 March	(75)	(15)
	505	145

(c) (i) £300,000

(ii) £9,000

Workings:

	Contract A £000	Contract B £000
Contract price	2,000	550
Cost incurred to date	(1,200)	(406)
Cost to completion	(400)	(174)
Estimated total contract profit/(loss)	400	(30)
Recognised	300[1]	(30)[2]

Notes:

1. $400 \times \left(\dfrac{1200}{1600}\right)$

2. The full amount of loss is allowed for.

Contract B

	£
Degree of completion, based on cost incurred = 406/580 total cost = 70%	
Revenue to be credited to income statement (£550,000 × 70%)	385,000
Cost to be charged to income statement (£580,000 × 70%)	(406,000)
Provision for future losses (balancing figure)	(9,000)
Contract loss	(30,000)

9

Process Costing

Process Costing

9.1 Introduction

In this chapter, you will learn about another costing method: process costing. Process costing is used by organisations where a number of production processes are involved and the output of one process is the input to a later process, this continuing until the final product is completed. Examples of industries where process costing might be applied are food processing, chemicals and brewing. The final product is said to be homogeneous (i.e., each unit is identical and cannot be distinguished from another unit) and is usually manufactured for inventory from which sales are made to customers. Unlike job costing, the product is not customer specific and the range of products available is likely to be limited, but it is likely that the customer base will be large.

9.2 Process accounts

When using process costing, the process is the collection point for costs incurred. This means that materials and labour costs will be identified with the particular process to which they relate. The method is best explained by a simple example.

Example

During August a processing company incurred the following costs in its three processes:

	Process 1 £	Process 2 £	Process 3 £
Direct materials	6,000	4,000	9,000
Direct labour	1,000	2,000	3,000
Direct expenses	2,000	3,000	4,000
Production overhead	1,000	2,000	3,000

The quantities of input and output were as follows:

	Process 1 kg	Process 2 kg	Process 3 kg
Input	500	200	300
Output	500	700	1,000

The input quantities shown above do not include the output from the previous process. The output from process 1 is transferred to process 2, which in turn transfers its output to process 3 which after further processing results in the final product.

The process accounts will appear as follows:

Process 1

	kg	£		kg	£/kg	£
Materials	500	6,000	Output	500	20.00	10,000
Labour		1,000				
Expenses		2,000				
Overheads		1,000				
	500	10,000		500		10,000

Process 2

	kg	£		kg	£/kg	£
Process 1	500	10,000	Output	700	30.00	21,000
Materials	200	4,000				
Labour		2,000				
Expenses		3,000				
Overheads		2,000				
	700	21,000		700		21,000

Process 3

	kg	£		kg	£/kg	£
Process 2	700	21,000	Output	1,000	40.00	40,000
Materials	300	9,000				
Labour		3,000				
Expenses		4,000				
Overheads		3,000				
	1,000	40,000		1,000		40,000

You should note the layout of the process account. It is a ledger account with debit and credit entries, but it is different from financial accounting ledger accounts because it includes other columns. On the debit side, there is a column for the quantity as well as the values, and on the credit side as well as the quantity column there is a column showing the cost per unit. The value per unit of output is calculated by dividing the cost by the number of units.

When preparing process accounts, it is important that the quantity columns are completed first and balanced *before* attempting to value the units. This example was a simple one, but as this chapter progresses and introduces more complications you will see why this technique is recommended.

Note too that the total cost of process 1 is attributed to its output and that this is then transferred to process 2. This procedure is repeated in process 2. The output from process 3 is finished goods.

9.3   Losses in process

The majority of process industries expect there to be a loss in the production process.

 A certain amount of loss is expected and therefore unavoidable and this is referred to in cost accounting terminology as a *normal loss*.

This loss may occur through evaporation or may be a form of defective production. The extent of the normal loss may be estimated using past records and experience. As a loss, the only value that the organisation can derive from it is its scrap value (if it has any). It is therefore considered good practice to regard the net cost (after deducting any scrap sale proceeds if applicable) of producing the normal loss as a cost of the process and to attribute it to the remaining units. The following example of a single process shows how this is achieved.

The costs of the process are as follows:

	Process 1 £
Direct materials	6,000
Direct labour	1,000
Direct expenses	2,000
Production overhead	1,000

The input quantity was 500 kg and the expected or normal loss was 10 per cent of input. Actual output was 450 kg. The process account would appear as follows:

	kg	£		kg	£/kg	£
Materials	500	6,000	Output	450	22.22	10,000
Labour		1,000	Normal loss	50	–	–
Expenses		2,000				
Overheads		1,000				
	500	10,000		500		10,000

Process 1

The total costs of the process (£10,000) have been attributed to the output of 450 kg. This has the effect of increasing the cost per kg of good output to compensate for the cost of producing the unavoidable normal loss.

If the normal loss could be sold for scrap at a value of £5 per kg, then this would reduce the net cost of producing the normal loss. The effect of this on the entries in the process account is as follows:

Process 1						
	kg	£		kg	£/kg	£
Materials	500	6,000	Output	450	21.67	9,750
Labour		1,000				
Expenses		2,000	Normal loss	50	5.00	250
Overheads		1,000				
	500	10,000		500		10,000

Note now the credit side of the process account shows the scrap value of the normal loss. The net cost of the process is reduced by the £250 scrap value to £9,750 and this is attributed to the output. The effect is to reduce the cost per kg of the output to £21.67.

The double entry for the normal loss is usually made in a scrap account.

Scrap account				
	kg	£		£
Process 1 – normal loss	50	250	Receivable/cash	250

9.4 Abnormal losses and gains

We have seen that the normal loss is an estimate of the loss expected to occur in a particular process. This estimate may be incorrect and a different amount of loss may occur.

 If the actual loss is greater than the normal loss then the excess loss is referred to as an *abnormal loss*.

 If the actual loss is less than the normal loss then the difference is referred to as an *abnormal gain*.

The following example illustrates the calculations and entries in the process account when an abnormal loss occurs.

Example

Input 500 kg of materials costing	£6,000
Labour cost	£1,000
Expenses cost	£2,000
Overhead cost	£1,000

Normal loss is estimated to be 10 per cent of input.
Losses may be sold as scrap for £5 per kg.
Actual output was 430 kg.

The process account is shown below.

Remember that, earlier in the chapter, we recommended that you should insert the units into the process account first, and then balance them off. In this example, this results in a balancing value on the credit side of 20 kg, which is the abnormal loss.

Process account

	kg	£		kg	£/kg	£
Materials	500	6,000	Output	430	21.67	9,317
Labour		1,000	Normal loss	50	5.00	250
Expenses		2,000	Abnormal loss	20	21.67	433
Overheads		1,000				
	500	10,000		500		10,000

The valuation per kg of £21.67 is calculated as follows

$$\frac{\text{Cost incurred} - \text{scrap value of normal loss}}{\text{Expected output}} = \frac{£10,000 - £250}{450} = £21.67$$

The abnormal loss units are valued at the same rate per unit as the good output units. The normal loss is valued at its scrap value only.

The next step is to prepare the scrap and abnormal loss accounts. These are shown below.

Scrap account

	£		£
Process – normal loss	250	Receivable/cash: (50 + 20) × £5	350
Abnormal loss transfer	100		
	350		350

The scrap balance now represents the total of 70 kg scrapped, with a total scrap value of £350.

Abnormal loss account

	£		£
Process	433	Scrap account: 20 × £5	100
		Income statement	333
	433		433

The resulting balance on the abnormal loss account is the net cost of producing an excess loss (i.e., after deducting the scrap sale proceeds). It has now been highlighted separately for management attention, and the balance is transferred to the income statement.

If the actual loss is smaller than the amount expected, then an abnormal gain is said to have occurred. The abnormal gain is the extent to which the loss is smaller than expected. If we consider the same example again, except that the actual output achieved was 470 kg, we can see that the following process account results. Remember to balance the units column first. The normal loss is the same, because the input is the same.

Process account

	kg	£		kg	£/kg	£
Materials	500	6,000	Output	470	21.67	10,183
Labour		1,000				
Expenses		2,000	Normal loss	50	5.00	250
Overheads		1,000				
Abnormal gain	20	433				
	520	10,433		520		10,433

Note that the balancing value in the quantity column is now on the debit side. It represents the abnormal gain. The calculation of the cost per unit remains the same, but now there is an additional entry on the debit side.

Exercise 9.1

Following the principles that you have learned so far, attempt to produce the scrap and abnormal gain accounts yourself, before you look at the accounts which follow.

 Solution

Scrap account				
	£			£
Process – normal loss	250	Bank/receivables: (50 − 20) × £5		150
		Abnormal gain		100
	250			250

Abnormal gain account			
	£		£
Scrap	100	Process	433
Income statement	333		
	433		433

Note that the balance carried down in the scrap account is only £150. This represents the cash available from the sale of the loss. The loss which actually occurred was only 30 kg.

In the abnormal gain account the balance of £333 represents the net benefit of producing a smaller loss than expected (this is after deducting the scrap sale proceeds which would have been received if the normal loss had occurred).

9.5 Closing work in progress: the concept of equivalent units

To calculate a unit cost of production it is necessary to know how many units were produced in the period. If some units were only partly processed at the end of the period, then these must be taken into account in the calculation of production output. The concept of equivalent units provides a basis for doing this. The work in progress (the partly finished units) is expressed in terms of how many equivalent complete units it represents. For example, if there are 500 units in progress which are 25 per cent complete, these units would be treated as the equivalent of 500, 25% = 125 complete units.

A further complication arises if the work in progress has reached different degrees of completion in respect of each cost element. For example, you might stop the process of cooking a casserole just as you were about to put the dish in the oven. The casserole would probably be complete in respect of ingredients, almost complete in respect of labour, but most of the overhead cost would be still to come in terms of the cost of the power to cook the casserole.

It is common in many processes for the materials to be added in full at the start of processing and for them to be converted into the final product by the actions of labour and related overhead costs. For this reason, labour and overhead costs are often referred to as conversion costs.

> Conversion cost is the 'cost of converting material into finished product, typically including direct labour, direct expense and production overhead'. *CIMA Terminology*

To overcome the problem of costs being incurred at different stages in the process, a separate equivalent units calculation is performed for each cost element. An example will help to make this clear. For simplicity, losses have been ignored. These will be introduced in the next example.

Example

Input materials	1,000 kg @ £9 per kg
Labour cost	£4,800
Overhead cost	£5,580
Outputs	Finished goods: 900 kg
	Closing work in progress: 100 kg

The work in progress is completed:

100% as to material
60% as to labour
30% as to overhead

Now that you are beginning to learn about more complications in process costing, this is a good point to get into the habit of producing an input/output reconciliation as the first stage in your workings. This could be done within the process account, by balancing off the quantity columns in the way that we have done so far in this chapter. However, with more complex examples it is better to have total quantity columns in your working paper and do the 'balancing off' there.

In the workings table which follows, the first stage is to balance the input and output quantities, that is, check that the total kg input is equal to the total kg output. Then, each part of the output can be analysed to show how many equivalent kg of each cost element it represents.

				Equivalent kg to absorb cost		
Input	*kg*	*Output*	*kg*	*Materials*	*Labour*	*Overhead*
Materials	1,000	Finished goods	900	900	900	900
		Closing WIP	100	(100%) 100	(60%) 60	(30%) 30
	1,000		1,000	1,000	960	930
		Costs		£9,000	£4,800	£5,580
		Cost/eq. unit		£9	£5	£6

For the equivalent unit calculations there is a separate column for each cost element. The number of equivalent units is found by multiplying the percentage completion by the number of kg in progress. For example, equivalent kg of labour in progress is 100 kg × 60% = 60 equivalent kg.

The number of equivalent units is then totalled for each cost element and a cost per equivalent unit is calculated.

These costs per equivalent unit are then used to value the finished output and the closing work in progress.

The process account is shown below, together with the calculation of the value of the closing work in progress. Note that this method may be used to value the finished output, but it is easier to total the equivalent unit costs (£9 + £5 + £6) and use the total cost of £20 multiplied by the finished output of 900 kg.

Closing WIP valuation		£
Materials	100 equivalent units × £9	900
Labour	60 equivalent units × £5	300
Overheads	30 equivalent units × £6	180
		1,380

Process account

	kg	£		kg	£/kg	£
Materials	1,000	9,000	Finished goods	900	20.00	18,000
Labour		4,800	WIP	100	13.80	1,380
Overheads		5,580				
	1,000	19,380		1,000		19,380

The next example follows the same principles but it includes process losses. Work through the equivalent units table carefully and ensure that you understand where each figure comes from.

Example: Closing work in progress

Data concerning process 2 last month was as follows:

Transfer from process 1	400 kg at a cost of	£2,150
Materials added	3,000 kg	£6,120
Conversion costs		£2,344
Output to finished goods		2,800 kg
Output scrapped		400 kg
Normal loss		10 per cent of materials added in the period

The scrapped units were complete in materials added but only 50 per cent complete in respect of conversion costs. All scrapped units have a value of £2 each.

There was no opening work in progress, but 200 kg were in progress at the end of the month, at the following stages of completion:

80 per cent complete in materials added
40 per cent complete in conversion costs

You are required to write up the accounts for the process.

Solution

The first step is to produce an input/output reconciliation as in the last example. Notice that the losses are not complete. You will need to take account of this in the equivalent units columns. And remember that the normal loss units do not absorb any of the process costs. They are valued at their scrap value only, so they must not be included as part of the output to absorb costs.

Input	kg	Output	kg	Process 1 transfer	Materials added	Conversion costs
				Equivalent kg to absorb cost		
Process 1 transfer	400	Finished goods	2,800	2,800	2,800	2,800
Material added	3,000	Normal loss	300	–	–	–
		Abnormal loss[1]	100	100	100	50
		Work in progress	200	200	160	80
	3,400		3,400	3,100	3,060	2,930
				£	£	£
		Costs				
		Incurred in period		2,150	6,120	2,344
		Scrap value of normal loss[2]		(600)		
				1,550	6,120	2,344
		Cost per unit	£3.30	0.50	2.00	0.80

Notes:
1. The abnormal loss is inserted in the output column as a balancing figure. Losses are 50 per cent complete in conversion costs. Therefore, the 100kg of abnormal loss represents 50 equivalent complete kg in respect of conversion costs.
2. By convention, the scrap value of normal loss is usually deducted from the first cost element.

For each cost element the costs incurred are divided by the figure for equivalent kg produced. For example, the cost per kg for materials added = £6,120/3,060 = £2 per kg.

The unit rates can now be used to value each part of the output. For example, the 160 equivalent kg of materials added in the work in progress are valued at 160 × £2 = £320. The 80 equivalent kg of conversion costs in work in progress are valued at 80 × £0.80 = £64.

Valuation	Total	Process 1 transfer	Materials added	Conversion costs
	£	£	£	£
Finished goods	9,240	1,400	5,600	2,240
Abnormal loss	290	50	200	40
Work in progress	484	100	320	64

It is now possible to draw up the relevant accounts using these valuations of each part of the process output.

Exercise 9.2

See if you can complete the process accounts before looking at the rest of the solution. Remember that the normal loss is valued at its scrap value.

Solution

Process 2 account

	kg	£		kg	£
Process 1	400	2,150	Finished goods	2,800	9,240
Materials added	3,000	6,120	Normal loss	300	600
Conversion costs		2,344	Abnormal loss	100	290
			Work in progress	200	484
	3,400	10,614		3,400	10,614

Abnormal loss account				
	£			£
Process 2	290	Scrap account		200
		Income statement		90
	290			290

Scrap account				
	£			£
Process 2	600	Bank/receivables: (300 + 100) × £2		800
Abnormal loss account	200			
	800			800

9.6 Previous process costs

A common problem that students experience when studying process costing is understanding how to deal with previous process costs. An important point that you should have grasped by now is that production passes through a number of sequential processes. Unless the process is the last in the series, the output of one process becomes the input of the next. A common mistake is to forget to include the previous process cost as an input cost in the subsequent process.

You should also realise that all of the costs of the previous process (materials, labour and overhead) are combined together as a single cost of 'input material' or 'previous process costs' in the subsequent process.

In the workings for the example in Section 9.5, we assumed that the work in progress must be 100 per cent complete in respect of Process 1 costs. This is also an important point to grasp. Even if the Process 2 work had only just begun on these units, there cannot now be any more cost to add in respect of Process 1. Otherwise the units would not yet have been transferred out of Process 1 into Process 2.

9.7 Opening work in progress

Opening work in progress consists of incomplete units in process at the beginning of the period. Your syllabus requires you to know how to value work in progress using the average cost method. With this method, opening work in progress is treated as follows:

1. The opening work in progress is listed as an additional part of the input to the process for the period.
2. The cost of the opening WIP is added to the costs incurred in the period.
3. The cost per equivalent unit of each cost element is calculated as before, and this is used to value each part of the output. The output value is based on the average cost per equivalent unit, hence the name of this method.

The best way to see how this is done is to work through some examples. The last two examples in this chapter include some opening work in progress. Work through them carefully, and try to learn the layout of the working paper so that you can use it quickly to do any workings that you need in the assessment. It will save you valuable time!

Example: Opening work in progress

The following information is available for Process 3 in June:

			Process 2 input		Materials added in Process 3		Conversion costs	
	Units	Cost	%	£	%	£	%	£
		£						
Opening WIP	100	692	100	176	60	300	30	216
Closing WIP	80		100		70		35	
Input costs:								
Input from process 2	900	1,600						
Materials added in process 3		3,294						
Conversion costs		4,190						

Degree of completion and cost spans the Process 2 input / Materials added / Conversion columns.

Normal loss is 10 per cent of input from process 2; 70 units were scrapped in the month, and all scrap units realise £0.20 each.

Output to the next process was 850 units.

You are required to complete the account for process 3 in June.

Solution

As before, the first step is to complete an input/output reconciliation and then to extend this to calculate the number of equivalent units for each cost element.

Input	Units	Output	Units	Process 2 input	Materials added	Conversion costs
				Equivalent units to absorb cost		
Opening WIP[1]	100	To process 4	850	850	850	850
Process 2[2]	900	Normal loss	90	–	–	–
		Abnormal gain[3]	(20)	(20)	(20)	(20)
		Closing WIP[4]	80	80	56	44
	1,000		1,000	910	886	874
				£	£	£
		Costs				
		Opening WIP[5]		176	300	216
		Input costs		1,600	3,294	4,190
		Normal loss value		(18)		
				1,758	3,594	4,406
			£	£	£	£
		Cost per unit	11.029	1.932	4.056	5.041
		Evaluation[6]				
		To process 4	9,375	1,642	3,448	4,285
		Abnormal gain	(221)	(39)	(81)	(101)
		Closing WIP	604	155	227	222

Notes:

1. The opening WIP is included as part of the input in the input/output reconciliation. The degree of completion of the opening WIP is not relevant, because we are going to average its cost over all units produced in the period.
2. Note that we are not told the quantity of material added because it does not affect the number of basic units processed.
3. The number of units scrapped is less than the normal loss. There is thus an abnormal gain.

4. The equivalent units of closing WIP takes account of the degree of completion for each cost element.
5. The opening WIP is included in the statement of costs, so that its value is averaged over the equivalent units produced in the period.
6. In the evaluation section, the unit rate for each cost element is multiplied by the number of equivalent units in each part of the output. These values can then be used to complete the process account.

Process 3 account

	Units	£		Units	£
Opening WIP	100	692	Process 4	850	9,375
Process 2	900	1,600	Normal loss	90	18
Materials added		3,294	Closing WIP	80	604
Conversion costs		4,190			
Abnormal gain	20	221			
	1,020	9,997		1,020	9,997

 ## Exercise 9.3

To give yourself some extra practice, draw up the abnormal gain account and the scrap account.

 ## Solution

Abnormal gain account

	£		£
Scrap stock (20 × £0.20)	4	Process 3	221
Income statement	217		
	221		221

Scrap account

	£		£
Normal loss	18	Bank/receivable: (90 − 20) × £0.20	14
		Abnormal gain	4
	18		18

9.8 Process costing: a further example

You must try to get as much practice as possible in preparing process cost accounts, and you will find it much easier if you use a standard format for the working papers. Although you will not be required to reproduce the workings in the assessment, for your own benefit you need to work quickly through the available data to produce the required answer.

Work carefully through the next example – or better still try it for yourself before looking at the suggested solution. Notice that the scrapped units are not complete. You will need to take account of this in the equivalent units calculations.

Example

The following information is available for process 2 in October:

			Process 1 input		Materials added in process 2		Conversion costs	
	Units	Cost £	%	£	%	£	%	£
Opening WIP	600	1,480	100	810	80	450	40	220
Closing WIP	350		100		90		30	
Input costs:								
Input from process 1	4,000	6,280						
Materials added in process 2		3,109						
Conversion costs		4,698						

Degree of completion and cost is the spanning header over the Process 1 input / Materials added in process 2 / Conversion costs columns.

Normal loss is 5 per cent of input from process 1.
300 units were scrapped in the month. The scrapped units had reached the following degrees of completion.

Materials added	90%
Conversion cost	60%

All scrapped units realised £1 each.
Output to the next process was 3,950 units.
You are required to complete the account for process 2 and for the abnormal loss or gain in October.

Solution

The first step is to prepare an input/output reconciliation to see if there was an abnormal loss or abnormal gain. This is found as a balancing figure in the output column.

Input	Units	Output	Units	Process 1 input	Materials added	Conversion costs
Opening WIP	600	To process 3	3,950	3,950	3,950	3,950
Process 1	4,000	Normal loss	200	–	–	–
		Abnormal gain	100	100	90	60
		Closing WIP	350	350	315	105
	4,600		4,600	4,400	4,355	4,115
		Costs		£	£	£
		Opening WIP		810	450	220
		Input costs		6,280	3,109	4,698
		Normal loss value		(200)		
				6,890	3,559	4,918
				£	£	£
		Cost per unit	3.578	1.566	0.817	1.195
		Evaluation				
		To process 3	14,133	6,186	3,227	4,720
		Abnormal loss	303	157	74	72
		Closing WIP	931	548	257	126

Equivalent units to absorb cost is the spanning header over the Process 1 input / Materials added / Conversion costs columns.

Process 2 account

	Units	£		Units	£
Opening WIP	600	1,480	Process 3	3,950	14,133
Process 1	4,000	6,280	Normal loss	200	200
Materials added		3,109	Abnormal loss	100	303
Conversion costs		4,698	Closing WIP	350	931
	4,600	15,567		4,600	15,567

Abnormal loss account

	£		£
Process 2	303	Scrap account	100
		Income statement	203
	303		303

Scrap account

	£		£
Normal loss	200	Bank/receivables:	300
		(200 + 100) × £1	
Abnormal loss	100		
	300		300

9.9 Contrasting process costing and specific order costing

Now that you have a clear picture of how process costing works you are in a position to think about the differences between process costing and specific order costing methods.

 Remember that *specific order costing* is the collective term for the costing methods that you learned about in the last chapter: job, batch and contract costing.

Process costing can be contrasted with specific order costing methods such as job, batch and contract costing in a number of ways:

- since there is a continuous flow of identical units, individual cost units cannot be separately identified in a process costing environment. In a specific order costing environment, each cost unit is different from all others;
- costs incurred are averaged over the units produced in a process costing system. In contrast to a specific order costing system, it is not possible to allocate costs to specific cost units;
- each cost unit usually undergoes the same process or sequence of processes. In specific order costing environments, each cost unit often involves different operations or processes, depending on the customer's requirements;
- in process costing environments, items are usually produced to replenish inventory, rather than for a specific customer's requirements.

9.10 Summary

Having read this chapter, the main points that you should understand are as follows.

1. The process costing method is appropriate for organisations that produce a continuous flow of identical units. The costs incurred are averaged over the number of units produced in the period in order to determine the cost per unit.

2. There may be more than one process involved in process costing. The output of one process becomes the input of the next process in the sequence.

3. A normal loss is the expected level of loss for the period. The normal loss does not absorb any process costs. If it is saleable it is valued at its scrap value, otherwise the normal loss will have zero value.

4. The scrap value of the normal loss is conventionally deducted from the cost of the first cost element in the analysis, which is usually either materials cost or previous process cost.

5. If losses are greater than the normal loss, the extra loss is called an abnormal loss. If losses are lower than the normal loss the difference is called an abnormal gain.

6. Abnormal losses and gains are valued at the same unit rate as good output. Their scrap values do not affect the main process account but are accounted for in a separate abnormal loss or abnormal gain account.

7. Where there are incomplete units in the process at the end of the period, that is, when there is closing work in progress, it is necessary to determine the number of equivalent units of production in order to calculate the production cost per unit.

8. There are a number of ways in which process costing can be contrasted with specific order costing methods such as job, batch and contract costing.

Revision Questions

? Question 1 Multiple choice

1.1 Process B had no opening WIP. 13,500 units of raw material were transferred in at £4.50 per unit. Additional material at £1.25 per unit was added in process. Labour and overheads were £6.25 per completed unit and £2.50 per unit incomplete. If 11,750 completed units were transferred out, what was the closing WIP in process B?

(A) £ 77,625
(B) £14,437.50
(C) £141,000
(D) £21,000

1.2 In a process account, abnormal losses are valued:

(A) at their scrap value.
(B) at the same rate as good production.
(C) at the cost of raw materials.
(D) at good production cost less scrap value.

1.3 A chemical process has a normal wastage of 10 per cent of input. In a period, 2,500 kg of material were input and there was an abnormal loss of 75 kg.
What quantity of good production was achieved?

(A) 2,175 kg
(B) 2,250 kg
(C) 2,325 kg
(D) 2,475 kg

1.4 In process costing, where losses have a positive scrap value, when an abnormal gain arises the abnormal gain account is:

(A) credited with the normal production cost of the abnormal gain units.
(B) debited with the normal production cost of the abnormal gain units and credited with the scrap value of the abnormal gain units.
(C) credited with the normal production cost of the abnormal gain units and debited with the scrap value of the abnormal gain units.
(D) credited with the normal production cost of the abnormal gain units and credited with the scrap value of the abnormal gain units.

Data for questions 1.5–1.7

X plc makes one product, which passes through a single process. Details of the process are as follows:

> Materials: 5,000 kg at 50 p per kg
> Labour: £800
> Production overheads 200% of labour

Normal losses are 20 per cent of input in the process, and without further processing any losses can be sold as scrap for 30 p per kg.

The output for the period was 3,800 kg from the process.

There was no work in progress at the beginning or end of the period.

1.5 What value will be credited to the process account for the scrap value of the normal loss?

   (A) £300
   (B) £530
   (C) £980
   (D) £1,021

1.6 What is the value of the abnormal loss?

   (A) £60
   (B) £196
   (C) £230
   (D) £245

1.7 What is the value of the output?

   (A) £3,724
   (B) £4,370
   (C) £4,655
   (D) £4,900

Data for questions 1.8–1.10

A product is manufactured as a result of two processes, A and B. Details of process B for the month of August were as follows:

Materials transferred from process A	10,000 kg valued at £40,500
Labour costs	1,000 hours @ £5.616 per hour
Overheads	50% of labour costs
Output transferred to finished goods	8,000 kg
Closing work in progress	900 kg

Normal loss is 10 per cent of input and losses do not have a scrap value.

Closing work in progress is 100 per cent complete for material, and 75 per cent complete for both labour and overheads.

1.8 What is the value of the abnormal loss (to the nearest £)?

   (A) Nil
   (B) £489
   (C) £544
   (D) £546

1.9 What is the value of the output (to the nearest £)?

(A) £39,139
(B) £43,488
(C) £43,680
(D) £43,977

1.10 What is the value of the closing work in progress (to the nearest £)?

(A) £4,403
(B) £4,698
(C) £4,892
(D) £4,947

Data for questions 1.11 and 1.12

The following data relates to a process for the latest period:

Opening work in process	1,000 litres valued at £1,500
Input	30,000 litres costing £15,000
Conversion costs	£10,000
Output	24,000 litres
Closing work in process	3,500 litres

Losses in process are expected to be 10 per cent of period input. They are complete as to input material costs but are discovered after 60 per cent conversion. Losses have a scrap value of £0.20 per litre.

Closing work in process is complete as to input materials and 80 per cent complete as to conversion.

1.11 The number of material-equivalent units was:

(A) 24,000
(B) 28,000
(C) 30,000
(D) 31,000

1.12 The number of conversion-equivalent units was:

(A) 27,100
(B) 27,300
(C) 28,000
(D) 30,100

Data for questions 1.13 and 1.14

PP Ltd makes one product, which passes through a single process. The details of the process for period 2 were as follows.

There were 400 units of opening work in progress, valued as follows:

Material	£49,000
Labour	£23,000
Production overheads	£3,800

No losses are expected in the process.

During the period, 900 units were added to the process, and the following costs occurred:

Material	£198,000 (900 units)
Labour	£139,500
Production overheads	£79,200

There were 500 units of closing work in progress, which were 100 per cent complete for material, 90 per cent complete for labour and 40 per cent complete for overheads. No losses were incurred in the process.

PP Ltd uses weighted average costing.

1.13 How many equivalent units are used when calculating the cost per unit in relation to labour?

(A) 450
(B) 850
(C) 1,250
(D) 1,300

1.14 The value of completed output for the period was

(A) £171,555
(B) £201,500
(C) £274,488
(D) £322,400

Question 2 Short objective-test questions

2.1 When the actual loss in a process is less than the expected loss for the period, there is an:

abnormal loss ☐
abnormal gain ☐

2.2 Input to a process last period was 5,000 kg. There was no opening work in progress but 800 kg were in process at the end of the period. Normal loss is 20 per cent of input. During the period, 4,100 kg were transferred to the next process.

(a) During the period, there was an:
abnormal loss ☐
abnormal gain ☐
(b) The abnormal loss/gain amounted to [＿＿＿＿] kg

2.3 Last period, an abnormal gain of 50 kg arose in process 1. Normal loss was 400 kg. The cost of good output from process 1, after allowing for the abnormal gain, was £3.50 per kg. Scrap from process 1 can be sold for £0.20 per kg.

The scrap account in respect of process 1 for the period is shown below.

Scrap account			
	£		£
Process 1	**A**	Abnormal gain	**B**
		Balance c/d	**C**

The values to be entered as A, B and C in the scrap account are:
A [＿＿＿＿]   B [＿＿＿＿]   C [＿＿＿＿]

2.4 In process 2 at the end of a period, 200 units are in progress. They are 100 per cent complete in respect of materials, 50 per cent complete in respect of labour and 20 per cent complete in respect of overhead. The cost of an equivalent complete unit for the period was £4 for materials, £3 for labour and £2 for overhead. Complete the following table to show the value of the work in progress at the end of the period.

	Equivalent units in progress	Valuation £
Materials		
Labour		
Overhead		

2.5 In the following process, all losses were fully processed and scrap units from the process can be sold for £3 per unit.

The values to be entered as A and B in the process account below are:

A [　　　　　]　　B [　　　　　]

Process account [extract]

	Units	£
Finished goods	4,000	88,000
Normal loss	90	**A**
Abnormal loss	50	**B**

Data for questions 2.6 and 2.7

T makes one product in a single process. Details for last period are as follows.
Opening work in process = 300 units valued as follows.

	£
Material cost	1,296
Conversion cost	462

900 units were added during the period and costs incurred were as follows.

	£
Material cost	3,960
Conversion cost	1,890

At the end of the period, there were 200 units of work in process that had reached the following degree of completion.

Material cost	100%
Conversion cost	60%

No losses occur in the process and weighted average costing is used.

2.6 How many equivalent units will be used when calculating the cost per unit in relation to conversion cost?

[　　　　　　　　　]

2.7 To the nearest £, what was the value of the work in process at the end of the period?

£ [   ]

? **Question 3** Process costing

A firm operates a process, the details of which for the period were as follows:

- There was no opening work in progress.
- During the period, 8,250 units were received from the previous process at a value of £453,750, labour and overheads were £350,060 and material introduced was £24,750.
- At the end of the period, the closing work in progress was 1,600 units, which were 100 per cent complete in respect of materials, and 60 per cent complete in respect of labour and overheads.
- The balance of units were transferred to finished goods.

Requirements

(a) The number of equivalent units of labour and overheads produced during the period was [   ]

(b) In the process account for the period, the following values will be credited:
  (i) finished goods value: £ [   ]
  (ii) closing work in progress value: £ [   ]

? **Question 4** Process costing with abnormal losses

Chemical Processors manufacture Wonderchem using two processes – mixing and distillation. The following details relate to the distillation process for a period:

No opening work in progress	
Input from mixing	36,000 kg at a cost of £166,000
Labour for period	£43,800
Overheads for period	£29,200

Closing WIP of 8,000 kg, which was 100 per cent complete for materials and 50 per cent complete for labour and overheads.

The normal loss in distillation is 10 per cent of fully complete production. Actual loss in the period was 3,600 kg, fully complete, which was scrapped.

Requirements

(a) The abnormal loss for the period was [   ] kg.

(b) The number of equivalent kg produced during the period was:

materials: [   ] equivalent kg.

labour and overhead: [   ] equivalent kg.

(c) (i) The value of the abnormal loss is £ [   ]
   (ii) (*Tick the correct box*): This value is entered in the process account as a:

   debit ☐
   credit ☐

(d) The values to be credited in the process account in respect of the following outputs for the period are:

finished goods   £ [＿＿＿＿＿＿]

normal loss   £ [＿＿＿＿＿＿]

closing work in progress   £ [＿＿＿＿＿＿]

Question 5 Process costing with opening work in progress

A company operates an expensive processing plant to produce a single product from one process. At the beginning of October, 3,400 completed units were still in the processing plant awaiting transfer to finished goods. They were valued as follows:

	£	
Direct material	25,500	
Direct wages	10,200	
Production overhead	20,400	(200% of direct wages)

During October, 37,000 further units were put into process and the following costs charged to the process:

	£
Direct materials	276,340
Direct wages	112,000
Production overhead	224,000

A total of 36,000 units were transferred to finished goods and 3,200 units remained in work in progress at the end of October, which were complete as to material and half complete as to labour and production overhead. The normal level of scrap (1,200 units) occurred during the process.

Requirements

(a) The number of equivalent units produced during the period was:

materials   [＿＿＿＿＿＿]

labour and overhead   [＿＿＿＿＿＿]

(b) The value of the outputs from the process during the period was:

finished goods £ [＿＿＿＿＿＿]

closing work in progress £ [＿＿＿＿＿＿]

Question 6 Process account

Complete the following account for process 3 last period. The work in progress was complete as to materials and 50 per cent complete as to labour and overhead.

Process 3 account

	Units	£		Units	£
Process 2 input	2,000	8,000	Finished goods	1,800	[＿＿＿＿]
Labour and overhead		3,800	Work in progress	200	[＿＿＿＿]
	2,000	11,800		2,000	11,800

Solutions to Revision Questions

☑ Solution 1

For some of these multiple-choice questions you will need to use some fairly extensive workings. In the assessment, you will not be awarded marks for the workings, but do not be tempted to rush them: they are an important part of answering the question, and they will be of no use to you if you cannot read them!

1.1   Answer: (B)

Closing WIP in process B = (13,500 − 11,750) units = 1,750 units

Unit value = £4.50 + £1.25 + £2.50 = £8.25

Closing WIP value = £8.25 × 1,750 = £14,437.50

1.2   Answer: (B)

Abnormal losses are valued at the same rate as good production, so that their occurrence does not affect the cost of good production.

1.3   Answer: (A)

	kg
Input	2,500
Normal loss (10%)	(250)
Abnormal loss	(75)
Good production	2,175

1.4   Answer: (C)

The abnormal gain account shows the net benefit of the abnormal gain. The scrap value must be debited to the abnormal gain account to allow for the 'forgone' scrap value of the normal loss units which did not arise.

1.5   Answer: (A)

Normal loss 5,000 kg × 20% = 1,000 kg @ 30 p = £300

1.6   Answer: (C)

Abnormal loss	kg
Input	5,000
Normal loss	(1,000)
Output	(3,800)
Abnormal loss	200

Production costs	£
Materials	2,500
Labour	800
Production overheads	1,600
	4,900

$$\text{Cost per kg} = \frac{£4,900 - £300}{4,000^*} = £1.15 \text{ per kg}$$

*Output $3,800 +$ abnormal loss $200 = 4,000$ kg

Abnormal loss $£1.15 \times 200$ kg $= £230$.

1.7   Answer: (B)

Value of output $= £1.15 \times 3,800$ kg $= £4,370$.

Equivalent unit table for 1.8–1.10

	Units	%	Materials EU	%	Labour/overheads EU
Output	8,000	100	8,000	100	8,000
Normal loss	1,000		–		–
Abnormal loss	100	100	100	100	100
Closing work in progress	900	100	900	75	675
Total equivalent units	10,000		9,000		8,775
Costs			£40,500		£8,424
Equivalent unit cost			£4.50		£0.96

1.8   Answer: (D)

Value of abnormal loss $= 100 \times (£4.50 + £0.96) = £546$.

1.9   Answer: (C)

Value of output $= 8,000 \times (£4.50 + £0.96) = £43,680$.

1.10   Answer: (B)

Closing work in progress:	£
$900 \times £4.50$	4,050
$675 \times £0.96$	648
	4,698

1.11 Answer: (B)

Workings for 1.11 are shown as part of solution 1.12.

1.12 Answer: (A)

				Equivalent litres		
				Input		Conversion
Input	Litres	Output	Litres	material		costs
Opening WIP	1,000	Finished output	24,000	24,000		24,000
Input	30,000	Normal loss	3,000	–		–
		Abnormal loss	500	500	(60%)	300
		Closing WIP	3,500	3,500	(80%)	2,800
	31,000		31,000	28,000		27,100

1.13 Answer: (C)

Workings are shown as part of solution 1.14.

1.14 Answer: (D)

Equivalent units table

		Materials		Labour		Production o/h	
Description	Units	%	EU	%	EU	%	EU
Output	800	100	800	100	800	100	800
Closing WIP	500	100	500	90	450	40	200
EU			1,300		1,250		1,000
			£		£		£
Costs – Period			198,000		139,500		79,200
Opening WIP			49,000		23,000		3,800
Total cost			247,000		162,500		83,000
Cost per equivalent unit			190		130		83

Value of completed output = 800 × (£190 + £130 + £83) = £322,400.

Solution 2

2.1 When the actual loss in a process is less than the expected loss for the period, there is an *abnormal gain*.

2.2

	kg
Transferred to next process	4,100
Normal loss (20% × 5,000)	1,000
Closing work in process	800
Abnormal gain	**(900)**
	5,000

2.3   A   £80;   B   £10;   C   £70.

Scrap account			
	£		£
Process 1 – normal loss		Abnormal gain	**10**
(400 kg × £0.20)	**80**	(50 × £0.20)	
		Balance c/d	70
	80		80

2.4

	Equivalent units in progress	Valuation £
Materials	**200** (×£4)	800
Labour	**100** (×£3)	300
Overhead	**40** (×£2)	80
		1,180

2.5   A   £270;   B   £1,100.

Process account [extract]			
	Units		£
Finished goods	4,000		88,000
Normal loss	90	(×£3)	**270**
Abnormal loss	50	(×£22*)	**1,100**

*Abnormal loss units are valued at the same rate as good output (£88,000/ 4,000 = £22).

2.6   Number of equivalent units of conversion cost = 1,120.
Workings are shown as part of solution 2.7.

2.7   Value of work in process at the end of the period = £1,128.

Equivalent units table
Since no losses occur in the process, output can be calculated as follows.
Output = 300 units opening WIP + 900 units input − 200 units closing WIP = 1,000 units

		Materials		Conversion cost	
Description	Units	%	EU	%	EU
Output	1,000	100	1,000	100	1,000
Closing WIP	200	100	200	60	120
			1,200		1,120
			£		£
Costs incurred in period			3,960		1,890
Opening WIP			1,296		462
Total cost			5,256		2,352
Cost per equivalent unit			4.38		2.10

Value of closing WIP = (200 × £4.38) + (120 × £2.10) = £1,128.

Solution 3

- You can use the standard layout for the working paper that you should have become accustomed to when working through this chapter. You can then pick out the relevant parts that you need for your answers.
- There are no losses, therefore the question is quite straightforward.
- The transfer to finished goods is calculated as follows: 8,250 units input, less 1,600 units in progress, equals 6,650 units to finished goods.

(a) 7,610

(b) (i) £691,600

(ii) £136,960

Workings:

				Equivalent units produced		
Input	Units	Output	Units	*Previous process*	*Materials added*	*Labour and o/h*
Previous process	8,250	Finished goods	6,650	6,650	6,650	6,650
		Closing WIP	1,600	1,600	1,600	960 (60%)
	8,250	Equiv. units produced	8,250	8,250	8,250	7,610
		Costs	£	£	£	£
		Period costs		453,750	24,750	350,060
		Cost per equiv. unit	104	55	3	46
		Valuation				
		Finished goods	691,600			
		Closing WIP	136,960	88,000	4,800	44,160
				(1,600 × £55)	(1,600 × £3)	(960 × £46)

 Solution 4

- Read the question carefully. The normal loss calculation is based on the completed production rather than on the more usual basis of input to the process.
- The losses are completely processed, therefore you can use the total cost per unit to value the abnormal loss.

(a) The abnormal loss for the period was 800 kg.

Workings:

	kg
Input	36,000
Less: Closing WIP	(8,000)
Production	28,000
Normal loss: 10% × 28,000 kg	2,800
Actual loss	3,600
∴ Abnormal loss	800

(b) Materials: 33,200 equivalent kg.
   Labour and overhead: 29,200 equivalent kg.

(c) (i) £6,000
   (ii) Credit.

(d) Finished goods: £183,000
   Normal loss: £0
   Closing work in progress: £50,000
   Workings:

Input	kg	Output	Total kg	Material kg	Labour kg	Overhead kg
				Equivalent units		
From mixing	36,000	Finished goods	24,400	24,400	24,400	24,400
		Abnormal loss	800	800	800	800
			25,200	25,200	25,200	25,200
		Normal loss	2,800	–	–	–
		Closing WIP:				
		Material (100%)	8,000	8,000		
		Labour (50%)			4,000	
		Overheads (50%)				4,000
			36,000	33,200	29,200	29,200
		Cost (£)	239,000	166,000	43,800	29,200
		Cost per unit (£)	7.50	5.00	1.50	1.00
		Evaluation (£)				
		Finished goods	183,000			
		Abnormal loss	6,000			
		Closing WIP	50,000	40,000	6,000	4,000

☑ Solution 5

- There is opening work in progress to deal with in this question, so you will probably find it easiest to use the full working schedule, beginning with an input/output reconciliation. Although you will not be awarded any marks for these workings, they will help you to achieve the required 100 per cent accuracy.
- Do not be confused by the fact that the opening work in progress consists of complete units. Simply deal with it using the method that you learned in this chapter, that is include it as part of the input and include its value in the cost section of your working schedule.

(a) Materials: 39,200
   Labour and overhead: 37,600.

(b) Finished goods: £628,200
   Closing work in progress: £40,240.

Workings:

Input	Units	Output	Units	Equivalent units produced Materials	Labour	Overhead
Opening WIP	3,400	Finished goods	36,000	36,000	36,000	36,000
Further units	37,000	Normal loss	1,200	–	–	–
		Closing WIP	3,200	3,200	1,600	1,600
	40,400		40,400	39,200	37,600	37,600
		Cost	£	£	£	£
		Opening WIP	56,100	25,500	10,200	20,400
		Period costs	612,340	276,340	112,000	224,000
			668,440	301,840	122,200	244,400
		Cost per unit	17.45	7.70	3.25	6.50
		Evaluation				
		Finished goods	628,200			
		Closing WIP	40,240	24,640	5,200	10,400

☑ **Solution 6**

- You will need to prepare a statement of equivalent units and calculate the cost per equivalent unit.
- There are no losses to be accounted for, so all of the cost incurred is to be divided over the completed units and the units in progress.
- Be accurate with your workings. Although they will not be awarded marks, they will help you to achieve the necessary 100 per cent accuracy.

Input	Units	Output	Units	Equivalent units to absorb cost Materials	Labour/OH
Process 2 input	2,000	Finished goods	1,800	1,800	1,800
		Closing WIP	200	200	(50%) 100
	2,000		2,000	2,000	1,900
		Costs	£	£	£
		Incurred in period		8,000	3,800
		Cost per unit	6	4	2
		Evaluation			
		Finished goods			
		(1,800 × £6)	10,800		
		Closing WIP	1,000	800	200

		Process 3 account			

	Units	£		Units	£
Process 2 input	2,000	8,000	Finished goods	1,800	10,800
Labour and overhead		3,800	Work in progress	200	1,000
	2,000	11,800		2,000	11,800

10

Presenting Management Information

Presenting Management Information

10

LEARNING OUTCOMES

After completing this chapter you should be able to:

▸ explain the difference between subjective and objective classifications of expenditure and the importance of tracing costs both to products/services and to responsibility centres;

▸ construct coding systems that facilitate both subjective and objective classification of costs;

▸ prepare financial statements that inform management;

▸ explain why gross revenue, value added, contribution, gross margin, marketing expense, general and administration expense, etc. might be highlighted in management reporting;

▸ compare and contrast management reports in a range of organisations including commercial enterprises, charities and public sector undertakings.

10.1 Introduction

In this chapter, you will be learning about the effective presentation of management accounting reports to managers so that they have the information they need to be able to manage their area of responsibility in the most effective way.

You will be learning how these reports might be structured and about a range of different performance measures that might be highlighted in management reports in a variety of different types of organisation.

10.2 Subjective and objective classification

In chapter 1 of this text, you learned that the classification of costs involved arranging the costs into logical groups by nature, purpose or responsibility.

You saw that classification by nature involves grouping costs according to whether they are material cost, labour cost or expenses. This classification is referred to as *subjective classification*.

281

Classification by purpose involves grouping costs according to the reason they are incurred, for example, whether they are a direct or indirect cost of a particular cost object. This classification is referred to as *objective classification*.

10.2.1 Responsibility centres

Classification by responsibility involves grouping costs according to which individual manager or management team is responsible for the control of the cost. A responsibility accounting system divides an organisation into several parts, or responsibility centres, with an individual manager responsible for the operation and performance of each responsibility centre.

10.2.2 Reporting management accounting information

The different systems of classification allow expenditure to be reported in different ways, according to the reason why the information is being provided.

For example, managers might be interested in assessing the profitability of a particular product or service, in which case, costs might be classified by purpose (objective classification) so that they can be traced to individual products or services.

Alternatively, managers might be interested in assessing the expenditure incurred by a particular responsibility centre within the organisation. In this situation, it would be more useful to trace expenditure to individual responsibility centres rather than to particular products or services.

10.3 Coding of costs

 The CIMA *Terminology* defines a code as a 'brief, accurate reference designed to assist classification of items by facilitating entry, collation and analysis'.

The coding system is based on the selected cost classifications. It provides a way of expressing the classification of each cost or item of expenditure in a shortened symbolised form.

10.3.1 Composite codes

The CIMA *Terminology* describes the use of composite symbols in codes. For example, let us consider the hypothetical composite symbol 298.311.

The first three digits might indicate the nature of the expenditure.

 Remember this is the subjective classification of the expenditure.

2 – labour
9 – semi-skilled
8 – grade 8

Anyone who is familiar with the coding system would be able to identify that the expenditure was incurred on grade 8 semi-skilled labour.

The last three digits might indicate the cost object to be charged, for example, a particular cost unit or cost centre.

Remember this is the objective classification of the expenditure.

3 – indirect cost
1 – north east factory
1 – machining department

The code can indicate that the expenditure is to be charged as indirect labour to the machining department in the north east factory.

The code number 298.311 is much clearer than this lengthy description of where the cost is to be charged.

10.3.2 The advantages of a coding system

Some of the advantages of a well-designed coding system are as follows.

- A code is usually briefer than a description. The example in the previous section demonstrates this advantage very clearly. This saves time in a manual system and reduces the data storage capacity required in a computerised system.
- A coding system enables costs to be accumulated for each code number so that they can be logically grouped for reporting to managers.
- A code reduces ambiguity. Two people might each use a quite different description for the same item of expenditure but a code will be more precise.
- A code is more suitable than a description in computerised systems so that data processing is facilitated.

 Exercise 10.1

The XY Manufacturing Company uses a four digit code to classify its expenditure items.

- The first digit indicates the responsibility centre to be charged.
  1 = responsibility centre 1, 2 = responsibility centre 2 and so on.
- The second digit indicates the machine group within the responsibility centre that has incurred the cost.
  1 = machine group 1, 2 = machine group 2 and so on.
- The last two digits indicate the nature of the expenditure.
  For example, 01 = direct materials, 02 = indirect materials, 03 = direct labour, 11 = depreciation, 12 = power cost and so on.

(a) State the code number that would be used for the following two expenditure items.

   (i) Direct labour cost incurred in machine group 4 within responsibility centre 2
   (ii) Power cost incurred on machine group 1 within responsibility centre 1

(b) State the expenditure that is represented by the code number 2202.

 Solution

(a) (i) 2403
    (ii) 1112
(b) Indirect material cost incurred in machine group 2 within responsibility centre 2

10.3.3 The requirements for an efficient coding system

(a) The code should be unique and certain, that is, each item should have only one possible code number which can easily be identified from the structure of the code.

(b) The coding system should be comprehensive and elastic, that is, it should be possible to identify a code for every item and the coding system should be capable of expanding to accommodate new items.

(c) The code should be as brief as possible, having regard to the amount of detail which is needed in the analysis of the items being coded.

(d) To minimise errors, the code should incorporate check digits so that a computerised system can detect coding errors.

(e) The maintenance of the coding system should be centrally controlled. It should not be possible for individuals to independently add new codes to the existing coding system.

(f) Wherever possible, all codes should be of the same length. This makes errors easier to spot and it assists computerised data processing.

10.4 Preparing financial statements that inform management

The usefulness of a financial statement is greatly enhanced if it highlights subtotals, totals and performance measures that are relevant to the recipient. This enables the manager who receives the information to focus on the most relevant information from a point of view of management action.

A performance measure will be particularly relevant if it is controllable by the manager for whom the report is prepared, that is if the manager is able to take action to influence the measure, and if an improvement in the performance measure would improve the performance of the responsibility centre or the organisation overall.

Let us look now at a number of performance measures that you might see highlighted in management reports.

10.4.1 Value added

Value added is a performance measure which is sometimes used as an alternative to profit. Traditionally, value added is calculated as follows.

Value added = sales revenue − cost of materials and bought-in services

Since value added excludes all bought-in costs paid to people from outside the organisation, it effectively focuses on the additional revenue created by the organisation's own internal efforts. For this reason it is sometimes used as the basis for labour incentive schemes.

You might sometimes see value added calculated by 'working backwards' from the profit figure:

Value added = profit + interest + all conversion costs

You should remember from the last chapter that conversion costs are the costs of converting raw material into the finished product. Conversion costs include direct labour and production overhead costs.

This calculation method is intended to give the same result for the value added. However, it will only do so if bought-in overhead costs are treated as non-conversion costs.

> ✎ If you have to calculate value added in an assessment question then you should use the traditional method of calculation, i.e. sales revenue – cost of materials and bought-in services.

10.4.2 Contribution

You should remember from earlier in this text that contribution is calculated as follows.

Contribution = sales revenue – variable costs

Contribution is often highlighted in management reports when it is important for managers to be able to see whether individual cost objects are generating sufficient revenue to cover the variable costs they incur.

Highlighting contribution can also help managers to see the potential effect on profit of an increase or decrease in activity. For example, if it is assumed that variable costs are linear and that the selling price per unit is constant, then the contribution earned will change in direct proportion to the change in activity.

Example: a product contribution analysis

This example will demonstrate why it might be important to highlight the contribution earned by each product.

	Product A £000	Product B £000	Product C £000	Total £000
Gross revenue	931	244	954	2,129
Variable costs:				
Direct material and labour	547	87	432	1,066
Variable production overhead	54	58	179	291
Variable marketing expense	9	3	7	19
Total variable cost	610	148	618	1,376
Contribution	321	96	336	753
Fixed production overhead	43	35	34	112
Fixed marketing expense	38	10	40	88
Fixed general and administration expense	60	56	60	176
Profit/(loss)	180	(5)	202	377
Contribution to sales (PV) ratio	34.5%	39.3%	35.2%	

This product contribution analysis reveals the following:

- Product B appears to be incurring a loss. Its contribution is not sufficient to cover the fixed production, marketing, general and administration expenses attributed to it.
- However the product is earning a contribution. If the fixed costs attributed to product B are costs that would be incurred anyway, even if product B was discontinued, then it may be worth continuing the sale and production of product B since it does earn a

contribution of £96,000 towards these fixed costs. If product B was discontinued then this £96,000 contribution would be forgone.

- Although product B is earning a contribution, it does not at present generate sufficient contribution to cover its fair share of support costs such as marketing, general and administration overhead. The profitability of product B does require management attention.
- Product B earns the highest contribution to sales ratio. This means that if gross sales revenue of product B can be increased without affecting the fixed costs, the resulting increase in contribution will be higher than with the same sales increase on products A and C. Thus the key to product B's profitability might be to increase the volume sold.

10.4.3 Gross margin

Gross margin is the difference between the sales revenue and the direct production or purchasing costs incurred. Indirect costs or overheads are then deducted from the gross margin to determine the net profit.

The gross margin percentage is also useful. It is the gross margin calculated as a percentage of the sales revenue and it helps to highlight the relationship between sales revenues and production/purchasing costs.

Look at the following example.

Example: a gross margin analysis

The following extract is taken from the monthly managerial report of the DD Organisation.

	Month 1	Month 2	Month 3	Month 4
	£000	£000	£000	£000
Gross sales revenue	896	911	919	935
Direct cost of goods sold	699	713	722	737
Gross margin	197	198	197	198
Gross margin percentage	22.0%	21.7%	21.4%	21.2%

This gross margin analysis focuses managers' attention on the relationship between the sales value and the direct cost of sales, before indirect costs or overheads are taken into account. This analysis reveals the following:

- Although the gross sales revenue is steadily increasing, the gross margin is relatively constant each month.
- The gross margin percentage is steadily decreasing each month. If the gross margin percentage could have been maintained at 22% the total gross margin earned would have been higher.
- Perhaps selling prices are being increased but the reduction in the gross margin percentage might be the result of a failure to increase selling prices sufficiently in line with increasing direct costs.
- Alternatively the sales volume might be increasing but direct costs are not being contained as the sales increase.

10.5 Managerial reports in a service organisation

There is a very wide variety of service organisations, ranging from private sector organisations such as hotels and courier services, to public sector organisations such as hospitals and schools.

One aspect of services that can present difficulties for the information provider is establishing a suitable cost unit.

10.5.1 Establishing a suitable cost unit

Many service organisations produce an intangible 'output', that is, their output has no physical substance and it cannot be physically seen and touched. In order to maintain effective cost control it is essential to establish a measurable cost unit for which we can ascertain and monitor the costs.

In Chapter 1 we saw how composite cost units are often used to monitor and control the costs in service operations. Any cost unit can be used as long as it can be objectively measured and its cost can be determined and compared from one period to another and if possible from one organisation to another.

 Exercise 10.2

Suggest a composite cost unit that could be used in each of these service organisations:
(i) hotel; (ii) hospital; (iii) haulage contractor.

 Solution

  (i) Hotel: bed-night or room-night.
 (ii) Hospital: in-patient day.
(iii) Haulage contractor: tonne-kilometre.

10.5.2 Establishing the cost per unit

Once a suitable cost unit has been selected, the cost for each unit can be determined using an averaging method:

$$\text{Average cost per unit of service} = \frac{\text{Total costs incurred in period}}{\text{Number of units of service supplied in the period}}$$

10.5.3 The instantaneous and perishable nature of services

Many services are provided instantaneously rather than for inventory; for example, a restaurant meal is cooked as it is ordered by the customer. This brings with it particular management problems of planning and control but it does mean that the incidence of work in progress is very low, that is, it is rarely necessary to value part-finished units of service at the end of an accounting period.

Many services also 'perish' immediately; for example, if a cinema seat is vacant when a film is showing it cannot be stored in inventory for a later sale. The opportunity to gain revenue from that seat at that particular showing of the film has been lost forever. Therefore, capacity utilisation becomes a very important issue for managers in many service organisations.

Example: managerial reporting in a consultancy business

As you read through this example, notice that we are applying all of the principles of cost analysis that you have already learned about in this *Learning System*. The only difference is that the principles are being applied to determine the cost of intangible services, rather than of tangible products.

Mr G and Mrs H have recently formed a consultancy business and they wish to establish the following rates to charge clients:

- an hourly rate for productive client work;
- an hourly rate for time spent travelling to/from the clients' premises;
- a rate per mile for expenses incurred in travelling to/from the clients' premises.

Pricing policy
Mr G and Mrs H have decided that their pricing policy will be based on the cost per hour plus a 5 per cent profit mark-up. Travelling time will be charged to clients at one-third of the normal hourly rate. Travelling expenses will be charged to clients at cost.

Activity estimates
Mr G and Mrs H each expect to work for 8 hours per day, 5 days per week, 45 weeks per year. They refer to this as 'available time'.

- Twenty-five per cent of the available time will be spent dealing with administrative matters relating to the general running of the business.
- In the first year, 22.5 per cent of the available time will be idle, that is, no work will be done in this time.
- The remainder of the available time is expected to be chargeable to clients.
- Travelling time will amount to 25 per cent of the chargeable time, during which a total of 18,000 miles will be travelled.

Cost estimates
- Mr G and Mrs H each wish to receive a salary of £25,000 in the first year of trading.
- Other costs to be incurred in the first year of trading:

	£
Electricity	1,200
Fuel for vehicles	1,800
Depreciation of vehicles	6,000
Insurance – professional liability and office	600
Vehicle insurance and road tax	1,080
Office rent and rates	8,400
Telephone expenses	3,000
General office expenses	8,900
Servicing and repair of vehicles	1,200

Requirement
Prepare a summary report for Mr G and Mrs H which states the client charge rates that they wish to establish.

Solution

If you look back to Section 10.5.2 you will be reminded that we need to know two things in order to establish the cost per unit of service:

(1) the total costs incurred in the period;
(2) the number of units of service supplied in the period.

We need to classify the costs provided to determine the total cost associated with travelling, and that associated with providing consultancy services.

	Consultancy £	Travelling £
Salaries	50,000	
Electricity	1,200	
Fuel		1,800
Depreciation		6,000
Insurance	600	
Vehicle insurance, etc.		1,080
Office rent and rates	8,400	
Telephone expenses	3,000	
General office expenses	8,900	
Servicing vehicles, etc.		1,200
	72,100	10,080

Now we need to determine the number of units of service by which each of these cost totals is to be divided. The calculation of the rate per mile for travelling expenses is relatively straightforward:

$$\text{Rate per mile} = \frac{\text{Total travelling expenses}}{\text{Miles travelled}} = \frac{£10,080}{18\,000} = £0.56 \text{ per mile}$$

The calculation of the hourly rate for productive work and travelling time is a little more complicated. The first step is to determine the number of units of service supplied that is, the chargeable hours. We need to look at the activity estimates provided in order to analyse the available time.

		Hours
Total available hours for the first year = 2 people × 8 hours × 5 days × 45 weeks		3,600
Less: administration time	25.0%	
idle time	22.5%	
	47.5% × 3,600	(1,710)
Time chargeable to clients		1,890
Productive time spent with clients (75%)		1,417.5
Travelling time (25%)		472.5

Travelling time will be charged at one-third of the normal hourly rate, therefore we need to calculate a 'weighted' figure for chargeable time.

$$\text{Weighted chargeable time} = 1,417.5 + \frac{472.5}{3} = 1,575 \text{ hours}$$

Now we can combine the consultancy services costs and the weighted chargeable time to determine an hourly rate for each type of work.

PRESENTING MANAGEMENT INFORMATION

$$\text{Cost per chargeable hour} = \frac{£72,100}{1,575} = £45.78$$

Hourly rate for productive client work = £45.78 + 5% profit mark-up = £48.07 per hour, say £48 per hour

$$\text{Hourly rate for travelling time} = \frac{£48.07}{3} = £16.02 \text{ per hour, say } £16 \text{ per hour}$$

Summary report: client charge rates
To: Mr G and Mrs H
From: AN Other
Date: xx.xx.xx
Subject: Client charge rates

REPORT

In response to your request, in accordance with the cost and activity data provided, I detail below the required charge rates to clients.

Hourly rate for productive client work   £48
Hourly rate for travelling time   £16
Rate per mile for travelling expenses   £0.56

 Exercise 10.3

The following data is available for the Central Hospital for the latest period.

Use this data to calculate the following cost control measures for the monthly management report, to the nearest penny.

(a) Operating theatre cost per hour
(b) Admission costs per patient
(c) Patient care cost per night

Activity data

Number of patients	1,040
Number of patient nights	4,750
Number of operating theatres	5
Number of days theatres in use during month	26
Number of hours theatres used per day	15

Cost data   £

Operating theatre costs in total	510,000
Updating patient records on admission	33,900
Bed scheduling costs	20,833
Nursing	1,077,000
Patient catering costs	244,200
Medical supplies	120,000
Patient laundry costs	100,000
Other patient care costs	60,900

Solution

(a) Number of theatre hours = 5 theatres × 26 days × 15 hours = 1,950

Operating theatre cost per hour = £510,000/1,950 = £261.54

(b) *Admission costs* £

Updating patient records	33,900
Bed scheduling	20,833
Total admission costs	54,733

Admission costs per patient = £54,733/1,040 = £52.63

(c) *Patient care costs* £

Nursing	1,077,000
Patient catering costs	244,200
Medical supplies	120,000
Patient laundry costs	100,000
Other patient care costs	60,900
Total patient care costs	1,602,100

Patient care cost per patient night = £1,602,100/4,750 = £337.28

10.5.4 Managerial reporting in a charity: example

The TW Care Charity has just completed an overseas aid programme to assist homeless orphans. Cost and revenue data concerning the programme are as follows.

	£
Income from donations	157,750
Grants received from government and others	62,000
Fundraising costs	23,900
Direct staff costs, including travel and insurance	68,800
Medical supplies and temporary accommodation	78,120
Food, blankets and clothes	17,100
Transport costs	24,300
Other direct costs	9,800
Apportioned administrative support costs	13,200

Requirement

Prepare a statement to enable managers to monitor the total net cost of the aid programme, highlighting any subtotals that you think may be useful to the managers.

 **Solution**

TW Care Charity
Report on overseas aid programme

	£	£
Income from donations		157,750
Grants received from government and others		62,000
Gross revenue		219,750
Less fundraising costs		23,900
Net revenue		195,850
Direct staff costs, including travel and insurance	68,800	
Medical supplies and temporary accommodation	78,120	
Food, blankets, clothes	17,100	
Transport costs	24,300	
Other direct costs	9,800	
Total direct cost		198,120
Net direct cost of programme		(2,270)
Apportioned administrative support costs		13,200
Total net cost of programme		15,470

Points to note about the statement are as follows.

- The fundraising costs are netted off against the gross revenue. Managers can use the resulting net revenue to monitor the effectiveness of the fundraising activities undertaken.
- Direct costs of the programme are highlighted separately. Managers are able to see whether the net revenue from the fundraising efforts was sufficient to cover the directly identifiable costs of undertaking the programme. In this case, the direct costs exceeded the net fundraising revenue by £2,270.
- Administrative support costs are apportioned so that managers can see the final net impact of this programme on the charity's resources.

10.6 Summary

Having read this chapter the main points you should understand are as follows.

1. Costs can be classified according to their nature, purpose or responsibility.
2. Classification by nature is known as subjective classification.
3. Classification by purpose is known as objective classification.
4. A coding system provides a means of expressing the classification of expenditure in a shortened symbolised form, and a means of accumulating data for analysis purposes.
5. Value added focuses on the value created by an organisation's own efforts. It can be calculated as: sales revenue less cost of materials and bought-in services, or as profit plus interest plus all conversion costs.
6. The output of service organisations is often intangible and 'instantly perishable'. With many services it is impossible to produce the service to hold in inventory for sale at a later date. Capacity utilisation is therefore important.
7. Composite cost units are often used to monitor and control costs in a service organisation.

Revision Questions

? Question 1 Multiple choice

1.1 State which of the following are characteristics of managerial reports prepared in a service organisation:

  (i) a low incidence of work in progress at the end of a period
 (ii) the use of composite cost units
(iii) the use of equivalent units

(A) (i) only
(B) (i) and (ii) only
(C) (ii) only
(D) (i), (ii) and (iii)

1.2 Which of the following is a correct calculation of value added:

(A) Sales revenue − variable production costs
(B) Sales revenue − direct labour costs
(C) Sales revenue − all bought-in costs
(D) Sales revenue − all variable costs.

1.3 An item of expenditure has the composite code number 109.433. The digits 109 indicate the nature of the expenditure, that is, whether it is material, labour or expense. This is:

(A) classification by cost behaviour
(B) classification by responsibility
(C) objective classification
(D) subjective classification

1.4 Records for a passenger limousine company reveal the following data for last period.

No. of passengers	Miles travelled
80	4
40	5
90	6
100	7
140	8
180	9
150	10

The drivers' wages cost incurred was £1,100.
The drivers' wages cost per passenger mile was (to the nearest penny):

(A) £0.03
(B) £0.18
(C) £1.41
(D) £22.45

Question 2 Short objective-test questions

2.1 Match the organisations with the most appropriate cost unit by writing (a), (b), (c), (d) or (e) in the box provided.

Organisations

- Hotel ☐
- Transport service ☐
- College ☐
- Restaurant ☐
- Accountancy service ☐

Cost units

(a) Enrolled student
(b) Meal served
(c) Chargeable hour
(d) Room night
(e) Tonne-kilometre

2.2 Happy Stays hotel has 345 rooms. During the latest week, the following data was collected concerning unoccupied rooms.

Day	Number of unoccupied rooms
Monday	77
Tuesday	43
Wednesday	26
Thursday	31
Friday	17
Saturday	12
Sunday	88

(a) The number of occupied room nights during the week was ⬚.
(b) The overall percentage room occupancy rate during the week was ⬚ % (to the nearest whole number).

❓ **Question 3** Managerial reporting for a service organisation

Happy Returns Ltd operates a haulage business with three vehicles. The following estimated operating costs and performance data are available:

Petrol	£0.50 per km on average
Repairs	£0.30 per km
Depreciation	£1.00 per km, plus £50 per week per vehicle
Drivers' wages	£300.00 per week per vehicle
Supervision costs	£550.00 per week
Loading costs	£6.00 per tonne

During week 26 it is expected that all three vehicles will be used, 280 tonnes will be loaded and a total of 3,950 km travelled (including return journeys when empty) as shown in the following table:

Journey	Tonnes carried (one way)	Kilometres (one way)
1	34	180
2	28	265
3	40	390
4	32	115
5	26	220
6	40	480
7	29	90
8	26	100
9	25	135
	280	1,975

Requirements

(a) The total variable operating cost incurred in week 26 was £ ☐ .

(b) The total fixed operating cost incurred in week 26 was £ ☐ .

(c) The total cost for week 26, including administration cost, amounted to £13,265. To the nearest penny, the average total cost per tonne-kilometre for week 26 was £ ☐ .

❓ **Question 4** Managerial reporting for a service organisation

The Ludford Hotel and Conference Centre is used for conference bookings and private guest bookings. Conference bookings use some bedrooms each week, the balance being available for private guests.

Data has been collected relating to private guest bookings (i.e., non-conference bookings) which are summarised below for a 10-week period.

Week	Double rooms available for private guest bookings	Number of guests	Average stay (nights)
1	55	198	2.1
2	60	170	2.6
3	72	462	1.4
4	80	381	3.2
5	44	83	5.6
6	62	164	3.4
7	80	348	2.6
8	54	205	1.7
9	80	442	1.8
10	24	84	3.2

Some of the costs for private guest bookings vary with the number of guests, regardless of the length of their stay, while others vary with the number of rooms available in any week.

Variable cost per guest	£17.50
Variable cost per week per room available	£56.00

The general fixed cost for private guest bookings per week is £8,100.

Requirements

(a) To the nearest penny, the total costs for private guests' bookings for the 10-week period is £ _____ .

(b) To the nearest whole number, the number of private guest-nights achieved in the 10-week period is _____ .

(c) The number of private guest-nights available for the 10-week period is _____ .

Solutions to Revision Questions

10

✓ Solution 1

Do not rush the narrative multiple choice questions. Take the time to read each question carefully because some of the distractors seem very similar when they are read in a hurry.

1.1 Answer: (B)

Many services are consumed as soon as they are made available to the customer. They cannot be held in inventory for sale at a later date. Therefore there is a low incidence of work in progress at the end of a period.

Composite cost units are often used because they are more useful for control purposes, for example in a haulage company a cost per tonne mile might be more useful for planning and control purposes than a simple cost per tonne.

Equivalent units are more likely to be used in process costing.

1.2 Answer: (C)

Direct labour is not a bought-in cost therefore options A, B and D are incorrect.

1.3 Answer: (D)

Classification by the nature of the expenditure is known as subjective classification.

1.4 Answer: (B)

No. of passengers	Miles travelled	Passenger miles
80	4	320
40	5	200
90	6	540
100	7	700
140	8	1,120
180	9	1,620
150	10	1,500
Total passenger miles		6,000

Drivers' wages cost per passenger mile = £1,100/6,000 = £0.18

Solution 2

2.1
- Hotel (d)
- Transport service (e)
- College (a)
- Restaurant (b)
- Accountancy service (c)

2.2   (a) The number of occupied room nights during the week was 2,121.
   (b) The overall percentage room occupancy rate during the week was 88 per cent.

Workings:
Number of room nights available = 345 × 7 nights = 2,415 room nights
Total number of unoccupied room nights = 294
Number of occupied room nights = 2,415 − 294 = 2,121

Percentage occupancy = 2,121/2,415 = 88%

 Solution 3

- This question provides an example of the use of a composite cost unit. The cost per tonne-kilometre is the cost of transporting 1 tonne for 1 km.

(a) £8,790
(b) £1,600
(c) £0.20

Workings:
Tonne-kilometres

Journey	Tonnes carried	km	Tonne-km
1	34	180	6,120
2	28	265	7,420
3	40	390	15,600
4	32	115	3,680
5	26	220	5,720
6	40	480	19,200
7	29	90	2,610
8	26	100	2,600
9	25	135	3,375
	280	1,975	66,325

			£
Variable operating costs			
Loading: 280 × £6 =			1,680
		£ per km	
Running costs:	Petrol	0.50	
	Repairs	0.30	
	Depreciation	1.00	
		1.80 × 3,950	7,110
			8,790
Fixed operating costs		£	
Depreciation (3 × £50)		150	
Supervision		550	
Drivers' wages (3 × £300)		900	
			1,600
Total operating cost			10,390

$$\text{Average total cost per tonne-kilometre} = \frac{£13,265}{66,325} = £0.20$$

 ## Solution 4

- You will be using a composite cost unit in this question as well: a guest night. The cost per guest night is the cost incurred by the hotel for one guest to stay for one night. In this example, the number of guest nights is calculated as:

  No. of guest nights = no. of guests × average no. of nights stayed

- You will need to prepare some preliminary workings in part (a). The totals to be calculated for the 10-week period are:
  (i) the number of rooms available (you need this in order to calculate the costs incurred);
  (ii) the number of guests (this is also needed for the cost calculation);

(a) £159,613.50
(b) 6,064
(c) 8,554

Workings:

Week	Rooms	Guests	Average stay	Guest nights
1	55	198	2.1	415.8
2	60	170	2.6	442.0
3	72	462	1.4	646.8
4	80	381	3.2	1,219.2
5	44	83	5.6	464.8
6	62	164	3.4	557.6
7	80	348	2.6	904.8
8	54	205	1.7	348.5
9	80	442	1.8	795.6
10	24	84	3.2	268.8
	611	2,537		6,063.9

Total costs for private guests' bookings = (611 × £56) + (2,537 × £17.50)
  + (10 × £8,100) = £159,613.50
Guest nights available = 611 rooms × 7 nights × 2 guests = 8,554.

11

Financial Planning
and Control

Financial Planning and Control

11

LEARNING OUTCOMES

After completing this chapter, you should be able to:

▶ explain why organisations set out financial plans in the form of budgets, typically for a financial year;

▶ prepare functional budgets for material usage and purchase, labour and overheads, including budgets for capital expenditure and depreciation;

▶ prepare a master budget: income statement, balance sheet and cash flow statement, based on the functional budgets;

▶ interpret budget statements and advise managers on financing projected cash short-falls and/or investing projected cash surpluses;

▶ prepare a flexed budget based on the actual levels of sales and production and calculate appropriate variances;

▶ compare and contrast fixed and flexed budgets;

▶ explain the use of budgets in designing reward strategies for managers.

11.1 Introduction

In this chapter, you will learn about budgets: what they are for, how they are prepared, and their use in planning and controlling the activities of an organisation.

11.2 The purposes of budgeting

Budgets have two main roles:

(1) they act as authorities to spend, that is, they give authority to budget managers to incur expenditure in their part of the organisation;

(2) they act as comparators for current performance, by providing a yardstick against which current activities can be monitored.

These two roles are combined in a system of budgetary planning and control.

FINANCIAL PLANNING AND CONTROL

11.2.1 Budgetary planning and control

Planning the activities of an organisation ensures that the organisation sets out in the right direction. Individuals within the organisation will have definite targets which they will aim to achieve. Without a formalised plan the organisation will lack direction and managers will not be aware of their own targets and responsibilities. Neither will they appreciate how their activities relate to those of other managers within the organisation.

A formalised plan will help to ensure a coordinated approach, and the planning process itself will force managers to continually think ahead, planning and reviewing their activities in advance.

However, the budgetary process should not stop with the plan. The organisation has started out in the right direction but to ensure that it continues on course it is the management's responsibility to exercise control.

Control is best achieved by comparison of the actual results with the original plan. Appropriate action can then be taken to correct any deviations from the plan.

The comparison of actual results with a budgetary plan, and the taking of action to correct deviations, is known as feedback control.

The two activities of planning and control must go hand in hand. Carrying out the budgetary planning exercise without using the plan for control purposes is performing only part of the task.

11.2.2 What is a budget?

 A budget could be defined as 'a quantified plan of action relating to a given period of time'.

For a budget to be useful it must be quantified. For example, it would not be particularly useful for the purposes of planning and control if a budget was set as follows:

'We plan to spend as little as possible in running the printing department this year'; or 'We plan to produce as many units as we can possibly sell this quarter'.

These are merely vague indicators of intended direction; they are not quantified plans. They will not provide much assistance in management's task of planning and controlling the organisation.

These 'budgets' could perhaps be modified as follows:

'Budgeted revenue expenditure for the printing department this year is £60,000'; and 'Budgeted production for the quarter is 4,700 units'.

The quantification of the budgets has provided:

(a) a definite target for planning purposes; and
(b) a yardstick for control purposes.

11.2.3 The budget period

You may have noticed that in each of these 'budgets' the time period was different. The first budget was prepared for a year and the second budget was for a quarter. The time period for which a budget is prepared and used is called the budget period. It can be any length to suit management purposes but it is usually one year.

The length of time chosen for the budget period will depend on many factors, including the nature of the organisation and the type of expenditure being considered. Each budget period can be subdivided into control periods, also of varying lengths, depending on the level of control which management wishes to exercise. The usual length of a control period is one month.

11.2.4 Strategic planning, budgetary planning and operational planning

It will be useful at this stage to distinguish in broad terms between three different types of planning:

(1) strategic planning;
(2) budgetary planning;
(3) operational planning.

These three forms of planning are interrelated. The main distinction between them relates to their timespan which may be short term, medium term or long term.

The short term for one organisation may be the medium or long term for another, depending on the type of activity in which it is involved.

Strategic planning

Strategic planning is concerned with preparing long-term action plans to attain the organisation's objectives.

Strategic planning is also known as corporate planning or long-range planning.

Budgetary planning

Budgetary planning is concerned with preparing the short- to medium-term plans of the organisation. It will be carried out within the framework of the strategic plan. An organisation's annual budget could be seen as an interim step towards achieving the long-term or strategic plan.

Operational planning

Operational planning refers to the short-term or day-to-day planning process. It is concerned with planning the utilisation of resources and will be carried out within the framework set by the budgetary plan. Each stage in the operational planning process can be seen as an interim step towards achieving the budget for the period.

Operational planning is also known as tactical planning.

Remember that the full benefit of any planning exercise is not realised unless the plan is also used for control purposes. Each of these types of planning should be accompanied by the appropriate control exercise covering the same time span.

11.3 The preparation of budgets

The process of preparing and using budgets will differ from organisation to organisation. However there are a number of key requirements in the design of a budgetary planning and control process.

11.3.1 Coordination: the budget committee

The need for coordination in the planning process is paramount. The interrelationship between the functional budgets (e.g. sales, production, purchasing) means that one budget cannot be completed without reference to several others.

For example, the purchasing budget cannot be prepared without reference to the production budget, and it may be necessary to prepare the sales budget before the production budget can be prepared. The best way to achieve this coordination is to set up a budget committee. The budget committee should comprise representatives from all functions in the organisation. There should be a representative from sales, a representative from marketing, a representative from personnel and so on.

The budget committee should meet regularly to review the progress of the budgetary planning process and to resolve problems that have arisen. These meetings will effectively bring together the whole organisation in one room, to ensure a coordinated approach to budget preparation.

11.3.2 Participative budgeting

 The CIMA *Terminology* defines participative budgeting as a 'budgeting process where all budget holders have the opportunity to participate in setting their own budgets'.

This may also be referred to as 'bottom-up budgeting'. It contrasts with imposed or top-down budgets where the ultimate budget holder does not have the opportunity to participate in the budgeting process. The advantages of participative budgeting are as follows:

- *Improved quality of forecasts* to use as the basis for the budget. Managers who are doing a job on a day-to-day basis are likely to have a better idea of what is achievable, what is likely to happen in the forthcoming period, local trading conditions, etc.
- *Improved motivation.* Budget holders are more likely to want to work to achieve a budget that they have been involved in setting themselves, rather than one that has been imposed on them by more senior managers. They will own the budget and accept responsibility for the achievement of the targets contained therein.

Detail on the behavioural aspects of budgeting is outside the scope of the *Fundamentals of Management Accounting* syllabus.

The main disadvantage of participative budgeting is that it tends to result in a more extended and complex budgetary process. However, the advantages are generally accepted to outweigh this.

11.3.3 Information: the budget manual

Effective budgetary planning relies on the provision of adequate information to the individuals involved in the planning process.

Many of these information needs are contained in the budget manual.

A budget manual is a collection of documents which contains key information for those involved in the planning process. Typical contents could include the following:

(a) An introductory explanation of the budgetary planning and control process including a statement of the budgetary objective and desired results.

Participants should be made aware of the advantages to them and to the organisation of an efficient planning and control process. This introduction should give participants an understanding of the workings of the planning process, and of the sort of information that they can expect to receive as part of the control process.

(b) A form of organisation chart to show who is responsible for the preparation of each functional budget and the way in which the budgets are interrelated.

(c) A timetable for the preparation of each budget. This will prevent the formation of a 'bottleneck', with the late preparation of one budget holding up the preparation of all others.

(d) Copies of all forms to be completed by those responsible for preparing budgets, with explanations concerning their completion.

(e) A list of the organisation's account codes, with full explanations of how to use them.

(f) Information concerning key assumptions to be made by managers in their budgets, for example, the rate of inflation, key exchange rates, etc.

(g) The name and location of the person to be contacted concerning any problems encountered in preparing budgetary plans. This will usually be the coordinator of the budget committee (the budget officer) and will probably be a senior accountant.

11.3.4 Early identification of the principal budget factor

The principal budget (key budget) factor is the factor which limits the activities of the organisation. The early identification of this factor is important in the budgetary planning process because it indicates which budget should be prepared first.

The principal budget factor was referred to in Chapter 4 as the limiting factor.

For example, if sales volume is the principal budget factor, then the sales budget must be prepared first, based on the available sales forecasts. All other budgets should then be linked to this.

Alternatively machine capacity may be limited for the forthcoming period and therefore machine capacity is the principal budget factor. In this case, the production budget must be prepared first and all other budgets must be linked to this.

Failure to identify the principal budget factor at an early stage could lead to delays at a later stage when managers realise that the targets they have been working with are not feasible.

11.3.5 The interrelationship of budgets

The critical importance of the principal budget factor stems from the fact that all budgets are interrelated. For example, if sales is the principal budget factor this is the first budget to be prepared. This will then provide the basis for the preparation of several other budgets including the selling expenses budget and the production budget.

However, the production budget cannot be prepared directly from the sales budget without a consideration of inventory policy. For example, management may plan to increase finished goods inventory in anticipation of a sales drive. Production quantities would then have to be higher than the budgeted sales level. Similarly, if a decision is taken to reduce the level of material inventories held, it would not be necessary to purchase all of the materials required for production.

11.3.6 Using computers in budget preparation

A vast amount of data is involved in the budgetary planning process and managing this volume of data in a manual system is an onerous and cumbersome task.

A computerised budgetary planning system will have the following advantages over a manual system:

- computers can easily handle the volume of data involved;
- a computerised system can process the data more rapidly than a manual system;
- a computerised system can process the data more accurately than a manual system;
- computers can quickly and accurately access and manipulate the data in the system.

Organisations may use specially designed budgeting software. Alternatively, a well-designed spreadsheet model can take account of all of the budget interrelationships described above.

The model will contain variables for all of the factors about which decisions must be made in the planning process, for example, sales volume, unit costs, credit periods and inventory volumes.

If managers wish to assess the effect on the budget results of a change in one of the decision variables, this can be accommodated easily by amending the relevant variable in the spreadsheet model. The effect of the change on all of the budgets will be calculated instantly so that managers can make better informed planning decisions.

> This process of reviewing the effect of changes in the decision variables is called 'what-if?' analysis. For example, managers can rapidly obtain the answer to the question, 'What if sales volumes are 10 per cent lower than expected?'.

Budgetary planning is an iterative process. Once the first set of budgets has been prepared, those budgets will be considered by senior managers. The criteria used to assess the suitability of budgets may include adherence to the organisation's long-term objectives, profitability and liquidity. Computerised spreadsheet models then provide managers with the ability to amend the budgets rapidly, and adjust decision variables until they feel that they have achieved the optimum plan for the organisation for the forthcoming period.

11.3.7 The master budget

> The master budget is a summary of all the functional budgets. It usually comprises the budgeted income statement, budgeted balance sheet and budgeted cash flow statement.

It is this master budget which is submitted to senior managers for approval because they should not be burdened with an excessive amount of detail. The master budget is designed to give the summarised information that they need to determine whether the budget is an acceptable plan for the forthcoming period.

11.4 Preparation of functional budgets

The best way to see how budgets are prepared is to work through an example.

Example: Preparing a functional budget

A company manufactures two products, Aye and Bee. Standard cost data for the products for next year are as follows:

	Product Aye per unit	Product Bee per unit
Direct materials:		
X at £2 per kg	24 kg	30 kg
Y at £5 per kg	10 kg	8 kg
Z at £6 per kg	5 kg	10 kg
Direct wages:		
Unskilled at £6 per hour	10 hours	5 hours
Skilled at £10 per hour	6 hours	5 hours

Budgeted inventories for next year are as follows:

	Product Aye units	Product Bee units
1 January	400	800
31 December	500	1,100

	Material X kg	Material Y kg	Material Z kg
1 January	30,000	25,000	12,000
31 December	35,000	27,000	12,500

Budgeted sales for next year: product Aye 2,400 units; product Bee 3,200 units.

You are required to prepare the following budgets for next year:

(a) production budget, in units;
(b) material usage budget, in kilos;
(c) material purchases budget, in kilos and £;
(d) direct labour budget, in hours and £.

Solution

(a) *Production budget for next year*

	Product Aye units	Product Bee units
Sales units required	2,400	3,200
Closing inventory at end of year	500	1,100
	2,900	4,300
Less opening inventory	400	800
Production units required	2,500	3,500

(b) *Material usage budget for next year*

	Material X kg	Material Y kg	Material Z kg
Requirements for production:			
Product Aye[1]	60,000	25,000	12,500
Product Bee	105,000	28,000	35,000
Total material usage	165,000	53,000	47,500

> *Note 1*: Material X for product Aye:
> 2,500 units produced × 24 kg = 60,000 kg
> The other material requirements are calculated in the same way.

(c) *Material purchases budget for next year*

	Material X kg	Material Y kg	Material Z kg	Total
Material required for production	165,000	53,000	47,500	
Closing inventory at end of year	35,000	27,000	12,500	
	200,000	80,000	60,000	
Less opening inventory	30,000	25,000	12,000	
Material purchases required	170,000	55,000	48,000	
Standard price per kg	£2	£5	£6	
Material purchases value	£340,000	£275,000	£288,000	£903,000

(d) *Direct labour budget for next year*

	Unskilled labour hours	Skilled labour hours	Total
Requirements for production:			
Product Aye[1]	25,000	15,000	
Product Bee	17,500	17,500	
Total hours required	42,500	32,500	
Standard rate per hour	£6	£10	
Direct labour cost	£255,000	£325,000	£580,000

> *Note 1:* Unskilled labour for product Aye:
> 2,500 units produced × 10 hours = 25,000 hours
> The other labour requirements are calculated in the same way.

11.4.1 Budget interrelationships

This example has demonstrated how the data from one functional budget becomes an input in the preparation of another budget. The last budget in the sequence, the direct labour budget, would now be used as an input to other budgets. The material purchases budget will also provide input data for other budgets.

For example, the material purchases budget would probably be used in preparing the payables budget, taking account of the company's intended policy on the payment of suppliers. The payables budget would indicate the payments to be made to suppliers, which would then become an input for the cash budget, and so on.

The cash budget is the subject of the next section of this chapter.

11.5 The cash budget

The cash budget is one of the most vital planning documents in an organisation. It will show the cash effect of all of the decisions taken in the planning process.

Management decisions will have been taken concerning such factors as inventory policy, credit policy, selling price policy and so on. All of these plans will be designed to meet the objectives of the organisation. However, if there are insufficient cash resources to finance the plans they may need to be modified or perhaps action might be taken to alleviate the cash restraint.

A cash budget can give forewarning of potential problems that could arise so that managers can be prepared for the situation or take action to avoid it.

 The use of forecasts to modify actions so that potential threats are avoided or opportunities exploited is known as feedforward control.

There are four possible cash positions that could arise:

Cash position	Possible management action
• *Short-term deficit*	Arrange a bank overdraft, reduce receivables and inventories, increase payables
• *Long-term deficit*	Raise long-term finance, such as long-term loan capital or share capital
• *Short-term surplus*	Invest short term, increase receivables and inventories to boost sales, pay suppliers early to obtain cash discount
• *Long-term surplus*	Expand or diversify operations, replace or update non-current assets

Notice that the type of action taken by management will depend not only on whether a deficit or a surplus is expected, but also on how long the situation is expected to last.

For example, management would not wish to use surplus cash to purchase non-current assets, if the surplus was only short term and the cash would soon be required again for day-to-day operations.

Cash budgets therefore forewarn managers of whether there will be cash surpluses or cash deficits, and how long the surpluses or deficits are expected to last.

11.5.1 Preparing cash budgets

Before we work through a full example of the preparation of a cash budget, it will be useful to discuss a few basic principles.

(a) The format for cash budgets

There is no definitive format which should be used for a cash budget. However, whichever format you decide to use it should include the following:

(i) *A clear distinction between the cash receipts and cash payments for each control period.* Your budget should not consist of a jumble of cash flows. It should be logically arranged with a subtotal for receipts and a subtotal for payments.

(ii) *A figure for the net cash flow for each period.* It could be argued that this is not an essential feature of a cash budget. However, you will find it easier to prepare and use a cash budget if you include the net cash flow. Also, managers find in practice that a figure for the net cash flow helps to draw attention to the cash flow implications of their actions during the period.

(iii) *The closing cash balance for each control period.* The closing balance for each period will be the opening balance for the following period.

(b) Depreciation is not included in cash budgets

Remember that depreciation is not a cash flow. It may be included in your data for overheads and must therefore be excluded before the overheads are inserted into the cash budget.

(c) Allowance must be made for bad and doubtful debts

Bad debts will never be received in cash and doubtful debts may not be received. When you are forecasting the cash receipts from customers you must remember to adjust for these items, if necessary.

Example: cash budget

Watson Ltd is preparing its budgets for the next quarter. The following information has been drawn from the budgets prepared in the planning exercise so far:

Sales value		
	June (estimate)	£12,500
	July (budget)	£13,600
	August	£17,000
	September	£16,800
Direct wages	£1,300 per month	
Direct material purchases	June (estimate)	£3,450
	July (budget)	£3,780
	August	£2,890
	September	£3,150

Other information
- Watson sells 10 per cent of its goods for cash. The remainder of customers receive one month's credit.
- Payments to material suppliers are made in the month following purchase.
- Wages are paid as they are incurred.
- Watson takes one month's credit on all overheads.

- Production overheads are £3,200 per month.
- Selling, distribution and administration overheads amount to £1,890 per month.
- Included in the amounts for overhead given above are depreciation charges of £300 and £190, respectively.
- Watson expects to purchase a delivery vehicle in August for a cash payment of £9,870.
- The cash balance at the end of June is forecast to be £1,235.

You are required to prepare a cash budget for each of the months July to September.

Solution

Watson Ltd cash budget for July to September

	July £	August £	September £
Sales receipts:			
10% in cash	1,360	1,700	1,680
90% in one month	11,250	12,240	15,300
Total receipts	12,610	13,940	16,980
Payments			
Material purchases (one month credit)	3,450	3,780	2,890
Direct wages	1,300	1,300	1,300
Production overheads[1]	2,900	2,900	2,900
Selling, distribution and administration overhead[1]	1,700	1,700	1,700
Delivery vehicle	–	9,870	–
Total payments	9,350	19,550	8,790
Net cash inflow/(outflow)	3,260	(5,610)	8,190
Opening cash balance	1,235	4,495	(1,115)
Closing cash balance at the end of the month	4,495	(1,115)	7,075

Note 1: Depreciation has been excluded from the overhead payment figures because it is not a cash item.

11.5.2 Interpretation of the cash budget

This cash budget forewarns the management of Watson Limited that their plans will lead to a cash deficit of £1,115 at the end of August. They can also see that it will be a short-term deficit and can take appropriate action.

They may decide to delay the purchase of the delivery vehicle or perhaps negotiate a period of credit before the payment will be due. Alternatively overdraft facilities may be arranged for the appropriate period.

The important point to appreciate is that management should take appropriate action for a forecast short-term deficit. For example, it would not be appropriate to arrange a five year loan to manage a cash deficit that is expended to last for only one month.

If it is decided that overdraft facilities are to be arranged, it is important that due account is taken of the timing of the receipts and payments within each month.

For example, all of the payments in August may be made at the beginning of the month but receipts may not be expected until nearer the end of the month. The cash deficit could then be considerably greater than it appears from looking only at the month-end balance.

If the worst possible situation arose, the overdrawn balance during August could become as large as £4,495 − £19,550 = £15,055. If management had used the month-end balances as a guide to the overdraft requirement during the period then they would not have arranged a large enough overdraft facility with the bank. It is important therefore, that they look in detail at the information revealed by the cash budget, and not simply at the closing cash balances.

 ## Exercise 11.1

Practise what you have just learned about cash budgets by attempting this exercise before you look at the solution.

The following information relates to XY Ltd:

Month	Wages incurred £000	Materials purchases £000	Overhead £000	Sales £000
February	6	20	10	30
March	8	30	12	40
April	10	25	16	60
May	9	35	14	50
June	12	30	18	70
July	10	25	16	60
August	9	25	14	50

(a) It is expected that the cash balance on 31 May will be £22,000.
(b) The wages may be assumed to be paid within the month they are incurred.
(c) It is company policy to pay suppliers for materials three months after receipt.
(d) Credit customers are expected to pay two months after delivery.
(e) Included in the overhead figure is £2,000 per month which represents depreciation on two cars and one delivery van.
(f) There is a one-month delay in paying the overhead expenses.
(g) Ten per cent of the monthly sales are for cash and 90 per cent are sold on credit.
(h) A commission of 5 per cent is paid to agents on all the sales on credit but this is not paid until the month following the sales to which it relates; this expense is not included in the overhead figures shown.
(i) It is intended to repay a loan of £25,000 on 30 June.
(j) Delivery is expected in July of a new machine costing £45,000 of which £15,000 will be paid on delivery and £15,000 in each of the following two months.
(k) Assume that overdraft facilities are available if required.

You are required to prepare a cash budget for each of June, July and August.

Solution

Cash budget for June, July and August

	June £	July £	August £
Receipts			
Receipts from credit sales[1]	54,000	45,000	63,000
Cash sales[2]	7,000	6,000	5,000
	61,000	51,000	68,000
Payments			
Wages	12,000	10,000	9,000
Materials[3]	30,000	25,000	35,000
Overhead[4]	12,000	16,000	14,000
Commission[5]	2,250	3,150	2,700
Loan repayment	25,000		
Payments for new machine		15,000	15,000
	81,250	69,150	75,700
Net cash inflow/(outflow)	(20,250)	(18,150)	(7,700)
Opening balance	22,000	1,750	(16,400)
Closing balance	1,750	(16,400)	(24,100)

Explanatory notes

1. The cash received from credit sales is 90 per cent of the sales made 2 months before, that is, for June, 90 per cent of April sales = 90 per cent × £60,000.
2. Cash sales are 10 per cent of the sales made in the month.
3. March purchases are paid for three months later in June, and so on.
4. May overheads, less depreciation = £14,000 − £2,000 = £12,000. These are paid in cash in June, and so on.
5.

	May	June	July
Credit sales (90%)	£45,000	£63,000	£54,000
5% commission	£2,250	£3,150	£2,700

These amounts for commission are paid 1 month later, that is, in June, July and August.

11.6 A complete exercise

Now that you have seen how to prepare functional budgets and cash budgets, have a go at the following exercise. It requires you to work from basic data to produce a number of functional budgets, as well as the master budget, that is, budgeted cash flow, income statement and balance sheet.

Exercise 11.2

C Ltd makes two products, Alpha and Beta. The following data is relevant for year 3:

| Material prices: | Material M | £2 per unit |
| | Material N | £3 per unit |

Direct labour is paid £10 per hour.

Production overhead cost is estimated to be £200,000, which includes £25,000 for depreciation of property and equipment. Production overhead cost is absorbed into product costs using a direct labour hour absorption rate.

Each unit of finished product requires:

	Alpha	*Beta*
Material M	12 units	12 units
Material N	6 units	8 units
Direct labour	7 hours	10 hours

The sales director has forecast that sales of Alpha and Beta will be 5,000 and 1,000 units, respectively, during year 3. The selling prices will be:

| Alpha | £182 per unit |
| Beta | £161 per unit |

She estimates that the inventory at 1 January, year 3, will be 100 units of Alpha and 200 units of Beta. At the end of year 3 she requires the inventory level to be 150 units of each product.

The production director estimates that the raw material inventories on 1 January, year 3, will be 3,000 units of material M and 4,000 units of material N. At the end of year 3 the inventories of these raw materials are to be:

| M: | 4,000 units |
| N: | 2,000 units |

The finance director advises that the rate of tax to be paid on profits during year 3 is likely to be 30 per cent. Selling and administration overhead is budgeted to be £75,000 in year 3, which includes £5,000 for depreciation of equipment.

A quarterly cash-flow forecast has already been completed and is set out below:

	1	2	3	4
Quarter, year 3	£	£	£	£
Receipts	196,000	224,000	238,000	336,000
Payments:				
Materials	22,000	37,000	40,000	60,000
Direct wages	100,000	110,500	121,000	117,000
Overhead	45,000	50,000	70,000	65,000
Taxation	5,000			
Machinery purchase			120,000	

The company's balance sheet at 1 January, year 3, is expected to be as follows:

	£ Cost	£ Depreciation	£ Net
Non current assets			
Land	50,000	–	50,000
Buildings and equipment	400,000	75,000	325,000
	450,000	75,000	375,000
Current assets			
Inventories			
– raw materials	20,000		
– finished goods	15,000		
		35,000	
Receivables		25,000	
Cash at bank		10,000	
		70,000	
Current liabilities			
Payables	9,000		
Taxation	5,000		
		14,000	
			56,000
			431,000
Financed by			
Share capital			350,000
Retained earnings			81,000
			431,000

You are required to prepare the company's budgets for year 3 including a budgeted income statement for the year and a balance sheet at 31 December, year 3.

 Solution

Note the order in which the budgets are prepared. The sales budget determines production requirements, which in turn determines materials usage, which in turn determines materials purchases and then payments to suppliers. Since the sales budget is prepared first, sales are termed the principal (key) budget factor.

Sales budget for the year ended 31 December, year 3

	Alpha	Beta	Total
Sales volume	5,000	1,000	
Selling price	£182	£161	
Sales revenue	£910,000	£161,000	£1,071,000

Production budget for the year ended 31 December, year 3

	Alpha units	Beta units
Required by sales	5,000	1,000
Required closing inventory	150	150
	5,150	1,150
Less expected opening inventory	100	200
Production required	5,050	950

Raw materials usage budget for the year ended 31 December, year 3

	Materital M units	Material N units
Required by production of Alpha[1]	60,600	30,300
Required by production of Beta	11,400	7,600
Total raw material usage	72,000	37,900

Note 1: The material usage for Alpha is determined as follows:

	Units
Material M: 5,050 × 12	60,600
Material N: 5,050 × 6	30,300

The material requirements for Beta are calculated in the same way.

Raw materials purchases budget for the year ended 31 December, year 3

	Material M units	Material N units	Total
Raw materials required by production	72,000	37,900	
Required closing inventory	4,000	2,000	
	76,000	39,900	
Less expected opening inventory	3,000	4,000	
Quantity to be purchased	73,000	35,900	
Price per unit	£2	£3	
Value of purchases	£146,000	£107,700	£253,700

Direct labour budget for the year ended 31 December, year 3

	Labour hours	Rate per hour £	Labour cost £
Product Alpha – 5,050 units	35,350	10	353,500
Product Beta – 950 units	9,500	10	95,000
	44,850		448,500

Production cost budget: preliminary workings

$$\text{Production overhead absorption rate} = \frac{£200,000}{44,850} = £4.459 \text{ per labour hour}$$

Overhead absorbed by Alpha = 35,350 hours × £4.459 = £157,626
Overhead absorbed by Beta = 9,500 hours × £4.459 = £42,361

Production cost budget for the year ended 31 December, year 3

	Alpha £	Beta £
Direct materials		
– M²	121,200	22,800
– N	90,900	22,800
Direct wages	353,500	95,000
Production overhead	157,626	42,361
	723,226	182,961
Cost per unit (used for closing inventory valuation)	£143.21	£192.59

Note 2: The direct material cost for Alpha is determined as follows:

Material	Usage (units)	£
M	60,600 @ £2	121,200
N	30,300 @ £3	90,900

The material cost for Beta is calculated in the same way.

Cash budget for the year ended 31 December, year 3

Quarter	1 £	2 £	3 £	4 £
Receipts	196,000	224,000	238,000	336,000
Payments:				
Materials	22,000	37,000	40,000	60,000
Direct wages	100,000	110,500	121,000	117,000
Overhead	45,000	50,000	70,000	65,000
Taxation	5,000			
Machinery purchase			120,000	
Total payments	172,000	197,500	351,000	242,000
Net cash inflow/(outflow)	24,000	26,500	(113,000)	94,000
Balance b/fwd[3]	10,000	34,000	60,500	(52,500)
Balance c/fwd	34,000	60,500	(52,500)	41,500

Note 3: The balance b/fwd in quarter 1 is the cash at bank on the forecast balance sheet for 1 January, year 3.

Budgeted income statement for the year ended 31 December, year 3

	£	£
Revenue		1,071,000
Opening inventory of raw materials[4]	20,000	
Purchases of raw materials	253,700	
	273,700	
Closing inventory of raw materials[5]	14,000	
	259,700	
Direct wages	448,500	
Production overhead	200,000	
Production cost of goods completed	908,200	
Opening inventory of finished goods[4]	15,000	
	923,200	
Closing inventory of finished goods[5]	50,370	
Production cost of goods sold		872,830
Gross profit		198,170
Selling and administration overhead		75,000
Net profit before taxation		123,170
Taxation		36,951
		86,219
Retained earnings b/f		81,000
Retained earnings c/f		167,219

Note 4: The opening inventory figures for raw materials and finished goods are taken from the opening balance sheet.

Note 5: The closing inventories are calculated as follows:

	£
Raw materials:	
M: 4,000 × £2	8,000
N: 2,000 × £3	6,000
	14,000
Finished goods:	
Alpha: 150 × £143.21	21,481.50
Beta: 150 × £192.59	28,888.50
	50,370.00

Budgeted balance sheet at 31 December, year 3

	Cost £	Depreciation £	Net £
Non-current assets			
Land	50,000	–	50,000
Buildings and equipment[6]	520,000	105,000	415,000
	570,000	105,000	465,000
Current assets			
Inventories			
– raw materials	14,000		
– finished goods	50,370		
		64,370	
Receivables[7]		102,000	
Cash at bank		41,500	
		207,870	
Current liabilities			
Payables[8]	118,700		
Taxation	36,951		
		155,651	
			52,219
			517,219
Financed by			
Share capital			350,000
Retained earnings			167,219
			517,219

	£000
Note 6: Buildings and equipment	
Opening cost balance	400
Purchases during year	120
	520
Opening depreciation balance	75
Production depreciation	25
Selling depreciation	5
	105
Note 7: Receivables	
Opening balance	25
Sales	1,071
Receipts (cash budget)	(994)
	102

	£	£
Note 8: Closing payables balance		
Opening balance of payables		9,000
Material purchases from budget		253,700
Overhead, excluding depreciation:*		
Production		175,000
Selling and administration		70,000
		507,700
Less payments (from cash budget):		
Materials	159,000	
Overhead	230,000	
		389,000
Closing balance of payables		118,700

*The depreciation must be excluded from the overhead because it is not a cash item, i.e. it is not a payment which must be made to suppliers.

11.7 Rolling budgets

> The CIMA *Terminology* defines a rolling budget as a 'budget continuously updated by adding a further accounting period (month or quarter) when the earliest accounting period has expired. Its use is particularly beneficial where future costs and/or activities cannot be forecast accurately'.

For example, a budget may initially be prepared for January to December, year 1. At the end of the first quarter, that is, at the end of March, year 1, the first quarter's budget is deleted. A further quarter is then added to the end of the remaining budget, for January to March, year 2. The remaining portion of the original budget is updated in the light of current conditions. This means that managers have a full year's budget always available and the rolling process forces them continually to plan ahead.

A system of rolling budgets is also known as *continuous budgeting*. Rolling budgets can be particularly useful when future events cannot be forecast reliably.

It is not necessary for all of the budgets in a system to be prepared on a rolling basis. For example, many organisations will use a rolling system for the cash budget only.

In practice, most organisations carry out some form of updating process on all their budgets, so that the budgets represent a realistic target for planning and control purposes. The formalised budgetary planning process will still be performed on a regular basis to ensure a coordinated approach to budgetary planning.

11.8 Budgets for non-operating functions

So far in this chapter, we have been concentrating mainly on budgets for operating functions. You have seen that once the principal budget factor has been identified and budgeted, most of the operating budgets can be linked to and coordinated with this one. The level of expenditure is thus directly linked to the level of activity.

Budgets for non-operating functions such as computer services, and research and development are only indirectly linked to activity levels. Determining the level of expenditure to be included in these non-operating budgets is not quite so straightforward.

11.8.1 Incremental budgeting

Many non-operating budgets are set using an incremental approach. This means that the budget for each period is based on the budget or actual results for the previous period, adjusting for any expected changes and inflation.

This approach is unlikely to result in the optimum allocation of resources. It tends to perpetuate inefficient and unnecessary practices, and may result in *budget slack*, which is unnecessary expenditure built into the budget.

11.8.2 Zero-based budgeting

Zero-based budgeting (ZBB) was developed as an alternative to the incremental approach.

 The CIMA *Terminology* defines ZBB as a 'method of budgeting that requires all costs to be specifically justified by the benefits expected.'

Zero-based budgeting is so called because it requires each budget to be prepared and justified from zero, instead of simply using last year's budget or actual results as a base. Incremental levels of expenditure on each activity are evaluated according to the resulting incremental benefits. Available resources are then allocated where they can be used most effectively.

The major advantage of ZBB exercises is that managers are forced to consider alternative ways of achieving the objectives for their activity and they are required to justify the activities which they currently undertake. This helps to eliminate or reduce the incidence of *budget slack*, which is the intentional overestimation of expenses and/or underestimation of revenues in the budgeting process.

A detailed discussion of ZBB is outside the scope of your *Fundamentals of Management Accounting* syllabus, but you should be aware that there are a number of different approaches to budgetary planning.

11.9 Budgetary control information

You have now learned about the basic principles underlying the budgetary planning process. You have seen how budgets are created to guide and coordinate the activities of individuals within the organisation, to ensure that the organisation starts out in the right direction.

In the remainder of this chapter, you will see how budgets are used for control purposes to ensure that the organisation continues in the right direction.

Budgetary control is achieved by comparing the actual results with the budget. The differences are calculated as variances and management action may be taken to investigate and correct the variances if necessary or appropriate.

FINANCIAL PLANNING AND CONTROL

- If costs are higher or revenues are lower than the budget, then the difference is an adverse variance.
- If costs are lower or revenues are higher than the budget, then the difference is a favourable variance.

11.9.1 Budget centres

 The CIMA *Terminology* defines a budget centre as a 'section of an entity for which control may be exercised through prepared budgets'.

Each budget centre is often a responsibility centre. Each centre will have its own budget and a manager will be responsible for managing the centre and controlling the budget. This manager is often referred to as the budget holder. Regular budgetary control reports will be sent to each budget holder so that they may monitor their centre's activities and take control action if necessary.

11.9.2 Budgetary control reports

If managers are to use the budgets to control effectively, they must receive regular control information.

The budgetary control reports should be:

(a) *Timely*. The information should be made available as soon as possible after the end of the control period. Corrective action will be much more effective if it is taken soon after the event, and adverse trends could continue unchecked if budgetary reporting systems are slow.

(b) *Accurate*. Inaccurate control information could lead to inappropriate management action. There is often a conflict between the need for timeliness and the need for accuracy. More accurate information might take longer to produce. The design of budgetary reporting systems should allow for sufficient accuracy for the purpose to be fulfilled.

(c) *Relevant to the recipient*. Busy managers should not be swamped with information that is not relevant to them. They should not need to search through a lot of irrelevant information to reach the part which relates to their area of responsibility. The natural reaction of managers in this situation could be to ignore the information altogether.

The budgetary reporting system should ideally be based on the *exception principle* which means that management attention is focused on those areas where performance is significantly different from budget. Subsidiary information could be provided on those items which are in line with the budget.

Many control reports also segregate controllable and non-controllable costs and revenues, that is, the costs and revenues over which managers can exercise control are highlighted separately in the reports from those over which they have no control.

A number of accounting packages have the facility to record actual and budget details against each account code for each budget centre. These may then be printed in the form of a report.

(d) *Communicated to the correct manager*. Control information should be directed to the manager who has the responsibility and authority to act upon it. If the information is communicated to the wrong manager its value will be immediately lost and any adverse trends may continue uncorrected. Individual budget holders' responsibilities must be clearly defined and kept up to date in respect of any changes.

11.10 Fixed and flexible budgets

When managers are comparing the actual results with the budget for a period, it is important to ensure that they are making a valid comparison. The use of flexible budgets can help to ensure that actual results are monitored against realistic targets.

11.10.1 Flexible budgets: an example

An example will demonstrate how flexible budgets may be used.

A company manufactures a single product and the following data show the actual results for costs for the month of April compared with the budgeted figures.

Operating statement for April

	Actual	*Budget*	*Variance*
Units produced	1,000	1,200	(200)
	£	£	£
Direct material	16,490	19,200	2,710
Direct labour	12,380	13,200	820
Production overhead	24,120	24,000	(120)
Administration overhead	21,600	21,000	(600)
Selling and distribution o/head	16,200	16,400	200
Total cost	90,790	93,800	3,010

Note: Variances in brackets are *adverse*.

Looking at the costs incurred in April, a cost saving of £3,010 has been made compared with the budget. However, the number of units produced was 200 less than budget so some savings in expenditure might be expected. It is not possible to tell from this comparison how much of the saving is due to efficient cost control, and how much is the result of the reduction in activity.

The type of budget being used here is a fixed budget. A fixed budget is one which remains unchanged regardless of the actual level of activity. In situations where activity levels are likely to change, and there is a significant proportion of variable costs, it is difficult to control expenditure satisfactorily with a fixed budget.

If costs are mostly fixed, then changes in activity levels will not cause problems for cost comparisons with fixed budgets.

A flexible budget can help managers to make more valid comparisons. It is designed to show the allowed expenditure for the actual number of units produced and sold. Comparing this flexible budget with the actual expenditure, it is possible to distinguish genuine efficiencies.

11.10.2 Preparing a flexible budget

Before a flexible budget can be prepared, managers must identify which costs are fixed and which are variable. The allowed expenditure on variable costs can then be increased or decreased as the level of activity changes. You will recall that fixed costs are those costs which will not increase or decrease over the relevant range of activity. The allowance for these items will therefore remain constant.

We can now continue with the example.

Management has identified that the following budgeted costs are fixed:

	£
Direct labour	8,400
Production overhead	18,000
Administration overhead	21,000
Selling and distribution overhead	14,000

It is now possible to identify the expected variable cost per unit produced.

	Original budget (a)	Fixed cost (b)	Variable cost (c) = (a) − (b)	V'ble cost per unit = (c)/1,200
Units produced	1,200			
	£	£	£	£
Direct material	19,200	–	19,200	16
Direct labour	13,200	8,400	4,800	4
Production overhead	24,000	18,000	6,000	5
Administration overhead	21,000	21,000	–	–
Selling and distribution o/head	16,400	14,000	2,400	2
	93,800	61,400	32,400	27

Now that managers are aware of the fixed costs and the variable costs per unit it is possible to 'flex' the original budget to produce a budget cost allowance for 1,000 units produced.

The budget cost allowance for each item is calculated as follows:

Cost allowance = Budgeted fixed cost
+ (number of units produced × variable cost per unit)

For the costs that are wholly fixed or wholly variable, the calculation of the budget cost allowance is fairly straightforward. The remaining costs are semi-variable, which you will recall means that they are partly fixed and partly variable. For example, the budget cost allowance for direct labour is calculated as follows:

Cost allowance for direct labour = £8,400 + (1,000 × £4) = £12,400

A full flexible budget can now be produced.

Flexible budget comparison for April

| | Cost allowances | | | | |
	Fixed	Variable	Total	Actual cost	Variance
	£	£	£	£	£
Direct material	–	16,000	16,000	16,490	(490)
Direct labour	8,400	4,000	12,400	12,380	20
Production overhead	18,000	5,000	23,000	24,120	(1,120)
Administration overhead	21,000	–	21,000	21,600	(600)
Selling and distn. o/h	14,000	2,000	16,000	16,200	(200)
Total cost	61,400	27,000	88,400	90,790	(2,390)

Note: Variances in brackets are adverse.

This revised analysis shows that in fact the cost was £2,390 higher than would have been expected from a production volume of 1,000 units.

The cost variances in the flexible budget comparison are almost all adverse. These over-spendings were not revealed when a fixed budget was used and managers may have been under the false impression that costs were being adequately controlled.

11.10.3 The total budget variance

If we now produce a statement showing the fixed budget, the flexible budget and the actual results together, it is possible to analyse the total variance between the original budget and the actual results.

	Fixed budget	Flexible budget	Actual results	Expenditure variances
	£	£	£	£
Direct material	19,200	16,000	16,490	(490)
Direct labour	13,200	12,400	12,380	20
Production overhead	24,000	23,000	24,120	(1,120)
Administrative overhead	21,000	21,000	21,600	(600)
Selling and distribution overhead	16,400	16,000	16,200	(200)
	93,800	88,400	90,790	(2,390)

5,400 Volume variance   (2,390) Expenditure variance

3,010 Total variance

The total variance is therefore made up of two parts:

(1) the volume variance of £5,400 favourable, which is the expected cost saving resulting from producing 200 units less than budgeted;

(2) the expenditure variance of £2,390 adverse, which is the net total of the over- and under-expenditure on each of the costs for the actual output of 1,000 units.

 Notice that the volume variance is the saving in standard variable cost: 200 units $\times$ £27 per unit $=$ £5,400.

In Chapter 5, you learned how some of the expenditure variances can be analysed between their price and usage elements – for example, how much of the variance is caused by paying the wrong price per hour of labour (the labour rate variance), or per kilogram of material (the material price variance), and how much is caused by using the wrong quantity of material or labour (the usage and efficiency variances).

11.10.4 Using flexible budgets for planning

You should appreciate that while flexible budgets can be useful for control purposes they are not particularly useful for planning. The original budget must contain a single target level of activity so that managers can plan such factors as the resource requirements and the product pricing policy. This would not be possible if they were faced with a range of possible activity levels – although managers will of course consider a range of possible activity levels *before* they select the target budgeted activity level.

The budget can be designed so that the fixed costs are distinguished from the variable costs. This will facilitate the preparation of a budget cost allowance for control purposes at the end of each period, when the actual activity is known.

11.10.5 Flexible budgets: another example

Now that you have got the idea of how a flexible budget can be prepared, work through the following example to consolidate your understanding.

In this example, as in practice, you will need to investigate the cost behaviour patterns to determine which costs are fixed, which are variable and which are semi-variable.

The first step in investigating cost behaviour patterns is to look at the cost data. You should be able to easily spot any fixed costs because they remain constant when activity levels change.

The easiest way to identify the behaviour patterns of non-fixed costs is to divide each cost figure by the related activity level. If the cost is a linear variable cost, then the cost per unit will remain constant. For a semi-variable cost the unit rate will reduce as the activity level increases, because the same basic amount of fixed costs is being spread over a greater number of units.

You will then need to recall how to use the high–low method to determine the fixed and variable elements of any semi-variable costs. Look back to Chapter 1 if you have forgotten how the high–low method works.

Example

Lawrence Ltd operates a system of flexible budgets and the flexed budgets for expenditure for the first two quarters of year 3 were as follows:

Flexed budgets – quarters 1 and 2

	Quarter 1	Quarter 2
Activity		
Sales units	9,000	14,000
Production units	10,000	13,000
Budget cost allowances	£	£
Direct materials	130,000	169,000
Production labour	74,000	81,500
Production overhead	88,000	109,000
Administration overhead	26,000	26,000
Selling and distribution overhead	29,700	36,200
Total budget cost allowance	347,700	421,700

Despite a projected increase in activity, the cost structures in quarters 1 and 2 are expected to continue during quarter 3 as follows:

(a) The variable cost elements behave in a linear fashion in direct proportion to volume. However, for production output in excess of 14,000 units the unit variable cost for production labour increases by 50 per cent. This is due to a requirement for overtime working and the extra amount is payable only on the production above 14,000 units.
(b) The fixed cost elements are not affected by changes in activity levels.
(c) The variable elements of production costs are directly related to production volume.
(d) The variable element of selling and distribution overhead is directly related to sales volume.

You are required to prepare a statement of the budget cost allowances for quarter 3, when sales were 14,500 units and production was 15,000 units.

Solution

If you divide each cost figure by the relevant activity figure, you will find that the only wholly variable cost is direct material, at £13 per unit.

You can also see that the only wholly fixed cost is administration overhead since this is a constant amount for both activity levels, £26,000.

For the remaining costs you will need to use the high–low method to determine the fixed and variable elements.

Production labour

	Production, units	£
Quarter 2	13,000	81,500
Quarter 1	10,000	74,000
Change	3,000	7,500

$$\text{Variable cost per unit} = \frac{£7,500}{3,000} = £2.50 \text{ per unit}$$
$$\text{Fixed cost} = £81,500 - (£2.50 \times 13,000) = £49,000$$

Production overhead

	Production, units	£
Quarter 2	13,000	109,000
Quarter 1	10,000	88,000
Change	3,000	21,000

$$\text{Variable cost per unit} = \frac{£21,000}{3,000} = £7 \text{ per unit}$$

$$\text{Fixed cost} = £109,000 - (£7 \times 13,000) = £18,000$$

Selling and distribution overhead

Note that the example data says that selling and distribution overhead is related to sales volume.

	Sales, units	£
Quarter 2	14,000	36,200
Quarter 1	9,000	29,700
	5,000	6,500

$$\text{Variable cost per unit sold} = \frac{£6,500}{5,000} = £1.30 \text{ per unit}$$

$$\text{Fixed cost} = £36,200 - (£1.30 \times 14,000) = £18,000$$

We can now prepare a statement of the budget cost allowances for quarter 3.

	Quarter 3 Budget cost allowance	
	£	£
Direct material (15,000 units × £13)		195,000
Production labour:[1]		
Fixed	49,000	
Variable up to 14,000 units (14,000 × £2.50)	35,000	
Variable above 14,000 units (1,000 × £3.75)	3,750	
		87,750
Production overhead:		
Fixed	18,000	
Variable (15,000 × £7)	105,000	
		123,000
Administration overhead: fixed		26,000
Selling and distribution overhead:		
Fixed	18,000	
Variable (14,500 × £1.30)[2]	18,850	
		36,850
Total budget cost allowance		468,600

Note 1: The unit variable cost for production labour increases by 50 per cent for production over 14,000 units.

Note 2: The flexible budget allowance for selling and distribution overhead must be based on the sales volume of 14,500 units.

11.10.6   Extrapolating outside the relevant range

In the preceding example, you were told that the cost structures would remain unaltered despite the increase in activity. In practice, if you need to do a similar extrapolation outside the range for which you have available data, you should always state the assumption that the observed behaviour patterns will still be applicable.

11.10.7   Example: producing a flexible budget control statement

G Limited produces and sells a single product. The budget for the latest period is as follows.

	£
Sales revenue (12,600 units)	277,200
Variable costs	
Direct material	75,600
Direct labour	50,400
Production overhead	12,600
Fixed costs	
Production overhead	13,450
Other overhead	10,220
	162,270
Budget profit	114,930

The actual results for the period were as follows.

	£
Sales revenue (13,200 units)	303,600
Variable costs	
Direct material	78,350
Direct labour	51,700
Production overhead	14,160
Fixed costs	
Production overhead	13,710
Other overhead	10,160
	168,080
Actual profit	135,520

Required

Prepare a flexible budget control statement and comment on the results.

Solution

The budgeted sales revenue and the budget cost allowances for the variable costs are increased by a factor of 13,200/12,600 to derive the flexed budget for the actual activity achieved during the period. The budget cost allowance for the fixed costs remains unaltered.

Flexible budget control statement for the latest period

	Original budget	Flexed budget	Actual results	Variance
Activity (units)	12,600	13,200	13,200	
	£	£	£	£
Sales revenue	277,200	290,400	303,600	13,200
Variable costs				
Direct material	75,600	79,200	78,350	850
Direct labour	50,400	52,800	51,700	1,100
Production overhead	12,600	13,200	14,160	(960)
Fixed costs				
Production overhead	13,450	13,450	13,710	(260)
Other overhead	10,220	10,220	10,160	60
	162,270	168,870	168,080	790
Profit	114,930	121,530	135,520	13,990

Note: variances in brackets are adverse

Comments

1. The total budget variance can be analysed as follows.

	£	£
Sales volume variance* (£121,530 − £114,930)		6,600
Sales price variance	13,200	
Expenditure variance	790	
		13,990
Total budget variance (£135,520 − £114,930)		20,590

*You can calculate the sales volume variance separately as a check on the budget figures: increase in sales volume above budget × standard contribution per unit = (13,200 − 12,600) × £((277,200 − 75,600 − 50,400 − 12,600)/12,600) = 600 units × £11 standard contribution = £6,600 favourable

2. The favourable sales price variance indicates that a higher selling price than standard was charged for the units sold. Despite the higher price the sales volume achieved was higher than budgeted.
3. Expenditure on direct material, direct labour and other overhead costs was lower than the budget cost allowance for the activity level achieved. It is not possible to tell from the data provided whether the savings were achieved as a result of a lower price or a lower usage of resources.
4. Expenditure on production overhead costs, both fixed and variable, was higher than the budget cost allowance for the activity level achieved.

11.11   Using budgets as a basis for rewards

Budgets may be used as a basis for reward strategies for managers. In this situation, the budget acts as a target for achievement and the budget holder's success in meeting the budget might be rewarded by the payment of a bonus.

11.11.1   Example

The maintenance manager has a budget cost allowance each period based on the actual number of maintenance hours worked in the period. He is paid a bonus of 10% of any savings he achieves against the flexible budget cost allowance.

Budgeted fixed maintenance costs are £17,800 per period and the budgeted variable maintenance cost allowance is £14 per maintenance hour worked.

The number of maintenance hours worked in the latest period was 120 and the actual total maintenance cost incurred was £17,600.

Requirement

Calculate the amount of any bonus payable to the manager.

Solution

Flexible budget cost allowance = £17,800 + (£14 × 120 hours) = £19,480
Actual maintenance cost incurred   £17,600
Savings achieved against the flexible budget cost allowance   £1,880

Bonus payable = 10% × £1,880 = £188

11.11.2   Factors to consider in the design of budget reward schemes

The potential to earn a bonus by the achievement of a budget target can create a powerful incentive for budget holders. However, a number of factors should be considered in the design of reward strategies.

- A flexible budget system should be used where appropriate so that the budget holder's performance is monitored against a realistic revenue and expenditure target for the actual level of activity achieved.
- Managers who are responsible for setting their own budgets in a participative budgeting system might set easy targets for themselves and build in budgetary slack in order to improve their chances of earning a bonus. If the targets are not realistic as a result of this budget padding then the budget will not be useful as a planning or control document.
- Managers who are aiming to achieve a bonus based on their short-term budget performance might be tempted to cut back on expenditure which is necessary for the longer-term strategy of the organisation, for example, training and development expenditure, that is, the budget reward system might encourage short termism.
- Managers might become demotivated if they fail to achieve their budget targets, and thus do not earn a bonus, due to factors which are outside their control. A manager should not be monitored against any budget target over which they are not able to exercise control.

Therefore a reward system based on the achievement of budget targets should be designed and operated with due regard for the possible impact on managers' behaviour.

11.12 Summary

Having read this chapter, the main points that you should understand are as follows.

1. A budget is a quantified plan of action relating to a given period of time. An organisation's annual budget is set within the framework of the long-term strategic plans.

2. The budget committee coordinates the preparation of budgets and issues the budget manual which provides information to those involved in the planning and control process.

3. The principal (key) budget factor is the factor which limits the activities of the organisation. The budget for the principal factor should be prepared first.

4. The master budget is the summary of all the functional budgets, usually including a budgeted income statement, balance sheet and cash flow statement.

5. Cash budgets allow for feedforward control by forewarning managers of the cash effect of all their planning decisions.

6. Rolling or continuous budgets are continuously updated by adding a further period when the earliest period has expired.

7. Incremental budgeting involves using the prior period's budget or actual results as a basis for the next year's budget. Zero-based budgeting begins each year's budget from scratch.

8. A fixed budget is prepared for a single activity level. A flexible budget is more useful for control because it recognises cost and revenue behaviour patterns and the budget cost allowance for each cost and revenue is designed to change as the volume of activity changes.

9. Budgets may be used as a basis for reward strategies for managers.

Revision Questions

❓ **Question 1** Multiple choice

1.1 When preparing a production budget, the quantity to be produced equals:

    (A) sales quantity + opening inventory + closing inventory.
    (B) sales quantity − opening inventory + closing inventory.
    (C) sales quantity − opening inventory − closing inventory.
    (D) sales quantity + opening inventory − closing inventory.

1.2 A job requires 2,400 actual labour hours for completion and it is anticipated that there will be 20 per cent idle time. If the wage rate is £10 per hour, what is the budgeted labour cost for the job?

    (A) £19,200
    (B) £24,000
    (C) £28,800
    (D) £30,000.

1.3 The term 'budget slack' refers to:

    (A) the extended lead time between the preparation of the functional budgets and the master budget.
    (B) the difference between the budgeted output and the breakeven output.
    (C) the additional capacity available which can be budgeted for.
    (D) the deliberate overestimation of costs and underestimation of revenues in a budget.

1.4 Of the four costs shown below, which would not be included in the cash budget of an insurance firm?

    (A) depreciation of non-current assets
    (B) commission paid to agents
    (C) office salaries
    (D) capital cost of a new computer.

1.5 The following details have been extracted from the receivables collection records of C Limited:

Invoice paid in the month after sale	60%
Invoice paid in the second month after sale	25%
Invoice paid in the third month after sale	12%
Bad debts	3%

Invoices are issued on the last day of each month.

Customers paying in the month after sale are entitled to deduct a 2 per cent settlement discount.

Credit sales values for June to September are budgeted as follows:

June	July	August	September
£35,000	£40,000	£60,000	£45,000

The amount budgeted to be received from credit sales in September is

(A) £47,280
(B) £47,680
(C) £48,850
(D) £49,480.

1.6 A flexible budget is:

(A) a budget which, by recognising different cost behaviour patterns, is designed to change as the volume of activity changes.
(B) a budget for a defined period of time which includes planned revenues, expenses, assets, liabilities and cash flow.
(C) a budget which is prepared for a period of one year which is reviewed monthly, whereby each time actual results are reported, a further forecast period is added and the intermediate period forecasts are updated.
(D) a budget of semi-variable production costs only.

1.7 The following extract is taken from the production cost budget of S Limited:

Production (units)	2,000	3,000
Production cost (£)	11,100	12,900

The budget cost allowance for an activity level of 4,000 units is

(A) £7,200
(B) £14,700
(C) £17,200
(D) £22,200.

1.8 A master budget comprises:

(A) the budgeted income statement.
(B) the budgeted cash flow, budgeted income statement and budgeted balance sheet.
(C) the budgeted cash flow.
(D) the entire set of budgets prepared.

1.9 A recent budgetary control report shows the following information:

	Fixed budget £	Flexible budget £	Actual results £
Total sales revenue	585,847	543,776	563,945
Total variable costs	440,106	418,482	425,072
Total contribution	145,741	125,294	138,873

The sales volume contribution variance for the period was:

(A) £6,868 adverse
(B) £13,579 favourable
(C) £20,447 adverse
(D) £42,071 adverse

1.10 Budgeted sales of product Y next period are 8,690 units. Each unit of product Y requires 8 kg of material Z. Budgeted inventories are as follows:

	Product Y units	Material Z kg
Opening inventory	875	6,300
Closing inventory	920	6,180

The budgeted purchases of material Z, in kg, next period are:

(A) 8,615
(B) 69,280
(C) 69,760
(D) 69,880

Question 2 Short objective-test questions

2.1 *Tick the correct box.*
A participative budgeting system may also be described as a:

bottom-up budget ☐
top-down budget ☐

2.2 Which of the following items of information would be contained in the budget manual? (Tick all that are correct.)

(a) An organisation chart. ☐
(b) The timetable for budget preparation. ☐
(c) The master budget. ☐
(d) A list of account codes. ☐
(e) Sample forms to be completed during the budgetary process. ☐

2.3 Is the following statement *true* or *false?*
The principal budget factor is always the forecast sales volume.

True ☐
False ☐

2.4 Assuming that sales volume is the principal budget factor, place the following budgets in the order that they would be prepared in the budgetary planning process. Indicate the correct order by writing 1, 2, 3, etc. in the boxes provided.

☐ Sales budget
☐ Materials purchases budget
☐ Materials inventory budget

FINANCIAL PLANNING AND CONTROL

☐ Production budget
☐ Finished goods inventory budget
☐ Materials usage budget.

2.5 PR Ltd's cash budget forewarns of a short-term surplus. Which of the following would be appropriate actions to take in this situation? (Select all that are correct).

(a) Increase receivables and inventory to boost sales. ☐
(b) Purchase new non-current assets. ☐
(c) Repay long-term loans. ☐
(d) Pay suppliers early to obtain a cash discount. ☐

2.6 Each finished unit of product H contains 3 litres of liquid L. Ten per cent of the input of liquid L is lost through evaporation in the production process. Budgeted output of product H for June is 3,000 units. Budgeted inventories of liquid L are:

- Opening inventory, 1 June   1,200 litres
- Closing inventory, 30 June   900 litres

The required purchases of liquid L for June are [＿＿＿＿＿] litres.

2.7 *Tick the correct box.*

A system of budgeting whereby the budget is continuously updated by adding a further accounting period when the earliest accounting period has expired, is known as a system of:

rolling budgets   ☐
incremental budgets   ☐

2.8 The totals from KM Ltd's budgetary control report for February are as follows;

	Fixed budget	*Flexible budget*	*Actual results*
	£	£	£
Total sales revenue	124,310	135,490	134,580
Total variable costs	93,480	98,450	97,920
Total contribution	30,830	37,040	36,660

Complete the following table, ticking the box to indicate whether the variance is adverse or favourable.

	£	Adverse	Favourable
Sales price variance	[＿＿＿]	☐	☐
Sales volume contribution variance	[＿＿＿]	☐	☐
Total expenditure variance	[＿＿＿]	☐	☐
Total budget variance	[＿＿＿]	☐	☐

2.9 Which of the following best describes the principle of reporting by exception?

Sending budget reports only to those exceptional managers who are able to understand their content. ☐

Providing detailed reports only on those areas of the business that are performing exceptionally well and providing only subsidiary information about other areas of the business. □

Providing detailed reports only on those areas of the business that are not performing according to budget and providing only subsidiary information about aspects that are in line with budget. □

2.10 F Limited uses a flexible budgeting system to control the costs incurred in its staff canteen.

The budget cost allowance for consumable materials is flexed according to the average number of employees during the period.

Complete the following equation by inserting '+', '−' or '×' as appropriate in the boxes:

Flexible budget = budgeted fixed □ (budgeted variable □ average no.)
cost allowance   cost   (cost per employee   of employees)
for consumable
materials

2.11 The following extract is taken from the catering costs budget of a company that provides training courses.

Number of delegates	120	170
Catering cost	£1,470	£2,020

In a flexible budget for 185 delegates, the budget cost allowance for catering costs will be £ ⬜

2.12 The distribution manager is paid a bonus of 5% of any savings he achieves against a flexible budget cost allowance for distribution costs each period.

The budget cost allowances for distribution costs for the previous two periods were as follows.

Tonnes distributed	Budget cost allowance £
11,200	118,400
16,100	152,700

In the latest period, the number of tonnes distributed was 13,200 and the distribution cost incurred was £130,900.

The bonus payable to the distribution manager for the period is £ ⬜

? Question 3 Functional budgets

An ice cream manufacturer is in the process of preparing budgets for the next few months, and the following draft figures are available:

Sales forecast	
June	6,000 cases
July	7,500 cases
August	8,500 cases
September	7,000 cases
October	6,500 cases

Each case uses 2.5 kg of ingredients and it is policy to have inventories of ingredients at the end of each month to cover 50 per cent of next month's production.

There are 750 cases of finished ice cream in inventory on 1 June and it is policy to have inventories at the end of each month to cover 10 per cent of the next month's sales.

Requirements

(a) The production budget (in cases) for June and July will be:

June
July

(b) The ingredient purchases budget (in kg) for August will be

Question 4 Cash budget

A small manufacturing firm is to commence operations on 1 July. The following estimates have been prepared:

	July	August	September
Sales (units)	10	36	60
Production (units)	40	50	50
Opening inventory (units) NIL			

It is planned to have raw material inventories of £10,000 at the end of July, and to maintain inventories at that level thereafter.

Selling prices, costs and other information:

	Per unit £
Selling price	900
Material cost	280
Labour cost	160
Variable overheads	40

Fixed overheads are expected to be £5,000 per month, including £1,000 depreciation.

Settlement terms on sales: 10 per cent cash, the balance payable the month following sale. Labour is paid in the month incurred, and all other expenditures the following month.

Requirements

(a) The budgeted cash receipts from sales are:

July   £
August   £
September   £

(b) The budgeted cash payments for raw materials are:

July   £
August   £
September   £

(c) The total of the budgeted cash payments for labour and overhead in August is £ ☐ .

(d) A cash budget can be used to give forewarning of potential cash problems that could arise so that managers can take action to avoid them. This is known as:

feedforward control ☐
feedback control ☐

(e) A cash budget is continuously updated to reflect recent events and changes to forecast events. This type of budget is known as a:

flexible budget ☐
rolling budget ☐

Question 5 Flexible budget

The Arcadian Hotel operates a budgeting system and budgets expenditure over eight budget centres as shown below. Analysis of past expenditure patterns indicates that variable costs in some budget centres vary according to occupied room nights (ORN), while in others the variable proportion of costs varies according to the number of visitors (V).

The budgeted expenditures for a period with 2,000 ORN and 4,300 V were as follows:

Budget centre	Variable costs vary with:	Budgeted expenditure £	Partial cost analysis — Budget expenditure includes:
Cleaning	ORN	13,250	£2.50 per ORN
Laundry	V	15,025	£1.75 per V
Reception	ORN	13,100	£12,100 fixed
Maintenance	ORN	11,100	£0.80 per ORN
Housekeeping	V	19,600	£11,000 fixed
Administration	ORN	7,700	£0.20 per ORN
Catering	V	21,460	£2.20 per V
General overheads	–	11,250	all fixed
		112,485	

In period 9, with 1,850 ORN and 4,575 V, actual expenditures were as follows:

Budget centre	Actual expenditure £
Cleaning	13,292
Laundry	14,574
Reception	13,855
Maintenance	10,462
Housekeeping	19,580
Administration	7,930
Catering	23,053
General overheads	11,325
	114,071

Requirements

(a) The total budget cost allowances for the following costs in the flexible budget for period 9 are:

	£
Cleaning	
Laundry	
Reception	
Maintenance	
Housekeeping	
General overheads	

(b) The total budget cost allowance in the flexible budget for period 9 is £113,521.

The total expenditure variance for period 9 is £ [   ]. The variance is:

adverse   ☐
favourable   ☐

Solutions to Revision Questions

☑ Solution 1

- In question 1.2 you cannot simply add 20 per cent to the actual labour hours to allow for the idle time. The idle time is 20 per cent of the hours to be paid for, so you will need to think more carefully about how to make the adjustment.
- In question 1.5 remember that the 3 per cent bad debts will never be received in cash.

1.1 Answer: (B)

Requirements for closing inventory increase the amount to be produced, so these must be added. The available opening inventory reduces production requirements, so this must be deducted.

1.2 Answer: (D)

Idle time is 20 per cent of the total hours to be paid for. Therefore, hours to be paid for = 2,400/0.8 = 3,000. Budgeted labour cost = 3,000 × £10 = £30,000.

1.3 Answer: (D)

A manager might build some slack into a budget to provide some 'leeway' to disguise unnecessary spending.

1.4 Answer: (A)

Depreciation is not a cash flow.

1.5 Answer: (D)

Amount to be received in September is:

	£
60% of August sales less 2% discount:	
£60,000 × 60% × 98%	35,280
25% of July sales: £40,000 × 25%	10,000
12% of June sales: £35,000 × 12%	4,200
	49,480

1.6 Answer: (A)

A flexible budget is designed to show the budgeted costs and revenues at different levels of activity.

1.7   Answer: (B)

Increase in cost	£1,800
Increase in production	1,000 units
Variable costs: £1,800/1,000	£1.80/unit

	£
Variable cost of 2,000 units	3,600
Total cost of 2,000 units	11,100
Fixed cost	7,500
Variable cost of 4,000 units	7,200
Fixed cost	7,500
	14,700

1.8   Answer: (B).

1.9   Answer: (C)

The sales volume contribution variance is the reduction in the budgeted contribution for the period.
Sales volume contribution variance = £(125,294 − 145,741) = £20,447 adverse

1.10   Answer: (C)

Product Y production budget	*Units*
Sales volume	8,690
Closing inventory	920
	9,610
Less opening inventory	875
Production required	8,735
Materials usage budget	*kg*
Production units 8,735 × 8 kg	69,880
Material Z purchases budget	*kg*
Required for production	69,880
Closing inventory	6,180
	76,060
Less opening inventory	6,300
Budgeted purchases	69,760

✓ Solution 2

2.1   A participative budgeting system may also be described as a *bottom-up* budget.

2.2   (a), (b), (d) and (e) would be contained in a budget manual. The master budget (c) is the end result of the budgetary planning process.

2.3   *False.* The forecast sales volume will often be the principal budget factor or limiting factor, but this is not always the case.

2.4   1. Sales budget
   2. Finished goods inventory budget
   3. Production budget

4. Materials usage budget
5. Materials inventory budget
6. Materials purchases budget

2.5 (a) and (d) would be appropriate actions in this situation. Actions (b) and (c) would not be appropriate because they would involve investing the surplus funds for too long.

2.6

	Litres
Liquid L required for finished output (3,000 units × 3 litres)	9,000
Evaporation loss $\left(\times \dfrac{10}{90}\right)^{*}$	1,000
Total required input of liquid L	10,000
Less: reduction in inventory	300
Required purchases of liquid L	9,700

*evaporation loss is 10 per cent of *input*

2.7 A system of budgeting whereby the budget is continuously updated by adding a further accounting period when the earliest accounting period has expired is known as a system of *rolling budgets*. It is also known as a *continuous budgeting* system.

2.8

	£	
Sales price variance[1] £(134,580 − 135,490)	910	Adverse
Sales volume contribution variance[2] £(37,040 − 30,830)	6,210	Favourable
Expenditure variance[3] £(98,450 − 97,920)	530	Favourable
Total budget variance[4] £(36,660 − 30,830)	5,830	Favourable

Notes:

1. The sales price variance is the difference between the sales revenue that was achieved and the sales revenue that would be expected for the actual activity level that occurred (that is, the sales revenue in the flexible budget).
2. The sales volume contribution variance is the additional standard contribution that arose as a result of the change in the sales volume from the original budget.
3. The expenditure variance is the difference between the actual expenditure and the expenditure that would be expected for the actual activity achieved.
4. The total budget variance is the difference between the original budget contribution and the actual contribution achieved.

2.9 Exception reporting involves providing detailed reports only on those areas of the business that are not performing according to budget and providing only subsidiary information about aspects that are in line with budget. This ensures that management do not receive too much information and that their attention is focused where control action is most needed.

2.10 Flexible budget = budgeted fixed $\boxed{+}$ (budgeted variable $\boxed{\times}$ average no.)
cost allowance   cost   (cost per employee   of employees)
for consumable
materials

2.11 In a flexible budget for 185 delegates the budget cost allowance for catering costs will be **£2,185**

Delegates	£
170	2,020
120	1,470
50	550

Variable catering cost per delegate = £550/50 = £11
Fixed catering cost = £2,020 − £(170 × 11) = £150
Budget cost allowance for 185 delegates = £150 + £(185 × 11) = £2,185.

2.12 The bonus payable to the distribution manager for the period is £75.

Tonnes distributed	Budget cost allowance £
11,200	118,400
16,100	152,700
4,900	34,300

Variable distribution cost per tonne delivered   = £34,300/4,900 = £7
Fixed distribution cost = £118,400 − (11,200 × £7) = £40,000
Budget cost allowance for 13,200 tonnes delivered   = £40,000 + (13,200 × £7)
     = £132,400
Savings against budget cost allowance   = £132,400 − £130,900
     = 1,500
Bonus payable   = 5% × £1,500 = £75

☑ Solution 3

- Use a clear columnar layout for your budget workings. Although your workings will not earn marks, clear workings help you to avoid arithmetical errors because 100 per cent accuracy is vital.
- Do not forget to adjust for the budgeted movement in inventory in parts (a) and (b). A common error is to get the opening and closing inventory calculations the wrong way round.

(a) June: 6,000
     July: 7,600
(b) August: 19,125

Workings:
Production budget (in cases)

	June	July	August	September
Cases to be sold	6,000	7,500	8,500	7,000
Closing inventory	(7,500 × 10%) 750	(8,500 × 10%) 850	(7,000 × 10%) 700	(6,500 × 10%) 650
Opening inventory	(750)	(750)	(850)	(700)
Production budget	6,000	7,600	8,350	6,950

Ingredients purchases budget (in kg)

		August
Quantity to be used in production	(8,350 × 2.5)	20,875
Quantity in closing inventory	(6,950 × 2.5 × 50%)	8,687.5
Quantity in opening inventory	(8,350 × 2.5 × 50%)	(10,437.5)
Ingredients purchases budget		19,125.0

 ## Solution 4

- Remember to exclude depreciation from the fixed overhead figures. Depreciation is not a cash flow.
- Read the wording of the question carefully to determine the timing of each cash flow.

(a)

July	£900
August	£11,340
September	£34,560

Workings:

	£	£
July: 10% × (10 × £900)		900
August: 90% × July sales (10 × £900)	8,100	
10% × August sales (36 × £900)	3,240	
		11,340
September: 90% × August sales (36 × £900)	29,160	
10% × September sales (60 × £900)	5,400	
		34,560

(b)

July	£0
August	£21,200
September	£14,000

Workings:
Cash payments each month are for the previous month's purchases. Therefore, no payments are made in July.

	£	£
August: payment for July closing inventory	10,000	
payment for July usage (40 × £280)	11,200	
		21,200
September: payment for August usage (50 × £280)		14,000

(c) £13,600

Workings:

	£
August labour cost paid in month incurred (50 × £160)	8,000
July variable overhead cost paid in August (40 × £40)	1,600
Fixed overhead cash cost (£5,000 − £1,000 depreciation)	4,000
	13,600

(d) This is known as *feedforward* control.
(e) This type of budget is known as a *rolling* budget.

✓ Solution 5

- A common error in this type of question is to calculate the expenditure variance (part (b)) by comparing the actual results with the budget supplied in the question. This is the budget for quite different activity levels, so the flexed budget should be used instead.

(a)

	£
Cleaning	12,875
Laundry	15,506
Reception	13,025
Maintenance	10,980
Housekeeping	20,150
General overheads	11,250

Workings:

	Activity (ORN/V)	Variable cost per unit £	Variable cost allowance £	Fixed cost allowance £	Total budget cost allowance £
Cleaning	1,850	2.50	4,625	8,250[1]	12,875
Laundry	4,575	1.75	8,006	7,500[2]	15,506
Reception	1,850	0.50[3]	925	12,100	13,025
Maintenance	1,850	0.80	1,480	9,500[4]	10,980
Housekeeping	4,575	2.00[5]	9,150	11,000	20,150
General o/heads	–	–	–	11,250	11,250

		£
1.	Total budget cost allowance for 2,000 ORN	13,250
	Less variable allowance (2,000 × £2.50)	5,000
	Fixed cost allowance	8,250
2.	£15,025 − (4,300 × £1.75) = £7,500	

3.

	£
Total budget cost allowance for 2,000 ORN	13,100
Less fixed allowance	12,100
Variable cost allowance for 2,000 ORN	1,000
Variable cost allowance per ORN: $\dfrac{£1,000}{2,000}$	£0.50

4. $£11,100 - (2,000 \times £0.80) = £9,500$

5. $\dfrac{(£19,600 - £11,000)}{4,300} = £2$ per visitor

(b) £550 adverse

Workings:

	£	
Flexible budget expenditure	113,251	
Actual expenditure	114,071	
Expenditure variance	550	adverse

Preparing for the
Assessment

Preparing for the Assessment

This chapter is intended for use when you are ready to start revising for your assessment. It contains:

- ► Details of the format of the assessment.
- ► A summary of useful revision techniques.
- ► Guidance on how to tackle the assessment.
- ► A bank of assessment-standard revision questions and suggested solutions.
- ► Two mock assessments. These should be attempted when you consider yourself to be ready for the assessment, and you should simulate assessment conditions when you attempt them.

Format of the assessment

The assessment for *Fundamentals of Management Accounting* is a two hour computer-based assessment (CBA) comprising 50 objective test questions with one or more parts. There will be no choice of questions and all questions should be attempted if time permits. There is no penalty for incorrect answers.

Objective test questions are used. The most common type is multiple choice, where the candidate is required to select the correct answer from a list of possible options. Other types of objective test questions that may be used include true/false questions, matching pairs of text and graphic, sequencing and ranking, labelling diagrams and single and multiple numeric entry. Candidates answer the questions by pointing and clicking the mouse, moving objects around the screen, typing numbers, or a combination of these responses.

CIMA are continuously developing the question styles within the cba system and you are strongly advised to try the online demo at www.cimaglobal.com/cba. This will enable you to gain familiarity with the assessment software and to keep track of the latest style of questions being used. You are also advised to keep an eye on the articles in the 'Study Notes' section of *Financial Management* magazine which will forewarn of any changes in question styles.

Revision technique

Planning

The first thing to say about revision is that it is an addition to your initial studies, not a substitute for them. In other words, don't coast along early in your course in the hope

353

of catching up during the revision phase. On the contrary, you should be studying and revising concurrently from the outset. At the end of each week, and at the end of each month, get into the habit of summarising the material you have covered to refresh your memory of it.

As with your initial studies, planning is important to maximise the value of your revision work. You need to balance the demands for study, professional work, family life and other commitments. To make this work, you will need to think carefully about how to make best use of your time.

Begin by comparing the estimated hours you will need to devote to revision with the hours available to you in the weeks leading up to the assessment. Prepare a written schedule setting out the areas you intend to cover during particular weeks, and break that down further into topics for each day's revision. To help focus on the key areas try to establish which areas you are weakest on, so that you can concentrate on the topics where effort is particularly needed.

Do not forget the need for relaxation, and for family commitments. Sustained intellectual effort is only possible for limited periods, and must be broken up at intervals by lighter activities. And do not continue your revision timetable right up to the moment when you enter the assessment room; you should aim to stop work a day or even two days before the assessment. Beyond this point, the most you should attempt is an occasional brief look at your notes to refresh your memory.

Getting down to work

By the time you begin your revision you should already have settled into a fixed work pattern: a regular time of day for doing the work, a particular location where you sit, particular equipment that you assemble before you begin and so on. If this is not already a matter of routine for you, think carefully about it now in the last vital weeks before the assessment.

You should have notes summarising the main points of each topic you have covered. Begin each session by reading through the relevant notes and trying to commit the important points to memory.

Usually this will be just your starting point. Unless the area is one where you already feel very confident, you will need to track back from your notes to the relevant chapter(s) in the *Learning System*. This will refresh your memory on points not covered by your notes and fill in the detail that inevitably gets lost in the process of summarisation.

When you think you have understood and memorised the main principles and techniques, attempt some assessment questions. At this stage of your studies, you should normally be expecting to complete the questions in something close to the actual time allocation allowed in the assessment. After completing your effort, check the solution provided and add to your notes any extra points it reveals.

Tips for the final revision phase

As the assessment looms closer, consider the following list of techniques and make use of those that work for you:

- Summarise your notes into a more concise form, perhaps on index cards that you can carry with you for revision on the way to work.
- Go through your notes with a highlighter pen, marking key concepts and definitions.

- Summarise the main points in a key area by producing a wordlist, mind map or other mnemonic device.
- On areas that you find difficult, rework questions that you have already attempted, and compare your answers with those provided in the *Learning System*.
- Rework questions you attempted earlier in your studies with a view to completing them within the time limits.
- In the week preceding the assessment, quickly go through any recent articles in the 'Study Notes' section of *Financial Management* magazine, paying particular attention to those relevant to your subject.
- Avoid late-night study, as your assessment is based on daytime performance, not night-time performance.
- Make sure that you cover the whole syllabus in your revision, as all questions in the assessment are compulsory.

How to tackle the assessment

Assessment day

- Before leaving for the assessment you should ensure that you know where you are going: plan your route and ensure that you have the necessary documentation and your calculator with you. It is advisable to bring a second calculator and some spare batteries!
- Arrive early and settle into your assessment environment. You will have enough nerves on the day without compounding them by arriving late.

The assessment

Multiple-choice questions

Multiple-choice questions (MCQs) are broken down into two parts; the problem or task to be solved, and the options you must choose from. There is only ever one correct answer: the other options are known as distractors.

Your approach to MCQs should be as follows:

- For numerical MCQs, in the majority of cases you will need to do some rough workings.
- Never rush to select your answer; some options might *initially* look plausible, but on closer scrutiny turn out to be distractors. Unless you are certain of the answer, look carefully at *all* the options before choosing.
- If you are finding the MCQ difficult and you are taking up too much time, move on to the next one.
- Time permitting, revisit those MCQs which you left unanswered and refer to your original workings.
- Remember: you must *never* omit to answer any question in the assessment as there is no penalty for an incorrect answer.

Other types of question

- Prepare neat workings where necessary *for your own benefit*. Only your final answers will be marked, not workings, methods or justifications. However, your workings will help you to achieve the necessary 100 per cent accuracy.
- Check your answer carefully. If you have typed in your answer, check the figures are typed correctly.
- *Never* omit to answer a question. There is no penalty for an incorrect answer.

Revision Questions

The following table indicates the main learning outcome covered by each question in the bank that follows. Once you have revised each topic you can attempt the relevant question(s). However you should be aware that some questions relate to more than one learning outcome.

Learning outcome	Question number(s)
Explain why organizations need to know how much products, processes and services cost and why they need costing systems;	5
Explain the idea of a cost object;	5
Explain the concept of a direct cost and an indirect cost;	6,13
Explain why the concept of cost needs to be qualified as direct, full, marginal, etc. in order to be meaningful;	7
Distinguish between the historical cost of an asset and the economic value of an asset to an organisation;	11
Apply first-in-first-out (FIFO), last-in-first-out (LIFO) and average cost (AVCO) methods of accounting for stock, calculating stock values and related gross profit;	8, 9, 10, 12
Explain why FIFO is essentially a historical cost method, while LIFO approximates economic cost;	11
Prepare cost statements for allocation and apportionment of overheads, including between reciprocal service departments;	14,18,19
Calculate direct, variable and full costs of products, services and activities using overhead absorption rates to trace indirect costs to cost units;	14, 15, 16, 17, 18, 19, 20, 53
Explain the use of cost information in pricing decisions, including marginal cost pricing and the calculation of 'full cost' based prices to generate a specified return on sales or investment;	21, 53, 54
Explain how costs behave as product, service or activity levels increase or decrease;	1, 2, 4
Distinguish between fixed, variable and semi-variable costs;	1, 4

Explain step costs and the importance of time-scales in their treatment as either variable or fixed;	2
Compute the fixed and variable elements of a semi-variable cost using the high-low method and 'line of best fit' method;	3
Explain the contribution concept and its use in Cost–Volume–Profit (CVP) analysis;	22, 23, 24
Calculate and interpret the breakeven point, profit target, margin of safety and profit/volume ratio for a single product or service;	22, 23, 24, 27, 28
Prepare breakeven charts and profit/volume graphs for a single product or service;	25, 26, 29
Calculate the profit maximising sales mix for a multi-product company that has limited demand for each product and one other constraint or limiting factor;	30, 31
Explain the difference between ascertaining costs after the event and planning by establishing standard costs in advance;	32
Explain why planned standard costs, prices and volumes are useful in setting a benchmark for comparison and so allowing managers' attention to be directed to areas of the business that are performing below or above expectation;	32
Calculate standard costs for the material, labour and variable overhead cost elements of cost of a product or service;	33
Calculate variances for material, labour, variable overhead, sales prices and sales volumes;	34, 35, 36, 37, 38, 39, 40
Prepare a statement that reconciles budgeted contribution with actual contribution;	41
Interpret statements of variances for variable costs, sales prices and sales volumes including possible inter-relations between cost variances, sales price and volume variances, and cost and sales variances;	42, 43
Discuss the possible use of standard labour costs in designing incentive schemes for factory and office workers;	44
Explain the principles of manufacturing accounts and the integration of the cost accounts with the financial accounting system;	45, 46, 47, 48
Prepare a set of integrated accounts, given opening balances and appropriate transactional information, and show standard cost variances;	49, 50
Compare and contrast job, batch, contract and process costing;	18, 51
Prepare ledger accounts for job, batch and process costing systems;	52, 53, 54, 56, 57, 58, 59
Prepare ledger accounts for contract costs;	55
Explain the difference between subjective and objective classifications of expenditure and the importance of tracing costs both to products/services and to responsibility centres;	60
Construct coding systems that facilitate both subjective and objective classification of costs;	61
Prepare financial statements that inform management;	62
Explain why gross revenue, value added, contribution, gross margin, marketing expense, general and administration expense, etc. might be highlighted in management reporting;	63

Compare and contrast management reports in a range of organisations including commercial enterprises, charities and public sector undertakings;	6, 62, 64
Explain why organisations set out financial plans in the form of budgets, typically for a financial year;	65
Prepare functional budgets for material usage and purchase, labour and overheads, including budgets for capital expenditure and depreciation;	68, 69, 70, 73
Prepare a master budget: income statement, balance sheet and cash flow statement, based on the functional budgets;	66, 67, 71, 74
Interpret budget statements and advise managers on financing projected cash shortfalls and/or investing projected cash surpluses;	76
Prepare a flexed budget based on the actual levels of sales and production and calculate appropriate variances;	75
Compare and contrast fixed and flexed budgets;	72
Explain the use of budgets in designing reward strategies for managers.	77

Question 1 Cost behaviour

The following data have been collected for four cost types – W, X, Y, Z – at two activity levels:

Cost type	Cost 100 units £	Cost 140 units £
W	8,000	10,560
X	5,000	5,000
Y	6,500	9,100
Z	6,700	8,580

Where V = variable, SV = semi-variable and F = fixed, assuming linearity, the four cost types W, X, Y and Z are, respectively:

	W	X	Y	Z
(A)	V	F	SV	V
(B)	SV	F	V	SV
(C)	V	F	V	V
(D)	SV	F	SV	SV

Question 2 Step fixed costs

Which of the following costs would be classified as step costs (tick all that apply)?

(i) The cost of materials is £3 per kg for purchases up to 10,000 kg. From 10,001 kg to 15,000 kg the cost is £2.80 per kg. Thereafter the cost is £2.60 per kg. ☐

(ii) The cost of supervisory labour is £18,000 per period for output up to 10,000 units. From 10,001 units to 15,000 units the cost is £37,000 per period. Thereafter the cost is £58,000 per period. ☐

(iii) The cost of machine rental is £4,500 per period for output up to 3,000 units. From 3,001 units to 6,000 units the cost is £8,700 per period. Thereafter the cost is £12,200 per period. ☐

(iv) The mileage charge for a rental car is £0.05 per mile up to 400 miles. From 401 miles to 700 miles the charge is £0.07 per mile. Thereafter the cost is £0.08 per mile. ☐

Question 3 High–low method

The following data relate to the overhead expenditure of a contract cleaner at two activity levels:

Square metres cleaned	12,750	15,100
Overheads	£73,950	£83,585

What is the estimate of the overheads if 16,200 square metres are to be cleaned?

(A) £88,095
(B) £89,674
(C) £93,960
(D) £98,095.

Question 4 Cost behaviour patterns

Select the correct equation below.

AG Ltd rents an office photocopier for £300 per month. In addition, the cost incurred per copy taken is 2 pence. If £ y = total photocopying cost for the month and x = the number of photocopies taken, the total photocopying cost for a month can be expressed as:

$y = 300 + 2x$ ☐
$y = 300x + 2$ ☐
$y = 300 + 0.02x$ ☐

Question 5 Cost object

Which of the following could be used as a cost object in an organisation's costing system (tick all that apply)?

(i) Customer number 879 ☐
(ii) Department A ☐
(iii) The finishing process in department A ☐

(iv) Product H ☐
 (v) Employee number 776 ☐
(vi) Order processing activity ☐

? **Question 6** Direct cost and indirect cost

Which of the following costs would a local council classify as a direct cost of providing a door-to-door refuse collection service (tick all that apply)?

 (i) Depreciation of the refuse collection vehicle ☐
 (ii) Wages paid to refuse collectors ☐
(iii) Cost of leaflets sent to customers to advertise refuse collection times and dates ☐
(iv) Employer's liability insurance premium to cover all council employees ☐

? **Question 7** Full cost

Is the following statement true or false?

'The only cost that is really useful in setting a selling price for a particular service to be provided is the full cost'.

True ☐   False ☐

? **Question 8** Inventory valuation

ABC Ltd had an opening inventory value of £880 (275 units valued at £3.20 each) on 1 April.

The following receipts and issues were recorded during April:

8 April	Receipts 600 units	£3.00 per unit
12 April	Issues 200 units	
15 April	Receipts 400 units	£3.40 per unit
30 April	Issues 925 units	

Using the FIFO or LIFO method, what was the total value of the issues on 30 April?

	FIFO	LIFO
(A)	£2,850	£2,935
(B)	£2,850	£2,960
(C)	£2,890	£2,935
(D)	£2,890	£2,960

? **Question 9** Inventory valuation

The effect of using the last in, first out (LIFO) method of inventory valuation rather than the first in, first out (FIFO) method in a period of rising prices is

 (A) to report lower profits and a lower value of closing inventory.
 (B) to report higher profits and a higher value of closing inventory.
 (C) to report lower profits and a higher value of closing inventory.
 (D) to report higher profits and a lower value of closing inventory.

Question 10 Inventory valuation

Is the following statement *true* or *false?*

With all average price systems where it is required to keep prices up to date, the average price must be recalculated each time an issue is made from inventory. True ☐   False ☐

Question 11 Economic value

The R Organisation is experiencing rapid inflation in its raw material prices. Which of the following inventory valuation methods is most likely to ensure that the prices at which material issues are charged to cost of production approximate the economic cost of the materials?

First In, First Out (FIFO)   ☐
Last In, Last Out (LIFO)   ☐
Average cost (AVCO)   ☐

Question 12 Inventory valuation methods

The following extract is taken from the stores ledger record for material M:

Date September	Qty	Receipts Price	£	Qty	Issues Price	£	Qty	Balance Price	£
1							12		18.00
3	6	2.10	12.60				18		30.60
7	8	2.35	18.80				26		49.40
12				5		**A**			
14				8		**B**			**C**

The values that would be entered on the stores ledger record as A, B and C are:

(a) Using FIFO:
A £ [ ]
B £ [ ]
C £ [ ]

(b) Using LIFO:
A £ [ ]
B £ [ ]
C £ [ ]

(c) Using weighted average (AVCO):
A £ [ ]
B £ [ ]
C £ [ ]

Question 13 Direct cost

Wages paid to which of the following would be classified as direct labour costs of the organisation's product or service (tick all that apply):

A driver in a taxi company   ☐
A carpenter in a construction company   ☐
An assistant in a factory canteen   ☐
A hair stylist in a beauty salon.   ☐

? **Question 14** Cost attribution

A method of accounting for overheads involves attributing them to cost units using predetermined rates. This is known as

(A) overhead allocation.
(B) overhead apportionment.
(C) overhead absorption.
(D) overhead analysis.

? **Question 15** Overhead absorption

A company absorbs overheads on standard machine hours which were budgeted at 11,250 with overheads of £258,750. Actual results were 10,980 standard machine hours with overheads of £254,692.

Overheads were:

(A) under-absorbed by £2,152.
(B) over-absorbed by £4,058.
(C) under-absorbed by £4,058.
(D) over-absorbed by £2,152.

? **Question 16** Overhead absorption rates

XX Ltd absorbs overheads based on units produced. In one period, 23,000 units were produced, actual overheads were £276,000 and there was £46,000 under absorption.

The budgeted overhead absorption rate per unit was:

(A) £10
(B) £12
(C) £13
(D) £14.

? **Question 17** Overhead absorption

Tick the box to indicate whether the overhead was over- or under-absorbed, and insert the value of the under- or over-absorption.

XY operates a standard absorption costing system. Data for last period are as follows:

Budgeted labour hours	48,500
Actual standard labour hours	49,775
Budgeted overheads	£691,125
Actual overheads	£746,625

To the nearest whole number, the overhead for the period was £ ☐

under-absorbed   ☐
over-absorbed.   ☐

? **Question 18** Overhead analysis

TRI-D Ltd has three production departments – Extrusion, Machining and Finishing – and a service department known as Production Services which works for the production departments in the ratio of 3:2:1.

The following data, which represent normal activity levels, have been budgeted for the period ending 31 December 20X6:

	Extrusion	Machining	Finishing	Production Services	Total
Direct labour hours	7,250	9,000	15,000		31,250
Machine hours	15,500	20,000	2,500	2,000	40,000
Floor area (m²)	800	1,200	1,000	1,400	4,400
Equipment value	£160,000	£140,000	£30,000	£70,000	£400,000
Employees	40	56	94	50	240

Requirements

(a) The template being used by the management accountant to analyse the overheads for the period is shown below:

Cost allocated	Basis	Extrusion £	Machining £	Finishing £	Production Services £	Total £
Indirect wages	Allocated					102,000
Apportioned						
Depreciation	Equipment value		A			84,000
Rates	Floor area	B				22,000
Power				C		180,000
Personnel					D	60,000
Other						48,000
					109,600	
Production services		E			(109,600)	
					–	496,000

The values that would be entered on the overhead analysis sheet at A to E are:

A [   ]
B [   ]
C [   ]
D [   ]
E [   ]

(b) After completion of the allocation, apportionment and reapportionment exercise, the total departmental overheads are:

Extrusion	Machining	Finishing
£206,350	£213,730	£75,920

Calculate appropriate overhead absorption rates (to two decimal places) for the period ending 31 December 20X6 and tick the box to indicate in each case whether labour hours or machine hours are to be used as the absorption basis:

(i) Extrusion department: £ ☐   for each: labour hour ☐
                                            machine hour ☐

(ii) Machining department: £ ☐   for each: labour hour ☐
                                            machine hour ☐

(iii) Finishing department: £ ☐   for each: labour hour ☐
                                            machine hour ☐

(c) Which of the following are specific order costing systems:

    (i) Contract costing   ☐
   (ii) Batch costing   ☐
  (iii) Process costing   ☐
  (iv) Job costing.   ☐

? Question 19 Overhead analysis

(a) The management accountant of X Ltd is preparing the budgeted overhead analysis sheet for the year 20X2/X3. The company has two production cost centres (Machining and Assembly) and two service departments (Stores and Maintenance). The directly attributable production overheads have already been allocated to the cost centres but other costs need to be apportioned. A section of the template being used by the management accountant and other information are shown below:

Overhead analysis sheet 20X2/3

Costs	Basis of apportionment	Machining £	Assembly £	Stores £	Maintenance £	Total £
Various	Allocated	1,105,000	800,000	90,000	350,000	2,345,000
Rent	Area occupied		**A**			750,000
Personnel dept			**B**			60,000
Equipment dep'n		**C**				200,000

Other information

	Departments			
	Machining	Assembly	Stores	Maintenance
Employees	75	210	25	40
Area occupied (square metres)	10,000	6,000	3,000	1,000
Cost of equipment £	1,200,000	150,000	50,000	200,000
Machine hours	500,000	50,000		
Direct labour hours	30,000	120,000		

The values that would be entered on the overhead analysis sheet in the boxes A, B and C are:

A   £ ☐
B   £ ☐
C   £ ☐

(b) When the allocation and apportionment exercise had been completed by the management accountant, the analysis showed:

	Machining £	Assembly £	Stores £	Maintenance £	Total £
Total	2,250,000	1,900,000	250,000	800,000	5,200,000

The management accountant has now established the workloads of the service departments. The service departments provide services to each other as well as to the production departments as shown below:

	Machining	Assembly	Stores	Maintenance
Stores	30%	30%	–	40%
Maintenance	45%	30%	25%	–

After the apportionment of the service department overheads to the production departments (and acknowledging the reciprocal servicing), the total overhead for the machining department will be £ [_____] (to the nearest £000).

Question 20 Elements of cost

Data concerning one unit of product B produced last period are as follows.

Direct material 3 kg @ £9 per kg
Direct labour: department A   4 hours @ £14 per hour
               department B   6 hours @ £11 per hour
Machine hours: department A   3 hours
                department B   2 hours

Production overhead is absorbed at a rate of £7 per direct labour hour in department A and £6 per machine hour in department B.

(a) The direct cost per unit of product B is £ [_____]
(b) The full production cost per unit of product B is £ [_____]

Question 21 Pricing to achieve a specified return on investment

Data for product Q are as follows.

Direct material cost per unit	£54
Direct labour cost per unit	£87
Direct labour hours per unit	11 hours
Production overhead absorption rate	£7 per direct labour hour
Mark-up for non-production overhead costs	3%

10,000 units of product Q are budgeted to be sold each year. Product Q requires an investment of £220,000 and the target rate of return on investment is 14 per cent per annum.

The selling price for one unit of product Q, to the nearest penny is £ [_____].

? **Question 22** Breakeven analysis

Data for questions 22 and 23

JJ Ltd manufactures a product which has a selling price of £14, a variable cost of £6 per unit. The company incurs annual fixed costs of £24,400. Annual sales demand is 8,000 units.

New production methods are under consideration, which would cause a 30 per cent increase in fixed costs and a reduction in variable cost to £5 per unit. The new production methods would result in a superior product and would enable sales to be increased to 8,500 units per annum at a price of £15 each.

If the change in production methods were to take place, the breakeven output level would be:

(A) 122 units higher
(B) 372 units higher
(C) 610 units lower
(D) 915 units higher

? **Question 23** Breakeven analysis

If the organisation implements the new production methods and wishes to achieve the same profit as that under the existing method, how many units would need to be produced and sold annually to achieve this?

(A) 7,132 units
(B) 8,000 units
(C) 8,500 units
(D) 9,710 units

? **Question 24** Breakeven analysis

X Ltd produces and sells a single product, which has a contribution to sales ratio of 30 per cent. Fixed costs amount to £120,000 each year.

The number of units of sale required each year to break even:

(A) is 156,000.
(B) is 171,428.
(C) is 400,000.
(D) cannot be calculated from the data supplied.

? **Question 25** Breakeven graph

The following graph relates to questions 25 and 26

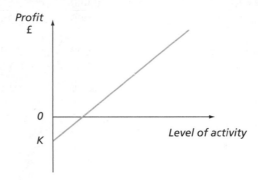

Point K on the graph indicates the value of:

    (A) semi-variable cost.
    (B) total cost.
    (C) variable cost.
    (D) fixed cost.

Question 26 Breakeven graph

This graph is known as a:

    (A) conventional breakeven chart.
    (B) contribution breakeven chart.
    (C) semi-variable cost chart.
    (D) profit–volume chart.

Question 27 Cost analysis

A company makes a single product which generates a contribution to sales ratio of 30 per cent. In a period when fixed costs were £30,000 the net profit was £56,400. Direct wages are 20 per cent of variable costs.

    The direct wages cost for the period was £ [   ].

Question 28 Breakeven analysis

Tick the correct boxes.

A company makes and sells a single product. If the fixed costs incurred in making and selling the product increase:

	Increase	Decrease	Stay the same
(a) the breakeven point will	☐	☐	☐
(b) the contribution to sales ratio will	☐	☐	☐
(c) the margin of safety will	☐	☐	☐

Question 29 Cost behaviour/breakeven chart

Z plc operates a single retail outlet selling direct to the public. Profit statements for August and September are as follows:

	August £	September £
Sales	80,000	90,000
Cost of sales	50,000	55,000
Gross profit	30,000	35,000
Less:		
Selling and distribution	8,000	9,000
Administration	15,000	15,000
Net profit	7,000	11,000

The data for August has been used to draw the following breakeven chart:

Contribution breakeven chart

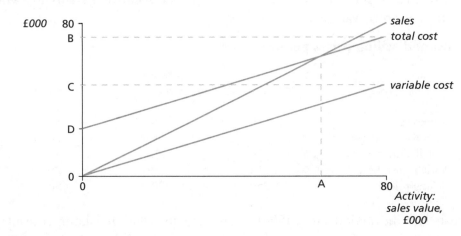

Requirements

The values of A–D read from the chart would be:

A £ [   ]

B £ [   ]

C £ [   ]

D £ [   ] .

? Question 30 Limiting factor

The following budgeted information is available for a company that manufactures four types of specialist paints:

	Product W per batch £	Product X per batch £	Product Y per batch £	Product Z per batch £
Selling price	20.00	15.00	15.00	17.50
Variable overhead	9.60	6.00	9.60	8.50
Fixed overhead	3.60	3.00	2.10	2.10
Profit	6.80	6.00	3.30	6.90
Machine hours per batch	12	9	6	11

All four products use the same machine.

In a period when machine hours are in short supply, the product that makes the most profitable use of machine hours is:

(A) Product W

(B) Product X

(C) Product Y

(D) Product Z.

? **Question 31** Limiting factor decision-making

Triproduct Ltd makes and sells three types of electronic security systems for which the following information is available:

Standard cost and selling prices per unit

	Day scan	Product Night scan	Omni scan
	£	£	£
Materials	70	110	155
Manufacturing labour	40	55	70
Installation labour	24	32	44
Variable overheads	16	20	28
Selling price	250	320	460

Fixed costs for the period are £450,000 and the installation labour is available for 25,000 hours only in a period and is paid £8 per hour.

Both manufacturing and installation labour are variable costs.

The maximum demand for the products is:

Day scan	2,000 units
Night scan	3,000 units
Omni scan	1,800 units

Requirements

(a) The shortfall in hours of installation labour each period is ☐ hours.

(b) In order to maximise profits for the next period, the optimum production plan is:

Day scan	☐ units
Night scan	☐ units
Omni scan	☐ units.

? **Question 32** Standard costing

Which of the following are *not* provided by a system of standard costing and variance analysis?

(A) Unit standard costs as a benchmark for comparison.
(B) Variances to direct managers' attention where control action will be most worthwhile.
(C) Actual unit costs to be incurred in the future.
(D) Unit standard costs for budgetary planning.

? **Question 33** Standard cost

JR Limited produces product H. The standard cost card indicates that each unit of H requires 4 kg of material W and 2 kg of material X at a standard price of £1 and £5 per kg, respectively.

Standard direct labour hours required per unit are 14 at a standard rate of £8 per hour. Variable production overheads are absorbed at a rate of £4 per direct labour hour.

The standard variable production cost of one unit of product H is £ ☐ .

Question 34 Variance analysis
Data for questions 34–36

PP Ltd has prepared the following standard cost information for one unit of product X:

Direct materials	2 kg @ £13/kg	£26.00
Direct labour	3.3 hours @ £12/hour	£39.60
Variable overheads	3.3 hours @ £2.50	£8.25

Actual results for the period were recorded as follows:

Production	12,000 units
Materials – 26,400 kg	£336,600
Labour – 40,200 hours	£506,520
Variable overheads	£107,250

All of the materials were purchased and used during the period.
The direct material price and usage variances are:

	Material price	*Material usage*
(A)	£6,600F	£31,200A
(B)	£6,600F	£31,200F
(C)	£31,200F	£6,600A
(D)	£31,200A	£6,600A

Question 35 Variance analysis

The direct labour rate and efficiency variances are:

	Labour rate	*Labour efficiency*
(A)	£24,120F	£7,200F
(B)	£24,120A	£7,200A
(C)	£24,120A	£7,560A
(D)	£31,320A	£7,200A

Question 36 Variance analysis

The variable overhead expenditure and efficiency variances are:

	Expenditure	*Efficiency*
(A)	£6,750A	£1,500A
(B)	£6,750A	£1,500F
(C)	£8,250A	£1,500A
(D)	£8,250F	£1,500F

Question 37 Materials variances

In a period, 11,280 kg of material were used at a total standard cost of £46,248. The material usage variance was £492 adverse. What was the standard allowed weight of material for the period?

(A) 11,520 kg
(B) 11,280 kg
(C) 11,394 kg
(D) 11,160 kg.

Question 38 Labour variances

In a period, 6,500 units were made and there was an adverse labour efficiency variance of £26,000. Workers were paid £8 per hour, total wages were £182,000 and there was a nil rate variance.

How many standard labour hours were allowed per unit?

(A) 3
(B) 3.5
(C) 4
(D) They cannot be calculated without more information.

Question 39 Variance analysis

During a period, 25,600 labour hours were worked at a standard rate of £7.50 per hour. The direct labour efficiency variance was £8,250 adverse.

The number of standard hours produced was [   ].

Question 40 Sales variances

Budgeted sales of product V are 4,800 units per month. The standard selling price and variable cost of product V are £45 per unit and £22 per unit respectively.

During June the sales revenue achieved from actual sales of 4,390 units of product V amounted to £231,900.

(a) The sales price variance for product V for June was £ [   ] adverse/favourable (delete as appropriate).

(b) The sales volume contribution variance for product V for June was £ [   ] adverse/favourable (delete as appropriate).

❓ **Question 41** Profit reconciliation

The following variances have been calculated for the latest period:

	£
Sales volume contribution variance	11,245 (F)
Material usage variance	6,025 (F)
Labour rate variance	3,100 (A)
Variable overhead expenditure variance	2,415 (A)

All other variances were zero. The budgeted contribution for the period was £48,000. The actual contribution reported for the period was £ [＿＿＿＿＿＿＿] .

❓ **Question 42** Variance interpretation I

The direct labour efficiency variance for the latest period was adverse. Which of the following reasons could have contributed to this variance? (tick all that apply).

- (a) Output was higher than budgeted ☐
- (b) The purchasing department bought poor quality material which was difficult to process ☐
- (c) The original standard time for the output was set too low ☐
- (d) The hourly labour rate was higher than had been expected when the standard was set ☐
- (e) Employees were more skilled than specified in the standard ☐

❓ **Question 43** Variance interpretation II

The sales volume contribution variance for the latest period was favourable. Which of the following reasons could have contributed to this variance? (tick all that apply).

- (a) A lower selling price was charged than standard ☐
- (b) The variable cost per unit was lower than standard, which led to a higher actual contribution per unit than standard ☐
- (c) Demand for the product was greater than had been expected ☐

❓ **Question 44** Labour incentive scheme

A company operates a premium bonus system by which employees receive a bonus of 75 per cent of the time saved compared with a standard time allowance (at the normal hourly rate).

Details relating to employee X are shown below:

Actual hours worked	42
Hourly rate of pay	£10
Output achieved	400 units of product Y
Standard time allowed per unit of Y	7 minutes

The bonus payable to employee X (to the nearest £) is:

(A) £35
(B) £47
(C) £70
(D) £82.

❓ Question 45 Integrated accounts

A company operates an integrated cost and financial accounting system. The accounting entries for the return to stores of unused direct materials from production would be:

	Debit	*Credit*
(A)	Work in progress account	Stores control account
(B)	Stores control account	Work in progress account
(C)	Stores control account	Finished goods account
(D)	Cost of sales account	Work in progress account

❓ Question 46 Integrated accounts

ABC Ltd operates an integrated cost accounting system. The production overhead control account at 31 July, which is ABC Ltd's year-end, showed the following information:

Production overhead control account

	£		£
Trade payables	50,000	Work in progress	120,000
Bank	20,000	?	5,000
Depreciation	5,000		
Salaries	40,000		
Materials	10,000		
	125,000		125,000

The £5,000 credit entry represents the value of the transfer to:

(A) the income statement for the under-recovery of production overheads.
(B) the income statement for the over-recovery of production overheads.
(C) the work in progress account for the under-recovery of production overheads.
(D) the following period.

❓ Question 47 Integrated accounts

Wages incurred last period amounted to £33,400, of which £27,400 were direct wages and £6,000 were indirect production wages. Wages paid in cash were £31,700.

Which of the following entries would arise as a result of these transactions? (Tick all that are correct.)

			£	
(a)	Debit	Wages control account	33,400	☐
(b)	Debit	Wages control account	31,700	☐
(c)	Debit	Work in progress account	27,400	☐
(d)	Debit	Production overhead control account	6,000	☐
(e)	Credit	Wages control account	33,400	☐
(f)	Credit	Wages control account	31,700	☐
(g)	Credit	Work in progress account	27,400	☐
(h)	Credit	Production overhead control account	6,000	☐

? **Question 48** Integrated accounting system

WYZ Limited operates an integrated accounting system.
The following information was available for period 7:

	£
Cost of finished goods produced	1,241,500
Direct wages	173,400
Direct material issues	598,050
Indirect material issues	32,800
Direct material purchases on credit	617,300
Production overheads (actual expenditure)	359,725
Depreciation of production machinery	35,000

At the beginning of the period, the relevant account balances were:

Account	£
Work in progress control	125,750
Direct material stores control	48,250

Production overheads are absorbed on the basis of 280 per cent of direct wages cost. Any production overheads under- or over-absorbed for the period are transferred to the income statement at the end of the period.

Requirements

(a)

Direct material stores control account (extract)			
	£		£
Balance b/f	**A**	Work in progress	**B**
Payables	**C**	Production overhead control	**D**

The values that would be entered as A–D in the above account extract are:

A £ ☐

B £ ☐

C £ ☐

D £ ☐

(b) (i) The production overheads for the period were:

under-absorbed ☐
over-absorbed ☐

(ii) The value of the under-/over-absorption was £ ☐

(iii) This amount will be transferred as a:

credit ☐
debit ☐

in the income statement at the end of the period.

Question 49 Standard cost bookkeeping

A company uses standard costing and an integrated accounting system. The double entry to record a favourable labour rate variance is:

	Debit	*Credit*
(A)	Work in progress account	Labour rate variance account
(B)	Labour rate variance account	Work in progress account
(C)	Wages control account	Labour rate variance account
(D)	Labour rate variance account	Wages control account

Question 50 Standard cost bookkeeping

STD Ltd operates an integrated standard costing system for its single product. All inventories are valued at standard price.

During a period the following variances were recorded:

	Favourable £	*Adverse* £
Material price		3,950
Material usage	1,925	
Labour rate		1,325
Labour efficiency	1,750	

(a) Tick the correct boxes to show the entries that will be made to record the material price variance.

	Debit	*Credit*	*No entry in this account*
Materials control account	☐	☐	☐
Material price variance account	☐	☐	☐
Work in progress account	☐	☐	☐

(b) Tick the correct boxes to show the entries that will be made to record the material usage variance.

	Debit	*Credit*	*No entry in this account*
Materials control account	☐	☐	☐
Material usage variance account	☐	☐	☐
Work in progress account	☐	☐	☐

(c) The labour force was paid at a:

higher hourly rate than standard ☐
lower hourly rate than standard ☐.

(d) Tick the correct boxes to show the entries that will be made to record the labour efficiency variance.

	Debit	Credit	No entry in this account
Wages control account	☐	☐	☐
Labour efficiency variance account	☐	☐	☐
Work in progress account	☐	☐	☐

Question 51 Specific order costing

PZ Ltd undertakes work to repair, maintain and construct roads. When a customer requests the company to do work, PZ Ltd supplies a fixed price to the customer, and allocates a works order number to the customer's request. This works order number is used as a reference number on all documentation to enable the costs of doing the work to be collected.

PZ Ltd's financial year ends on 31 December. At the end of December 20X1, the data shown against four of PZ Ltd's works orders were as follows:

Works order number	488	517	518	519
Date started	1.11.X0	1.10.X1	14.11.X1	20.11.X1
Estimated completion date	28.2.X2	30.7.X2	31.1.X2	31.1.X2
Selling price	£450,000	£135,000	£18,000	£9,000

The most appropriate costing method for accounting for each of the four works order numbers is:

Works order number	Contract costing	Job costing
(i) 488	☐	☐
(ii) 517	☐	☐
(iii) 518	☐	☐
(iv) 519	☐	☐

Question 52 Job costing

An accountant is to set up in private practice. She anticipates working a 35-hour week and taking four weeks' holiday per year. General expenses of the practice are expected to be £20,000 per year, and she has set herself a target of £40,000 a year salary.

Assuming that only 75 per cent of her time worked will be chargeable to clients, what should she quote (to the nearest £) for a job anticipated to take 50 hours?

(A) £1,587
(B) £1,786
(C) £2,381
(D) £2,976.

Question 53 Job costing

A company has been asked to quote for a job. The company aims to make a net profit of 30 per cent on sales. The estimated cost for the job is as follows:

Direct materials	10 kg @ £10 per kg
Direct labour	10 hours @ £10 per hour

Variable production overheads are recovered at the rate of £4 per labour hour.

Fixed production overheads for the company are budgeted to be £200,000 each year and are recovered on the basis of labour hours. There are 10,000 budgeted labour hours each year.

Other costs in relation to selling, distribution and administration are recovered at the rate of £50 per job.

The company quote for the job should be:

(A) £572
(B) £637
(C) £700
(D) £833.

 Question 54 Job/batch costing

Acme Electronics Ltd makes specialist electronic equipment to order. There are three main departments: Preparation, Etching and Assembly. Preparation and Etching are departments which use a considerable amount of machinery while Assembly is mainly a manual operation using simple hand tools.

For period 7, the following budgets have been prepared:

	Production overheads	
Department	£	Activity
Preparation	165,000	3,000 machine hours
Etching	98,000	1,400 machine hours
Assembly	48,600	1,800 labour hours

During the period, an enquiry is received for a batch of 200 control units for which the following estimates have been made:

Total direct materials	£26,500
Preparation	260 machine hours
	90 labour hours at £8 per hour
Etching	84 machine hours
	130 labour hours at £7 per hour
Assembly	180 labour hours at £6 per hour

Requirements

(a) (i) The prime cost of the batch of 200 control units is £ [   ]

    (ii) The production overhead cost of the batch of 200 control units is:

        Preparation Department overheads: £ [   ]

        Etching Department overheads: £ [   ]

        Assembly Department overheads: £ [   ]

(b) After an addition has been made to the batch cost to cover administrative overheads, the total cost of the batch of 200 control units is £65,100.

   If the company wishes to achieve a 30 per cent profit margin on sales, the price per control unit which should be quoted is £[＿＿＿＿].

? **Question 55** Specific order costing

SS Developments Ltd is currently converting a former hospital into residential apartments.

The contract commenced on 1 March 20X0 and is expected to take a year and a half to complete. The contract value is £10 million. SS Developments Ltd's financial year runs from 1 January to 31 December.

The contract account for the building of the apartments includes the following data at 31 December 20X0:

	£000
Materials delivered direct to site	1,200
Materials issued from head office stores	200
Plant delivered to site at cost	900
Estimated costs to completion	2,640

Depreciation on plant is to be provided at the rate of 20 per cent on cost each year. The estimated value of the materials on site at 31 December 20X0 was £180,000.

The company recognises profit on contracts according to the proportion of the total estimated contract cost that is represented by the cost incurred to date.

Requirements
(a) The total materials cost of the contract to 31 December 20X0 is £[＿＿＿＿].
(b) The net book value of the plant on site at 31 December 20X0 is £[＿＿＿＿].
(c) The total cost incurred to date, including the cost of materials and plant depreciation, is £3,360,000. The profit to be recognised on the contract is £[＿＿＿＿].

? **Question 56** Process costing
Data for sub-questions 56.1–56.3
A company produces a single product that passes through two processes. The details for process 1 are as follows:

Materials input	20,000 kg at £2.50 per kg
Direct labour	£15,000
Production overheads	150 per cent of direct labour

Normal losses are 15 per cent of input in process 1 and without further processing any losses can be sold as scrap for £1 per kg.

The output for the period was 18,500 kg from process 1.

There was no work in progress at the beginning or at the end of the period.

56.1 What value (to the nearest £) will be credited to the process 1 account in respect of the normal loss?

(A) Nil
(B) £3,000
(C) £4,070
(D) £5,250.

56.2 What is the value (to the nearest £) of the abnormal loss/gain for the period in process 1?

(A) £6,104
(B) £6,563
(C) £7,257
(D) £7,456.

56.3 What is the value (to the nearest £) of the output to process 2?

(A) £88,813
(B) £90,604
(C) £91,956
(D) £94,063.

? Question 57 Process costing

A cleansing detergent is manufactured by passing raw material through two processes. The details of the process costs for Process 1 for April were as follows:

Opening work in progress	5,000 litres valued as follows:	
	Material cost	£2,925
	Conversion costs	£6,600
Raw material input	50,000 litres valued at a cost of	£37,500
Conversion costs		£62,385

Normal loss is 3% of the input during the period and has a scrap value of £0.20 per litre. It is company policy to deduct the income from the sale of normal loss from that period's materials cost.

Actual output to Process 2	49,000 litres
Closing work in progress	4,000 litres, which were 100% complete for materials and 40% complete for conversion costs.

A template that could be used to calculate the cost of the output from Process 1 is shown below. The template has been partially completed.

	Costs	Equivalent litres	Cost per equivalent litre
	OWIP + Period = Total	Transfer out + Abnormal loss + CWIP = Total	
Materials	£2,925 + A	500	£0.75
Conversion	= £68,985	= 51,100	£1.35

OWIP = Opening work in progress
CWIP = Closing work in progress

(a) The value to be inserted in the table at **A** is £ _____
(b) The total value of the transfers to process 2 is £ _____
(c) The value of the abnormal loss is £ _____
(d) The value of the closing work in progress is £ _____.

? **Question 58** Process costing

Industrial Solvents Ltd mixes together three chemicals – A, B and C – in the ratio 3:2:1 to produce Allklean, a specialised anti-static fluid. The chemicals cost £8, £6 and £3.90 per litre, respectively.

In a period, 12,000 litres in total were input to the mixing process. The normal process loss is 5 per cent of input and in the period there was an abnormal loss of 100 litres, while the completed production was 9,500 litres. There was no opening work in progress (WIP) and the closing WIP was 100 per cent complete for materials and 40 per cent complete for labour and overheads. Labour and overheads were £41,280 in total for the period. Materials lost in production are scrapped.

Requirements

(a) The number of equivalent litres of labour and overhead produced during the period was _____ equivalent litres.
(b) The cost per equivalent litre of materials produced was £ _____.

? **Question 59** Process costing

A company manufactures a variety of liquids which pass through a number of processes. One of these products, P, passes through processes 1, 2 and 3 before being transferred to the finished goods warehouse.

The following process 3 data is available for October:

	£
Work in process at 1 October is 6,000 units, valued as:	
Transfer from process 2	14,400
Materials added	2,160
Wages and overhead	2,880
	19,440
Transfer from process 2 during October:	
48,000 units	110,400
Transferred to finished goods: 46,500 units	
Costs incurred:	
Materials added	27,180
Wages and overhead	54,720
Work in process at 31 October: 4,000 units	
Degree of completion:	
Materials added: 50%	
Wages and overhead: 30%	

Normal loss in process: 6% × (units in opening WIP *plus* transfers from process 2 *less* closing WIP)

At a certain stage in the process, it is convenient for the quality control inspector to examine the product and, where necessary, to reject it. Rejected products are sold for £0.80 per unit. During October an actual loss of 7 per cent was incurred, with product P having reached the following stage of production:

Direct materials added: 80%
Wages and overhead: 60%

Requirements

The cost per equivalent unit produced was:

(a) process 2 input: £ ☐ per equivalent unit
(b) material added: £ ☐ per equivalent unit
(c) wages and overhead: £ ☐ per equivalent unit.

? Question 60 Subjective classification

Tick the relevant box to indicate whether the following statement is true or false.

'The classification of expenditure items according to the cost centre or cost unit to be charged is known as subjective classification'.

True ☐   False ☐

? Question 61 Code number

In the composite code number 544.221, the first three digits indicate the nature of the expenditure and the last three digits indicate the cost object to be charged with the expenditure.

Delete as appropriate in the following statements.

(a) 544 indicates the **objective/subjective** classification of the expenditure item.
(b) 221 indicates the **objective/subjective** classification of the expenditure item.

? Question 62 Managerial reporting in a service organisation

Speedee Ltd has three main divisions – a motor-cycle courier service, a domestic parcel delivery service, and a bulk parcel service for industry.

The following information is available for a period:

	Courier service	Domestic parcels	Bulk parcels
Sales (£000)	205	316	262
Distance travelled (000 km)	168	82	54

Variable costs vary both with the distance travelled and also the type of vehicle used, and are £307,800 for the company as a whole. A technical estimate shows that the various vehicles used for the three services incur variable costs per kilometre in the ratio of 1:3:5, respectively, for the courier service, domestic parcels and bulk parcels.

Requirements

The contribution for each service for the period is:

(a) courier service: £ _____
(b) domestic parcels: £ _____
(c) bulk parcels: £ _____ .

 Question 63 Value added

An extract from the performance report of the F Division for the latest period is as follows.

	£	£
Sales revenue		289,500
Cost of goods sold		
Material costs	89,790	
Labour costs	72,340	
Production overhead	54,030	
		216,160
Gross margin		73,340
Marketing overhead	21,890	
General and administration overhead	38,120	
		60,010
Net profit		13,330

The following salary costs are included within the overhead costs.

	Salary cost included
Production overhead	£10,710
Marketing overhead	£14,560
General and administration overhead	£21,330

For the F Division for the latest period, the value added was £ _____ .

Question 64 Managerial reporting in a charity

As part of its fundraising and awareness-raising activities a charity operates a number of retail shops, selling new and donated second-hand goods.

Data for the latest period for the Southmere shop are as follows.

	£
Sales income	
New goods	6,790
Donated goods sold to customers	4,880
Purchase cost of new goods	3,332
Cost of laundering and cleaning selected donated goods	120
Delivery cost paid for new goods	290
Other income: low-quality donated goods sold for recycling	88
Salary costs	810
Amount paid to valuer to assess selected donated items	30
General overhead costs	1,220

(a) The gross margin generated by second-hand donated goods sold was £ ⬚

(b) The gross margin generated by new goods sold was £ ⬚

? **Question 65** The role of budgets

Which of the following is *not* a main role of a budget?

- (A) A budget gives authority to budget managers to incur expenditure in their area of responsibility.
- (B) A budget provides a means for an organisation to expand its activities.
- (C) A budget coordinates the activities of various parts of the organisation.
- (D) A budget acts as a comparator for current performance.

? **Question 66** Principal budget factor

A principal budget factor is:

- (A) the highest value item of cost.
- (B) a factor which limits the activities of an undertaking.
- (C) a factor common to all budget centres.
- (D) a factor controllable by the manager of the budget centre.

? **Question 67** IT in the budget process

Which of the following are benefits of using a computerised budget system as opposed to a manual one (tick all that are correct):

- (a) ☐ data used in drawing up the budget can be processed more quickly.
- (b) ☐ budget targets will be more acceptable to the managers responsible for their achievement.
- (c) ☐ changes in variables can be incorporated into the budget more quickly.
- (d) ☐ the principal budget factor can be identified before budget preparation begins.
- (e) ☐ continuous budgeting is only possible using a computerised system.

? **Question 68** Production budget

AB Ltd is currently preparing its production budget for product Z for the forthcoming year. The sales director has confirmed that he requires 120,000 units of product Z. Opening inventory is estimated to be 13,000 units and the company wishes to reduce inventory at the end of the year by 50 per cent. How many units of product Z will need to be produced?

- (A) 113,500 units
- (B) 120,000 units
- (C) 126,500 units
- (D) 133,000 units.

? **Question 69** Material budget

A company is currently preparing a material usage budget for the forthcoming year for material Z that will be used in product XX. The production director has confirmed that the production budget for product XX will be 10,000 units.

Each unit of product XX requires 4 kg of material Z. Opening inventory of material Z is budgeted to be 3,000 kg and the company wishes to reduce inventory at the end of the year by 25 per cent.

What is the *usage* budget for material Z for the forthcoming year?

(A) 34,750 kg
(B) 39,250 kg
(C) 40,000 kg
(D) 40,750 kg.

? **Question 70** Functional budgets

Budgeted sales of product P for next month are 4,000 units. Each unit of P requires 2 kg of raw material. Other budget information for next month is as follows:

Raw materials	
Opening inventories	3,000 kg
Closing inventories	4,500 kg
Finished product P	
Opening inventories	2,400 units
Closing inventories	1,800 units

The budgeted purchases of raw material for next month should be:

(A) 8,000 kg
(B) 8,300 kg
(C) 9,500 kg
(D) 12,500 kg.

? **Question 71** Cash budget

The following details have been extracted from the receivables collection records of X Ltd:

Invoices paid in the month after sale	60%
Invoices paid in the second month after sale	20%
Invoices paid in the third month after sale	15%
Bad debts	5%

Credit sales for June to August are budgeted as follows:

June	£100,000
July	£150,000
August	£130,000

Customers paying in the month after sale are entitled to deduct a 2 per cent settlement discount. Invoices are issued on the last day of the month. The amount budgeted to be received in September from credit sales is

(A) £115,190
(B) £116,750
(C) £121,440
(D) £123,000.

Question 72 Budgetary control

Tick the correct box.
A budget which is designed to show the allowed expenditure for the actual level of activity achieved is known as

a rolling budget ☐
a flexible budget ☐
a fixed budget ☐

Question 73 Functional budgets

RD Ltd is in the process of preparing its budgets for 20X2. The company produces and sells a single product, Z, which currently has a selling price of £100 for each unit.

The budgeted sales units for 20X2 are expected to be as follows:

J	F	M	A	M	J	J	A	S	O	N	D
5,000	5,500	6,000	6,000	6,250	6,500	6,250	7,000	7,500	7,750	8,000	7,500

The company expects to sell 7,000 units in January 20X3.

The selling price for each unit will be increased by 15 per cent with effect from 1 March 20X2.

A total of 1,000 units of finished goods are expected to be in inventory at the end of 20X1. It is company policy to hold a closing inventory balance of finished goods equal to 20 per cent of the following month's sales.

Each unit of Z produced requires 3 kg of material X, which currently costs £5 per kg. This price is expected to increase by 10 per cent on 1 June 20X2.

Inventory of raw material at the end of 20X1 is expected to be 3,750 kg. The company requires the closing inventory of raw materials to be set at 20 per cent of the following month's production requirements.

The production of each unit of Z requires 4 hours of skilled labour and 2 hours of unskilled labour.

Requirements
(a) The sales budget for quarter 1 is £⬚.
(b) The production budget for quarter 4 is ⬚ units.
(c) The material usage budget for quarter 2 is ⬚ kg.
(d) The material purchase budget for quarter 1 is £⬚.
(e) The direct labour budget for quarter 3 is ⬚ hours.

Question 74 Cash budget

The following data and estimates are available for ABC Limited for June, July and August:

	June £	July £	August £
Sales	45,000	50,000	60,000
Wages	12,000	13,000	14,500
Overheads	8,500	9,500	9,000

The following information is available regarding direct materials:

	June £	July £	August £	September £
Opening inventory	5,000	3,500	6,000	4,000
Material usage	8,000	9,000	10,000	

Notes
1. Ten per cent of sales are for cash: the balance is received the following month.
2. Wages are paid in the month in which they are incurred.
3. Overheads include £1,500 per month for depreciation. Overheads are settled in the month following.
4. Purchases of direct materials are paid for in the month purchased.

Requirements

(a) The budget value of direct materials purchases is:

June: £ ☐
July: £ ☐
August: £ ☐.

(b) The budgeted cash receivable from customers in August is £ ☐.
(c) The budgeted cash payable for wages and overhead in July is £ ☐.

Question 75 Flexible budgets

S Ltd makes a single product for which the budgeted costs and activity for a typical month are as follows:

Budgeted production and sales	15,000 units

Budgeted unit costs	£
Direct labour	46
Direct materials	30
Variable overheads	24
Fixed overheads	80
	180

The standard selling price of the product is £220 per unit.

Requirements

(a) During October, only 13,600 units were produced. The total budget cost allowance contained in the flexed budget for October is £ [   ].

(b) During November, 14,500 units were produced and sold at the standard selling price, and the following actual costs were incurred:

	£
Direct labour	658,000
Direct materials	481,400
Variable overheads	334,600
Fixed overheads	1,340,000
	2,814,000

(i) The sales volume contribution variance for November was £ [   ]

    adverse   ☐

    favourable   ☐.

(ii) The total expenditure variance for November was £ [   ]

    adverse   ☐

    favourable   ☐.

? **Question 76** Interpreting cash budgets

CB Ltd's cash budget forewarns of a short-term cash deficit. Which of the following would be appropriate actions to take in this situation (tick all that apply)?

(a) Arrange a bank overdraft   ☐

(b) Reduce receivables   ☐

(c) Increase inventories   ☐

(d) Sell more shares in the company   ☐

? **Question 77** Using budgets in management reward strategies

The maintenance manager is paid a bonus of 5 per cent of any savings he achieves against the flexible budget cost allowance for maintenance costs in the period.

The flexible budget cost allowance for the latest two periods was as follows.

	Activity level Machine hours	Budget cost allowance £
Period 4	3,800	11,040
Period 5	4,320	11,976

During period 6, the actual maintenance expenditure was £10,990 and 4,090 machine hours were worked.

The bonus paid to the maintenance manager in period 6 is (to the nearest penny) £ [   ].

Solutions to Revision Questions

 Solution 1

- Cost type X is clearly fixed for this range of activity levels.
- For the other costs, divide the total cost by the number of units at the head of the column. Variable costs result in a constant amount per unit of output. Semi-variable costs result in a varying amount per unit of output.

Answer: (B)

Cost type	Cost per unit @ 100 units £	Cost per unit @ 140 units £	
W	80	75.43	semi-variable
Y	65	65.00	variable
Z	67	61.29	semi-variable

 Solution 2

- It might help to actually draw a rough sketch graph of each cost described. Then tick the boxes of the costs whose behaviour patterns resemble a flight of stairs.

Costs (ii) and (iii) are step costs. The total expenditure on these costs remains constant for a range of activity levels until a critical activity level is reached. At this point, the cost increases to a new level and then remains constant for a further range of activity levels.

Costs (i) and (iv) are non-linear variable costs. The gradient of a graph of cost (i) will become less steep as activity increases. The gradient of a graph of cost (iv) will become more steep as activity increases.

 Solution 3

- You need to be completely familiar with the high–low method. The data shows that the technique can be applied in service situations as well as in manufacturing.
  Answer: (A)

1. Find the variable overheads per square metre:

   Extra m² cleaned = 15,100 − 12,750 = 2,350
   Extra overhead cost = £83,585 − £73,950 = £9,635
   Variable overhead per m² = £9,635/2,350 = £4.10

2. Find the fixed overhead:

	£
Total overheads of cleaning 12,750 m²	= 73,950
Variable overheads = 12,750 × £4.10	= 52,275
Fixed overhead	= 21,675

3. Total overheads for 16,200 m²:

	£
Variable overhead = 16,200 × £4.10	= 66,420
Fixed overhead	= 21,675
	88,095

 ## Solution 4

- Do not be confused by the use of the y and x notation. You simply need to think through how to calculate the total cost of a semi-variable cost.
- Total semi-variable cost = fixed cost + (variable cost per unit × no. of units)

Answer: $y = 300 + 0.02x$

 ## Solution 5

- An organisation's costing system is designed to provide the basic cost information that managers need in order to make operational and strategic planning and control decisions. For this purpose they may need to know the cost of a wide variety of items, ranging from a particular product or service to an individual customer.

All of the items described could be used as a cost object.

The CIMA *Terminology* provides the following description of a cost object: 'for example a product, service, centre, activity, customer or distribution channel in relation to which costs are ascertained'.

 ## Solution 6

- A direct cost is a cost which can be specifically attributed to a single cost object without the need for any potentially arbitrary apportionments.

Costs (i), (ii) and (iii) are direct costs of the service because they can be specifically attributed to the service provided.

Cost (iv) is an indirect cost of the service because it applies to all council employees, not only to those who are providing the refuse collection service.

Solution 7

- Think carefully before you answer a true/false question like this. For a statement to be true it must apply in all circumstances.

The statement is false.

Although the full cost, which includes absorbed overhead, shows the long run average cost that will be incurred per unit of service provided, it might be necessary to consider the marginal or incremental cost when making a special, one-off pricing decision.

 Solution 8

- You will need to produce some clear workings for your own benefit, since workings will not be awarded marks. You might like to draw up full inventory records to ensure greater accuracy.

Answer: (D)

Under FIFO the 200 units issued on 12 April would have been priced at £3.20 from the opening inventory. Therefore the remaining 75 units from the opening inventory make up the first part of the batch issued on 30 April:

	£
75 units at £3.20	240
600 units at £3.00	1,800
250 units at £3.40	850
925	2,890 (FIFO)

Under LIFO, the 200 units issued on 12 April would have been priced at £3.00 from the latest batch in inventory at that date (received 8 April). Therefore, the 400 units remaining from the £3.00 batch received on 8 April will be a part of the issues made on 30 April:

	£
400 units at £3.40	1,360
400 units at £3.00	1,200
125 units at £3.20	400
925	2,960 (LIFO)

 Solution 9

- Read the question carefully to ascertain whether prices are rising or falling

Answer: (A)

The issues to production will have been charged at the most recent, higher prices–lower profit figure.

The remaining inventory will be valued at the earlier, cheaper prices–lower inventory value.

Solution 10

- Think before you answer! An issue from inventory at the average price will not alter the average price of the items remaining in inventory.

  False. The average price must be recalculated each time a purchase is made at a different price.

 # Solution 11

- You should appreciate that, although the LIFO method results in issues from stores being valued at the most recent prices paid, the costs used are still historical costs.

Since the LIFO method uses the most recent prices to value issues from inventory it is most likely to ensure that the prices charged to cost of production approximate the economic cost of the materials.

 # Solution 12

- Remember the need for total accuracy. Prepare as many workings as you need to help you, but note that workings will not be awarded any marks. Our workings will help you to detect any errors you may have made.

(a)

		£
A	5 units × £1.50 (from opening inventory)	**7.50**
B	7 units × £1.50 (remaining units from opening inventory)	10.50
	1 unit × £2.10 (from September 3 receipts)	2.10
	8	**12.60**
C	5 units × £2.10 (remaining units from September 3)	10.50
	8 units × £2.35 (September 7 receipts)	18.80
		29.30

(b)

		£
A	5 units × £2.35 (from September 7 receipts)	**11.75**
B	3 units × £2.35 (remaining units from September 7)	7.05
	5 units × £2.10 (from September 3 receipts)	10.50
	8	**17.55**
C	1 unit × £2.10 (remaining unit from September 3)	2.10
	12 units × £1.50 (opening inventory)	18.00
		20.10

(c) Weighted average price of inventory on 7 September $= £\dfrac{49.40}{26} = £1.90$

    A   5 units × £1.90 = **£9.50**

    B   8 units × £1.90 = **£15.20**

    C   83 units × £1.90 = **£24.70**.

Solution 13

- Direct wages are those paid to employees working directly on the organisation's output. Their wages can be traced to specific cost units.

   The wages paid to the driver, carpenter and hair stylist are all direct labour costs. The wages paid to the canteen assistant are indirect wages because the assistant is not working directly on the organisation's output.

 Solution 14

- Take your time and read all the options. This is not a difficult question but it would be easy to rush and select the wrong answer.

Answer: (C)

   Overhead allocation is the allotment of whole items of cost to cost units or cost centres. Overhead apportionment is the sharing out of costs over a number of cost centres according to the benefit used. Overhead analysis refers to the whole process of recording and accounting for overheads.

 Solution 15

- First you need to calculate the overhead absorption rate per standard machine hour. Remember that this is always based on the budgeted data.
- Next you must use the absorption rate to calculate the overhead absorbed, and then compare this with the overhead incurred to determine the over- or under-absorption.

Answer: (A)

$$\text{Overhead absorption rate} = \frac{£258,750}{11,250} = £23 \text{ per standard machine hour}$$

	£
Overhead absorbed = 10,980 std. hours × £23	252,540
Overhead incurred	254,692
Under absorption	2,152

 Solution 16

- Use the under-absorption to adjust the actual overhead incurred, to determine the overhead absorbed. Since there was an under absorption, the actual overhead incurred must be greater than the overhead absorbed.
- Lastly, divide the overhead absorbed by the number of units produced.

Answer: (A)

	£000
Actual incurred	276
Under absorption	46
Absorbed	230
No. of units	23,000

Rate per unit = £230,000/23,000 = £10.

 ## Solution 17

- Remember that the overhead absorption rate (OAR) is based on the budgeted data.
- Overheads absorbed for the period = OAR × actual standard labour hours achieved.

$$OAR = \frac{£691,125}{48,500} = £14.25$$

	£
Overhead absorbed during period	
49,775 × £14.25	709,293.75
Overhead incurred	746,625.00
Overhead under-absorbed	37,331 (to nearest whole number).

Solution 18

- The basic data on labour and machine hours seems to indicate that the Extrusion and Machining departments are machine-intensive, so a machine hour rate would be most appropriate. The Finishing department appears to be labour-intensive, so a labour hour rate would be more suitable.

(a) A: $\dfrac{£140,000}{£400,000} \times £84,000 = \textbf{£29,400}$

B: $\dfrac{800}{4,400} \times £22,000 = \textbf{£4,000}$

C: $\dfrac{2,500}{40,000} \times £180,000 = \textbf{£11,250}$

D: $\dfrac{50}{240} \times £60,000 = \textbf{£12,500}$

E: $\dfrac{3}{(3 + 2 + 1)} \times £109,600 = \textbf{£54,800}.$

(b) **Overhead absorption rates**

Extrusion $\dfrac{£206,350}{15,500 \text{ machine hours}}$ = **£13.31 for each machine hour**

Machining $\dfrac{£213,730}{20,000 \text{ machine hours}}$ = **£10.69 for each machine hour**

Finishing $\dfrac{£75,920}{15,000 \text{ labour hours}}$ = **£5.06 for each labour hour.**

(c)   (i) Contract costing
    (ii) Batch costing
    (iii) Job costing

☑ Solution 19

- You will need a systematic approach in part (b), with neat workings to help you achieve 100 per cent accuracy.

(a) A: Rent cost apportioned to Assembly Department $= \dfrac{6,000}{20,000} \times £750,000 =$ **£225,000**

    B: Personnel cost apportioned to Assembly Department $= \dfrac{210}{350} \times £60,000 =$ **£36,000**

    C: Using an apportionment basis of cost of equipment, depreciation cost apportioned to Machining Department $= \dfrac{1,200,000}{1,600,000} \times £200,000 =$ **£150,000**

(b) **£2,850,000** (to the nearest 000)

Workings:

	Machining £	Assembly £	Stores £	Maintenance £
Initial allocation	2,250,000	1,900,000	250,000	800,000
Apportion stores	75,000	75,000	(250,000)	100,000
Apportion maintenance	405,000	270,000	225,000	(900,000)
Apportion stores	67,500	67,500	(225,000)	90,000
Apportion maintenance	40,500	27,000	22,500	(90,000)
Apportion stores	6,750	6,750	(22,500)	9,000
Apportion maintenance	4,050	2,700	2,250	(9,000)
Apportion stores	675	675	(2,250)	900
Apportion maintenance	405	270	225	(900)
Apportion stores	68	67	(225)	90
Apportion maintenance	40	27	23	(90)
Total apportioned	2,849,988			

PREPARING FOR THE ASSESSMENT

 Solution 20

- The full production cost includes production overheads absorbed using the predetermined rates provided in the question

(a) The direct cost per unit of product B is £149
(b) The full production cost per unit of product B is £189

Working	£	£
Direct material (3 kg × £9)		27
Direct labour		
Department A (4 hours × £14)	56	
Department B (6 hours × £11)	66	
		122
Total direct cost		149
Production overhead		
Department A (4 labour hours × £7)	28	
Department B (2 machine hours × £6)	12	
		40
Full production cost		189

 Solution 21

- Remember to add on the target return for one unit of Q and not the total required return from all 10,000 units.

The selling price for one unit of product Q, to the nearest penny, is £227.62

	£ per unit
Direct material cost	54.00
Direct labour cost	87.00
Total direct cost	141.00
Production overhead absorbed = 11 hours × £7	77.00
Total production cost	218.00
Mark-up for non-production costs = 3% × £218.00	6.54
Full cost	224.54
Profit mark-up (see working)	3.08
Selling price	227.62

Working:

Target return on investment in product Q = £220,000 × 14% = £30,800
Target return per unit of product Q = £30,800/10,000 units = £3.08.

Solution 22

- Calculate the breakeven point before and after the change in production methods, using the formula:

$$\text{Breakeven point in units} = \frac{\text{Fixed costs}}{\text{Contribution per unit}}$$

Answer: (A)

Existing situation:

$$\text{Breakeven point} = \frac{£24,400}{£8} = 3,050 \text{ units}$$

Working:

Contribution per unit	£
Selling price	14
Variable cost	(6)
Contribution	8

New production methods:

$$\text{Breakeven point} = \frac{£24,400 \times 1.3}{£10} = 3,172 \text{ units}$$

Working:

Contribution per unit	£
Selling price	15
Variable cost	(5)
Contribution	10

Increase in number of units: $3,172 - 3,050 = 122$.

 ## Solution 23

- First calculate the existing profit level.
- Using the new cost and selling price, calculate the required sales volume using the formula:

$$\text{Required sales volume} = \frac{(\text{Fixed costs} + \text{required profit})}{\text{Contribution per unit}}$$

Answer: (A)

$$\frac{£31,720 + £39,600}{£15 - £5} = 7,132 \text{ units}$$

(Working for existing profit: 8,000 units $\times$ £8 = £64,000 contribution less fixed costs £24,400 = £39,600.)

PREPARING FOR THE ASSESSMENT

 ## Solution 24

- Do not rush this question. You can probably easily calculate the breakeven point in terms of sales value, but then you will need to stop and think carefully.

Answer: (D)

$$\text{Breakeven point in terms of sales value} = \frac{£120,000}{0.3} = £400,000.$$

This must now be divided by the selling price.

The breakeven point in terms of units cannot be derived because we do not know the unit selling price.

 ## Solution 25

- The single line drawn on the graph represents profits or losses earned for a range of activity levels.

Answer: (D)

Point K indicates the loss incurred at zero activity. At this point, the loss incurred is equal to the fixed cost.

 ## Solution 26

- Profit-volume chart is the name given to a graph which indicates the profits or losses earned for a range of activity levels.

Answer: (D)

Charts A and B would include lines for costs and revenues. Chart C would be depicted by a single line, starting at a point above the origin on the vertical axis. This point represents the total fixed cost incurred at zero activity.

 ## Solution 27

- Remember that contribution for a period is equal to the fixed costs plus the profit for the period.
- Once you have calculated the contribution you can use the C/S ratio to derive the sales value, and that will lead you to the variable costs and thus the direct wages for the period.

$$\text{Contribution} = £30,000 + £56,400 = £86,400$$

$$\frac{\text{Contribution}}{\text{Sales}} = 0.3$$

$$\text{Sales} = \frac{£86,400}{0.3} = £288,000$$

$$\text{Variable costs} = \text{sales value} - \text{contribution} = £288,000 - £86,400 = £201,600$$

$$\text{Direct wages} = 20\% \times £201,600 = £40,320.$$

Solution 28

- For a given level of sales, the margin of safety and the breakeven point will always move in the 'opposite direction' to each other. If one increases then the other decreases.
- The contribution to sales ratio is not affected by the level of fixed costs incurred.

(a) The breakeven point will *increase*.
(b) The contribution to sales ratio will *stay the same*.
(c) The margin of safety will *decrease*.

 ## Solution 29

- You will need to use the contribution to sales (C/S) ratio in this question, in calculating the breakeven sales value. Once you have calculated the variable costs as a percentage of sales value you should be able to use this to determine the C/S ratio.
- The contribution breakeven chart that has been drawn shows the variable cost line instead of the fixed cost line. This means that contribution can be read directly from the chart.

Workings:

	August £	September £	Change £
Sales	80,000	90,000	10,000
Cost of sales	50,000	55,000	5,000
Selling and distribution	8,000	9,000	1,000
Administration	15,000	15,000	nil

(i) Cost of sales:
  Variable   £5,000/£10,000 = 50p/£1 of sales (50% of sales)
  Fixed   £50,000 − (50% × £80,000) = £10,000
(ii) Selling and distribution:
  Fixed   nil
  Variable   £1,000/£10,000 = 10p/£1 of sales (10% of sales)
(iii) Administration:
  Fixed   £15,000
  Variable   nil

A: $\text{Breakeven sales value} = \dfrac{\text{Fixed costs}}{\text{C/S ratio *}} = \dfrac{£25,000}{0.4} = £62,500$

  *Variable costs have been calculated to be 60 per cent of sales. Therefore, the C/S ratio is 40 per cent.

B: Total cost of £80,000 sales value = **£73,000** (from original data).
C: Total variable cost for £80,000 sales value = £80,000 × 0.6 = **£48,000**.
D: Total fixed cost = cost of sales £10,000 + administration £15,000 = **£25,000**.

Solution 30

- The products must be ranked in order of their contribution per machine hour used.

Answer: (B)

	Product W £	Product X £	Product Y £	Product Z £
Contribution per batch	10.40	9.00	5.40	9.00
Contribution per machine hour	10.40/12	9.00/9	5.40/6	9.00/11
=	0.8667	1.0000	0.9000	0.8182
Ranking	3rd	1st	2nd	4th

 # Solution 31

- The best production plan in part (b) is that which will maximise the contribution from the installation labour. The products must therefore be ranked in order of their contribution per hour.

(a) **2,900 hours**.

   Workings:
   Hours of installation labour required to satisfy maximum demand

	Hours
Day scan*: 2,000 units × 3 hours/unit	6,000
Night scan: 3,000 units × 4 hours/unit	12,000
Omni scan: 1,800 units × 5.5 hours/unit	9,900
	27,900
Available hours	25,000
Shortfall	2,900

   * Hours of installation labour for Day scan $= \dfrac{£24}{£8} = 3$ hours.

(b) Day scan 2,000 units
   Night scan 2,275 units
   Omni scan 1,800 units

Workings:

	Day scan	Night scan	Omni scan
	£	£	£
Selling price	250	320	460
Variable costs			
Material	(70)	(110)	(155)
Manufacturing labour	(40)	(55)	(70)
Installation labour	(24)	(32)	(44)
Variable overheads	(16)	(20)	(28)
Contribution per unit	100	103	163
Installation hours required	3	4	5.5
Contribution per installation hour	£33.33	£25.75	£29.64
Production priority	1st	3rd	2nd

Best production plan

	Units		Hours used
Day scan to maximum demand	2,000	(×3.0)	6,000
Omni scan to maximum demand	1,800	(×5.5)	9,900

This leaves $(25,000 - 6,000 - 9,900) = 9,100$ installation labour hours for Night scan.

Therefore, production of Night scan $= \dfrac{9,100}{4} = 2,275$ units.

 ## Solution 32

Answer: (C)

Although standard costs are based on estimates of what might happen in the future, a standard costing system does not provide actual future costs.

 ## Solution 33

• This is a straightforward exercise in accumulating costs using the data provided.
The standard variable production cost of one unit of product H is £182

		£ per unit
Direct material W	(4 kg × £1)	4
Direct material X	(2 kg × £5)	10
Direct labour	(14 × £8)	112
Variable production overhead	(14 × £4)	56
Total variable production cost		182

Solution 34

- Remember that all the 'quantity' variances (material usage, labour efficiency and variable overhead efficiency) are valued at the standard rate rather than at the actual rate. Therefore the material usage variance in kg should be multiplied by the standard price per kg to determine the monetary value of the material usage variance.

Answer: (A)

	£
Material price variance	
Standard cost of materials used 26,400 kg × £13	343,200
Actual cost	336,600
	6,600 F

	Kg
Material usage variance	
Standard usage 12,000 units × 2 kg	24,000
Actual usage	26,400
	2,400 × £13/kg = £31,200 A

 Solution 35

- Once again, remember to use the standard rate per hour to evaluate the labour efficiency variance.

Answer: (B)

	£
Labour rate variance	
Standard cost of hours used 40,200 × £12	482,400
Actual labour cost	506,520
	24,120 A

	Hours
Labour efficiency variance	
Standard time 12,000 units × 3.3 hours	39,600
Actual time	40,200
	600 × £12/hour = £7,200 A

 Solution 36

- Remember that the variable overhead efficiency variance is directly related to the labour efficiency variance

Answer: (A)

	£
Variable overhead expenditure variance	
40,200 hours of variable overhead should cost (×£2.50)	100,500
But did cost	107,250
	6,750 adverse

Variable overhead efficiency variance

Efficiency variance in hours, from labour efficiency variance	600	adverse
× standard variable overhead rate per hour	×£2.50	
	£1,500	adverse

 ## Solution 37

- The usage must have been higher than standard because the usage variance is adverse.
- Remember that the usage variance is equal to the excess usage multiplied by the standard price per kg of material.

Answer: (D)

Standard price per kilogram of material: $\dfrac{£46,248}{11,280} = £4.10$

Number of kilograms excess usage: $\dfrac{£492}{£4.10} = 120 \, \text{kg}$.

Standard usage: $11,280 \, \text{kg} - 120 \, \text{kg} = 11,160 \, \text{kg}$.

Solution 38

- The adverse efficiency variance means that the actual time taken was higher than the standard allowance.
- Notice that there was a nil rate variance. This means that the actual rate per hour was the same as the standard rate per hour.
- There are a number of ways of calculating the correct solution. You might have used a different method – it does not matter as long as you arrive at the correct answer!

Answer: (A)

$$\text{Excess hours above standard time} = \text{efficiency variance/standard rate per hour}$$
$$= \frac{£26,000}{8} = 3,250 \text{ hours}$$
$$\text{Actual hours worked} = \frac{£182,000}{£8} = 22,750 \text{ hours}$$
$$\text{Standard hours for actual output} = 22,750 - 3,250$$
$$= 19,500 \text{ hours}$$
$$\text{Standard hours for one unit} = \frac{19,500}{6,500} = 3 \text{ hours}.$$

Solution 39

- 'Backwards' variance questions are a good way of testing whether you really understand the logic of the variance calculations.
- If you got this question wrong, go back and study variance analysis again to ensure that you can calculate all the required variances quickly and accurately.

Actual labour hours worked	25,600
Adverse efficiency variance in hours $\left(\dfrac{£8,250}{£7.50} \right)$	1,100
Standard hours expected for production achieved	**24,500**

Solution 40

- Remember that the sales volume contribution variance is evaluated using the standard contribution per unit.

(a) The sales price variance for product V for June was £34,350 favourable
(b) The sales volume contribution variance for product V for June was £9,430 adverse

	£	
4,390 units should sell for (×£45)	197,550	
But did sell for	231,900	
Sales price variance	34,350	favourable
Actual sales volume	4,390	units
Budget sales volume	4,800	units
Sales volume variance in units	410	adverse
× standard contribution per unit £(45 − 22)	×£23	
Sales volume contribution variance	£9,430	adverse

 ## Solution 41

- Adverse variances are deducted from the budgeted contribution to derive the actual contribution. Favourable variances are added because they would increase the contribution above the budgeted level.

The actual contribution reported for the period was **£59,755**.

£48,000 + £(11,245 + 6,025 − 3,100 − 2,415) = £59,755.

 ## Solution 42

Only (b) and (c) could have contributed to an adverse direct labour efficiency variance.

(a) Higher output would not in itself cause an adverse efficiency variance. In calculating the efficiency variance the expected labour hours would be flexed according to the actual output achieved.
(b) If material was difficult to process the number of labour hours taken might have been higher than standard. This would result in an adverse labour efficiency variance.
(c) If the original standard time was set too low then actual times are likely to be higher than standard, thus resulting in an adverse labour efficiency variance.
(d) A higher hourly labour rate would cause an adverse labour rate variance, not an adverse efficiency variance.
(e) Using employees who are more skilled than specified in the standard is more likely to result in a favourable direct labour efficiency variance.

Solution 43

- Reason (a) is an example of an inter-relationship between variances; the adverse sales price variance could have resulted in the favourable sales volume contribution variance.

Reasons (a) and (c) could have contributed to a favourable sales volume contribution variance. A lower sales price might encourage more customers to buy which, as with (c), might increase sales volumes above budget and a favourable sales volume contribution variance would result.

A higher actual contribution than the standard per unit (reason (b)) would not result in a favourable sales volume contribution variance, since the variance is evaluated at the standard contribution per unit.

 Solution 44

- First calculate the standard time allowed and compare this with the time taken. You can convert all times to minutes or to hours, whichever you find easier.
- Next read the question carefully to determine the bonus. Every bonus scheme is different, so do not assume that this one is calculated in the same way as the last scheme you met!

Answer: (A)

Standard time allowed = 400 units × 7 minutes	2,800 minutes
Actual time taken = 42 hours × 60 minutes	2,520 minutes
Time saved against standard allowance	280 minutes

Bonus payable = 75% × (280/60) × £10 = £35.

 Solution 45

- Remember: if you are reduced to guessing, then eliminate first the options that are obviously incorrect. For example, option D must be incorrect because direct materials returned to stores unused cannot yet have become part of cost of sales.

Answer: (B)

This is the reverse of the entries that would have been made when the direct materials were first issued to production.

 Solution 46

- Ensure that you read the introduction to the question carefully. We need to know that this is the company's year-end, in order to be able to select the correct entry.

Answer: (A)

Since this is the year-end, the balance on the overhead control account would be transferred to the income statement, rather than carried forward to the following period.

The debit side of the account (the overhead incurred) is greater than the credit side of the account (the overhead absorbed into work in progress). Therefore, the overhead is under-recovered or under-absorbed.

Solution 47

- You might find it easiest to quickly sketch the T-accounts from the data provided, then you can simply pick out the correct journal entries and tick them.
- Wages incurred are higher than the wages paid, so there must be an accrual for the period, but you are not asked about the accounting entries for this element of the transactions.

The correct choices are:

(b) Debit   wages control account: £31,700
Wages actually paid are debited to the wages control account and credited to the bank or cash account.

(c) Debit   work in progress account: £27,400

(d) Debit   production overhead control account: £6,000

(e) Credit   wages control account: £33,400
Direct wages incurred are credited to the wages control account and debited to work in progress. Indirect wages incurred are credited to the wages control account and debited to the production overhead control account, pending their later absorption into work in progress.

 # Solution 48

- In part (b), you might like to draw up your own production overhead control account. Although you would not earn marks for this, it might help you to collect together all the information you need to calculate the under- or over-absorption.

(a) A   £48,250
    B   £598,050 (direct materials issued to work in progress)
    C   £617,300
    D   £32,800 (indirect materials issued).

(b) The production overheads for the period were *over*-absorbed by £57,995. This amount will be transferred as a *credit* in the income statement at the end of the period.

Working:

Production overhead control account			
	£		£
Payables	359,725	Work in progress (280% × £173,400)	485,520
Provision for depreciation	35,000		
Indirect materials	32,800		
Over-absorption	57,995		
	485,520		485,520

 # Solution 49

- A favourable variance is always credited to the relevant variance account, so you can easily eliminate options (B) and (D) as incorrect.

Answer: (C)

As a general rule, all variances are entered in the accounts at the point at which they arise. The labour rate variance is therefore recorded in the wages control account.

Solution 50

- Remember that adverse variances are always debited in the relevant variance account, and favourable variances are always credited in the variance account.

(a)

	Debit	Credit	No entry in this account
Materials control account		✓	
Material price variance account	✓		
Work in progress account			✓

(b)

	Debit	Credit	No entry in this account
Materials control account			✓
Material usage variance account		✓	
Work in progress account	✓		

(c) The labour force was paid at a *higher hourly rate than standard*. (Because the labour rate variance is adverse.)

(d)

	Debit	Credit	No entry in this account
Wages control account			✓
Labour efficiency variance account		✓	
Work in progress account	✓		

 Solution 51

- Do not confuse the term 'works order number' with 'job number'. A reference number (in this case the works order number) is used in the recording of costs in any specific order costing system, whether it is a job, batch or contract system.
- After our answer we have included some discussion, so that you can understand the reasoning behind the answers, for revision purposes. You would not add any such discussion or workings in the actual assessment.

  (i) Number 488 *contract* costing
 (ii) Number 517 *contract* costing
(iii) Number 518 *job* costing
(iv) Number 519 *job* costing

Discussion

Works order 488. This should be accounted for as a long-term contract since it spans three accounting years, and because the sums of money involved in the contract are large.

    Works order 517. This work spans a financial year-end with a significant sales value, so although the case for 'contract' status would not be as strong as for works order 488, this nevertheless would be appropriate.

    Works orders 518 and 519. Both of these are of small value, and both have durations of approximately 2 months, although spanning a financial year-end. In neither case, would the apportionment of profit over the 2 financial years be worthwhile, any profit being most likely to be taken at the end of the work. Should a loss be expected, however, this should be brought forward into the accounts of the first financial period covered. Long-term contract status would not be appropriate, however, so they should be accounted for using job costing.

Solution 52

- Use the information provided to determine the number of chargeable hours each year.
- Calculate the hourly rate that the accountant needs to charge to cover her expenses and salary, based on the number of chargeable hours.
- Apply the hourly rate to the job in question.

Answer: (C)

Chargeable hours each year will be $(52 - 4$ weeks$=)$ 48 weeks $\times$ 35 hours per week $= 1,680$ hours $\times 75\% = 1,260$ hours.

In these 1,260 hours, she must make £60,000 to cover her salary and general expenses. Therefore, her charge rate should be

$$\frac{£60,000}{1,260} = £47.62 \text{ per hour}$$

Thus, the quote for a 50-hour job should be £47.62/hour $\times$ 50 $=$ £2,381.

 # Solution 53

- Read the question carefully. Profit is calculated as a percentage of sales, not as a percentage of cost.

Answer: (C)

	£	
Direct materials 10 × £10	100	
Direct labour 10 × £10	100	
Prime cost	200	
Variable production overheads 10 × £4	40	
Fixed production overheads 10 × £20*	200	
Total production cost	440	
Other costs	50	
Total cost	490	70%
Profit	210	30%
Quote for the job	700	100%

*£200,000 overheads/10,000 hours = £20 per hour.

 # Solution 54

- Be careful when you are adding the profit percentage to the total cost in part (b). The question states that the company wishes to achieve 30 per cent profit margin on sales. Do not make the common mistake of simply adding 30 per cent to cost. This will not produce 30 per cent profit margin on sales.

(a) (i) **£29,210**

Workings:

	£	£
Direct materials		26,500
Labour		
Preparation: 90 × £8	720	
Etching: 130 × £7	910	
Assembly: 180 × £6	1,080	
		2,710
		29,210

(ii)

Preparation Department overheads	£14,300
Etching Department overheads	£5,880
Assembly Department overheads	£4,860

Workings:
Overhead absorption rates:

$$\text{Preparation:} \quad \frac{£165,000}{3,000} = £55 \text{ per machine hour}$$

$$\text{Etching:} \quad \frac{£98,000}{1,400} = £70 \text{ per machine hour}$$

$$\text{Assembly:} \quad \frac{£48,600}{1,800} = £27 \text{ per labour hour}$$

Overheads charged to batch

Preparation: 260 × £55	£14,300
Etching: 84 × £70	£5,880
Assembly: 180 × £27	£4,860

(b) **£465**

Workings:

	£
Batch cost	65,100
Profit (×30/70)	27,900
Sales value of batch	93,000
Selling price per unit (93,000/200)	**£465**

Solution 55

- When you are calculating the depreciation charge in part (b), don't forget that the contract has been in operation for only ten months.

(a) **£1,220,000**

(b) **£750,000**

(c) **£2,240,000**

Workings:

		£000
(a)	Materials delivered direct to site	1,200
	Materials issued from head office stores	200
		1,400
	Materials on site at 31 December 20X0	(180)
	Cost of material used on contract	1,220
(b)	Plant delivered to site at cost	900
	Depreciation $\left(900 \times 20\% \times \dfrac{10}{12}\right)$	150
	Net book value of plant at 31 December	750
(c)	Final contract value	10,000
	Cost incurred to date	3,360
	Cost to completion	2,640
	Estimated contract profit	4,000

Profit to be recognised on contract = £4,000,000 × (3,360,000/6,000,000 total cost)
= £2,240,000.

 Solution 56

- You may be able to solve this question without producing a reconciliation of the input and output volumes. We have shown a reconciliation so that you can use it for revision purposes.

56.1   Answer: (B)

20,000 kg input × 15% = 3,000 kg normal loss × £1 = £3,000

56.2   Answer: (D)

Input	Kg	Output	Kg	Kg to absorb cost
Materials	20,000	To process 2	18,500	18,500
		Normal loss	3,000	–
		Abnormal gain	(1,500)	(1,500)
	20,000		20,000	17,000

Costs	£
Materials input	50,000
Direct labour	15,000
Production overheads	22,500
Scrap value normal loss	(3,000)
	84,500
Cost per kg £84,500/17,000	4.9706

Value of abnormal gain = 1,500 kg × £4.9706 = £7,456.

56.3 Answer: (C)

Value of output = 18,500 kg × £4.9706 = £91,956.

 Solution 57

- Do not be put off by the slightly different layout of the working template.
- The question is in fact very straightforward. To perform the necessary valuations you simply need to use the unit rates supplied in the template.

(a) £37,200

Working:

	£
Raw material input	37,500
Less scrap value of normal loss (50,000 litres × 3% × £0.20)	(300)
Material cost for the period	37,200

(b) £102,900

Working:

Value of transfer to process 2 = 49,000 litres × (£0.75 + £1.35) = £102,900.

(c) £1,050

Working:

Value of abnormal loss = 500 litres × £(0.75 + 1.35) = £1,050.

(d) £5,160

Working:

Value of closing work in progress = (4,000 litres × £0.75)
$$+ [(4,000 × 40\%) \text{ litres} × £1.35]$$
$$= £3,000 + £2,160$$
$$= 5,160.$$

Solution 58

• The materials lost in production are scrapped. Therefore, no value is allocated to the normal loss. A common error would be to attempt to allocate a monetary value to the normal loss.

(a) 10,320 equivalent litres
(b) £7.00 per equivalent litre

Workings:

Material cost:		£
A	3/6 × 12,000 × £8.00	48,000
B	2/6 × 12,000 × £6.00	24,000
C	1/6 × 12,000 × £3.90	7,800
		79,800

Statement of equivalent litres

	Total	Materials	Labour and overheads
Completed production	9,500	9,500	9,500
Abnormal loss	100	100	100
Normal loss	600	–	–
Closing WIP:			
Material	1,800	1,800	–
Labour and overheads (40% × 1,800) − 720		–	720
Equivalent litres	12,000	11,400	10,320
Cost		£79,800	£41,280
Cost per equivalent litre	£11.00	£7.00	£4.00

 Solution 59

• You will find process costing questions much quicker and easier to answer if you learn a pro-forma layout for your working papers, but remember that you will earn no marks for your workings.
• When you are carrying out your equivalent units calculation, remember that any units that are now in process 3 must be complete as regards process 2 input.

The cost per equivalent unit produced was:

(a) process 2 input: £2.40 per equivalent unit
(b) material added: £0.60 per equivalent unit
(c) wages and overhead: £1.20 per equivalent unit

Workings:

Input	Units	Output	Units	Process 2 input	Material added	Wages and overhead
Opening WIP	6,000	Finished goods	46,500	46,500	46,500	46,500
Process 2	48,000	Normal loss	3000[1]	–	–	–
		Abnormal loss	500[2]	500	400	300
		Closing WIP	4,000	4,000	2,000	1,200
	54,000		54,000	51,000	48,900	48,000
		Costs	£	£	£	£
		Opening WIP		14,400	2,160	2,880
		Input costs		110,400	27,180	54,720
		Normal loss value		(2,400)	–	–
				122,400	29,340	57,600
		Cost per unit	4.20	2.40	0.60	1.20

Notes:
1. Normal loss = 6% × (6,000 + 48,000 − 4,000) = 3,000 units.
2. The abnormal loss is found as a balancing figure in the input/output reconciliation.

Solution 60

The statement is false. It describes objective classification.

Subjective classification is the classification of expenditure items according to the nature of the expenditure.

Solution 61

(a) 544 indicates the *subjective* classification of the expenditure item.
(b) 221 indicates the *objective* classification of the expenditure item.

Solution 62

- We are told that the various vehicles incur variable costs per kilometre in the ratio 1:3:5. Therefore, we need to calculate a weighted total number of kilometres travelled, in order to fairly share out the total variable costs incurred. We cannot simply calculate the variable cost per kilometre as (costs incurred ÷ kilometres travelled), because a kilometre travelled by a motor-cycle costs less than a kilometre travelled by a bulk parcel van or lorry.

(a) Courier service   £129,400
(b) Domestic parcels   £205,300
(c) Bulk parcels   £140,500

PREPARING FOR THE ASSESSMENT

Workings:

Weighted total kilometres travelled

Weight	Distance km	Weighted km
1	168,000	168,000
3	82,000	246,000
5	54,000	270,000
		684,000

Total variable costs = £307,800

Therefore, variable costs per weighted km = $£\dfrac{307,800}{684,000}$ = £0.45 per weighted km

Variable cost per service is therefore:

	£
Courier service: 168,000 × 0.45	75,600
Domestic parcels: 246,000 × 0.45	110,700
Bulk parcels: 270,000 × 0.45	121,500
	307,800

Thus, contribution per service is:

	Courier £	Domestic £	Bulk £
Sales	205,000	316,000	262,000
Variable costs	(75,600)	(110,700)	(121,500)
Contribution	129,400	205,300	140,500

 Solution 63

- Value added = sales revenue less materials costs and the cost of bought-in goods and services. Wages and salary costs are not bought-in costs and must be excluded from the overhead cost figures when calculating the value added.

For the F Division for the latest period, the value added was £132,270

	£	£	£
Sales revenue			289,500
Less materials cost		89,790	
Production overhead cost	54,030		
Less salaries included	10,710		
Bought-in production overhead cost		43,320	
Marketing overhead cost	21,890		
Less salaries included	14,560		
		7,330	
General and admin. overhead	38,120		
Less salaries included	21,330		
		16,790	
Total bought in goods and services			157,230
Value added			132,270

Solution 64

- The salary costs and general overhead costs cannot be specifically attributed to either type of goods therefore these costs should not be included in the calculation of gross margin.

(a) The gross margin generated by second-hand donated goods sold was £4,818

(b) The gross margin generated by new goods sold was £3,168

Second-hand donated goods	£	£
Sales income		
Sold to customers	4,880	
Sold for recycling	88	
		4,968
Cost of laundering, etc.	120	
Valuation costs	30	
		150
Gross margin		4,818
New goods	£	£
Sales income		6,790
Less: purchase cost	3,332	
delivery cost	290	
		3,622
Gross margin		3,168

 Solution 65

- Only three of the budget roles are correct here, but there are others that are not mentioned including communication, planning, resource allocation and motivation.

Answer: (B)

A budget does not provide a means for expansion. In fact, an organisation can budget to reduce its level of activity.

 Solution 66

- If you remember that the principal budget factor is sometimes referred to as the limiting factor, then you should not have too many problems in selecting the correct answer!

Answer: (B)

The principal budget factor is important because it must be identified at the start of the budgeting process. Once the budget for the limiting factor has been prepared, all other budgets must be coordinated with it.

Solution 67

- Although continuous budgeting is quicker and easier using a computerised system it can be accomplished with a manual system.

Options (a) and (c) are correct.

 # Solution 68

- Remember the formula to calculate budgeted production:

  Budgeted sales + Budgeted closing inventory − Budgeted opening inventory

Answer: (A)

	Units
Required by sales	120,000
Required closing inventory	6,500
Less opening inventory anticipated	(13,000)
Production level	113,500

 # Solution 69

- Did you read the question carefully and note that the material *usage* budget was required, not the material purchases budget?

Answer: (C)

10,000 units × 4 kg = 40,000 kg

 # Solution 70

- The first step is to calculate the required production volume, taking account of the budgeted change in finished goods inventories.
- Convert the production volume into material usage requirements, then adjust for the budgeted change in raw materials inventories to determine the budgeted purchases.

Answer: (B)

	Units
Budgeted sales of product P	4,000
Required decrease in finished goods inventory	600
Required production	3,400

	Kg
Raw materials usage budget (×2 kg)	6,800
Increase in raw materials inventories	1,500
Budgeted purchases of raw material	8,300

Solution 71

- Note that the 5 per cent bad debts will never be received in cash.
- Do not forget to allow for the 2 per cent settlement discount for those customers paying in September for August sales.

Answer: (C)

	£
Receipts in September from:	
June sales £100,000 × 15%	15,000
July sales £150,000 × 20%	30,000
August sales £130,000 × 60% less	
2% settlement discount	76,440
Total receipts in September	121,440

 # Solution 72

- Make sure that you are completely familiar with the descriptions of all of the types of budgeting covered in this *Learning System*.

A budget which is designed to show the allowed expenditure for the actual level of activity achieved is known as a *flexible budget*. A fixed budget is prepared for a single level of activity and a rolling budget is a continuously updated budget.

 # Solution 73

- You will need to produce quite a few workings for your own benefit.

(a) **£1,740,000**

Quarter 1 *Sales Budget*

	January	February	March	Total
Sales (units)	5,000	5,500	6,000	
Selling price for each unit	£100	£100	£115	
Sales (£)	£500,000	£550,000	£690,000	£1,740,000

(b) **23,100 units**

Quarter 4 *Production Budget*	units	
Required sales units	23,250	(7,750 + 8,000 + 7,500)
Add:		
Required closing inventory	1,400	(20% × 7,000 − January 20X3 sales units)
Less:		
Opening inventory	(1,550)	(20% × 7,750 − October sales units)
Production budget	23,100	

(c) **56,400 kg**

Quarter 2 *Material Usage Budget*

Quarter 2 production units	18,800*
Material usage for each unit	3 kg
Total quarter 2 material usage	56,400 kg

*It is calculated below as a result of the production budget.

Quarter 2 *Production Budget*	units	
Required sales units	18,750	(6,000 + 6,250 + 6,500)
Add:		
Required closing inventory	1,250	(20% × 6,250 − July sales units)
Less:		
Opening inventory	(1,200)	(20% × 6,000 − April sales units)
Production budget	18,800*	

(d) **£249,900**

Quarter 1 *Material Purchases Budget*

Quarter 1 material usage	50,100 kg	(16,700* × 3 kg)
Add:		
Required closing inventory	3,630 kg	(6,050* × 3 kg × 20%)
Less:		
Opening inventory	(3,750) kg	
Purchases	49,980 kg	
Price of each kg	£5.00	
Total material purchases budget	£249,900	

Quarter 1 *Production Budget*	units	
Required sales units	16,500	(5,000 + 5,500 + 6,000)
Add:		
Required closing inventory	1,200	(20% × 6,000 − April sales units)
Less:		
Opening inventory	(1,000)	
Production budget	16,700*	

April *Production Budget*	units	
Required sales units	6,000	
Add:		
Required closing inventory	1,250	(20% × 6,250 − May sales units)
Less:		
Opening inventory	(1,200)	(20% × 6,000 − April sales units)
Production budget	6,050*	

(e) **126,300 hours**

Quarter 3 *Production Budget*	units	
Required sales units	20,750	
Add:		
Required closing inventory	1,550	(20% × 7,750 − October sales units)
Less:		
Opening inventory	(1,250)	(20% × 6,250 − July sales units)
Production budget	21,050	
Total skilled labour		
hours required	84,200 hours	(21,050 × 4 hours)
Total unskilled labour		
hours required	42,100 hours	(21,050 × 2 hours)
Total hours required	126,300 hours	

 ## Solution 74

- Remember to exclude depreciation from your calculations of overhead cash payments. It is not a cash flow.

(a) June: £**6,500**
July: £**11,500**
August: £**8,000**

Workings:

	June £	July £	August £
Closing inventory	3,500	6,000	4,000
Material usage	8,000	9,000	10,000
	11,500	15,000	14,000
Less: opening inventory	5,000	3,500	6,000
Direct material purchases	6,500	11,500	8,000

(b) £51,000

(c) £20,000

Workings:

(b)

	£
Sales receipts in August:	
Cash sales (10% × £60,000)	6,000
Credit sales from July (90% × £50,000)	45,000
	51,000

(c) *Cash payments in July:*

	£
Wages	13,000
Overheads (June £8,500 less depreciation)	7,000
	20,000

Solution 75

- The flexed budgets are reasonably straightforward to produce: all variable costs are multiplied by a factor of 13,600 and 14,500, respectively, and fixed overheads remain unaltered by the change in activity.

(a) **£2,560,000**

Workings:	£
Direct labour: £46 × 13,600 units	625,600
Direct material: £30 × 13,600 units	408,000
Variable overheads: £24 × 13,600 units	326,400
Fixed overheads: original budget	
(£80 × 15,000 units)	1,200,000
	2,560,000

(b) (i) **£60,000** adverse

 (ii) **£164,000** adverse

Workings:	£	£
Actual cost		2,814,000
Budget cost allowance:		
Labour, materials and variable o/h		
£(46 + 30 + 24) × 14,500	1,450,000	
Fixed overhead – original budget	1,200,000	
		2,650,000
Expenditure variance		164,000 (A)

$$\text{Sales volume contribution variance} = \text{volume shortfall} \times \text{standard contribution per unit}$$
$$= 500 \text{ units} \times £(220 - 100)$$
$$= £60,000 \text{ adverse}$$

 Solution 76

- Be careful to select actions that are appropriate both for a deficit and for the short term.

Actions (a) and (b) would be appropriate actions.

 Action (c) would not be appropriate because increasing receivables would drain the cash balance still further. Action (d) is more suited to a long-term deficit, since share capital is a long term source of finance.

Solution 77

- The first step is to use the high-low method to determine the fixed and variable elements of the maintenance costs.
- Use the result to determine the budget cost allowance for period 6 and then compare this allowance with the actual expenditure during the period.

The bonus to be paid to the maintenance manager in period 6 is **£28.60**.

	Activity Hours	£
Using the high-low method:		
Period 4	3,800	11,040
Period 5	4,320	11,976
Change	520	936

Variable maintenance budgeted cost per hour = £936/520 = £1.80

Fixed maintenance cost budgeted per period = £11,976 − (4,320 × £1.80) = £4,200

	£
Fixed cost allowance for period 6	4,200
Variable cost (4,090 machine hours × £1.80)	7,362
Total budget cost allowance for period 6	11,562
Actual maintenance expenditure	10,990
Saving	572

Bonus payable = 5% × £572 = £28.60

Mock Assessment 1

Mock Assessment 1

Certificate in Business Accounting
Fundamentals of Management Accounting

You are allowed two hours to complete this assessment.

The assessment contains 50 questions.

All questions are compulsory.

Do not turn the page until you are ready to attempt the assessment under timed conditions.

Mock Assessment Questions

? Question 1

Which ONE of the following would be classified as direct labour?

☐ Personnel manager in a company servicing cars.
☐ Bricklayer in a construction company.
☐ General manager in a DIY shop.
☐ Maintenance manager in a company producing cameras.

? Question 2

The principal budget factor is the

☐ factor which limits the activities of the organisation and is often the starting point in budget preparation.
☐ budgeted revenue expected in a forthcoming period.
☐ main budget into which all subsidiary budgets are consolidated.
☐ overestimation of revenue budgets and underestimation of cost budgets, which operates as a safety factor against risk.

? Question 3

R Ltd absorbs overheads based on units produced. In one period, 110,000 units were produced and the actual overheads were £500,000. Overheads were £50,000 over-absorbed in the period.

The overhead absorption rate was £ [   ] per unit.

? Question 4

X operates an integrated cost accounting system. The Work-in-Progress Account at the end of the period showed the following information:

Work-in-Progress Account

	$		$
Stores ledger a/c	100,000	?	200,000
Wage control a/c	75,000		
Factory overhead a/c	50,000	Balance c/d	25,000
	225,000		225,000

The $200,000 credit entry represents the value of the transfer to the

☐ Cost of sales account.
☐ Material control account.
☐ Sales account.
☐ Finished goods inventory account.

Question 5

X Ltd absorbs overheads on the basis of machine hours. Details of budgeted and actual figures are as follows:

	Budget	Actual
Overheads	£1,250,000	£1,005,000
Machine hours	250,000 hours	220,000 hours

(a) Overheads for the period were:

under-absorbed ☐
over-absorbed ☐

(b) The value of the under/over absorption for the period was £ _____ .

Question 6

In an integrated bookkeeping system, when the actual production overheads exceed the absorbed production overheads, the accounting entries to close off the production overhead account at the end of the period would be:

	Debit	Credit	No entry in this account
Production overhead account	☐	☐	☐
Work in progress account	☐	☐	☐
Income statement	☐	☐	☐

Question 7

A retailer uses a Last In First Out (LIFO) inventory valuation system. Movements of item M for February are as follows.

		Units	£ per unit
1st February	Opening inventory balance	230	7.80
3rd February	Receipts	430	7.95
8th February	Issues	370	
14th February	Issues	110	
22nd February	Receipts	400	8.01

No other movements of item M occurred during the month.

(a) The value of the closing inventory of item M at the end of February is £ _____

(b) All units of item M were sold for £14 each. The gross profit achieved on item M during February was £ _____ .

Question 8

A Limited has completed the initial allocation and apportionment of its overhead costs to cost centres as follows.

Cost centre	Initial allocation
	£000
Machining	190
Finishing	175
Stores	30
Maintenance	25
	420

The stores and maintenance costs must now be reapportioned taking account of the service they provide to each other as follows.

	Machining	Finishing	Stores	Maintenance
Stores to be apportioned	60%	30%	–	10%
Maintenance to be apportioned	75%	20%	5%	

After the apportionment of the service department costs, the total overhead cost of the production departments will be (*to the nearest £000*):

Machining £ [   ]
Finishing £ [   ]

 # Question 9

The budgeted contribution for R Limited last month was £32,000. The following variances were reported.

Variance	£	
Sales volume contribution	800	adverse
Material price	880	adverse
Material usage	822	favourable
Labour efficiency	129	favourable
Variable overhead efficiency	89	favourable

No other variances were reported for the month.
The actual contribution earned by R Limited last month was £ [   ].

Question 10

The following scattergraph has been prepared for the costs incurred by an organisation that delivers hot meals to the elderly in their homes.

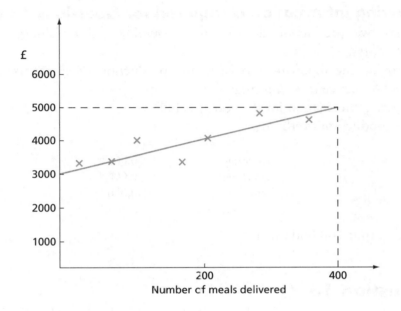

Based on the scattergraph:
(a) the period fixed cost is £ [_____]
(b) the variable cost per meal delivered is £ [_____].

Question 11

A company operates a differential piece-rate system and the following weekly rates have been set:

1–500 units	£0.20 per unit in this band
501–600 units	£0.25 per unit in this band
601 units and above	£0.55 per unit in this band

Details relating to employee A for the latest week are shown below:

Employee A
Actual output achieved	800 units
Actual hours worked	45

There is a guaranteed minimum wage of £5 per hour for a 40-hour week paid to all employees.

The amount payable (to the nearest £) to employee A is £ [_____].

Question 12

Overtime premium is

☐ the additional amount paid for hours worked in excess of the basic working week.

☐ the additional amount paid over and above the normal hourly rate for hours worked in excess of the basic working week.

☐ the additional amount paid over and above the overtime rate for hours worked in excess of the basic working week.

☐ the overtime rate.

The following information is required for Questions 13 and 14

X Ltd has two production departments, Assembly and Finishing, and one service department, Stores.

Stores provide the following service to the production departments: 60 per cent to Assembly and 40 per cent to Finishing.

The budgeted information for the year is as follows:

Budgeted production overheads:

Assembly	£100,000
Finishing	£150,000
Stores	£50,000

Budgeted output 100,000 units

? Question 13

The budgeted production overhead absorption rate for the Assembly Department will be £ [＿＿＿＿＿] per unit.

? Question 14

At the end of the year, the total of all of the production overheads debited to the Finishing Department Production Overhead Control Account was £130,000, and the actual output achieved was 100,000 units.

(a) The overheads for the Finishing Department were:

under-absorbed ☐
over-absorbed ☐

(b) The value of the under/over absorption was £ [＿＿＿＿＿].

? Question 15

R Ltd has been asked to quote for a job. The company aims to make a profit margin of 20% on sales. The estimated total variable production cost for the job is £125.

Fixed production overheads for the company are budgeted to be £250,000 and are recovered on the basis of labour hours. There are 12,500 budgeted labour hours and this job is expected to take 3 labour hours.

Other costs in relation to selling, distribution and administration are recovered at the rate of £15 per job.

The company quote for the job should be £ [＿＿＿＿＿].

? **Question 16**

Which of the following would NOT be included in a cash budget? Tick all that would NOT be included.

☐ Depreciation
☐ Provisions for doubtful debts
☐ Wages and salaries

The following information is required for Questions 17 and 18

X is preparing its budgets for the forthcoming year.
The estimated sales for the first 4 months of the forthcoming year are as follows:

Month 1	6,000 units
Month 2	7,000 units
Month 3	5,500 units
Month 4	6,000 units

40% of each month's sales units are to be produced in the month of sale and the balance is to be produced in the previous month.

50% of the direct materials required for each month's production will be purchased in the previous month and the balance in the month of production.

The direct material cost is budgeted to be $5 per unit.

? **Question 17**

The production budget for Month 1 will be ☐ units.

? **Question 18**

The material cost budget for Month 2 will be $ ☐.

? **Question 19**

When calculating the material purchases budget, the quantity to be purchased equals

☐ material usage + materials closing inventory − materials opening inventory
☐ material usage − materials closing inventory + materials opening inventory
☐ material usage − materials closing inventory − materials opening inventory
☐ material usage + materials closing inventory + materials opening inventory

? **Question 20**

The following extract is taken from the overhead budget of X Ltd:

	50%	75%
Budgeted activity		
Budgeted overhead	£100,000	£112,500

The overhead budget for an activity level of 80 per cent would be £ ☐.

? **Question 21**

Which of the following would be included in the cash budget, but would not be included in the budgeted income statement? Tick all that are correct.

- ☐ Repayment of a bank loan.
- ☐ Proceeds from the sale of a non-current asset.
- ☐ Bad debts write off.

? **Question 22**

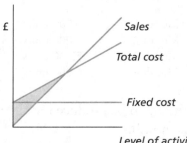

(a) This graph is known as a

- ☐ semi-variable cost chart.
- ☐ conventional breakeven chart.
- ☐ contribution breakeven chart.
- ☐ profit volume chart.

(b) The shaded area on the graph represents:

- ☐ loss
- ☐ fixed cost
- ☐ variable cost
- ☐ profit

? **Question 23**

The following details have been extracted from the payables records of X:

Invoices paid in the month of purchase	25%
Invoices paid in the first month after purchase	70%
Invoices paid in the second month after purchase	5%

Purchases for July to September are budgeted as follows:

July	$250,000
August	$300,000
September	$280,000

For suppliers paid in the month of purchase, a settlement discount of 5 per cent is received. The amount budgeted to be paid to suppliers in September is $ ☐.

Question 24

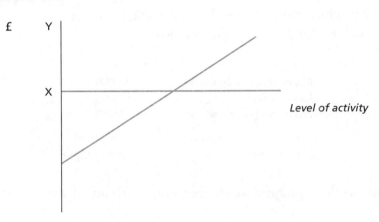

The difference in the values (£) between point X and point Y on the profit volume chart shown above represents:

☐ contribution
☐ profit
☐ breakeven
☐ loss

Question 25

Which one of the following statements is correct:

☐ Job costing can only be applied where work is undertaken on the customer's premises
☐ Batch costing can only be applied where every unit in the batch is separately identifiable
☐ Contract costing can only be applied where every contract is separately identifiable

Question 26

In a standard cost bookkeeping system, when the actual material usage has been greater than the standard material usage, the entries to record this is in the accounts are:

	Debit	Credit	No entry in this account
Material usage variance account	☐	☐	☐
Raw material control account	☐	☐	☐
Work in progress account	☐	☐	☐

? Question 27

R Ltd makes one product, which passes through a single process.
Details of the process for period 1 were as follows:

	£
Material cost – 20,000 kg	26,000
Labour cost	12,000
Production overhead cost	5,700
Output	18,800 kg
Normal losses	5% of input

There was no work-in-progress at the beginning or end of the period. Process losses have no value.

The cost of the abnormal loss (to the nearest £) is £ ⌷.

The following information is required for Questions 28–35

X Ltd operates a standard costing system. The following budgeted and standard cost information is available:

Budgeted production and sales	10,000 units
	£ per unit
Selling price	250
Direct material cost – 3 kg × £10	30
Direct labour cost – 5 hours × £8	40
Variable production overheads – 5 hours × £4	20

Actual results for the period were as follows:

Production and sales	11,500 units
	£
Sales value	2,817,500
Direct material – 36,000 kg	342,000
Direct labour – 52,000 hours	468,000
Variable production overheads	195,000

For all calculated variances, tick the correct box to indicate whether the variance is adverse or favourable.

? Question 28

The direct material price variance is £ ⌷

adverse ☐
favourable ☐

? **Question 29**

The direct material usage variance is £ ⬚

    adverse ☐
    favourable ☐

? **Question 30**

The direct labour rate variance is £ ⬚

    adverse ☐
    favourable ☐

? **Question 31**

The direct labour efficiency variance is £ ⬚

    adverse ☐
    favourable ☐

? **Question 32**

The variable production overhead expenditure variance is £ ⬚

    adverse ☐
    favourable ☐

? **Question 33**

The variable production overhead efficiency variance is £ ⬚

    adverse ☐
    favourable ☐

? **Question 34**

The sales volume contribution variance is £ ⬚

    adverse ☐
    favourable ☐

? **Question 35**

The sales price variance is £ ⬚

    adverse ☐
    favourable ☐

Question 36

X Ltd uses the FIFO method to charge material issue costs to production. Opening inventory of material M at the beginning of April was 270 units valued at £4 per unit.

Movements of material M during April were as follows.

4 April	Received 30 units at £4.10 per unit
9 April	Issued 210 units
14 April	Issued 80 units
22 April	Received 90 units at £4.20 per unit
24 April	Issued 40 units

(a) The total value of the issues to production during April was £ _____.

(b) The value of the closing inventory at the end of April was £ _____.

Question 37

X Ltd manufactures a product called the 'ZT'. The budget for next year was:

Annual sales	10,000 units
	£ per unit
Selling price	20
Variable cost	14
Fixed costs	3
Profit	3

If the selling price of the ZT were reduced by 10 per cent, the sales revenue that would be needed to generate the original budgeted profit would be £ _____.

Question 38

A company is faced with a shortage of skilled labour next period.

When determining the production plan that will maximise the company's profit next period, the company's products should be ranked according to their:

☐ profit per hour of skilled labour
☐ profit per unit of product sold
☐ contribution per hour of skilled labour
☐ contribution per unit of product sold

Question 39

Which of the following would contribute towards a favourable sales price variance (tick all that apply)?

(a) The standard sales price per unit was set too high ☐.

(b) Price competition in the market was not as fierce as expected ☐.

(c) Sales volume was higher than budgeted and therefore sales revenue was higher than budgeted ☐.

? Question 40

R Ltd has the following year-end information regarding one of its long-term contracts:

	£
Revenue credited to income statement	2,500,000
Profit recognised	750,000
Cash received	1,875,000
Costs to date	2,200,000
Future costs	220,000

(a) The cost charged to the income statement in respect of this contract was £ [_____].

(b) The value of the contract receivable is £ [_____].

? Question 41

The following data relate to a process for the latest period.

Opening work in progress	300 kg valued as follows
	Input material £1,000
	Conversion cost £200
Input during period	8,000 kg at a cost of £29,475
Conversion costs	£11,977
Output	7,000 kg
Closing work in progress	400 kg

Closing work in progress is complete as to input materials and 70 per cent complete as to conversion costs.

Losses are expected to be 10 per cent of input during the period and they occur at the end of the process. Losses have a scrap value of £2 per kg.

The value of the completed output (to the nearest £) is £ [_____].

? Question 42

Which of the following inventory valuation methods results in charges to cost of sales which are close to the economic cost?

First In, First Out (FIFO) ☐
Last In, First Out (LIFO) ☐
Average Cost (AVCO) ☐

Data for questions 43 and 44

A company makes a single product T and budgets to produce and sell 7,200 units each period. Cost and revenue data for the product at this level of activity are as follows.

	$ per unit
Selling price	53
Direct material cost	24
Direct labour cost	8
Other variable cost	3
Fixed cost	7
Profit	11

? Question 43

The contribution to sales ratio (P/V ratio) of product T (to the nearest whole number) is [   ] per cent.

? Question 44

The margin of safety of product T (to the nearest whole number) is [   ] per cent of budgeted sales volume.

Data for questions 45 and 46

The total figures from TY Division's budgetary control report are as follows.

	Fixed budget $	Flexed budget allowances $	Actual results $
Total sales revenue	520,000	447,000	466,500
Total variable cost	389,000	348,000	329,400
Total contribution	131,000	99,000	137,100

? Question 45

(a) The sales price variance for the period is $ [   ] **adverse/favourable**

(b) The sales volume contribution variance for the period is $ [   ] **adverse/favourable**

? Question 46

(a) The total expenditure variance for the period is $ [   ] **adverse/favourable**

(b) The total budget variance for the period is $ [   ] **adverse/favourable**

? Question 47

In an integrated bookkeeping system, the correct entries to record the depreciation of production machinery are:

	Debit	Credit	No entry in this account
Depreciation of production machinery	☐	☐	☐
Work in progress account	☐	☐	☐
Production overhead control account	☐	☐	☐

? **Question 48**

In an integrated bookkeeping system, the correct entries to record the issue of indirect materials for production purposes are:

	Debit	*Credit*	*No entry in this account*
Materials control account	☐	☐	☐
Work in progress account	☐	☐	☐
Production overhead control account	☐	☐	☐

? **Question 49**

H Limited budgets to produce and sell 4,000 units of product H next year. The amount of capital investment required to support product H will be £290,000 and H Limited requires a rate of return of 14 per cent on all capital invested.

The full cost per unit of product H is £45.90.

To the nearest penny, the selling price per unit of product H that will achieve the specified return on investment is £ [   ].

? **Question 50**

The Drop In Café sells specialist coffees to customers to drink on the premises or to take away.

The proprietors have established that the cost of ingredients is a wholly variable cost in relation to the number of cups of coffee sold whereas staff costs are semi-variable and rent costs are fixed.

Within the relevant range, as the number of cups of coffee sold increases (tick the correct box):

	increase	*decrease*	*stay the same*
(a) The ingredients cost per cup sold will	☐	☐	☐
(b) The staff cost per cup sold will	☐	☐	☐
(c) The rent cost per cup sold will	☐	☐	☐

MOCK ASSESSMENT 1

First Mock Assessment – Solutions

 ## Solution 1

Bricklayer in a construction company.

The bricklayer's wages can be identified with a specific cost unit therefore this is a direct cost. The wages paid to the other three people cannot be identified with specific cost units. Therefore they would be indirect costs.

 ## Solution 2

The principal budget factor is the factor which limits the activities of the organisation and is often the starting point in budget preparation.

 ## Solution 3

The overhead absorption rate was £5 per unit.

Workings:

	£
Actual overheads	500,000
Over-absorption	50,000
Overhead absorbed	550,000

Overhead absorption rate = £550,000/110,000 units = £5.

 ## Solution 4

Finished goods inventory account.

 ## Solution 5

Overheads for the period were *over-absorbed by £95,000.*

Workings:

Overhead absorption rate = £1,250,000/250,000 = £5 per hour

	£
Absorbed overhead = 220,000 hours × £5	1,100,000
Actual overhead incurred	1,005,000
Over-absorbed overhead	95,000

 ## Solution 6

	Debit	*Credit*	*No entry in this account*
Production overhead account		✓	
Work in progress account			✓
Income statement	✓		

✅ Solution 7

(a) The value of the closing inventory of item M at the end of February is £4,608

(b) All units of item M were sold for £14 each. The gross profit achieved on item M during February was £2,911.50.

Workings

Date	Qty	Receipts Price	£	Qty	Sales Price	£	Qty	Balance Price	£
1 Feb							230	7.80	1,794.00
3 Feb	430	7.95	3,418.50				230	7.80	1,794.00
							430	7.95	3,418.50
							660		5,212.50
8 Feb				370	7.95	2,941.50	230	7.80	1,794.00
							60	7.95	477.00
							290		2,271.00
14 Feb				60	7.95	477.00			
				50	7.80	390.00			
				110		867.00	180	7.80	1,404.00
22 Feb	400	8.01	3,204.00				180	7.80	1,400.00
							400	8.01	3,204.00
							580		4,608.00

(b)

	£
Sales revenue (480 units × £14)	6,720.00
Cost of goods sold (2,941.50 + 867.00)	3,808.50
Gross profit	2,911.50

✅ Solution 8

After the apportionment of the service department costs, the total overhead cost of the production departments will be (*to the nearest £000*):

Machining	£230,000
Finishing	£190,000

Workings

	Machining £000	Finishing £000	Stores £000	Maintenance £000
Apportioned costs	190.00	175.00	30.0	25.0
Stores apportionment	18.00	9.00	(30.0)	3.0
Maintenance apportionment	21.00	5.60	1.4	(28.0)
Stores apportionment	0.84	0.42	(1.4)	0.14
Maintenance apportionment	0.11	0.03	–	(0.14)
Total	229.95	190.05		

Solution 9

The actual contribution earned by R Limited last month was £31,360.

£(32,000 − 800 − 880 + 822 + 129 + 89) = £31,360.

 ## Solution 10

(a) The period fixed cost is £3,000
(b) The variable cost per meal delivered is £5

> *Workings*:
>
> $$\text{Variable cost per meal} = \frac{£5,000 - £3,000}{400 \text{ meals}} = £5$$

 ## Solution 11

The amount payable to employee A is £235.

> *Workings*:
>
> | Units | £ |
> |---|---|
> | 500 × 20p | 100 |
> | 100 × 25p | 25 |
> | 200 × 55p | 110 |
> | 800 | 235 |

 ## Solution 12

Overtime premium is the additional amount paid over and above the normal hourly rate for hours worked in excess of the basic working week.

 ## Solution 13

The budgeted production overhead absorption rate for the Assembly Department will be £1.30 per unit.

Workings:	*Assembly*
	£
Budgeted overheads	100,000
Reapportioned stores overhead 60% × £50,000	30,000
Total budgeted overhead	130,000
Budgeted output	100,000
OAR =	£130,000
	100,000
	= £1.30 per unit

Solution 14

The overheads for the Finishing Department were *over-absorbed by £40,000*.

Workings:

	Finishing
	£
Budgeted overheads	150,000
Reapportioned stores overhead 40% × £50,000	20,000
Total budgeted overhead	170,000
Budgeted output	100,000

$$OAR = \frac{£170,000}{100,000}$$

$$= £1.70 \text{ per unit}$$

	£
Absorbed overhead £1.70 × 100,000	170,000
Actual overhead incurred	130,000
Over-absorption	40,000

 ## Solution 15

The company quote for the job should be *£250*.

Workings:

	Job quote
	£
Variable production costs	125
Fixed production overheads $\left(\frac{250,000}{12,500} \times 3 \right)$	60
Selling, distribution and administration	15
Total cost	200
Profit margin 20%	50
Quote	250

 ## Solution 16

Depreciation and provisions for doubtful debts are not cash flows and would not be included in a cash budget.

Solution 17

The production budget for month 1 will be *6,600 units*.

Workings:

	Month 1 Units	Month 2 Units	Month 3 Units	Month 4 Units
Sales	6,000	7,000	5,500	6,000
Production				
40% in the month	2,400	2,800	2,200	2,400
60% in the previous month	4,200	3,300	3,600	
Production	6,600	6,100	5,800	

 # Solution 18

The material cost budget for Month 2 will be *$30,500*.

Workings:

Month 2   6,100 units produced @ $5 per unit = $30,500.

 # Solution 19

The quantity to be purchased equals material usage + materials closing inventory − materials opening inventory.

 # Solution 20

The overhead budget for an activity level of 80% would be *£115,000*.

Workings:
Using the high/low method

		£	
High	75%	112,500	
Low	50%	100,000	
Change	25%	12,500	− variable cost of 25%
	1%	500	− variable cost of 1%

Substitute into 75% activity	£
Total overhead	112,500
Variable cost element 75 × £500	37,500
Fixed cost element	75,000

Total overhead for 80% activity	
Variable cost element 80 × £500	40,000
Fixed cost element	75,000
Total overhead	115,000

Solution 21

The correct answers are:
- – repayment of a bank loan
- – proceeds from the sale of a non-current asset.

Both these items result in a cash flow and would therefore be included in the cash budget. However, they would not be included in the income statement. The bad debts write off would be included in the income statement, but not in the cash budget.

 Solution 22

(a) The graph is known as a conventional breakeven chart.
(b) The shaded area on the breakeven chart represents *loss*.

 Solution 23

The amount budgeted to be paid to suppliers in September is *$289,000*.

Workings:

	July $	August $	September $
Purchases	250,000	300,000	280,000
25% paid in the month of purchase	62,500	75,000	70,000
5% discount allowed	(3,125)	(3,750)	(3,500)
70% paid in the first month		175,000	210,000
5% paid in the second month			12,500
Budgeted payment			289,000

 Solution 24

The difference in the values (£) between point X and point Y on the profit volume chart represents *profit*.

 Solution 25

The correct statement is that contract costing can only be applied where every contract is separately identifiable. A separate account is maintained for each contract.

Job costing can be applied where work is undertaken on the organisation's own premises. For example job cost sheets can be used to collect the costs of the organisation's property repairs carried out by its own employees.

Batch costing can only be applied where every batch is separately identifiable, but the units within the batch will be identical.

Solution 26

	Debit	Credit	No entry in this account
Material usage variance account	✓		
Raw material control account			✓
Work in progress account		✓	

 # Solution 27

The cost of the abnormal loss is *£460*.

Workings:

	£
Direct material cost	26,000
Labour cost	12,000
Production overhead cost	5,700
	43,700

	Kg
Input	20,000
Normal loss	1,000
Expected output	19,000
Actual output	18,800
Abnormal loss	200

Cost per kg = £43,700/19,000 = £2.30
Cost of abnormal loss = £2.30 × 200 kg = £460.

 # Solution 28

The direct material price variance is *£18,000 favourable*.

Workings:

	£	
36,000 kg should cost (×£10)	360,000	
but did cost	342,000	
Variance	18,000	F

 # Solution 29

The direct material usage variance is *£15,000 adverse*.

Workings:

11,500 units should use (×3 kg)	34,500	kg
but did use	36,000	kg
Difference	1,500	kg
× std price per kg	×£10	
Variance	£15,000	A

Solution 30

The direct labour rate variance is *£52,000 adverse*.

Workings:

	£	
52,000 hours should cost (×£8)	416,000	
but did cost	468,000	
Variance	52,000	A

Solution 31

The direct labour efficiency variance is *£44,000 favourable*.

Workings:

11,500 units should take (×5 hours)	57,500	hours
but did take	52,000	hours
Difference	5,500	hours
× std rate per hour	× £8	
Variance	£44,000	F

Solution 32

The variable production overhead expenditure variance is *£13,000 favourable*.

Workings:

	£	
52,000 hours should have cost (× £4)	208,000	
but did cost	195,000	
Variance	13,000	F

Solution 33

The variable production overhead efficiency variance is *£22,000 favourable*.

Workings:

Variance in hours from labour efficiency variance	= 5,500	hours
× standard variable production overhead per hour	×£4	
Variance	£22,000	F

Solution 34

The sales volume contribution variance is *£240,000 favourable*.

Workings:

Actual sales volume	11,500	units
Budget sales volume	10,000	units
Variance in units	1,500	favourable
× standard contribution per unit £(250 − 30 − 40 − 20)	×£160	
Sales volume contribution variance	£240,000	favourable

Solution 35

The sales price variance is *£57,500 adverse*.

Workings:

	£
11,500 units should sell for (×£250)	2,875,000
But did sell for	2,817,500
Sales price variance	57,500 adverse

 # Solution 36

(a) The total value of the issues to production during April was *£1,329*.
(b) The value of the closing inventory at the end of April was *£252*.

Workings:

			£
(a) Issues:	9 April	210 units × £4	840
	14 April	60 units × £4	240
		20 units × £4.10	82
	24 April	10 units × £4.10	41
		30 units × £4.20	126
			1,329

(b) Inventory = 60 units × £4.20 = £252

 # Solution 37

The sales revenue that would be needed to generate the original budgeted profit would be *£270,000*.

Workings:
Fixed costs are not relevant because they will remain unaltered.
Original budgeted contribution = 10,000 units × £(20 − 14) = £60,000
Revised contribution per unit = £(18 − 14) = £4
Required number of units to achieve same contribution = £60,000/£4 = 15,000 units
Required sales revenue = 15,000 units × £18 revised price = £270,000

 # Solution 38

When determining the production plan that will maximise the company's profit next period, the company's products should be ranked according to their contribution per hour of skilled labour.

 # Solution 39

Only reason (b) would contribute to a favourable sales price variance.

Reason (a) would result in an adverse variance. Reason (c) would not necessarily result in any sales price variance because all the units could have been sold at standard price.

Solution 40

(a) The cost charged to the income statement in respect of this contract was *£1,750,000*.

Workings:

	£
Revenue credited	2,500,000
Profit recognised	750,000
Cost charged	1,750,000

(b) The value of the contract receivable is *£625,000*.

Workings:

	£
Revenue credited	2,500,000
Less cash received	1,875,000
Receivable balance	625,000

 Solution 41

The value of the completed output is £38,500

Workings:

	kg	Output	kg	Equivalent kg Input material		Conversion costs
Input		*Output*				
Opening WIP	300	Finished output	7,000	7,000		7,000
Input	8,000	Normal loss	800	–		–
		Abnormal loss	100	100		100
		Closing WIP	400	400	70%	280
	8,300		8,300	7,500		7,380

	£	£		£
Costs				
Opening WIP	1,200	1,000		200
Period costs	41,452	29,475		11,977
Normal loss	(1,600)	(1,600)		–
	41,052	28,875		12,177
Cost per equivalent kg	5.50	3.85		1.65

The value of the completed output is £5.50 × 7,000 kg = £38,500

 Solution 42

The LIFO inventory valuation method results in charges to cost of sales which are close to the economic cost.

Solution 43

The contribution to sales ratio (P/V ratio) of product T is 34 per cent.

Workings:
Contribution per unit of product T = $(53 − 24 − 8 − 3) = $18
Contribution to sales ratio = 18/53 = 34%

Solution 44

The margin of safety of product T is 61 per cent of budgeted sales volume.

Workings:
Period fixed costs = 7,200 × $7 = $50,400

$$\text{Breakeven point} = \frac{\$50,400}{\$18} = 2,800 \text{ units}$$

Margin of safety = (7,200 − 2,800) units = 4,400 units
Margin of safety as percentage of budgeted sales = 4,400/7,200 = 61%

 ## Solution 45

(a) The sales price variance is $(466,500 − 447,000) = $19,500 favourable
(b) The sales volume contribution variance is $(99,000 − 131,000) = $32,000 adverse

 ## Solution 46

(a) The total expenditure variance is $(329,400 − 348,000) = $18,600 favourable
(b) The total budget variance is $(137,100 − 131,000) = $6,100 favourable

 ## Solution 47

	Debit	Credit	No entry in this account
Depreciation of production machinery		✓	
Work in progress account			✓
Production overhead control account	✓		

 ## Solution 48

	Debit	Credit	No entry in this account
Materials control account		✓	
Work in progress account			✓
Production overhead control account	✓		

 ## Solution 49

The selling price per unit of product H that will achieve the specified return on investment is £56.05

Workings:
Required return from capital invested to support product H = £290,000 × 14%
= £40,600

Required return per unit of product H sold = £40,600/4,000 = £10.15
Required selling price = 45.90 full cost + £10.15 = £56.05

 ## Solution 50

Within the relevant range, as the number of cups of coffee sold increases:

(a) the ingredients cost per cup sold will stay the same.
(b) the staff cost per cup sold will decrease.
(c) the rent cost per cup sold will decrease.

Mock Assessment 2

Mock Assessment 2

Certificate in Business Accounting
Fundamentals of Management Accounting

You are allowed two hours to complete this assessment.

The assessment contains 50 questions.

All questions are compulsory.

Do not turn the page until you are ready to attempt the assessment under timed conditions.

Question 1

In an integrated accounting system, the accounting entries to complete the production overhead control account at the end of the period, when the production overheads absorbed exceed the actual production overhead incurred are:

	Debit	*Credit*	*No entry in this account*
Production overhead control account	☐	☐	☐
Work in progress account	☐	☐	☐
Finished goods account	☐	☐	☐
Income statement	☐	☐	☐

Question 2

A company expects to sell h units in the next accounting period, and has prepared the following breakeven chart.

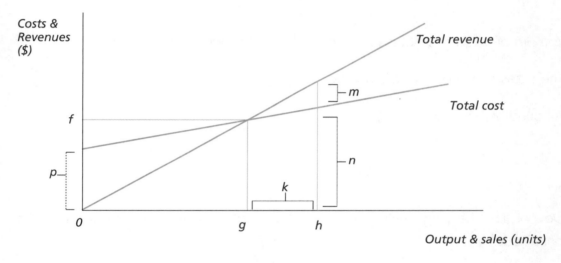

(a) The margin of safety is shown on the diagram by ☐ (insert correct letter).
(b) The effect of an increase in fixed costs, with all other costs and revenues remaining the same, will be

	increase	*decrease*	*stay the same*
m will	☐	☐	☐
k will	☐	☐	☐
f will	☐	☐	☐
p will	☐	☐	☐

Question 3

A company uses the repeated distribution method to reapportion service department costs. The use of this method suggests

☐ the company's overhead rates are based on estimates of cost and activity levels, rather than actual amounts.

☐ there are more service departments than production cost centres.

☐ the company wishes to avoid under- or over-absorption of overheads in its production cost centres.

☐ the service departments carry out work for each other.

? Question 4

The management accountant's report shows that fixed production overheads were over-absorbed in the last accounting period. The combination that is certain to lead to this situation is

Production activity	*and*	*Fixed overhead expenditure*
☐ lower than budget		☐ lower than budget
☐ higher than budget		☐ higher than budget
☐ as budgeted		☐ as budgeted

? Question 5

Which of the following costs would be classified as production overhead cost in a food processing company (tick all that apply)?

☐ The cost of renting the factory building.
☐ The salary of the factory manager.
☐ The depreciation of equipment located in the materials store.
☐ The cost of ingredients.

? Question 6

The normal loss in process 2 is valued at its scrap value. Extracts from the process account and the abnormal gain account for the latest period are shown below.

Process 2

	£		£
Opening WIP	1,847	Output to finished goods	
Conversion costs	14,555	−5,100 units	22,695
Input materials	6,490	Normal loss −100 units	120
Abnormal gain −220 units		Closing WIP	

Abnormal gain

	£		£
Income statement	A	Process 2	B

The values to be entered in the abnormal gain account for the period are:

A = £ [   ]

B = £ [   ]

The following information is required for questions 7 and 8

The incomplete process account relating to period 4 for a company which manufactures paper is shown below:

Process account

	Units	$		Units	$
Material	4,000	16,000	Finished goods	2,750	
Labour		8,125	Normal loss	400	700
Production overhead		3,498	Work in progress	700	

There was no opening work in process (WIP). Closing WIP, consisting of 700 units, was complete as shown:

Materials	100%
Labour	50%
Production overhead	40%

Losses are recognised at the end of the production process and are sold for $1.75 per unit.

 ## Question 7

Given the outcome of the process, which ONE of the following accounting entries is needed in each account to complete the double entry for the abnormal loss or gain?

	Debit	Credit	No entry in this account
Process account	☐	☐	☐
Abnormal gain account	☐	☐	☐
Abnormal loss account	☐	☐	☐

Question 8

The value of the closing WIP was $ ☐ .

Question 9

A machine operator is paid £10.20 per hour and has a normal working week of 35 hours. Overtime is paid at the basic rate plus 50%. If, in week 7, the machine operator worked 42 hours, the overtime premium paid to the operator would be £ ☐ .

Question 10

An engineering firm operates a job costing system. Production overhead is absorbed at the rate of £8.50 per machine hour. In order to allow for non-production overhead costs and profit, a mark up of 60% of prime cost is added to the production cost when preparing price estimates.

The estimated requirements of job number 808 are as follows:

Direct materials	£10,650
Direct labour	£3,260
Machine hours	140

The estimated price notified to the customer for job number 808 will be £ ☐ .

Question 11

The diagram represents the behaviour of a cost item as the level of output changes:

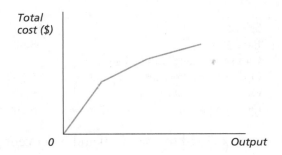

Which ONE of the following situations is depicted by the graph?

☐ Discounts are received on additional purchases of material when certain quantities are purchased.

☐ Employees are paid a guaranteed weekly wage, together with bonuses for higher levels of production.

☐ A licence is purchased from the government which allows unlimited production.

☐ Additional space is rented to cope with the need to increase production.

Question 12

A hospital's records show that the cost of carrying out health checks in the last five accounting periods have been as follows:

Period	Number of patients seen	Total cost £
1	650	17,125
2	940	17,800
3	1,260	18,650
4	990	17,980
5	1,150	18,360

Using the high–low method and ignoring inflation, the estimated cost of carrying out health checks on 850 patients in period 6 is £ _____.

Question 13

The principal budget factor for a footwear retailer is

☐ the cost item taking the largest share of total expenditure.

☐ the product line contributing the largest amount to sales revenue.

☐ the product line contributing the largest amount to business profits.

☐ the constraint that is expected to limit the retailer's activities during the budget period.

The following information is required for questions 14 and 15

Extracts from the budget of H, a retailer of office furniture, for the six months to 31 December show the following information:

	$
Sales	55,800
Purchases	38,000
Closing inventory finished goods	7,500
Opening inventory finished goods	5,500
Opening receivables	8,500
Opening payables	6,500

Receivables and payables are expected to rise by 10 and 5 per cent, respectively, by the end of the budget period.

Question 14

The estimated cash receipts from customers during the budget period are $ [_____].

Question 15

The profit mark-up, as a percentage of the cost of sales (to the nearest whole number) is ☐%.

Question 16

Which of the following actions are appropriate if a company anticipates a temporary cash shortage (tick all that apply)?

(i) ☐   issue additional shares;
(ii) ☐   request additional bank overdraft facilities;
(iii) ☐   sell machinery currently working at half capacity;
(iv) ☐   postpone the purchase of plant and machinery.

Question 17

A company manufactures three products, X, Y and Z. The sales demand and the standard unit selling prices and costs for the next accounting period, period 1, are estimated as follows:

	X	Y	Z
Maximum demand (000 units)	4.0	5.5	7.0
	£ per unit	£ per unit	£ per unit
Selling price	28	22	30
Variable costs:			
Raw material (£1 per kg)	5	4	6
Direct labour (£12 per hour)	12	9	18

(a) If supplies in period 1 are restricted to 90,000 kg of raw material and 18,000 hours of direct labour, the limiting factor would be

☐   direct labour.
☐   raw material.
☐   neither direct labour nor raw material.

(b) In period 2, the company will have a shortage of raw materials, but no other resources will be restricted. The standard selling prices and costs and the level of demand will remain unchanged.

In what order should the materials be allocated to the products if the company wants to maximise profit?

First: product ☐
Second: product ☐
Third: product ☐

Question 18

A performance standard which assumes efficient levels of operation, but which includes allowances for factors such as waste and machine downtime is known as:

☐ an allowable standard
☐ an attainable standard
☐ an ideal standard
☐ a current standard

The following information is required for questions 19 and 20

W makes leather purses. It has drawn up the following budget for its next financial period:

Selling price per unit	$11.60
Variable production cost per unit	$3.40
Sales commission	5% of selling price
Fixed production costs	$430,500
Fixed selling and administration costs	$198,150
Sales	90,000 units

Question 19

The margin of safety represents ☐ per cent of budgeted sales.

Question 20

The marketing manager has indicated that an increase in the selling price to $12.25 per unit would not affect the number of units sold, provided that the sales commission is increased to 8 per cent of the selling price.

These changes will cause the breakeven point (to the nearest whole number) to be ☐ units.

Question 21

Over long time periods of several years, supervisory labour costs will tend to behave as:

☐ linear variable costs
☐ step fixed costs
☐ fixed costs
☐ semi-variable costs

 # Question 22

A firm calculates the material price variance when material is purchased. The accounting entries necessary to record a favourable material price variance in the ledger are:

	Debit	Credit	No entry in this account
Material control account	☐	☐	☐
Work-in-progress control account	☐	☐	☐
Material price variance account	☐	☐	☐

 # Question 23

The accounting entries necessary to record an adverse labour efficiency variance in the ledger accounts are:

	Debit	Credit	No entry in this account
Wages control account	☐	☐	☐
Labour variance account	☐	☐	☐
Work-in-progress control account	☐	☐	☐

 # Question 24

The following graph shows the wages earned by an employee during a single day:

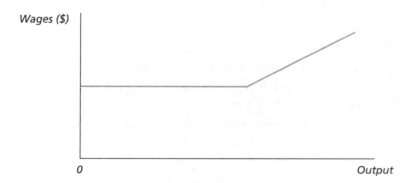

Which ONE of the remuneration systems listed below does the graph represent?

☐ Differential piecework.
☐ A flat rate per hour with a premium for overtime working.
☐ Straight piecework.
☐ Piecework with a guaranteed minimum daily wage.

Question 25

J absorbs production overheads on the basis of machine hours. The following budgeted and actual information applied in its last accounting period:

	Budget	Actual
Production overhead	$180,000	$178,080
Machine hours	40,000	38,760

(a) At the end of the period, production overhead will be reported as:

☐ under-absorbed
☐ over-absorbed

(b) The amount of the under/over-absorption will be $ ⬚ .

The following data are to be used to answer questions 26 and 27

A company's purchases during a recent week were as follows:

Day	Price per unit (S)	Units purchased
1	1.45	55
2	1.60	80
3	1.75	120
4	1.80	75
5	1.90	130

There was no inventory at the beginning of the week. 420 units were issued to production during the week. The company updates its inventory records after every transaction.

Question 26

Using a first in, first out (FIFO) method of costing issues from stores, the value of closing inventory would be $ ⬚ .

Question 27

If the company changes to the weighted average method of inventory valuation, the effect on closing inventory value and on profit for the week compared with the FIFO method will be:

(a) Closing inventory value will be: higher ☐
                                         lower ☐

(b) Gross profit for the week will be: higher ☐
                                         lower ☐

The following data are to be used to answer questions 28 and 29

The diagram shows the profit-volume chart for the latest accounting period. The company made a profit of $w during the period.

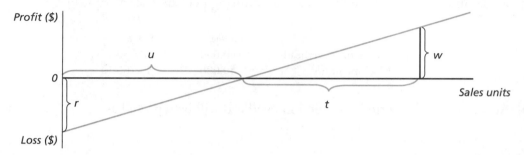

Question 28

An increase in the fixed costs per period (assuming the selling price per unit and the variable cost per unit remain unchanged), will cause:

	increase	*decrease*	*remain the same*
r to	☐	☐	☐
w to	☐	☐	☐
t to	☐	☐	☐
u to	☐	☐	☐

Question 29

The following results were achieved in the last accounting period:

$r = \$50,000$ $w = \$16,000$ $t = 800$ units $u = 2,500$ units

The company expects to make and sell an additional 1,400 units in the next accounting period. If variable cost per unit, selling price per unit and total fixed costs remain unchanged, profit will increase by $ ⬚ .

Question 30

Information concerning contract H7635 is as follows:

	£
Cost incurred to date	592,000
Cost to be incurred to complete contract	189,000
Value of work certified	800,000
Cash received from customer	640,000
Total contract value	1,015,000

No problems are foreseen on the contract and no profit has been recognised on the contract to date.

The formula used by the company when recognising profits on incomplete contracts is:

$$\text{Profit to be recognised} = \text{Final contract profit} \times \frac{\text{Revenue earned to date}}{\text{Final contract revenue}}$$

The profit to be recognised in the company's income statement in respect of contract H7635 is (to the nearest £) £ ⬚ .

Question 31

An advertising agency uses a job costing system to calculate the cost of client contracts. Contract A42 is one of several contracts undertaken in the last accounting period. Costs associated with the contract consist of:

Direct materials	$5,500
Direct expenses	$14,500

Design staff worked 1,020 hours on contract A42, of which 120 hours were overtime. One-third of these overtime hours were worked at the request of the client who wanted the contract to be completed quickly. Overtime is paid at a premium of 25 per cent of the basic rate of $24.00 per hour.

The prime cost of contract A42 is $ ⬚.

 Data for questions 32 and 33

Sales of product G are budgeted as follows.

	Month 1	Month 2	Month 3	Month 4	Month 5
Budgeted sales units	340	420	290	230	210

Company policy is to hold in inventory at the end of each month sufficient units of product G to satisfy budgeted sales demand for the forthcoming 2 months.

 Question 32

The budgeted production of product G in month 2 is ⬚ units.

Question 33

Each unit of product G uses 2 litres of liquid K. Company policy is to hold in inventory at the end of each month sufficient liquid K for the production requirements of the forthcoming month.

The budgeted purchases of liquid K in month 2 are ⬚ litres.

Question 34

The following data have been extracted from the budget working papers of GY Limited.

Production volume (units)	2,000	3,000
	£ per unit	£ per unit
Direct materials	6.00	6.00
Direct labour	7.50	7.50
Production overhead – department A	13.50	9.00
Production overhead – department B	7.80	5.80

(a) The total budgeted variable cost per unit is £ ⬚.
(b) The total budgeted fixed cost per period is £ ⬚.

Question 35

A company undertaking long-term building contracts has a financial year-end of 30 April. The following details on the purchase and use of machinery refer to contract A44, which was started on 1 May year 3 and is due for completion after 27 months.

1 July year 3:	Machine 1 was purchased at a cost of $55,000. It is to be used throughout the contract, and will be sold for $6,400 when the contract finishes.
1 October year 3:	Machine 2 was purchased at a cost of $28,600. The machine will be scrapped at the end of contract A44, and is not expected to have any saleable value.

If the company's policy is to charge depreciation in equal monthly amounts, the balance sheet value of machinery on contract A44 at 30 April year 4 will be $ [   ].

 Question 36

Data for product W are as follows.

Direct material cost per unit	£22
Direct labour cost per unit	£65
Direct labour hours per unit	5 hours
Production overhead absorption rate	£3 per direct labour hour
Mark-up for non-production overhead costs	8% of total production cost

The company requires a 15 per cent return on sales revenue from all products. The selling price per unit of product W, to the nearest penny, is £ [   ]

 Question 37

G repairs electronic calculators. The wages budget for the last period was based on a standard repair time of 24 minutes per calculator and a standard wage rate of $10.60 per hour.
   Following the end of the budget period, it was reported that:

Number of repairs	31,000
Labour rate variance	$3,100 (A)
Labour efficiency variance	Nil

Based on the above information, the actual wage rate per hour during the period was $ [   ].

? Question 38

Which ONE of the following factors could explain a favourable direct material usage variance?

A ☐ More staff were recruited to inspect for quality, resulting in a higher rejection rate.

B ☐ When estimating the standard product cost, usage of material had been set using ideal standards.

C ☐ The company had reduced training of production workers as part of a cost reduction exercise.

D ☐ The material price variance was adverse.

? Question 39

A company produces a single product B. The company budgets to sell 2,200 units of product B during period 4 and sales are budgeted to be 10 per cent higher in period 5. It is company policy to hold inventories of finished goods equal to 20 per cent of the following period's sales.

The budgeted production of product B for period 4 is [_____] units.

? Question 40

The following extract is taken from the delivery cost budget of D Limited:

| Miles travelled | 4,000 | 5,500 |
| Delivery cost | £9,800 | £10,475 |

The flexible budget cost allowance for 6,200 miles travelled is £[_____].

? Data for questions 41 to 49

Standard cost and revenue details for product C are as follows.

	£ per unit
Selling price	90.50
Direct material 12 kg at £1.70 per kg	20.40
Direct labour 3 hours at £14 per hour	42.00
Variable overhead	12.00

Budgeted sales and production for June were 47,200 units. However a machine breakdown occurred and as a result labour were idle for 150 hours and actual sales and production were 45,600 units.

Other actual data for June are as follows.

	£
Sales revenue	4,058,400
Direct material cost for 539,800 kg purchased and used	944,650
Direct labour cost for 134,100 hours, including 150 idle hours	1,850,580
Variable overhead cost	542,800

? Question 41

The sales price variance for June is £[_____]

adverse ☐

favourable ☐

Question 42

The sales volume contribution variance for June is £ _____

    adverse ☐
    favourable ☐

Question 43

The materials price variance for June is £ _____

    adverse ☐
    favourable ☐

Question 44

The materials usage variance for June is £ _____

    adverse ☐
    favourable ☐

Question 45

The idle time variance for June is £ _____

    adverse ☐
    favourable ☐

Question 46

The labour rate variance for June is £ _____

    adverse ☐
    favourable ☐

Question 47

The labour efficiency variance for June is £ _____

    adverse ☐
    favourable ☐

Question 48

The variable overhead expenditure variance for June is £ _____

    adverse ☐
    favourable ☐

Question 49

The variable overhead efficiency variance for June is £ _____

    adverse ☐
    favourable ☐

Question 50

A company provides a shirt laundering service. The standard cost and revenue for laundering one batch of shirts is as follows.

	£ per batch
Selling price	23
Materials cost (detergent, starch, etc.)	3
Labour cost	14
Variable overhead cost	1

Fixed costs incurred each month amount to £15,900.

The number of batches of shirts to be laundered to earn a profit of £4,300 per month is ☐ batches.

Second Mock Assessment – Solutions

 Solution 1

	Debit	Credit	No entry in this account
Production overhead control account	✓		
Work in progress account			✓
Finished goods account			✓
Income statement		✓	

 Solution 2

(a) The margin of safety is shown on the diagram by *k*. This is the difference between the expected sales level and the breakeven point.

(b) *m* will decrease (extra fixed cost = lower profit)
k will decrease (extra fixed cost = higher breakeven point = smaller margin of safety)
f will increase (extra fixed cost = higher breakeven point)
p will increase (p = fixed costs, which have increased)

 Solution 3

The use of this method suggests the service departments carry out work for each other.

 Solution 4

The combination that is certain to lead to over-absorption is production activity higher than budget *and* fixed overhead expenditure lower than budget.

Solution 5

The costs are all production overheads with the exception of the cost of ingredients, which is a direct cost.

 Solution 6

A = £715
B = £979

Workings:
Cost per complete unit in process 2 = £22,695/5,100 = £4.45
Cost of abnormal gain units = £4.45 × 220 = £979
Scrap value of normal loss per unit = £120/100 = £1.20
Forgone scrap value of abnormal gain = £1.20 × 220 units = £264
Transfer to income statement in respect of abnormal gain = £979 − £264 = £715

 Solution 7

Process account = credit; abnormal gain account = no entry in this account; abnormal loss account = debit.

Abnormal loss = (4,000 − 2,750 − 400 − 700) units = 150 units

 Solution 8

The value of the closing WIP was $4,158.

Statement of equivalent units

	Total units	Material equiv units	Labour equiv units	Production overhead equiv units
Finished goods	2,750	2,750	2,750	2,750
Normal loss	400	–	–	–
Abnormal loss	150	150	150	150
WIP c/fwd	700	700	350	280
		3,600	3,250	3,180
		$	$	$
Costs		16,000	8,125	3,498
Scrap value normal loss		(700)		
		15,300		
Cost per equivalent unit		$4.25	$2.50	$1.10

Statement of evaluation of WIP

	$
WIP c/fwd − material (700 × $4.25)	2,975
labour (350 × $2.50)	875
production overhead (280 × $1.10)	308
	4,158

Solution 9

The overtime premium paid to the operator would be £35.70.

    Overtime = 7 hours

    Overtime premium per hour = £5.10

    Overtime premium = £35.70

 Solution 10

The estimated price notified to the customer for job number 808 will be £23,446.

	£
Direct material	10,650
Direct labour	3,260
Prime cost	**13,910**
Production overhead (140 × £8.50)	1,190
Mark up on prime cost (60%)	8,346
	23,446

 Solution 11

Discounts are received on additional purchases of material when certain quantities are purchased. The graph depicts a variable cost where unit costs decease at certain levels of production.

 Solution 12

The estimated cost of carrying out health checks on 850 patients is £17,625.

	Patients	Total cost
		£
High	1,260	18,650
Low	650	17,125
	610	1,525

$$\text{Variable cost per patient} = \frac{£1,525}{610} = £2.50$$

At 650 patients:	£
Total cost	17,125
Total variable cost (650 × £2.50)	1,625
Total fixed cost	**15,500**
Total cost of 850 patients:	£
Fixed cost	15,500
Variable cost (850 × £2.50)	2,125
	17,625

 Solution 13

The principal budget factor for a footwear retailer is the constraint that is expected to limit the retailer's activities during the budget period.

Solution 14

The estimated cash receipts from customers during the budget period are $54,950.

$$\text{Cash received} = \text{Sales} + \text{opening receivables} - \text{closing receivables}$$
$$= \$(55,800 + 8,500 - 9,350)$$
$$= \$54,950.$$

 # Solution 15

The profit mark-up is 55%.

$$\text{Cost of sales} = \text{Opening inventory} + \text{purchases} - \text{closing inventory}$$
$$= \$(5,500 + 38,000 - 7,500)$$
$$= \$36,000$$

$36,000 + Mark up = $55,800

Mark Up = $19,800

$$\text{Mark Up\%} = \frac{19,800}{36,000} \times 100\% = 55\%.$$

 # Solution 16

The appropriate actions are (ii) and (iv). These are short term actions to cover a temporary cash shortage. Actions (i) and (iii) would be more appropriate for a longer term cash shortage.

 # Solution 17

(a) The limiting factor would be direct labour.

	X	Y	Z	Total
Material (kg)	20,000	22,000	42,000	84,000
Direct labour (hours)	4,000	4,125	10,500	18,625

(b) First: product *Y*; Second: product *X*; Third: product *Z*

	X	Y	Z
	£	£	£
Selling price	28	22	30
Variable cost	17	13	24
Contribution	11	9	6
Kg	5	4	6
Contribution per kg	£2.20	£2.25	£1.00
Ranking	2	1	3

Solution 18

A performance standard which assumes efficient levels of operation, but which includes allowances for factors such as waste and machine downtime is known as an attainable standard.

 Solution 19

The margin of safety represents 8.3% of budgeted sales.

$$\text{BEP} = \frac{\$(430,500 + 198,150)}{\$11.60 - \$(3.40 + 0.58)} = 82,500 \text{ units}$$

$$\text{Margin of safety} = \frac{90,000 - 82,500}{90,000} \times 100\% = 8.3\%$$

 Solution 20

These changes will cause the breakeven point to be 79,879 units.

$$\text{New BEP} = \frac{\$628,650}{\$12.25 - \$(3.40 + 0.98)} = 79,879 \text{ units.}$$

 Solution 21

Over long time periods of several years, supervisory labour costs will tend to behave as step fixed costs.

 Solution 22

Material control account = debit; work in progress = no entry in this account; material price variance account = credit.

The price variance is calculated at the point of purchase, therefore, the work in progress account is not affected. The favourable variance is credited to the variance account and debited in the material control account.

 Solution 23

Wages control account = no entry in this account; labour variance account = debit; work in progress control account = credit.

The efficiency variance is recorded at the point at which it arises, i.e. in the work in progress account rather than in the wages control account. The adverse variance is debited to the variance account.

 Solution 24

The graph represents piecework with a guaranteed minimum daily wage.

Solution 25

Production overhead will be reported as $3,660 under absorbed.

Machine hour rate = $180,000/40,000 = $4.50 per machine hour

	$
Overheads incurred	178,080
Overheads absorbed (38,760 × $4.50)	174,420
Under absorbed	3,660

 Solution 26

Using FIFO, the value of the closing inventory would be $76.

Units in inventory = 460 purchased − 420 issued = 40 units.

Issues would have been made at the earliest prices, therefore, the latest prices paid would be used to value remaining inventory = 40 units × $1.90 = $76.

 Solution 27

(a) Closing inventory value will be lower (prices are rising and FIFO uses latest prices to value items held in the stores)
(b) Gross profit for the week will be lower (higher average price charged to cost of sales)

 Solution 28

r will increase (r = loss at zero activity = fixed costs)
w will decrease (w = profit = lower if fixed costs increase)
t will decrease (t = margin of safety = lower if fixed costs increase)
u will increase (u = breakeven volume = higher if fixed costs increase)

 Solution 29

Profit will increase by $28,000.

Contribution per unit = (w + r)/(t + u) = $(16,000 + 50,000)/(800 + 2,500) = $20
Increase in profit = 1,400 additional units × $20 = $28,000

 Solution 30

The profit to be recognised in the company's income statement in respect of contract H7635 is £184,434.

Estimated final contract profit = £1,015,000 − £(592,000 + 189,000) = £234,000

$$\text{Profit to be recognised} = £234,000 \times \frac{£800,000}{£1,015,000}$$

$$= £184,434$$

Solution 31

The prime cost of contract A42 is $44,720.

	$
Direct materials	5,500
Direct expenses	14,500
Basic staff hours 1,020 hrs × $24	24,480
Overtime premium 40 hrs × $6	240
	44,720

 ## Solution 32

The budgeted production of product G in month 2 is 230 units.

Workings:

	units
Closing inventory month 2 (290 + 230)	520
Month 2 sales requirements	420
	940
Less opening inventory month 2 (420 + 290)	(710)
Budgeted production month 2	230 (i.e. month 4 sales volume)

 ## Solution 33

The budgeted purchases of liquid K in month 2 are 420 litres.

Workings:

Purchases each month will be the quantity required for production the following month. Production in month 3 = 210 units (month 5 sales), therefore, purchases in month 2 will be 210 × 2 litres = 420 litres.

 ## Solution 34

(a) The total budgeted variable cost per unit is £15.30
(b) The total budgeted fixed cost per period is £39,000

Workings:

Department A production overhead = fixed cost
                                 = 2,000 units × £13.50 or 3,000 units × £9.00
                                 = £27,000
Department B production overhead = semi-variable cost

Using the high-low method:

Units	Total cost
	£
3,000	17,400
2,000	15,600
1,000	1,800

Variable cost per unit = £1,800/1,000 = £1.80
Fixed cost = £17,400 − £(1.80 × 3,000) = £12,000
Total budgeted variable cost = £(6.00 + 7.50 + 1.80) = £15.30
Total budgeted fixed cost = £(27,000 + 12,000) = £39,000

Solution 35

The balance sheet value of machinery on contract A44 at 30 April year 4 is $55,060.

	Machine 1		Machine 2
	$		$
Cost	55,000		28,600
Depreciation $\frac{(55,000 - 6,400)}{25 \text{ months}} \times 10$		$\frac{28,600}{22 \text{ months}} \times 7$	
	19,440		9,100
	35,560		19,500

Net book value = $35,560 + $19,500 = $55,060

Solution 36

The selling price per unit of product W, to the nearest penny is £129.60

Workings:

	£ per unit
Direct material cost	22.00
Direct labour cost	65.00
Production overhead absorbed = 5 hours × £3	15.00
Total production cost	102.00
Mark-up for non-production costs = 8% × £102.00	8.16
Full cost	110.16
Profit mark-up = 15/85 × £110.16	19.44
Selling price	129.60

Solution 37

Labour efficiency variance = zero, therefore hours worked = standard hours for 31,000 repairs.

Hours worked = 31,000 × 24/60 = 12,400 hours
Adverse rate variance per hour = 3,100/12,400 = $0.25
Therefore, actual wage rate per hour = $10.60 + $0.25 = $10.85

Solution 38

Option D is the only factor that could explain a favourable direct material usage variance. Higher priced material may be of a higher quality than standard with the result that scrap and rejections were lower than standard.

Options A to C are all likely to result in an adverse direct material usage variance.

Solution 39

The budgeted production of product B for period 4 is 2,244 units.

	Units
Period 4 sales	2,200
Period 4 closing inventory (2,200 × 1.10 × 0.20)	484
Period 4 opening inventory (2,200 × 0.20)	(440)
Period 4 budgeted production	2,244

 Solution 40

The flexible budget cost allowance for 6,200 miles travelled is £10,790.

	Miles	£
High	5,500	10,475
Low	4,000	9,800
	1,500	675

Variable cost per mile = £675/1,500 = £0.45
Fixed cost = £10,475 − £(0.45 × 5,500) = £8,000
Total cost for 6,200 miles = £8,000 + £(0.45 × 6,200) = £10,790

 Solution 41

The sales price variance for June is £68,400 adverse.

Workings:

	£
45,600 units should sell for (×£90.50)	4,126,800
But did sell for	4,058,400
	68,400 adverse

 Solution 42

The sales volume contribution variance for June is £25,760 adverse

Workings:

Actual sales volume	45,600	units
Budget sales volume	47,200	units
Sales volume variance in units	1,600	units adverse
× standard contribution per unit	×£16.10	
	£25,760	adverse

Solution 43

The materials price variance for June is £26,990 adverse

Workings:

	£
539,800 kg should cost (×£1.70)	917,660
but did cost	944,650
	26,990 adverse

 # Solution 44

The materials usage variance for June is £12,580 favourable

Workings:

45,600 units produced should use (×12 kg)	547,200 kg
But did use	539,800 kg
Variance in kg	7,400 kg favourable
× standard price per kg	×£1.70
	£12,580 favourable

 # Solution 45

The idle time variance for June is £2,100 adverse

Workings:

Idle time variance = 150 hours idle × £14 standard labour cost per hour = £2,100 adverse

 # Solution 46

The labour rate variance for June is £26,820 favourable

Workings:

	£
134,100 hours should cost (×£14)	1,877,400
but did cost	1,850,580
	26,820 favourable

Solution 47

The labour efficiency variance for June is £39,900 favourable

Workings:

45,600 units produced should take (×3 hours)	136,800	hours
But did take (active hours)	133,950	hours
Variance in hours	2,850	hours favourable
× standard rate per hour	×£14	
	£39,900	favourable

 Solution 48

The variable overhead expenditure variance for June is £7,000 adverse

Workings:

	£	
133,950 active hours should cost (×£4)	535,800	
but did cost	542,800	
	7,000	adverse

 Solution 49

The variable overhead efficiency variance for June is £11,400 favourable

Workings:

Efficiency variance in hours from labour variance	2,850	hours favourable
× standard rate per hour	×£4	
	£11,400	favourable

 Solution 50

The number of batches of shirts to be laundered to earn a profit of £4,300 per month is 4,040 batches.

Workings:
Contribution per batch of shirts = £(23 − 3−14 − 1) = £5
Number of batches to achieve required profit = £(15,900 + 4,300)/£5 = 4,040 batches.

Index

Index